INTRODUCTION TO PROGRAMMING LANGUAGES

PROGRAMMING IN C, C++, SCHEME, PROLOG, C#, AND SOA

Yinong Chen and Wei-Tek Tsai
Arizona State University

KENDALL/HUNT PUBLISHING COMPANY
4050 Westmark Drive   Dubuque, Iowa 52002

Cover image © Corel 2003

Copyright © 2003, 2006 by Yinong Chen and Wei-Tek Tsai

ISBN 13: 978-0-7575-2974-0
ISBN 10: 0-7575-2974-7

Printed in the United States of America
10   9   8   7   6   5   4   3   2   1

CONTENTS

4 The Functional Programming Language, Scheme 179

5 The Logic Programming Language, Prolog   237

6 Fundamentals of Service-Oriented Computing Paradigm   309

PREFACE (SECOND EDITION)

The most important addition to the second edition is the inclusion of programming in Service-Oriented Architecture (SOA). Since the publication of the first edition in 2003, SOA programming has emerged as a new programming paradigm, which has demonstrated its strength and potential to become a dominating programming paradigm in the near future. All major computing companies, including HP, IBM, Intel, Microsoft, Oracle, SAP, Sun Microsystems, have moved into this new paradigm and are using the new paradigm to produce software and even hardware systems. The needs of the skill in SOA programming increase as the deployments of SOA applications increase. The new paradigm has not only the importance in the programming practice, not also contribution to the concepts and principles in programming theory. In fact, SOA programming applies a higher level of abstraction, which requires less technical details for building large software applications. The authors of the book are leading researchers and educators in SOA programming. The inclusion of the new chapter on C# and SOA programming makes the text unique, which allows teaching of the most contemporary programming concepts and practice. The new chapter also gives the text a new component to choose from, which adds flexibility for different courses to select different contents.

Furthermore, the existing chapters and sections in the first edition have been significantly improved, thanks to the feedbacks from the instructors who adopted the text and students who used the text in the past three years. Following new sections are added into the existing chapters,

2.5.5 Stack
2.7 Recursive structures
3.5 Exception handling
4.6.6 Compare and contrast imperative and functional programming paradigms
5.8 Additional topics in Prolog

Following sections are revised significantly in the second edition:

2.4.5 Enumeration type
2.5.4 Linked list using dynamic memory allocation
2.5.6 File and file operations
2.6 Functions and parameter passing
2.8 Modular design
A.2 Computer architectures and assembly programming

The second edition of the text consists of six chapters. A half-semester course (25 to 30 lecture hours) can teach two to three chapters and a full semester course can teach four to five chanters of choice from the text. Chapter 3 (C++) is closely related to chapter 2. If chapter 3 is selected as a component, chapter 2, or a part of chapter 2, should be selected too. Other chapters are relatively independent and can be selected freely to compose a course.

For a half-semester course, sensible course compositions could include: (chapters 1, 2, 3); (chapters 2, 3); (chapters 1, 2, 6); (chapters 2, 3, 6); (chapters 1, 4, 5); and (chapters 4, 5). For a full semester course, sensible course compositions could include: (chapters 1, 2, 3, 4, 5); (chapters 1, 2, 3, 4, 6); (chapters 1, 2, 3, 5, 6); and (chapters 2, 3, 4, 5, 6).

Please contact the authors for instructional support at <text.cse240@asu.edu>. Available materials include lecture slides in PowerPoint format, sample tests, and the solutions to assignments and tests.

Yinong Chen
Wei-Tek Tsai

PREFACE (FIRST EDITION)

This text is intended for computer science and computer engineering students in their sophomore year of study. It is assumed that students have completed a basic computer science course and have learned a high-level programming language like Pascal, C, C++, or Java.

Most parts of the contents presented in the text have been used in the "Introduction to Programming Languages" course taught by the author in the School of Computer Science at the University of the Witwatersrand at Johannesburg, and in the Computer Science and Engineering Department at Arizona State University. Being different from the existing texts on programming languages that either focus on teaching programming paradigms, principles, and the language mechanisms, or focus on language constructs and programming skills, this text takes a balanced approach on both sides. It teaches four programming languages representing four major programming paradigms. Programming paradigms, principles, and language mechanisms are used as the vehicle to facilitate learning of the four programming languages in a coherent way. The goals of such a programming course are to make sure that computer science students are exposed to different programming paradigms and language mechanisms, and obtain sufficient programming skills and experiences in different programming languages, so that they can quickly use these or similar languages in other courses.

Although there are many different programming paradigms, imperative, object-oriented, functional, and logic programming paradigms are the four major paradigms widely taught in computer science and computer engineering departments around the world. The four languages we will study in the text are the imperative C, object-oriented C++, functional Scheme, and logic Prolog.

By the end of the course, students should understand

- the language structures at different layers (lexical, syntactic, contextual, and semantic), the control structures and the execution models of imperative, object-oriented, functional, and logic programming languages;
- program processing (compilation versus interpretation) and preprocessing (macros and inlining);
- different aspects of a variable, including its type, scope, name, address, memory location, and value.

More specific features of programming languages and programming issues are explored in cooperation with the four selected languages. Students are expected to have understood and be able to

- write C programs with complex data types, including pointers, arrays, and generic structures, as well as programs with static and dynamic memory allocation;
- apply the object-oriented features such as inheritance and class hierarchy, polymorphism and typing, overloading, early versus late binding, as well as the constructors, the destructor and the management of static memory, stack and heap in C++;
- apply the functional programming style of parameter passing and write Scheme programs requiring multiple functions;
- apply the logic programming style of parameter passing, write Prolog facts, rules and goals, and use multiple rules to solve problems;
- be able to write programs requiring multiple subprograms/procedures to solve large programming problems;
- be able to write recursive subprograms/procedures in imperative, object-oriented, functional and logic programming languages

The text is organized into five chapters and three appendices. Chapter one discusses the programming paradigms, principles, and common aspects of programming languages. Chapter two uses C as the example of the imperative programming paradigm to teach how to write imperative programs. It is assumed that the students have basic understanding of a high-level programming language such as Pascal, C, C++, or Java. Chapter three extends the discussion and programming from C to C++. The chapter focuses on the main features of object-oriented programming paradigms, including class composition, inheritance, dynamic memory allocation and deallocation, late binding, polymorphism, and class hierarchy. Chapters four and five take a major paradigm shift to teach functional and logic programming, respectively. Students are not required to have any knowledge in functional and logic programming to learn from these two chapters. Assignments, programming exercises, and projects are given at the end of each chapter. The three appendices provide supplementary materials to the main text. In Appendix A, the basic computer architecture and assembly language programming are introduced. If students do not have basic computer science background, the material should be covered in the class. Appendix B first introduces basic Unix commands. If the class uses a Unix-based laboratory environment, students can read the appendix to get started with Unix. Then the appendix introduces the major programming language environments that can be used to support teaching the four programming languages. Appendix C gives the ASCII code table that is referred in various parts of the text. In the main text, the sections with an asterisk mark are optional and can be skipped if time does not permit to cover all the material. Chapters four and five are self-contained and can be taught independently, or in a different order.

I wish to thank all those who have contributed to the materials and to the formation of this text. Particularly, I would like to thank my colleagues, Scott Hazelhurst and Conrad Mueller, of the University of the Witwatersrand, and Richard Whitehouse of Arizona State University who shared their course materials with me. Parts of these materials were used in teaching the programming languages course and used in this text. Thomas Boyd, Joe DeLibero, and Renee Turban of Arizona State University reviewed the final draft of the text and made constructive suggestions and useful comments. My teaching assistants Ibraz Mohammed, Jianchun Fan, Harish Bashettihalli, and Rajanikanth Mitta, helped me in the past few years prepare the assignments and programming exercises. Raynette Brodie, the student consultant for Microsoft at Arizona State University, contributed the section "From C++ to C#" and the C# related materials in other sections. Peter Hallam, C# developer at Microsoft, made very useful comments on C# related topics. The major part of chapter five, sections 5.1 through 5.7, was reprinted (arranged by the publisher) from Tom Hankins and Thom Luce's book *Prolog Minimanual*.

I also would like to thank the editoral team, Jay Hays, Billee Jo Hefel, and Lynne Rogers at Kendall/ Hunt Publishing. Jay pushed me into the position to write the text, Billee Jo checked my progress constantly that made me finally meet the deadline, and Lynne completed the production process.

The text was written while I was carrying out a full university workload. I am thankful to my family, Wei, George, and Jane. I could not imagine that I would be able to complete the task without their generous support by allowing me to use most of the weekends in the past year to write the text.

Although I have used the materials in teaching the programming languages courses at the University of the Witwatersrand, Johannesburg and at Arizona State University for several years, the text was put together in a short period of time. There are certainly many errors of different kinds. I would appreciate it if you could send me any corrections, comments, or suggestions for improving the text. My email address dedicated to dealing with the responses to the text is <text.cse240@asu.edu>. Instructors who use the text can contact the author for instructional support, including lecture slides in PowerPoint format and the solutions to the assignments.

Yinong Chen

Basic Principles of Programming Languages

Although there exist many programming languages, the differences among them are insignificant compared to the differences among natural languages. In this chapter, we discuss the common aspects shared among different programming languages. These aspects include

- programming paradigms that define how computation is expressed;
- the main features of programming languages and their impact on the performance of programs written in the languages;
- a brief review of the history and development of programming languages;
- the lexical, syntactic and semantic structures of programming languages, data and data types, program processing and preprocessing, and the lifecycles of program development.

By the end of the chapter, you should have learned

- what are programming paradigms;
- an overview of different programming languages and the background knowledge of these languages;
- the structures of programming languages and how programming languages are defined at the syntactic level;
- data types, strong versus weak checking;
- the relationship between language features and their performances;
- the processing and pre-processing of programming languages, compilation versus interpretation, and different execution models of macros, procedures and inline procedures;
- the steps used for program development: requirement, specification, design, implementation, testing and the correctness proof of programs.

The chapter is organized as follows. Section 1.1 introduces the programming paradigms, performance, features, and the development of programming languages. Section 1.2 outlines the structures and design issues of programming languages. Section 1.3 discusses the typing systems, including types of variables, type equivalence, type conversion, and type checking during the compilation. Section 1.4 presents the preprocessing and processing of programming languages, including macro processing, interpretation and compilation. Finally, section 1.5 discusses the program development steps including specification, testing and correctness proof.

1.1 Introduction

1.1.1 Programming Concepts and Paradigms

Millions of programming languages have been invented, and several thousands of them are actually in use. Compared to natural languages that developed and evolved independently, programming languages are far more similar to each other. This is because

- different programming languages share the same mathematical foundation (e.g., Boolean algebra, logic);
- they provide similar functionality (e.g., arithmetic, logic operations, and text processing);
- they are based on the same kind of hardware and instruction sets;
- they have common design goals: find languages that make it simple for humans to use and efficient for hardware to execute;
- designers of programming languages share their design experiences.

Some programming languages, however, are more similar to each other, while some other programming languages are more different from each other. Based on their similarities or the paradigms, programming languages can be divided into different classes. In programming language's definition, **paradigm** is a set of basic principles, concepts, and methods of how computation or algorithm is expressed. The major paradigms we will study in this text are imperative, object-oriented, functional, and logic paradigms.

The **imperative**, also called the **procedural**, programming paradigm expresses computation by fully specified and fully controlled manipulation of named data in a step-wise fashion. In other words, data or values are initially stored in variables (memory locations), taken out of (read from) memory, and manipulated in ALU (arithmetic logic unit) and then stored back in the same or different variables (memory locations). Finally, the values of variables are sent to the I/O devices as output. The foundation of imperative languages is the **stored program concept** based computer hardware organization and architecture (von Neumann machine). The stored program concept will be further explained in the next chapter. Typical imperative programming languages include all assembly languages and earlier high-level languages like Fortran, Algol, Ada, Pascal, and C.

The **object-oriented** programming paradigm is basically the same as the imperative paradigm, except that related variables and operations on variables are organized into classes of **objects**. The access privileges of variables and methods (operations) in objects can be defined to reduce (simplify) the interaction among objects. Objects are considered the main building blocks of programs, which support the language features like inheritance, class hierarchy and polymorphism. Typical object-oriented programming languages include Smalltalk, C++, Java, and C#.

The **functional**, also called the **applicative**, programming paradigm expresses computation in terms of mathematical functions. Since we have been expressing computation in mathematical functions in many of the mathematical courses, functional programming is supposed to be easy to understand and simple to use. However, since functional programming is very different from imperative or object-oriented programming, and most programmers first get used to writing programs in imperative or object-oriented paradigm, it becomes difficult to switch to functional programming. The main difference is that there is no concept of memory locations in functional programming languages. Each function will take a number of values as input (parameters) and produce a single return value (output of the function). The return value cannot be stored for later use. It has to be used either as the final output or used immediately as the parameter value of another function. Functional programming is about defining functions and organizing the return values of one or more functions as the parameters of another function. Functional programming languages are mainly based on the **lambda-calculus** that will be discussed in chapter four. Typical functional programming languages include ML, SML, and Lisp/Scheme.

The **logic**, also called the **declarative**, programming paradigm expresses computation in terms of logic predicates. A logic program is a set of facts, rules, and questions. The execution process of a logic program is to compare a question to each fact and rule in the given fact and rulebase. If the question finds a match, we receive a yes-answer to the question. Otherwise, we receive a no-answer to the question. Logic programming is about finding facts, defining rules based on the facts, and writing questions to express the problems we wish to solve. Prolog is the only significant logic programming language.

It would be worthwhile to note that many languages belong to multiple paradigms. For example, we can say that C++ is an object-oriented programming language. However, C++ includes almost every feature of C and thus is an imperative programming language too. We can use C++ to write C programs. Java is more object-oriented, but still includes imperative features. For example, Java's primitive type variables do not obtain memory from the language heap like other objects. Lisp contains many non-functional features. Scheme can be considered a subset of Lisp with fewer non-functional features. Prolog's arithmetic operations are based on imperative paradigm.

Nonetheless, we will focus on the paradigm related features of the languages when we study the sample languages in the next four chapters. We will study the imperative features of C in chapter two, the object-oriented features of C++ in chapter three, functional features of Scheme, and logic features of Prolog in chapters four and five, respectively.

1.1.2 PROGRAM PERFORMANCE AND FEATURES OF PROGRAMMING LANGUAGES

A programming language's features include orthogonality or simplicity, available control structures, data types and data structures, syntax design, support for abstraction, expressiveness, type equivalence, and strong versus weak type checking, exception handling, and aliasing. These features will be further explained in the rest of the book. The performance of a program, including reliability, readability, writeability, reusability, and efficiency, is largely determined by the way the programmer writes the algorithm and selects the data structures, as well as other implementation details. However, the features of the programming language are vital in supporting and enforcing programmers to use proper language mechanisms in implementing the algorithms and data structures. Table 1.1 shows the influence of language's features on the performance of a program written in that language. The table indicates that simplicity, control structures, data types, and data structures have significant impact on all aspects of performance. Syntax design and the support for abstraction are important for readability, reusability, writeability and reliability. However, they do not have a significant impact on the efficiency of the program. Expressiveness supports writeability. However, it may have a negative impact on the reliability of the program. Strong type checking and restricted aliasing reduce the expressiveness of writing programs, but are generally considered to produce more reliable programs. Exception handling prevents the program from crashing due to unexpected circumstances and semantic errors in the program. All language features will be discussed in this book.

1.1.3 DEVELOPMENT OF PROGRAMMING LANGUAGES

The development of programming languages has been influenced by the development of hardware, the development of compiler technology and the user's need for writing high performance programs in terms of reliability, readability, writeability, reusability and efficiency. The hardware and compiler limitations have forced early programming languages to be close to the machine language. Machine languages are the native languages of computers and the first generation of programming languages used by humans to communicate with the computer.

Machine languages consist of instructions of pure binary numbers that are difficult for humans to remember. The next step in programming language development is the use of mnemonics that allows certain symbols to be used to represent frequently used bit patterns. The machine language with sophisticated use of mnemonics is called **assembly language**. An assembly language normally allows simple variables, branch to a label address, different addressing modes and macros that represent a number of instructions. An **assembler** is used to translate an assembly language program into a machine language

Table 1.1 The impact of language features on the performance of the programs

Performance Language features	Efficiency	Readability / Reusability	Writeability	Reliability
Simplicity / Orthogonality	✔	✔	✔	✔
Control structures	✔	✔	✔	✔
Data type and structures	✔	✔	✔	✔
Syntax design		✔	✔	✔
Support for abstraction		✔	✔	✔
Expressiveness			✔	✔
Strong checking				✔
Restricted aliasing				✔
Exception handling				✔

program. The typical work that an assembler does is: translate mnemonic symbols into corresponding binary numbers, substitute register numbers or memory locations for the variables, and calculate the destination address of branch instructions according to the position of the labels in the program.

This text will focus on introducing high-level programming languages in imperative, object-oriented, functional, and logic paradigms.

The first high-level programming language can be traced to Konrad Zuse's Plankalkül programming system in Germany in 1946. Konrad Zuse developed his Z-machines Z1, Z2, Z3, and Z4 in late 1930s and early 1940s and the Plankalkül system was developed on the Z4 machine at ETH (Eidgenossisch Technische Hochschule) in Zurich, with which Zuse designed a chess-playing program.

The first high-level programming language that was actually used in an electronic computing device was developed in 1949. The language was named Short Code. There was no compiler designed for the language, and programs written in the language had to be hand-compiled into the machine code.

The invention of the compiler was credited to Grace Hopper, who designed the first widely known compiler, called **A0** in 1951.

The first primitive compiler, called Autocoder, was written by Alick E. Glennie in 1952. It translated Autocode programs in symbolic statements into machine language for the Manchester Mark I computer. Autocode could handle single letter identifiers and simple formulas.

The first widely used language, Fortran (FORmula TRANslating), was developed by the team headed by John Backus at IBM between 1954 and 1957. Backus was also the system co-designer of the IBM 704 that ran the first Fortran compiler. Backus was later involved in the development of the language Algol and the Backus-Naur Form (BNF). BNF Form was a formal notation used to define the syntax of programming languages. Fortran II came in 1958. Fortran III came at the end of 1958, but it was never released to the public. Further versions of Fortran include ASA Fortran 66 (Fortran IV) in 1966, ANSI Fortran 77 (Fortran V) in 1978, ISO Fortran 90 in 1991 and ISO Fortran 95 in 1997. Different from assembly languages, the early versions of Fortran allowed different types of variables (real, integer, array), supported procedure call, and simple control structures.

Programs written in programming languages before the emergence of structured programming concepts were characterized as spaghetti programming or monolithic programming. **Structured programming** is a technique for organizing programs in a hierarchy of modules. Each module had a single entry and a single exit point. Control was passed downward through the structure without unconditional branches (e.g., *goto* statements) to higher levels of the structure. Only three types of control structures were used: sequential, conditional branch, and iteration.

Based on the experience of Fortran I, Algol 58 was announced in 1958. Two years later, Algol 60, the first block-structured language, was introduced. The language was revised in 1963 and 1968. Edsger Dijkstra was credited for the design of the first Algol 60 compiler. He was famous as the leader in introducing structured programming and in the abolition of the *goto* statement from programming.

Rooted in Algol, Pascal was developed by Niklaus Wirth between 1968 and 1970. He further developed Modula as the successor of Pascal in 1977, and then Modula-2 in 1980, and Oberon in 1988. Oberon language had Pascal-like syntax, but it was strongly typed. It also offered type extension (inheritance) that supported object-oriented programming. In Oberon-2, type-bound procedures (like *methods* in object-oriented programming languages) were introduced.

The C programming language was invented and first implemented by Dennis Ritchie at DEC between 1969 and 1973, as a system implementation language for the nascent Unix operating system. It soon became one of the dominant languages at the time and even today. The predecessors of C were the typeless language BCPL (Basic Combined Programming Language) by Martin Richards in 1967 and then the B written by Ken Thompson in 1969. C had a weak type checking structure to allow a higher level of programming flexibility.

Object-oriented programming concepts were first introduced and implemented in the Simula language, which was designed by Ole-Johan Dahl and Kristen Nygaard at the Norwegian Computing Center (NCC) between 1962 and 1967. The original version Simula I was designed as a language for discrete event simulation. However, its revised version, Simula 67, was a full-scale general purpose programming language. Although Simula never became widely used, the language was highly influential on the modern programming paradigms. It introduced important object-oriented concepts like classes and objects, inheritance, and late binding.

One of the object-oriented successors of Simula was Smalltalk, designed at Xerox PARC, led by Alan Kay. The versions developed included Smalltalk-72, Smalltalk-74, Smalltalk-76, and Smalltalk-80. Smalltalk also inherited functional programming features from Lisp.

Based on Simula 67 and C, a language called "C with classes" was developed by Bjarne Stroustrup in 1980 at Bell Labs, and then revised and renamed to C++ in 1983. C++ was considered a better C, e.g., with strong type checking, plus it supported data abstraction and object-oriented programming inherited from Simula 67.

Java was written by James Gosling, Patrick Naughton, Chris Warth, Ed Frank, and Mike Sheridan at Sun Microsystems. It was called Oak at first and then renamed Java when it was publicly announced in 1995. The predecessors of Java were C++ and Smalltalk. Java removed most non-object-oriented features of C++ and was a simpler and better object-oriented programming language. Its two-level program processing concept, i.e., compilation into an intermediate bytecode and then interpretation of the bytecode using a small virtual machine, made it the dominant language for programming Internet applications. Java was still not a pure object-oriented programming language. Its primitive types, integer, floating-point number, boolean, etc., were not classes, and their memory allocations were from the language stack, rather than from the language heap.

Microsoft's C# language was first announced in June 2000. The language was derived from C++ and Java. It was implemented as a full object-oriented language without "primitive" types. C# also emphasizes component-oriented programming which is a refined version of object-oriented programming. The idea is to be able to assemble software systems from prefabricated components.

Functional programming languages are relatively independent of the development process of imperative and object-oriented programming languages. The first and the most important functional programming language, Lisp, short for LISt Processing, was developed by John McCarthy at MIT. Lisp was first released in 1958. Then Lisp 1 appeared in 1959, Lisp 1.5 in 1962, and Lisp 2 in 1966. Lisp was developed specifically for artificial intelligence applications and was based on the lambda calculus. It inherited its algebraic syntax from Fortran and its symbol manipulation from Information Processing Language IPl. Several dialects of Lisp were designed later, for example, Scheme, InterLisp, FranzLisp, MacLisp, and ZetaLisp.

As a Lisp dialect, Scheme was first developed by G. L. Steele and G. J. Sussman in 1975 at MIT. Several important improvements were made in its later versions, including better scope rule, procedures (functions) as the first-class objects, removal of loops, and solely relying on recursive procedure calls to express loops. Scheme was standardized by IEEE in 1989.

Efforts began on developing a common dialect of Lisp, referred to as Common Lisp, in 1981. Common Lisp intended to be compatible to all existing versions of Lisp dialects and to create a huge commercial product. However, the attempt of trying to merge Scheme into Lisp failed, and Scheme remains an independent Lisp dialect today. Common Lisp was standardized by IEEE in 1992.

Other than Lisp, John Backus's FP language also belongs to the first functional programming languages. FP was not based on the lambda calculus, but based on a few rules for combining function forms. Backus felt that lambda calculus's expressiveness on computable functions was much broader than necessary. A simplified rule set could do a better job.

At the same time when FP was developed in the U.S., ML (Meta Language) appeared in the U.K. Like Lisp, ML was based on lambda calculus. However, Lisp was not typed (no variable needs to be declared) while ML was strongly typed, although users did not have to declare variables that could be inferentially determined by the compiler.

Miranda is a pure functional programming language developed by David Turner at the University of Kent in 1985-86. Miranda achieved referential transparency (side-effect free) by forbidding modification to global variables. It combines the main features of SASL and KRC with strong typing similar to that of ML. SASL and KRC are two earlier functional programming languages designed by Turner in 1976 and 1981, respectively.

There are many logic-based programming languages in existence. For example, ALF (Algebraic Logic Functional language) is an integrated functional and logic language based on Horn clauses for logic programming, and functions and equations for functional programming. Gödel is a strongly typed logic programming language. The type system is based on a many-sorted logic with parametric polymorphism. RELFUN extends Horn logic by using higher-order syntax, first-class finite domains, and expressions of non-deterministic, non-ground functions, explicitly distinguished from structures.

The most significant member in the family of logic programming languages is the Horn logic-based Prolog. Prolog was invented by Alain Colmerauer and Phillipe Roussel at the University of Aix-Marseille in 1971. The first version was implemented in 1972 using Algol. Prolog was designed originally for natural-language processing, but has become one of the most widely used languages for artificial intelligence. Many implementations appeared after the original work. Early implementations included C-Prolog, ESLPDPRO, Frolic, LM-Prolog, Open Prolog, SB-Prolog, and UPMAIL Tricia Prolog. Today, the common Prologs in use are AMZI Prolog, GNU Prolog, LPA Prolog, Quintus Prolog, SICSTUS Prolog, SNI Prolog, and SWI-Prolog.

1.2 STRUCTURES OF PROGRAMMING LANGUAGES

This section studies the structures of programming languages in terms of four structural layers: lexical, syntactic, contextual, and semantic.

1.2.1 LEXICAL STRUCTURE

Lexical structure defines the vocabulary of a language. Lexical units are considered the building blocks of programming languages. The lexical structures of all programming languages are similar and normally include the following kinds of units:

- **Identifiers**: Names that can be chosen by programmers to represent objects like variables, labels, procedures, and functions. Most programming languages require that an identifier start with an alphabetic letter and can be optionally followed by letters, digits, and some special characters.

- **Keywords**: Names reserved by the language designer and used to form the syntactic structure of the language.

- **Operators**: Symbols used to represent the operations. All general-purpose programming languages should provide certain minimum operators such as mathematical operators like +, -, *, /, relational operators like <, <=, ==, >, >=, and logic operators like AND, OR, NOT, etc.

- **Separators**: Symbols used to separate lexical or syntactic units of the language. Space, comma, colon, semicolon, and parentheses are used as separators.

- **Literals**: Values that can be assigned to variables of different types. For example, integer-type literals are integer numbers, character-type literals are any character from the character set of the language, and string-type literals are any string of characters.

- **Comments**: Any explanatory text embedded in the program. Comments start with a specific keyword or separator. When the compiler translates a program into machine code, all comments will be ignored.

1.2.2 SYNTACTIC STRUCTURE

Syntactic structure defines the grammar of forming sentences or statements using the lexical units. An imperative programming language normally offers the following kinds of statements:

- **Assignments**: An assignment statement assigns a literal value or an expression to a variable.

- **Conditional statements**: A conditional statement tests a condition and branches to a certain statement based on the test result (*true* or *false*). Typical conditional statements are *if-then*, *if-then-else*, and *switch* (*case*).

- **Loop statements**: A loop statement tests a condition and enters the body of the loop or exits the loop based on the test result (*true* or *false*). Typical loop statements are *for-loop* and *while-loop*.

The formal definition of lexical and syntactic structures will be discussed in section 1.2.5.

1.2.3 CONTEXTUAL STRUCTURE

Contextual structure (also called **static semantics**) defines the program semantics before dynamic execution. It includes variable declaration, initialization, and type checking.

Some imperative languages require that all variables be initialized when they are declared at the contextual layer, while some other languages do not require variables to be initialized when they are declared, as long as the variables are initialized before their values are used. This means that initialization can be done either at the contextual layer or at the semantic layer.

Contextual structure starts to deal with the meaning of the program. A statement that is lexically correct may not be contextually correct. For example:

```
string str = "hello";
int i = 0;
int j = i + str;
```

All declaration statements are lexically correct, but the last statement is contextually incorrect because it does not make sense to add an integer variable to a string variable.

More about data type, type checking, and type equivalence will be discussed in section 1.3.

1.2.4 Semantic Structure

Semantic structure describes the meaning of a program, or what the program does during the execution. The semantics of a language is often very complex. In most imperative languages, there is no formal definition of semantic structure. Informal descriptions are normally used to explain what each statement does. The semantic structures of functional and logic programming languages are normally defined based on the mathematical and logical foundation the languages are based on. For example, the meanings of Scheme procedures are the same as the meanings of the lambda expressions in lambda calculus on which Scheme is based, and the meanings of Prolog clauses are the same as the meanings of the clauses in Horn logic on which Prolog is based.

*1.2.5 BNF Notation

BNF (Backus-Naur Form) is a meta language that can be used to define the lexical and syntactic structures of another language. Instead of learning BNF language first and then using BNF to define a new language, let's first use BNF to define a simplified English language that we are familiar with and learn BNF from the definition itself.

A simple English sentence consists of a subject, a verb, and an object. A subject, in turn, consists of possibly one or more adjectives followed by a noun. The object basically has the same grammatical structure. The verbs and adjectives must come from the vocabulary. Formally, we can define a simple English sentence as follows:

<sentence>	::= <subject> <verb> <object>
<subject>	::= <noun> | <article> <noun> | <adjective> <noun> |
	<article> <adjective> <noun>
<adjective>	::= <adjective> | <adjective> <adjective>
<object>	::= <subject>
<noun>	::= **table** | **horse** | **computer**
<article>	::= **the** | **a**
<adjective>	::= **big** | **fast** | **good** | **high**
<verb>	::= **is** | **makes**

In the definitions, the symbol "::=" means that the name on the left-hand side is defined by the expression on the right-hand side. The name in a pair of angle brackets "< >" is **non-terminal**, which means that the name needs to be further defined. The vertical bar "|" represents an "or" relation. The boldfaced names are **terminal**, which means that the names need not be further defined. They form the vocabulary of the language.

Let's use the sentence definition to check whether the following sentences are syntactically correct.

fast high big computer is good table	1
the high table is a good table	2
a fast table makes the high horse	3
the fast big high computer is good	4
good table is high	5
a table is not a horse	6
is fast computer good	7

The first sentence is syntactically correct, although it does not make much sense. Three adjectives in the sentence are correct because the definition of an adjective recursively allows any number of adjectives to be used in the subject and the object of a sentence. The second and third sentences are also syntactically correct according to the definition.

The fourth and fifth sentences are syntactically incorrect because a noun is missing in the object of the sentences. The sixth sentence is incorrect because "not" is not a terminal. The last sentence is incorrect because the definition does not allow a sentence to start with a verb.

After we have a basic understanding of BNF, we can use it to define a small programming language. The first five lines define the lexical structure, and the rest defines the syntactic structure of the language.

<letter>	::=	a|b|c|d|e|f|g|h|i|j|k|l|m|n|o|p|q|r|s|t|u|v|w|x|y|z
<digit>	::=	0|1|2|3|4|5|6|7|8|9
<symbol>	::=	_|@|.|~|?|#|$
<char>	::=	<letter>|<digit>|<symbol>
<operator>	::=	+|-|*|/|%|<|>|==|<=|>=|and|or|not
<identifier>	::=	<letter>|<identifier><char>
<number>	::=	<digit>|<number><digit>
<item>	::=	<identifier>|<number>
<expression>	::=	<item>|(<expression>)|<expression><operator><expression>
<branch>	::=	if <expr> then {<block>} |
		if <expr> then {<block>} else {<block>}
<switch>	::=	switch <expr> {<sbody>}
<sbody>	::=	<cases> | <cases>; default : <block>
<cases>	::=	case <value> : <block> | <cases> ; case <value> : <block>
<loop>	::=	while <expr> do {<block>}
<assignment>	::=	<identifier> = <expression>;
<statement>	::=	<assignment>|<branch>|<loop>
<block>	::=	<statement>|<block>;<statement>

Now let's use the definition to check which of the following statements are syntactically correct.

sum = 0;	1
while sum1 <= 100 **do** {	2
sum1 = sum1 + (a1 + a2) * (3b % 4*b); }	3
if sum1 == 120 **then** 2sum - sum1 **else** sum2 +sum1;	4
p4#rd_2 = ((1a + a2) * (b3 % b4)) / (c7 - c8);	5
_foo.bar = (a1 + a2 - b3 - b4);	6
(a1 / a2) = (c3 - c4);	7

According to the BNF definition of the language, statements 1 and 2 are correct. Statements 3 and 4 are incorrect, because 3*b* and 2*sum* are neither acceptable identifiers nor acceptable expressions. Statement 5 is incorrect. Statement 6 is incorrect because an identifier must start with a letter. Statement 7 is incorrect because the left hand side of an assignment statement must be an identifier.

1.2.6 Syntax Graph

BNF notation provides a concise way to define the lexical and syntactic structures of programming languages. However, BNF notations, especially the recursive definitions, are not always easy to understand. A graphic form, called **syntax graph**, also known as **railroad tracks**, is often used to supplement the readability of BNF notation. For example, the identifier and the if-then-else statement corresponding to the BNF definitions can be defined using the syntax graphs in figures 1.1 and 1.2, respectively. The syntax graph in figure 1.1 requires that an identifier start with a letter, may exit with only one letter, or follow the loops to include any number of letters, digits, or symbols. In other words, to check the legitimacy of an identifier we need to travel through the syntax graph following the arrows and see if we can find a path that matches the given identifier. For example, we can verify that len_23 is a legitimate identifier as follows. We travel through the first <letter> once, travel through the second <letter> on the back track twice, travel through the <symbol> once, and finally travel through the <digit> twice, and then we exit the definition. On the other hand, if you try to verify that 23_len is a legitimate identifier, you would not be able to find a path to travel through the syntax graph.

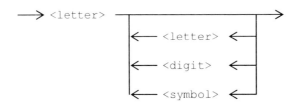

Figure 1.1 Definition of identifier

Using figure 1.2, we can precisely verify if a given statement is a legitimate if-then-else statement. The alternative route that bypasses the else branch in figure 1.2 signifies that the else branch is optional. Please note that the definition of the if-then-else statement here is not the same as the if-then-else statement in C language. The syntax graph definitions of various C statements can be found in chapter two.

Figure 1.2 Definition of if-then-else statement

In syntax graphs, we use the same convention that terminals are in boldfaced text and non-terminals are enclosed in a pair of angle brackets.

1.3 Data Types and Type Checking

In this section, we examine data types, type equivalence, and type checking that is part of the contextual structure of a programming language.

1.3.1 DATA TYPES AND TYPE EQUIVALENCE

A **data type** is defined by the set of primary values allowed and the operations defined on these values. A data type is used to declare variables, e.g., integer, real, array of integer, string, etc.

Type checking is the activity of ensuring that the data types of operands of an operator are legal or equivalent to the legal type.

Now the question is, what types are equivalent? For example, are *int* and *short* type, *int* and *float* type in C language equivalent? Are the following operations legal in C?

```
int i = 3; short j = 5; float n, k = 3.0;
n = i + j + k;
```

The answers to these questions are related to the type equivalence policy of programming languages. There are two major type equivalence policies: structural equivalence and name equivalence. If the **structural equivalence** policy is used, the two types are equivalent if they have the same set of values (data range) and the same operations. This policy follows the stored program concept and gives programmers the maximum flexibility to manipulate data. The **stored program concept** suggests that instruction and data are stored in computer memory as binary bit patterns and it is the programmer's responsibility to interpret the meanings of the bit patterns. Algol 68, Pascal, and C are examples of languages that use structural equivalence policy. For example, in the following C code, a type *salary* and a type age are defined:

```
typedef integer salary;
typedef integer age;
int i = 0; salary s = 60000; age a = 40;
i = s + a;
```

If structural equivalence policy is used, statement "i = s + a;" is perfectly legal because all three variables belong to types that are structurally equivalent. Obviously, adding an *age* value to a *salary* value and putting it into an integer type variable normally does not make sense and most probably is a programming error. Structural equivalence policy assumes programmers know what they are doing.

On the other hand, if **name equivalence** policy is used, two types are equivalent only if they have the same name. Since no programming language will normally allow two different data types to have the same name, this policy does not allow any variable of one type to be used in the place where a variable of another type is expected without explicit type conversion. If name equivalence policy is used, the statement "i = s + a;" is then illegal.

Ada, C++, and Java are examples where the name equivalence policy is used. Name equivalence enforces a much stronger discipline and is generally considered a good way to ensure the correctness of a program.

1.3.2 TYPE CHECKING AND TYPE CONVERSION

Besides type equivalence, type checking policy is another important characteristic of a programming language. We can vaguely differentiate strongly typed and weakly typed languages. In a (truly) **strongly typed language**

■ every name in a program must be associated with a single type that is known at the compilation time;
■ name equivalence is used;
■ every type inconsistency must be reported.

C++ and Java are strongly typed languages. Functional programming languages are normally weakly typed because mathematical functions are not typed. However, ML is strongly typed, although users did not have to declare variables that could be inferentially determined by the compiler.

On the other hand, in a **weakly typed language**

- not every name has to be associated with a single type at the compilation time;
- structural equivalence is used;
- a variable of a subtype is acceptable and implicit type conversion, called **coercion**, is allowed.

Type T1 is considered the **subtype** of T2, if the set of data of T1 is a subset of data of T2 and the set of operations of T1 is a subset of operations of T2. For example, an *integer* type can be considered a subtype of *floating-point* type. C, Scheme, and Prolog are weakly typed programming languages. Typeless languages like BCPL are weakly typed.

If a data type is a subtype of another type, it does not mean that the two types have the equivalent or similar structure. For example, in a 32-bit computer, an integer number 3 is represented in a simple binary form, as shown in the upper part of figure 1.3, while a floating-point number is normally represented in a three-segment format (IEEE 754 Standard) with the left-most bit representing the sign (positive or negative), the next 8 bits representing the exponent and the remaining 23 bits represents the fraction of the number, as shown in the lower part of figure 1.3

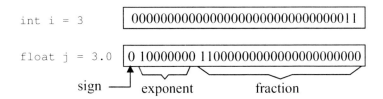

Figure 1.3 Integer and floating-point numbers have different internal structures

In a strongly typed programming language, you can still use different types of variables in a single expression. In this case, one has to do explicit type conversion. In C/C++, explicit type conversion is called **type casting**: the destination type in parentheses is placed before the variable that has an incompatible type. In the following statement, explicit conversion is used to convert variable s of *salary* type and variable a of *age* type into int type:

i = (int)s + (int)a;

Strong type checking basically trades flexibility for reliability. It is generally considered a good policy and is used in most recent programming languages.

1.3.3 ORTHOGONALITY

The word **orthogonality** refers to the property of straight lines meeting at right angles or independent random variables. In programming languages, orthogonality refers to the property of being able to systematically combine various language features. According to the way the features are combined, we can distinguish three kinds of orthogonality: compositional, sort, and number orthogonality.

Compositional orthogonality: If one member of the set of features S_1 can be combined with one member of the set of features S_2, then all members of S_1 can be combined with all members of S_2, as shown in figure 1.4.

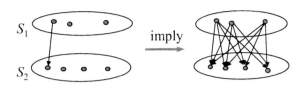

Figure 1.4 Compositional orthogonality

For example, assume that S_1 is the set of different kinds of declarations: (1) plain, (2) initializing, and (3) constant. For example

(1) typex i; (2) typex i = 5; (3) const typex i = 5;

Set S_2 is data types: **boolean, int, float, array**.

If the language is compositionally orthogonal, then we can freely combine these two sets of features in all possible ways:

■ Plain boolean, plain int, plain float, plain array

(1) boolean b; (2) int i; (3) float f; (4) array a[];

■ Initializing boolean, initializing int, initializing float and initializing array

(1) boolean b = true;
(2) int i = 5;
(3) float f = 4.5;
(4) array a[3] = {4, 6, 3};

■ Constant boolean, constant int, constant float, constant array

(1) const boolean b = true;
(2) const int i = 5;
(3) const float f = 7.5;
(4) const array a[3] = {1, 2, 8};

Sort orthogonality: If one member of the set of features S_1 can be combined with one member of the set of features S_2, then **this** member of S_1 can be combined with all members of S_2, as shown in figure 1.5.

For example, if we know that **int i** is allowed (the combination plain-int), according to the sort orthogonality, plain boolean, plain int, plain float, and plain array will be allowed, that is

(1) boolean b;
(2) int i;
(3) float f;
(4) array a[];

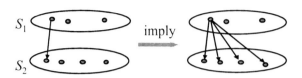

Figure 1.5 Sort orthogonality 1

However, since sort orthogonality does not allow other members of S_1 to combine with members of S_2, we cannot conclude that initializing and constant declarations can be applied to the data types in S_2.

The sort orthogonality can be viewed from the other side. If one member of the set S_1 can be combined with one member of the set S_2, then all members in S_1 can be combined with the members of S_2, as shown in figure 1.6.

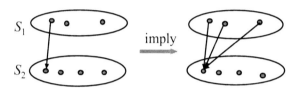

Figure 1.6 Sort orthogonality 2

For example, if the plain declaration can be combined with the **int** type, we conclude that the plain, initializing and constant declarations can be applied to the **int** type.

For example, if we know that **const array a** is allowed (the combination constant-array), according to the sort orthogonality, then plain array, initializing array, and constant array will be allowed:

(1) array a[];

(2) array a[3] = {1, 2, 8};

(3) const array a[3] = {1, 2, 8};

However, since the sort orthogonality does not allow other members of S_2 to combine with members of S_1, we cannot conclude that **boolean**, **int** and **float** type can be declared in three different ways.

Number orthogonality: If one member of the set of features S is allowed, then zero or multiple features of S are allowed. For example, if you can declare a variable in a particular place (in many languages, e.g., C++, and Java, you can put declarations anywhere in the program), you should be able to put zero (no declaration) or multiple declarations in that place. In a class definition, if you can define one member, you should be allowed to define zero or multiple members.

1.4 PROGRAM PROCESSING AND PREPROCESSING

This section discusses what preparations need to be done before the computer hardware can actually execute the programs written in a high-level programming language. Typical techniques used to do the preparation work are preprocessing, interpretation, and compilation.

1.4.1 INTERPRETATION AND COMPILATION

Interpretation of a program is the direct execution of one statement at a time sequentially by the interpreter. **Compilation**, on the other hand, first translates all statements of a program into assembly language code or machine code before any statement is executed. The compiler does not execute the program and we need a separate loader to load the program to the execution environment (hardware or a runtime system that simulates hardware). A compiler allows program modules to be compiled separately. A linker can be used to combine the machine codes separately compiled into one machine code program before we load the program to the execution environment. Figure 1.7 shows typical processing phases of programs using compilation.

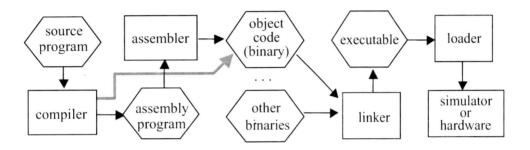

Figure 1.7 Compilation-based program processing

The advantage of interpretation is that a separate program-processing phase (compilation) is saved in the programming language development cycle. The interpreter can immediately and accurately locate the errors. However, the execution speed with interpretation is slower than the execution of machine code after the compilation. It is also more difficult to interpret programs written in very high-level languages.

To make use of the advantages of both compilation and interpretation, Java offers a combined solution to program processing. As shown in figure 1.8, Java source program is first translated by a compiler into an assembly language-like intermediate code, called **bytecode**. Then the bytecode is interpreted by an interpreter called **Java Virtual Machine** (JVM). The advantage of using the intermediate code is that the compiler will be independent of the machine on which the program is executed. Thus, only a single compiler needs to be written for all Java programs running on any machine. Another advantage is that the bytecode is a low level language that can be interpreted easily. It thus makes JVM small enough to be integrated into an Internet browser. In other words, Java bytecode programs can be transferred over the Internet and executed in the client's browser. This ability makes Java the dominant language for Internet application development and implementation.

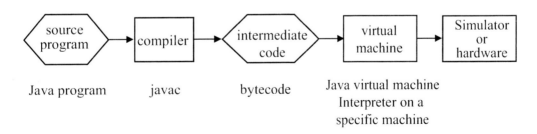

Figure 1.8 Java processing environment

Microsoft's .Net Framework extends the Java environment's compilation and interpretation processing into a two-step compilation process. As shown in figure 1.9, in the first compilation step, a high-level language program is compiled to a low-level language called **intermediate language** (IL). The IL is similar in appearance to an assembly language. Programs in IL language are managed and executed by the **common language runtime** (CLR). Similar to Java's bytecode, the purpose of IL is to make the CLR independent of the high-level programming languages. Compared to JVM, CLR has a richer type system, which makes it possible to support many different programming languages rather than one language only on JVM. Based on the type system, nearly any programming language, say X, can be easily integrated into the system. All we need to do is write a compiler that translates the programs of the X language into the IL intermediate language. Before an IL program can be executed, it must be translated to the machine code (instructions) of the processor on which the programs are executing. The translation job is done by a Just-In-Time (JIT) compiler embedded in CLR. The JIT compiler uses a strategy of compile-when-used and it dynamically allocates blocks of memory for internal data structures when each method is first called. In other words, Just-In-Time compilation lies between the complete compilation and statement-by-statement interpretation.

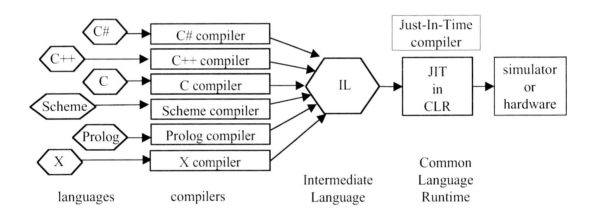

Figure 1.9 Microsoft's Visual Studio .Net programming environment

Unlike the Java environment, the .Net Framework is language agnostic. Although C# is considered its flagship, the .Net Framework is not designed for a specific language. Developers are open to use the common libraries and functionality of the environment, while coding their high-level application in the language of their choice.

1.4.2 Preprocessing: Macro and Inlining

Many programming languages allow programmers to write macros or inline procedures that preserve the structure and readability of programs while retaining the efficiency. The purpose of **program preprocessing** is to support macros and inline procedures. The preprocessing phase is prior to the code translation to the assembly or machine code. The preprocessor is normally a part of the compiler.

In different programming languages, macros can be defined in different ways. In Scheme, we can introduce a **macro** by simply adding a keyword macro in the head of a procedure definition. In C/C++, a macro is introduced by a construct, which is different from a procedure definition:

```
#define name body
```

The #define construct associates the code in the *body* part to the identifier *name* part. The body can be a simple expression or rather complex procedure-like code, where parameter passing is allowed. For example:

```
#define MAXVAL 100
#define QUADFN(a,b) a*a + b*b - 2*a*b
...
x = MAXVAL + QUADFN(5,16);
y = MAXVAL - QUADFN(1,3);
```

The last two statements will be replaced by the macro preprocessor as:

```
x = 100 + 5*5 + 16*16 - 2*5*16;
y = 100 - 1*1 + 3*3 - 2*1*3;
```

where MAXVAL is replaced by 100 and QUADFN(5,16) is replaced by a*a + b*b - 2*a*b, with parameter passing: a is given the value 5 and b is given the value 16, and a is given the value 1 and b is given the value 3, in the two statements respectively.

Macros are more efficient than procedure calls because the body part of the macro is copied into the statement where the macro is called. No control flow change will be necessary. This process is also called **inlining**. On the other hand, if the macro is implemented as a procedure/function:

```
#define MAXVAL 100
int QUADFN(a,b) {return a*a + b*b - 2*a*b;}
...
x = MAXVAL + QUADFN(5,16);
y = MAXVAL - QUADFN(1,3);
```

a procedure will cause a control flow change that usually needs to save the processor environment, including registers and the program counter (return address), onto the stack. This process sometimes is called **out-lining**. Obviously, inlining is much more efficient than out-lining.

Macro preprocessing is basically a very simple and straightforward substitution of the macro *body* for the macro *name*. It is the programmer's responsibility to make sure that such a simple substitution will produce correct code. A slight overlook could lead to programming error. For example, if we want to define a macro to obtain the absolute value of a variable, we write the following macro in C:

```
#define abs(a) ((a<0) ? -a : a)
```

where the C statement ((a<0) ? -a : a) returns -a if a<0, otherwise, it returns a.

This macro definition of the absolute-value function looks correct, but it is not. For example, if we call the macro in the following statement:

```
j = abs(2+5);      // we expect 7 to be assigned to j.
```

The statement does produce correct result. However, if we call the macro in the following statement:

```
j = abs(2-5);      // we expect +3 to be assigned to j.
```

The statement will produce an incorrect result. The reason is that the macro-processor will replace "abs(2-5)" by "((a<0) ? -a : a)" and then replace the parameter "a" by "2-5", resulting in the statement:

j = ((2-5 < 0) ? -2-5 : 2-5);

Since (2-5 < 0) is true, this statement will produce the result of -2-5 = -7, which is assigned to the variable j. Obviously, this result is incorrect, because we expect +3 to be assigned to j.

Let's examine a further example. If we write a statement:

j = abs(-2-5);

The macro-processor will replace "abs(-2-5)" by "((a<0) ? -a : a)" and then replace the parameter "a" by "-2-5", resulting in the statement:

j = ((-2-5 < 0) ? --2-5 : -2-5);

The "--2" in preprocessed statement may result in a compiler error.

The problem in this **abs(a)** macro is that we expect that the expression that replaces **a** to be a unit. All operations within the unit should be done before -a is performed. This is the case when we write a function or procedure. However, the macro replacement does not guarantee this order of operation and the programmer must understand the difference. A correct version of the **abs(a)** macro is:

```
#define abs(a) ((a<0) ? -(a) : a)        // correct version of abs(a) macro
```

Putting the "a" in a pair of parentheses guarantees that the operations within a are completed before -a is performed.

Due to the nature of simple textual replacement, a macro may cause side effects. A **side effect** is an unexpected or unwanted modification of a state. When we use a global variable to pass values between the caller procedure and the called procedure, a modification of the global variable in the called procedure is a side effect.

Let's examine the side effect in the correctly defined **abs(a)** macro discussed above. If we call the macro in the following code

```
i = 3;
j = abs(++i);        // we expect 4 to be assigned to j.
```

According to the way a macro is preprocessed, the following code will be produced by the macro processor:

```
i = 3;
j = ((++i < 0) ? -(++i) : ++i);
```

When the second statement is executed, variable i will be incremented twice: according to the definition of the expression ++i: variable i will be incremented every time before i is accessed. There is another similar expression in C/C++: i++, which increments variable i every time after i is accessed. Similarly, C/C++ have expressions --i and i--, etc.

In the statement above, variable i will be accessed twice: first when we assess (++i < 0), and then the second ++i will be accessed after the condition is assessed as false. As a result, number 5, instead of 4, will be assigned to the variable j.

Macros can be used to bring (in-line) a piece of assembly language code into a high-level language program. For example,

```
#define PORTIO __asm            \
    {                           \
    __asm mov al, 2             \
    __asm mov dx, 0xD007        \
    __asm out al, dx            \
    }
```

The back slash \ means that there is no line-break when performing macro replacement. When we make a macro call to **PORTIO** in the program, this macro call will be replaced by:

```
__asm { __asm mov al, 2 __asm mov dx, 0xD007 __asm out al, dx }
```

where __asm is the C/C++ keyword for assembly instructions. If the compiler is translating the program into assembly code, nothing needs to be done with a line that starts with __asm. If the compiler is translating the program into machine code, the compiler will call the assembler to translate this line into machine code.

The above discussion shows that macros are similar and yet different from procedures and functions, and that both writing macros (ensuring correctness) and using macros (understanding the possible side effects) can be difficult and challenging. Can we write and use macros (obtain better efficiency) exactly in the same way as we write and use procedures and functions (obtain the same simplicity)? Efforts have been made and we are making good progress. As mentioned before, in Scheme, we can write macros in the same way we write procedures. But we still cannot use macros exactly the same way we use procedures. This will be discussed in the chapter on Scheme programming. In C++, "inline" procedures/functions are allowed. All that is needed is to add a keyword **inline** in front of the definition of a procedure/function. For example:

```
inline int sum(int i, int j) {
    return i + j;
}
```

However, the inline procedure/function is slightly different from a macro. A macro call will always be replaced by the body of the macro definition. The macro processor will not check the semantics of the definition. On the other hand, for an inline procedure/function call, the compiler will try to replace the call by its body. There are two possibilities: If the procedure/function is simple enough, the compiler can do the replacement and can guarantee the correctness of the replacement, that is, the inlined code must work exactly in the same way as an ordinary procedure call. If the body of the procedure is too complicated, e.g., uses many variables and complex expressions, the compiler will not perform inlining. The inline procedure will work as an ordinary procedure.

Java has a similar mechanism called **final method**. If a method is declared **final**, it cannot be overridden in a subclass. This is because a call to a final method may have been replaced by its body during compilation, and thus late binding cannot associate the call to a method redefined in a subclass.

*1.5 Program Development

This section briefly introduces the main steps of the program development process, including requirement, specification, design, implementation, testing, proof, and related techniques. Understanding these steps and related techniques involved are extremely important. However, a more detailed discussion on these topics is beyond the scope of this text.

1.5.1 PROGRAM DEVELOPMENT PROCESS

Development of a program normally goes through the following process:

Requirement is an informal description, from the user's point of view, of the functionality of the program to be developed. Requirements are normally informal. For example, "I want the program to sort all numbers in an increasing order" is an informal requirement.

Specification is a formal or semi-formal description of the requirement from the developer's point of view. The specification describes what needs to be done at the functionality level. A formal specification is defined by a set of preconditions on the inputs and a set of postconditions on the outputs. For example, a formal specification of "sorting numbers" can be defined as follows:

Input: $(x_1, x_2, ..., x_n)$
Preconditions on inputs:

$(\forall x_i)(x_i \in I)$, where I is the set of all integer numbers.

Output: $(x_{i1}, x_{i2}, ..., x_{in})$
Postconditions on outputs:

$(\forall x_{ij})(\forall x_{ik})\ ((x_{ij} \in I \wedge x_{ij} \in I \wedge j < k) \rightarrow x_{ij} \leq x_{ik})$.

The **design** step translates what needs to be done (functional specification) into how to do it (procedural steps or algorithm). For example, devising a sorting algorithm to meet the specification belongs to the design step. An algorithm is usually written in a pseudo language that does not have mechanical details of a programming language. A pseudo language focuses on clear and accurate communication with humans, instead of humans and machines.

The **implementation** step actualizes or instantiates the design step using a real programming language. Writing programs in real programming languages is the main topic of this text and will be discussed in much more detail in the following chapters.

The **testing and correctness proof** step tries to show that the implementation does the work defined in the design step or in the specification step. The development process has to return to the implementation or design steps if the implementation does not meet the requirement of the design or the specification.

The **verification and validation** step tries to show that the implementation meets the specification or the user's requirements. The development has to return to design or specification steps if necessary.

In fact, numerous refined phases and iterations within and between these steps can occur during the entire development cycle.

1.5.2 PROGRAM TESTING

In this and the next subsections, we present more detail of the testing and correctness proof step, and related techniques in the program development process.

A **test case** is a set of inputs to a program and the expected outputs that the program will produce if the program is correct and the set of inputs is applied to the program. We also use the **input case** to refer to the input part of a test case. **Program testing** is the process of executing a program by applying pre-designed test cases with the intention of finding programming errors in a given environment. Testing is related to the environment. For example, assume that your program runs correctly on GNU GCC C/C++ environment. If you move your program to Visual Studio C/C++ environment, you need to retest your program because the environment has been changed. **Debugging** is the process of finding the locations and the causes of errors, and fixing them.

If a program has a limited number of possible inputs, we could choose all possible inputs as the test cases to test the program. This approach is called **exhaustive testing**. If the outputs are correct for all test cases, we basically proved the program's correctness.

However, in many cases, a program can take an unlimited number of inputs, or the number of test cases is too big to conduct exhaustive testing. We have two ways to deal with the problem: use incomplete testing or use a formal method to prove the program correctness.

If incomplete testing is used, the question is how we should choose (generate) the limited subset of test cases. Functional testing and structural testing are two major approaches used to generate incomplete test cases. In **functional testing**, we try to generate a subset of test cases that can cover (test) all functions or sub functions of the program under test. Functional testing is also called **black-box testing** because we generate test cases without looking into the structure or source code of the program under test. In **structural testing**, we try to generate a subset of test cases that can cover (test) particular structures of the program under test. For example, we can try to cover all

- statements in the program,
- branches of the control flow, or
- paths from the program's entry point to the program's exiting point.

Structural testing is also called **glass-box testing** or **white-box testing** because we need to have the detail of the control structure and the source code of the program under test.

Both functional testing and structural testing can be considered so-called partition testing. **Partition testing** tries to divide the input domain of the program under test into different groups, so that the inputs in the same group are equivalent in terms of their testing capacity. For example, if we are conducting functional testing, we can consider all inputs that will cause the same sub-function to be executed as a group. On the other hand, if we are conducting structural testing, we can consider all inputs that will cause the same program path to be executed as a group. Then, we choose

- one or several test cases from each group of inputs, and
- one or several inputs on the boundaries between the groups

to test the program. For example, if an integer input is partitioned into two groups: negative and non-negative, then zero is on the boundary and must be chosen as an input case. Obviously, if the partition is done properly, partition testing will have a fair coverage of all parts of the program under test.

Program testing is a topic that can take an entire semester to study. I do not attempt to teach the complete program testing theory and practice in this section. In the rest of the section, I will use a simple example to illustrate some of the important concepts related to the topic.

Example. The gcd function in the following C program is supposed to find the greatest common divisor of two non-negative integers.

```c
#include <stdio.h>
int gcd (int n0, int m0) {          // n0 >= 0 and m0 >= 0 and (n0 ≠ 0 or m0 ≠ 0)
    int n, m;
    n = n0;
    m = m0;
    while (n != 0 && n != m) {       // (n ≠ 0) AND (n ≠ m)
        if (n < m)
                m = m - n;
        else
                n = n - m;
    }
    return m;
```

```
}
void main() {
    int i, j, k;
    scanf("%d\n%d", &i, &j);        // input integers i and j from the keyboard
    k = gcd(i, j);                  // call function gcd
    printf("%d\n", k);              // output the greatest common divisor found
}
```

First, let's "randomly" picked up the following test cases to test the program.

Input	(i, j)	Expected Output k	Actual Output k
	(6, 9)	3	3
	(10, 5)	5	5
	(0, 4)	4	4
	(5, 7)	1	1
	(8, 29)	1	1

We find that the actual output equals to the expected output in all these test cases. Now the question is, is this program correct?

As we know that testing can never prove the correctness of a program unless all possible test cases have been used to test program. However, a set of test cases that can cover different parts of the program can certainly increase the confidence of the correctness of the program.

Now let's apply the structural testing to systematically generate a better set of test cases. We assume that we aim at covering all the branches in the gcd function. To make sure we cover all branches, we first draw the function's flowchart, as shown in figure 1.10. A **flowchart** is an abstraction of a program that outlines the control flows of the program in a graphic form. In the flowchart in figure 1.10, each branch is marked with a circled number.

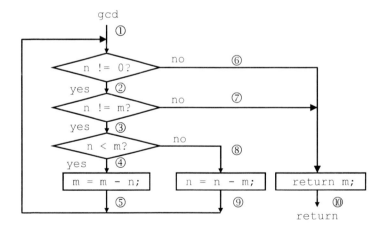

Figure 1.10 The flowchart of gcd function

To obtain a good coverage of the branches, we need to analyze the features of the input domain of the program. For the given program, the input domain has the following features:

- The program takes two non-negative integers as input. The boundary value is 0.
- The branches of the program are controlled by the relative values of a pair of integers. We should consider to choose equal and unequal pairs of numbers.
- The great common divisors are related the divisibility of integers, or the prime, and nonprime numbers. We should choose some prime number and some nonprime numbers.

Based on the analysis, we can choose, for example, these values for both i and j: boundary value 0, two prime numbers 2 and 3, and two nonprime numbers 9 and 10.

The combination of the two inputs generates following input cases:

(0, 0)   // This case is not allowed according to the precondition.

(0, 2), (0, 3), (0, 9), (0, 10)

(2, 0), (2 2), (2, 3), (2, 9), (2, 10)

(3, 0), (3, 2), (3, 3), (3, 9), (3, 10)

(9, 0), (9, 2), (9, 3), (9, 9), (9, 10)

(10, 0), (10, 2), (10, 3), (10, 9), (10, 10)

We can apply all these test cases to test the program. We can also reduce the number of test cases by partitioning the input cases into groups: Two input cases belong to the same group, if they cover the same branches in the same order. Table 1.2 lists the groups, a representative from each group, the expected output of the representative input case, and the branches covered by the groups.

Table 1.2 Input case partitions and the branch coverage

Groups partitioned	Representative	Expected gcd output	Branches covered
(0, 2),(0, 3),(0, 9),(0, 10)	(0, 2)	2	①⑥⑩
(2 2),(3, 3), (9, 9),(10, 10)	(2 2)	2	①②⑦⑩
(2, 0),(3, 0), (9, 0),(10, 0)	(2, 0)	2	①②③⑧⑨
(2, 3),(2, 9), (3, 10), (9, 10)	(2, 3)	1	①②③④⑤⑧⑨⑩
(2, 10), (3, 9)	(2, 10)	2	①②③④⑤⑦⑩
(3, 2),(9, 2), (10, 3),(10, 9)	(3, 2)	1	①②③⑧⑨④⑤⑩
(9, 3), (10, 2)	(9, 3)	3	①②③⑦⑧⑨⑩

If we choose the representative input from each group and the expected output as the test cases, we obtain a test case set can cover all the branches in the flowchart. Apply this set of test case, we will find that the input case (2, 0) will not be able to produce the expected output. In fact, a dead-looping situation will occur. Thus, we successfully find that the program is incorrect.

1.5.3 CORRECTNESS PROOF

To prove the correctness of a program, we need to prove that, for all predefined inputs (inputs that meet the preconditions), the program produces correct outputs (outputs that meet the postconditions).

Program proof consists of two steps: **partial correctness** and **termination**. A program is partially correct if an input that satisfies the preconditions is applied to the program, and if the program terminates, the output satisfies the postconditions. A program terminates, if for all inputs that meet the preconditions, the program will stop in finite execution steps. A program is totally correct (**total correctness**), if the program is partially correct and the program terminates.

The idea of partial correctness proof is to prove that, any input that meets the preconditions at the program entry point will be processed, step by step through the statements between the entry point and the exiting point, and the postconditions will be satisfied at the exiting point. Obviously, if there is no loop in the program, it is not too hard to do the step-by-step proof. However, if there is a loop in the program, the step-by-step approach won't work. In this case, we need use the loop invariant technique to drive the condition to be proved through the loop. A **loop invariant** is a condition that is true in each iteration of the loop. To prove a condition is a loop invariant, we can use mathematical induction: We prove that the condition is true when the control enters the loop for the first time (iteration 1). We assume that the condition is true at iteration k, and prove that the condition will be true at the iteration $k+1$.

Finding the loop invariant that can lead to the postconditions is the most challenging task of the correctness proof. You must have a deep understanding of the problem in order to define a proper loop invariant.

Proving the termination is easy if we design the loops following these guidelines. The loop variable

- is an enumerable variable, e.g., an integer;
- has a lower bound, e.g., will be greater than or equal to zero;
- will strictly decrease. Strictly decrease means that value of the loop variable must be strictly less than the value of the variable in the previous iteration. The "<" relation is strict while "≤" is not.

If you do not follow the guideline, you may have trouble proving the termination of even a simple program. In an exercise given at the end of the chapter, a very simple example is given where many input numbers have been tried and the program stops. However, nobody can prove so far the program terminates for all inputs.

Now let's use a similar example that we used in the last section to illustrate the proof concepts we discussed above. The program is given in a pseudo language. Since we don't have to actually execute the program, we don't have to give the program in a real programming language.

```
gcd (n0, m0)
// precondition: (n0 ≥ 0 ∧ m0 ≥ 0) ∧ (n0 ≠ 0 ∨ m0 ≠ 0) ∧ (n0, m0 are integer)
    n = n0;
    m = m0;
    while n ≠ 0 do
// loop invariant:    (n ≥ ∧ m ≥ 0) ∧ (n ≠ 0 ∨ m ≠ 0) ∧
//                    max{u: u|n and u|m} = max{u: u|n0 and u|m0}
        if n ≤ m
        then    m = m - n
        else    swap(n, m)
    output(m)
// postconditions: m = max{u: u|n0 and u|m0}
```

To prove the partial correctness, we need to prove, for any integer pair (n0, m0) that meets the preconditions, the loop invariant is true in every iteration of the loop. When the control completes all the iterations of the loop and reaches the exiting point of the program, the postconditions will be true. As I said, finding the loop invariant is the most difficult part. Now we are given the condition that should be a loop invariant, and we only need to prove that the condition is indeed a loop invariant. The given condition is

$$(n \geq \wedge\ m \geq 0) \wedge (n \neq 0 \vee m \neq 0) \wedge \max\{u: u|n \text{ and } u|m\} = \max\{u: u|n0 \text{ and } u|m0\}$$

We need to prove it is a loop invariant. We can use the mathematical induction to prove it in the following steps.

(1) Prove the condition is true at the iteration 1: It is obvious.

(2) Assume the condition is true at iteration k.

(3) Prove the condition is true in iteration k+1.

Since the conversion made in each iteration is

gcd(n, m) $\Rightarrow$ gcd(n, m - n), or

gcd(n, m) $\Rightarrow$ gcd(m, n)

According to mathematical facts

gcd(n, m) = gcd(n, m - n), and

gcd(n, m) = gcd(m, n)   .

Thus, from iteration k to iteration k+1, the condition will remain to be true. Therefore, we prove the condition is a loop invariant.

Next, we need to prove that the loop invariant leads to the postconditions. It can be easily seen from the program that if the loop invariant is true when the control leaves the loop, the postconditions will indeed be true. Thus, we have proved the partial correctness of the program.

To prove the program terminates, we can use the following facts:

(1) The loop variable is (n, m). The loop variable is enumerable.

(2) If we consider the dictionary order, that is

(n, m) > (n, m - n), if n $\geq$ m   // e.g. (3, 6) > (3, 3) in dictionary order

(n, m) > (m, n),   if n > m.   // (6, 3) > (3, 6) in dictionary order

we can see that there is strictly decreasing order on the loop variable (n, m) based on the dictionary order.

(3) There is a lower bound on the value that (n, m) can take, that is (0, 0).

Since the loop variable (n, m) is enumerable, it decreases strictly, and there is a lower bound (0, 0), the loop must terminate.

In an exercise given at the end of the chapter, a variation of the gcd program is suggested. Try to prove its partial correctness and its termination.

1.6 SUMMARY

In this chapter, we introduced in section 1.1 the concepts of the four major programming paradigms: imperative, object-oriented, functional, and logic paradigms. We looked at the impact of language features on the performance of the programs written in the language. We overviewed the development of languages and relationship of different languages. We then discussed in section 1.2 the structures of programs at four levels: lexical, syntactic, contextual, and semantic structures. We deliberated our discussion on the lexical and syntactic levels by introducing the BNF notation and syntax graph. We used BNF notation to define the lexical and syntactic structures of a simple programming language. In section

1.3, we studied the important concepts in programming languages, including data types, type checking, type equivalence, and type conversion. Orthogonality was used to examine the regularity and simplicity of programming languages. Finally, in section 1.4, we briefly discussed program processing via compilation, interpretation, and combination of the two techniques. The emphasis was on the macro and inline procedures/functions in C/C++. We studied how to define and use macros, and what their strengths and weakness are when compared to ordinary procedures/functions. In section 1.5, we overviewed the the program development process and discussed programming testing and proof techniques through examples.

1.7 HOMEWORK AND PROGRAMMING EXERCISES

1.   Multiple Choice. Choose only one answer in each question. Choose the best answer if more than one answer is acceptable.

1.1   Stored Program Concept (von Neumann machine) is one of the most fundamental concepts in computer science. What programming paradigm most-closely follows this concept?
      ❏ imperative   ❏ object-oriented   ❏ functional   ❏ logic

1.2   If you teach someone to make a pizza, you are in fact teaching
      ❏ imperative programming   ❏ functional programming

      If you teach someone to order a pizza from a restaurant, you are in fact teaching
      ❏ imperative programming   ❏ functional programming

1.3   Because of the hardware constraint, early programming languages emphasized on
      ❏ efficiency   ❏ orthogonality   ❏ reliability   ❏ readability

1.4   What factor is generally considered more important in modern programming language design?
      ❏ readability   ❏ writeability   ❏ efficiency   ❏ None

1.5   The main idea of structured programming is to
      ❏ reduce the types of control structures.   ❏ increase the types of control structures.
      ❏ make programs to execute faster.   ❏ use BNF to define the syntactic structure.

1.6   In the following pseudo code, which programming language allows the mixed use of data types?

      ```
      int i = 1; char c = 'a';      // declaration and initialization
      c = c + i;                    // execution of an assignment statement
      ```

      ❏ Ada   ❏ C   ❏ Java   ❏ All of them

1.7   In the layers of programming language structure, which layer performs type checking?
      ❏ lexical   ❏ syntactic   ❏ contextual   ❏ semantic

1.8   The contextual structure of a programming language defines
      ❏ how to form lexical units from characters.
      ❏ how to put lexical units together to form statements.
      ❏ the static semantics that will be checked by the compiler.
      ❏ the dynamic semantics of programs under execution.

1.9   Interpretation is NOT efficient if
      ❏ the source program is small.
      ❏ the source program is written in an assembly language.
      ❏ the difference between source and destination is small.
      ❏ multi-module programming is used.

1.10 Inlining (inline function) in C++ is implemented in such a way that
- ❏ the compiler decides whether to bring the body of the function into the caller.
- ❏ the compiler simply copies and pastes the body of the function in the place of the function call.
- ❏ the macro is implemented.
- ❏ inlining is considered a special case macro.

2. Compare and contrast the four programming paradigms: imperative, object-oriented, functional, and logic.

3. Use the library and Internet resources to compile a table of programming languages. The table must include all programming languages mentioned in the section on the development of programming languages. The table should contain the following columns:
- ■ name of the programming language,
- ■ year the language was first announced,
- ■ authors/inventors of the language,
- ■ predecessor languages (for example, C++ and Smalltalk are predecessors of Java),
- ■ programming paradigms (for example, Java belongs to imperative and object-oriented programming paradigms).

The table should be sorted by the year.

4. What is strong type checking, and what are its advantages? List a few languages that use nearly strong type checking in their program compilations.

5. What is weak type checking, and what are its advantages? List a few languages that use weak type checking in their program compilations.

6. What is orthogonality? What are the differences between compositional, sort, and number orthogonality?

7. Compare and contrast a macro and an inline function in C++. Which one is more efficient in execution time? Which one is easier for programmers to write?

8. Compare and contrast the C++ inline function and the Java's final method.

9. Which type equivalence leads to strong type checking, structural equivalence, or name equivalence? Explain your answer.

10. Use BNF notation to define a small programming language that includes the definition of variable, math-operator, math-expression, condition-operator, condition-expression, assignment statement, loop statement, switch statement, and a block of statements. A variable must start and end with a letter (an unusual requirement). A single letter is a valid variable. The definition of the expression must be able to handle nested expressions like $2*(x + y)$, and $5* ((u + v)*(x - y))$. The language must include the following statements:

Assignment: It assigns (the value of) a variable or an expression to a variable. For example, $x = 2*(y + z)$.

Conditional: if-then and if-then-else. The condition in the statement can be simply defined as an expression.

For-loop: e.g., for ($i = 0$; $i < 10$; $i=i+1$) {a block of statements}

Switch: It must have an unlimited number of cases.

Statement: A statement can be an assignment, conditional, for-loop or switch statement.

Block. One statement is a block, zero or multiple statements in curly braces and separated by ";" is also a block, according to number orthogonality. For example, $i=i+2$; is a block. {i=i+2; for (k=0; k<i; k=k+1) {i=i+1; s=2*i}} is also a block.

11. The following syntax graph defines the identifiers of a programming language, where *alpha* is the set of characters "a" through "z" and "A" through "Z", *digit* is the set of characters "0" through "9", and *underscore* is the character "_".

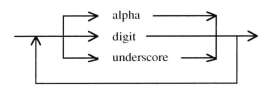

11.1 Which of the following strings can be accepted by the syntax graph (choose all correct answers)?
❏ _FooBar25_   ❏ 2_5fooBar_   ❏ Foo&Bar   ❏ 12.5   ❏ Foo2bar

11.2 Give the syntax graph that defines the identifiers always **starting** with a letter from the set *alpha*.

11.3 Give the BNF definition equivalent to the syntax graph of the question above.

12.   Given the C program below, answer the following questions.

```
#define min1(x,y) ((x < y) ? x : y)
#define min 10
#include <stdio.h>
int min2(int x, int y) {
        if (x < y) return x;
        else return y;
}
void main() {
        int a, b;
        scanf("%d %d", &a, &b);
        if (b < min)
                printf("input out of range\n");
        else {
                a = min1(a, b++);
                printf("a = %d, b = %d\n", a, b);
                a = min2(a, b++);
                printf("a = %d, b = %d\n", a, b);
        }
}
```

12.1 Give the exact C code of the statement "a = min1(a, b++);" after the macro processing.

12.2 Give the exact C code of the statement "a = min2(a, b++);" after the macro processing.

12.3   Give the exact C code of the statement "if (b < min)" after the macro processing.

12.4   Assume 60 and -30 are entered as inputs, what is the exact output of the program?

12.5   Assume 50 and 30 are entered as input, what is the exact output of the program?

13.   Assume a programming language has two sets of features. S_1 is the set of three different kinds of declarations: (1) plain, (2) initializing, and (3) constant. That is,

(1) typex i; (2) typex i = 5; (3) const typex i = 5;
S_2 is the set of data types: (a) bool, (b) int, (c) float, (d) array, (e) char

13.1   If the language guarantees sort orthogonality in figure 1.5, and we know that int i is allowed (the combination plain-int), list the allowed combinations of the features of the two sets that can be implied by the sort orthogonality.

13.2   If the language guarantee sort orthogonality in figure 1.6, and we know that const array a is allowed (the combination constant-array), list the allowed combinations of the features of the two sets that can be implied by the sort orthogonality.

13.3   If the language guarantees the compositional orthogonality, list the combinations of the two sets of features allowed. Write a simple C program that exercises all the declarations in this question. Each declared variable must be used at least once in the program. The purpose of the program is to test whether C supports compositional orthogonality. The program thus does not have to be semantically meaningful. Test the program on Visual Studio or GNU GCC, and submit a syntax error-free program. Note: a variable can only be declared once. You must use different variable names in the declarations.

14. Programming exercise.
     You are given the following simple C program.

```
*/ assign1.c is the file name of the program.
#include <stdio.h>              // use C style I/O library function
main () {                       // main function
        int i = 0, j = 0;  // initialization
        printf("Please enter a 5-digit integer \n");
        scanf("%d", &i);        // input an integer
        i = i % 10000;  // modulo operation
        printf("Please repeat the number you entered\n");
        scanf("%d", &j);        // input an integer
        j = j % 10000;          // modulo operation
        if (i == j)             // conditional statement
                printf("The number you entered is %d\n", i);
        else                    // else branch
                printf("The numbers you entered are different\n");
}
```

14.1 Enter the program in a development environment e.g., Visual C++ or GNU GCC. Save the file as assign1.c. If you are not familiar with any programming environment, please read section B.2 of Appendix B.

14.2 Compile and execute the program.

14.3 Read chapter two, section 2.1. Modify the given program. Change <stdio.h> to <iostream.h>. Change printf to cout and change scanf to cin, etc. Save the file as assign1.cpp

14.4 Compile and execute the program.

15. Macros are available in most high-level programming languages. The body of a macro is simply used to replace a macro-call during the preprocessing stage in compilation. A macro introduces an "inline" function that is normally more efficient than an "out-line" function. However, macros suffer from side-effect, unwanted or unexpected modifications of variables. Macros should be used cautiously. The main purpose of the following program is to demonstrate the differences between a function and a macro. Other purposes include learning different ways of writing comments, formatted input and output, variable declaration and initialization, unary operation ++, macro definition/call, function definition/call, if-then-else and loop structures, etc. Study the following program carefully and answer the following questions.

```
/* The purpose of this program is to compare and contrast a function to a macro. It shows the
side effect of a macro and an incorrect definition of a macro. The macros/functions abs1(x),
abs2(x) and  abs3(x) are supposed to return the absolute value of x.  */
#define abs1(a) ((a<0) ? -(a) : (a))     // macro definition
#define abs2(a) ((a<0) ? -a : a)         // macro definition
#include <stdio.h>
int abs3(int a) {                        // function definition
        return ((a<0) ? -(a) : (a));     // —> if(a < 0) return -a else return a;
}
void main() {
        int i1 = 0, i2 = 0, i3 = 0, j1 = 0, j2 = 0, j3 = 0;
        printf("Please enter 3 integers\n");
        scanf("%d %d %d", &i1, &i2, &i3);
        while (i1 != 123) {              // 123 is used as sentinel
                j1 = abs1(++i1 - 2);    // call a macro
                j2 = abs2(++i2 - 2);    // call a macro
                j3 = abs3(++i3 - 2);    // call a function
                printf("j1 = %d, j2 = %d, j3 = %d\n", j1, j2, j3);
                printf("Please enter 3 integers\n");
                scanf("%d %d %d", &i1, &i2, &i3);
        }
}
```

15.1 Desk check (manually trace) the program. What would be the outputs of the program when the following sets of inputs are applied to the program?

i1, i2, i3 = 9, 9, 9   j1, j2, j3 =
i1, i2, i3 = -5, -5, -5   j1, j2, j3 =
i1, i2, i3 = 0, 0, 0   j1, j2, j3 =

15.2 Enter the program into a programming environment and execute the program using the inputs given in the previous question. What are the outputs of the program?

15.3 Explain the side-effects that occurred in the program.

15.4 Which macro is incorrectly defined? Explain your answer.

15.5 Change the macros in the program into inline functions.

16. Consider the gcd program in section 1.5.3. What would happen if the else-branch swap(n, m) in the program is changed to n = n - m?

16.1 Can we still prove the partial correctness?

16.2 Can we prove the termination?

16.3 Write a C program to implement the original algorithm and find a set of test cases to test your program. The test case set must cover all the branches of the program.

17. Given the following algorithm

termination(n) // precondition: n is any integer
    while n ≠ 1 do
        if even(n)
        then   n := n/2
        else   n := 3n + 1
    output(n) // postcondition: n = 1

17.1 Prove the program is partially correct.

17.2 Discuss whether this program terminates or not.

17.3 Write a C program to implement the algorithm, generate a set of test cases that can cover all branches of the program, and use the set of test cases to test the program.

2

The Imperative Programming Languages, C/C++

As we discussed in chapter one, the imperative paradigm manipulates named data in a fully specified, fully controlled and step-wise fashion. It focuses on how to do the job instead of what needs to be done. Imperative programs are algorithmic in nature: do this, do that, and then repeat the operation n times, etc., similar to the instruction manuals of our home appliances. The coincidence between the imperative paradigm and the algorithmic nature makes the imperative paradigm the most popular paradigm among all possible different ways of writing programs. Another major strength of the imperative paradigm is its resemblance to the native language of the computer (von Neumann machine), which makes it efficient to translate and execute the high-level language programs in the imperative paradigm.

In this chapter, we study the imperative programming languages C/C++. We will focus more on C and the non-object-oriented part of C++. We will study the object-oriented part of C++ in the next chapter.

By the end of this chapter, you should

- ■ have a solid understanding of the imperative paradigm;
- ■ be able to apply the flow control structures of C language to write a program;
- ■ be able to explain the execution process of C programs on a computer;
- ■ be able to write programs with complex control structures including conditional, loop structures, function call, and parameter passing, and recursive structures;
- ■ be able to write programs with complex data types, including arrays, pointers, structures, and collection of structures.

The chapter is organized as follows. Section 2.1 gives a quick tutorial on C/C++ so that students can start their laboratory work on C. Section 2.2 introduces the C/C++ control structures. Sections 2.3, 2.4, and 2.5 discuss data declaration, scope and basic data types; constant, array, pointer and string; type construction, including enumeration type, union type, structured types, and file types. Section 2.5 also presents several large program examples using array, pointer, and structures. Section 2.6 studies the functions, function calls, and parameter passing mechanism in C language. Section 2.7 teaches a unique technique of understanding recursion and writing recursive programs in four easy steps. Finally, Section 2.8 briefly discusses how to construct C programs into modules and use modules to form larger programs.

Imperative programming is largely based on the computer architectures and assembly language programming. We thus briefly discuss the basic computer architectures as the background material in Appendix A.

37

2.1 Getting Started With C/C++

In this section, we first introduce how to write your first C/C++ program and how to perform input and output. You can develop your programs in different programming environments. Three most frequently used programming environments, GNU GCC and MS Visual Studio .Net, are introduced in Appendix B.

2.1.1 Write Your First C/C++ Program

A C program consists of one or more functions. There are two kinds of functions:

■ Built-in functions are pre-written and exist in **libraries**, for example, input and output functions (printf, scanf in C and cin, cout in C++), mathematical functions (abs, sin, cos, sqrt);

■ User defined functions are written by the programmers.

The main() is a function that all C/C++ programs must have, which is the entry point of a program, i.e., execution of all programs begin at the first statement of main function. The shortest and simplest C/C++ program is:

```
void main() { }
```

Obviously, this program does nothing. Usually, main will have some statements and invoke other user written or library functions to perform some job. For example:

```
/* My first program, file name hello.c
    This program prints "hello world" on the screen */
#include <stdio.h> // the library functions in stdio will be used
void main( ) {
    printf("hello, world\n");
}
```

The simple C program will call a library function printf to print

hello, world

The first two lines are comments. There are two ways to write comments in C/C++. Multi-line comments can be quoted in a pair of /* and */, while single line comments can simply follow double slashes //.

The third line of the program specifies what library package will be used. In this program, we use printf that is defined in the stdio package. In the print statement, "\n" is the "newline" control symbol that puts this output on a line by itself. Another useful control symbol is "\t" for tab.

A C/C++ function may return a value (like Pascal function) or return no value (like a Pascal procedure). A function may take zero or a number of parameters. The following are several forms of the main function:

```
main () { ... }
void main( ) { ... }
int main() {... return 0;}
void main (int argc, char *argv [ ]) {...}
```

The first and the second forms do not require the function to return a value. The third form requires the function to return an integer value. The fourth form does not require a return value but requires parameter inputs.

You may ask how do we or why do we need to pass values to the function that will be called before any other statements or functions are executed? The answer is that the parameters to the **main()** function allow it to take command line inputs, used to specify, e.g., the name of data file.

For example, if we compiled our first program **hello.c** into the executable code **hello.exe**, we can execute the program by simply typing the name **hello** and the **Enter** key. However, if we have a program, say, called **letterReader.exe** that reads a text file, say, **letter.txt**, then we need to execute the program by typing

letterReader letter.txt

where the file name "letter.txt" will be passed to the main function of the program **letterReader** as a parameter.

Unlike Java, C/C++ functions and variables may exist outside any class or functions. These functions and variables are **global**. Function **main()** is always a global function.

2.1.2 BASIC INPUT AND OUTPUT FUNCTIONS

Generally, input in C/C++ is reading from a file and output is writing to a file. The keyboard is considered the standard input file and the monitor screen is considered the standard output file. The functions **getchar()** and **putchar(x)** are the basic I/O library functions in C. **getchar()** fetches one character from the keyboard every time it is called, and returns that character as the value of the function. After it reaches the last character of a file, it returns **EOF** (end of file), signifying the end of the file. On the other hand, **putchar(x)** prints one character (the character stored in variable x) on the screen every time it is called. The following program reads a line of characters from the keyboard and prints it on the screen. Since both standard input and output are in fact files, a similar program can be used to copy the contents of one file to another.

```
#include <stdio.h>
main( ) {
    char c;                 // declare c as a character type variable
    c = getchar( );         // input one character from the keyboard
    while (c != '\n') {     // while c ≠ the newline control symbol
        putchar(c);         // print to screen
        c = getchar( );     // input another character from the keyboard
    }
}
```

2.1.3 FORMATTED INPUT AND OUTPUT FUNCTIONS

The basic input/output functions allow us to read and write a character at a time. They cannot be used to read and write other types of variables and cannot control the format of output.

The formatted input/output functions are **printf** and **scanf** that take an argument for formatting information. The following program demonstrates a simple use of the functions.

```
// The program takes a number from the keyboard, processes the number
// and then prints the result
```

```
#include <stdio.h>
main () {
    int i;              // i is an integer type variable
    float n = 5.0;      // n is floating-point type and is initialized to 5.0
    printf("Please enter an integer\n");
    scanf("%d", &i);          // An integer is expected from the keyboard
    if (i > n)
            n = n + i;
    else
            n = n - i;
    printf("i = %d\t n = %f\n", i, n);   //%d, \t, %f, and \n control formats
}
```

Assume a number 12 is entered when scanf is executed, the output of the program is

i = 12   n = 17.0

Generally, the formats of scanf and printf are

```
scanf ("control sequence", &variable1, &variable2, ... &variablek);
printf ("control sequence", expressions);
```

In the scanf function, the ampersand '&' is the address-of operator that returns the address of the variable. Using address-of operator in the argument of a function, e.g., &i in scanf, enforces parameter passing by reference. Parameter passing mechanisms will be explained in more detail later in Section 2.6.

In the printf function, the "expressions" is a list of expressions whose values are to be printed out. Each expression is separated by a comma.

The control sequence includes constant strings to be printed, e.g., "i = ", and control symbols to be used to convert the input/output from their numeric values that are stored in the computer to their character format displayed. The control symbol "%d" in the scanf and printf signifies that the next argument in the argument list is to be interpreted as a decimal number and "%f" signifies that the next argument is to be interpreted as a floating-point number. The other control characters include "%c" for characters and "%s" for strings of characters. The symbol "\n" and "\t" signify the "newline" that puts the next output on a new line, and "tab" that puts the next output after a tab. If there is no "newline" or "tab" at the end of the first output line, successive calls to printf (or putchar) will simply append the string or character to the previous output line.

In C++, a different library package and different I/O functions are used. When you use C++ specific features, your program name must have an extension .cpp for C++ program. If you use extension .c, your program will be considered to be a C program only, and you will obtain compilation error for C++ specific features.

```
#include <iostream.h>          // iostream.h is the C++ library I/O package
void main() {
    int i, j, sum;              // declaration
    cout << "Enter an integer" << endl; // prompt for input
    cin >> i;                   // read an integer and put in variable i
```

```
    cout << "Enter an integer" << endl;
    cin >> j;                      // read an integer and put in variable j
    sum = i + j;
    cout << "Sum is " << sum << endl; // print sum
}
```

A scenario of execution of the program is

```
Enter an integer
5
Enter an integer
7
Sum is 12
```

In the program, the functions **cin** and **cout** are C++ standard input and output functions. The function **endl** is the C++ **newline** function corresponding to C's **"\n"**.

In C formatted I/O, a programmer must specify the type of variables to be printed. In C++, the types are automatically recognized. This improvement simplifies printing statements in most cases. Unfortunately, we still have situations where we have to tell the program what type of data to print. For example, a character type in C/C++ is same as an integer type. How do we tell the program that we want to print a character or an integer? The solution is type casting. The following example shows how a character type variable c, initialized to 68 and corresponding to the ASCII character 'D', is printed as integer 68 and as character 'D' using **printf** and **std::cout**, respectively. The ASCII table is given in the Appendix C.

```
#include <iostream>          // <iostream> is a variation of <iostream.h>
void main(void) {
    char c = 68;
    printf("c = %d", c);
    printf("\tc = %c\n", c);
    std::cout<<"c = "<<(int) c;
    std::cout<<"\tc = "<<c<<std::endl;
}
```

The output of the program is

```
c = 68      c = D
c = 68      c = D
```

Please note that C++ I/O package **<iostream>** contains all C styled I/O functions and control symbols like **printf, scanf**, "\n" and "\t".

2.2 Control Structures in C/C++

In this section, we briefly review the basic control structures in C/C++, which are similar in all imperative programming languages. The topics we will discuss are

- operators and the order of evaluation,
- basic selection structures,
- multiple selection structures, and
- iteration structures.

Recursion structures are much more complex and will be discussed in Section 2.7 in full detail. Chapters 4 and 5 will have even more discussions on this topic.

2.2.1 OPERATORS AND THE ORDER OF EVALUATION

C/C++ provide a set of operators to allow programmers to write complex arithmetic and logical expressions. The **precedence** and **associativity** of C/C++ operators affect the grouping and evaluation of operands in expressions. Table 2.1 summarizes the precedence and associativity (the order in which the operands are evaluated) of C operators, listing them in order of precedence from highest to lowest. Operators with higher-precedence operators are evaluated first. If two operators have equal precedence (they appear at the same level in the table), they are evaluated according to their associativity, either from right to left or from left to right, as defined in the right column of the table.

Table 2.1 C/C++ Operators and Their Precedence

Operators	Type of Operation	Associativity
[ ] ( ) . –> postfix ++ and postfix --	Expression	Left to right
prefix ++ and prefix -- sizeof & * + - ~ !	Unary	Right to left
typecasts	Unary	Right to left
* / %	Multiplicative	Left to right
+ −	Additive	Left to right
<< >>	Logical bitwise shift	Left to right
< > <= >=	Relational	Left to right
== !=	Equality	Left to right
&	Bitwise-AND	Left to right
^	Bitwise-exclusive-OR	Left to right
|	Bitwise-inclusive-OR	Left to right
&&	Logical-AND	Left to right
||	Logical-OR	Left to right
? :	Conditional-expression	Right to left
= *= /= %= += −= <<= >>= &= ^= |=	Assignment	Right to left
,	Sequential evaluation	Left to right

Please note C/C++ use **lazy evaluation** policy, that is, an expression will be evaluated, only if its value is needed. For example, if we have an expression

(i == 0) && j++

the second operand, j++, will be evaluated only if i == 0 is true (nonzero). Thus, j will not be incremented if i == 0 is false (0).

2.2.2 BASIC SELECTION STRUCTURES (IF-THEN-ELSE AND THE CONDITIONAL EXPRESSION)

The basic selection structure in C/C++ is implemented by **if-then** and **if-then-else** statements, which can be defined by the syntax graph in figure 2.1.

Figure 2.1 Syntax graph for if-then-else in C/C++

In the syntax graph, **<block1>** and **<block2>** contain zero, one, or a block of statements enclosed within curly braces. The **<condition>** is any expression that evaluates to integer value. If the expression evaluates to 0 (considered "false"), **<block2>** will be executed, otherwise (any non-zero value will be considered "true"), **<block1>** will be executed. In the syntax graph, we omitted the arrow before the keyword if. In C, there is no Boolean type, while in C++ a Boolean type is predefined.

The following example illustrates the use of conditional structure and logic and relational operators.

```
if (a == b && c <= d)
    x = 0;
else {
    x = 1;
    y = 2;
}
```

The character sequence "&&" is a **logical operator** for AND. The character sequences "==" and "<=" are called **relational operators**. A complete set of arithmetic and logical operators are given in table 2.1.

C/C++ also provides a ternary **conditional operator** "?:" to form a **conditional expression**. The conditional operator takes three operands and performs similar selection function as if-then-else statement. The general form of the conditional operator is given in figure 2.2.

In the syntax graph, **<operand1>** and **<operand2>** can be any expression that return a value or a simple assignment statement, in which case, the assigned value will be considered the return value of the operand. When the conditional expression is executed, the **<condition>** is first tested. If it returns a non-zero or true value, **<operand1>** will be evaluated; otherwise, **<operand2>** will be evaluated.

$$\rightarrow \ (\rightarrow \ \text{<condition>} \rightarrow \ ? \rightarrow \ \text{<operand1>} \rightarrow \ : \ \rightarrow \ \text{<operand2>} \rightarrow \ ) \rightarrow \ ; \rightarrow$$

Figure 2.2 Syntax graph for the conditional operator in C/C++

The following example illustrates different ways of using the conditional expression and their effects. A conditional expression can be used as an expression in the right hand side of an assignment statement or as a standalone statement.

```
#include <stdio.h>
main() {
    int i,j,k;
```

```
    i = 0;                          // i = 0 represents the false value
    j = (i? 5 : 9);                 // 9 will be assigned to j
    i = 2;                          // i! = 0 represents the true value
    k = (i? 5 : 9);                 // 5 will be assigned to k
    printf("i = %d, j = %d, k = %d, \n", i, j, k):
}
```

2.2.3 MULTIPLE SELECTION STRUCTURE (SWITCH)

The basic selection statements select one out of two cases. If we have multiple choices, we need to use nested if-then-else statements. For example:

```
if (ch == '+')       x = a + b;
else if (ch == '-')  x = a - b;
else if (ch == '*')  x = a * b;
else if (ch == '/')  x = a / b;
else printf("invalid operator");
```

It is often more convenient in such situations that a multiple selection statement switch is used, as defined in figure 2.3.

The case statements label different actions we want to execute. The loop in the definition signifies that we can have any number of case statements (the number must be greater than or equal to one). The break statements, which exit the switch construct if a case is satisfied, are optional (there is a bypass route). The default case is performed if none of the other cases are satisfied. According to the definition, default is optional (there is bypass route). If default is not included and none of the cases match, no action will be executed. For example, the following piece of code selects one of the four operations.

```
switch (ch) {
    case '+': x = a + b; break;
    case '-': x = a - b; break;
    case '*': x = a * b; break;
    case '/': x = a / b; break;
    default: printf("invalid operator");
}
```

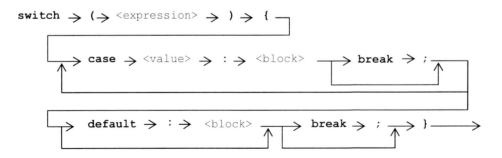

Figure 2.3 Syntax graph for switch in C/C++

Including the **break** statements in the code is not an efficiency issue that many people believe it to be. What would happen if any one of the four **break** statements is omitted? Let's examine the following program without the **break** statements.

```c
/* This C program demonstrates the switch statement without using breaks.
   The program is tested on MS Visual C++ platform */
#include <stdio.h>
void main() {
    char ch = '+';
    int f, a=10, b=20;
    printf("ch = %c\n", ch);
    switch (ch) {
            case '+': f = a + b; printf("f = %d\n", f);
            case '-': f = a - b; printf("f = %d\n", f);
            case '*': f = a * b; printf("f = %d\n", f);
            case '/': f = a / b; printf("f = %d\n", f);
            default: printf("invalid operator\n");
    }
    ch = '-';
    printf("ch = %c\n", ch);
    switch (ch) {
            case '+': f = a + b; printf("f = %d\n", f);
            case '-': f = a - b; printf("f = %d\n", f);
            case '*': f = a * b; printf("f = %d\n", f);
            case '/': f = a / b; printf("f = %d\n", f);
            default: printf("invalid operator\n");
    }
    ch = '*';
    printf("ch = %c\n", ch);
    switch (ch) {
            case '+': f = a + b; printf("f = %d\n", f);
            case '-': f = a - b; printf("f = %d\n", f);
            case '*': f = a * b; printf("f = %d\n", f);
            case '/': f = a / b; printf("f = %d\n", f);
            default: printf("invalid operator\n");
    }
    ch = '/';
    printf("ch = %c\n", ch);
    switch (ch) {
            case '+': f = a + b; printf("f = %d\n", f);
            case '-': f = a - b; printf("f = %d\n", f);
            case '*': f = a * b; printf("f = %d\n", f);
            case '/': f = a / b; printf("f = %d\n", f);
            default: printf("invalid operator\n");
    }
}
```

The **switch** statements in this program are all syntactically correct, but it does not implement the selection at all. The omission of the **break** statements leads to the execution of all the following cases of statements. The output of the program is

ch = +

f = 30

f = -10

f = 200

f = 0

invalid operator

ch = -

f = -10

f = 200

f = 0

invalid operator

ch = *

f = 200

f = 0

invalid operator

ch = /

f = 0

invalid operator

This rather "unexpected" output is due to the "jump-table" implementation of **switch** statements at the assembly language level as shown in figure 2.4.

The variable **ch** will be compared with the label values stored in the jump-table. If a match is found, the control will jump to the right address of the statement-table. Obviously, if no break statement appears at the end of each case, the machine would continue to execute the next statement. In some languages, e.g., Pascal, the compiler automatically adds a break statement at the end of each case. The advantage is the elimination of a possible error source and the drawback is that the programmer loses a bit of writeability -- in a rare case, a programmer may want to execute all the following cases once a condition is met.

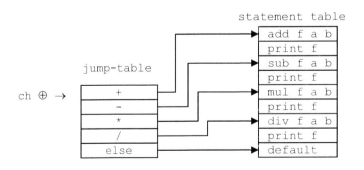

Figure 2.4 The assembly language level implementation of the **switch** statement

2.2.4 ITERATION STRUCTURES (WHILE, DO-WHILE AND FOR)

The basic looping structure in C/C++ is the **while-loop**. The syntax graph of a while-loop is given in figure 2.5.

$$\text{while} \rightarrow (\rightarrow \text{<condition>} \rightarrow) \rightarrow \text{<block>} \rightarrow$$

Figure 2.5 Syntax graph for while statement in C/C++

In a while-loop, the block of statements, called **loop body**, will repeatedly get executed as long as the condition statement produces a true (non-zero) value. However, there is no looping in the syntax definition. This is because there is only a semantic level looping for the while-statement, but no looping at the syntactic level. This is also true for the for-loop. On the other hand, there is a looping structure in the syntax graph of the switch statement, but there is no looping for the statement at the semantic level. The following program counts the number of inputs that are greater than 90. The program stops when a negative number is entered.

```
#include <stdio.h>
main () {
    int i, c = 0;
    scanf("%d", &i);
    while( i >= 0 ) {
        if (i > 90)
            c++;            // counting: same as c = c + 1;
        scanf("%d", &i);
    }
}
```

A variation of the while-loop is the **do-while-loop** that tests the condition after the loop body has been executed once. Using a do-while-loop, we only need one scanf statement for the example above:

```
#include <stdio.h>
main () {
    int i, c = 0;
    do {
        scanf("%d", &i);
        if (i > 90)
            c++;
    }
    while (i >= 0);
}
```

The **for-loop** can be considered a more compact form of the while-loop. It allows us to put the initialization, condition-test and increment parts of a loop in a single statement. The syntax graph of the for loop is given in figure 2.6.

In the syntax graph, the <initialization> and <increment> can be single statements or multiple statements separated by commas. The function of the **for-loop** is equivalent to the function of the following code with a **while-loop**:

```
<initialization>
while(<condition>) {
    <block>
    <increment>
}
```

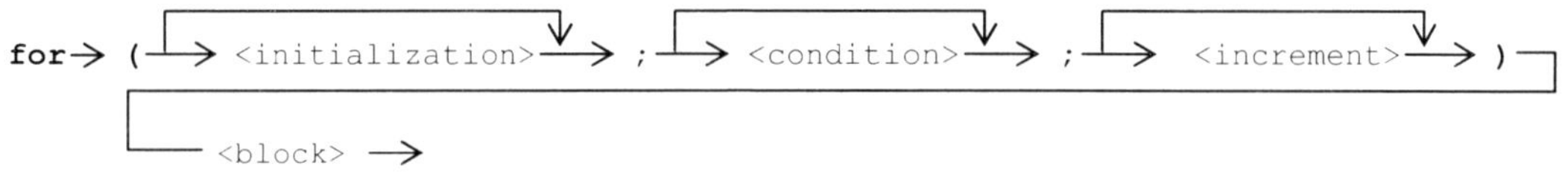

Figure 2.6 Syntax graph for the for statement in C/C++

For example, the following program does a similar job as the program with a **while-loop**, except that the program with a **while-loop** terminates if a negative number is entered, while the following program terminates when exactly **n** numbers are entered.

```
main () {
    int i, k, n = 10, c=0;
    for(k=0; k<n; k++) {
        scanf("%d", &i);
        if (i > 90)
            c++;
    }
}
```

All three components in the parentheses of a **for-loop** are optional. A **for-loop** with all three components absent creates an infinite loop:

```
for(;;) <block>
```

In some programming languages, e.g., Pascal, the loop iteration variable **k** and the loop boundary variable **n** may not be modified in the loop body, which means that the **for-loop** can only iterate a fixed number of times. In C/C++, both variables can be modified and thus the for-loop can iterate a variable number of times. However, it is not a good programming practice to modify any of the two variables even if we are allowed to modify them. Normally, we use a **while-loop** or a **do-while-loop** if the number of iterations is unknown and we use a **for-loop** if the number of iterations is fixed.

2.3 DATA AND BASIC DATA TYPES IN C/C++

The key concepts of data in a programming language include:

- Type: What values and operations are allowed on the type of data?
- Location: Where data is stored in memory?
- Address/Reference (of location in memory): How do we find the location where a particular piece of data is stored?
- Name: How do we conveniently access the locations of data?
- Value: What is stored in a memory location?
- Scope (visibility and life time): Where and when is a piece of data visible or accessible?

We will look at these concepts while studying basic data types in C/C++.

2.3.1 DECLARATION OF VARIABLES AND FUNCTIONS

At machine level, all data and instructions are stored in memory locations in sequences of binary bits: 001011. It is up to the programmer to manage and interpret the bit patterns.

A variable **declaration** in a high-level programming language binds a name to a location in memory and describes the attributes of the value in the location, so that the programmer can use the name to conveniently access the memory location and the value stored in the location. A variable declaration describes the following attributes of the value: .

- type
- scope
- qualifier (modifiability, e.g., constant)
- variable initialization

Typically, the compiler allocates memory for the variable and binds the name to that location when a variable is declared.

The general form of variable declaration in C/C++ is

qualifier typename variable_names separated by a comma.

For example:

int i = 0, j, k;
const double pi = 3.1415926;
float x = 3.0, y, z = 2.5;

The general form of function declaration in C/C++ is

typename function_name(typename name, ..., typename name){ <body> }

The **typename** before the **function_name** specifies the return-value type of the function. The list in the parentheses is the list of parameters with their types. If a function does not return a value, we can either write the type name **void** or write nothing. Similarly, if a function does not have any parameter, we can either write void or nothing in the parentheses.

For example, the following program declares a **max()** function that returns the larger value between two parameter values. The function is called twice in the **main()** function.

```
#include <stdio.h>
int max(int first, int second){                    // function declaration
```

```
        if (first > second)
               return first;
        else return second;
}
void main (void) {              // main function
    int i = 7, j = 5, k = 12, f;
    f = max(i, j);              // function call
    f = max(k, f);             // call the function again with different parameters
}
```

2.3.2 SCOPE RULE

The **scope rule** of a C/C++ declaration: the scope of a variable is from its declaration to the end of the block defined by a pair of curly braces. The idea of the scope rule is declare-before-use: any variables or functions must be declared before they can be used. For example:

```
{
    int height = 6; int width = 6;
    int area = height*width;

    . . .
} // block ends
```

In this example, the variable **area** is initialized to **height*width**, which are declared just before the **area** is declared. According to the scope rule, the declaration is correct. On the other hand, if we swap the order of the first two lines

```
{
    int area = height*width;
    int height = 6; int width = 6;

    . . .
} // block ends
```

we will have a compilation error complaining that **height** and **width** are not declared when their values are used.

There is a subtle difference between the scope rules of an imperative language and a functional language. In a functional language, the scope rule normally says that "the scope of a variable is within the block in which the variable is declared/defined." Should the scope rule of C/C++ say that "the scope of a variable is within the block in which the variable is declared," no compilation error would occur if the declaration of variable **area** is placed before **height** and **width**.

The declare-before-use principle is simple to understand and use for variables, but may cause problems for declarations of mutually recursive functions. For example, a function F calls function G and function G calls function F. In this case, which function should be declared first?

There are two possible solutions to this dilemma:

■ Multi-scan compilation: The compiler scans the program multiple times. For example, in the first round of scan, all names (variables and functions) are stored in a name-table, and in the second round of scan, binding between names and memory locations is made.

■ Forward declaration: Each function is declared in 2 steps: a forward declaration and a genuine decla-ration. The forward declaration makes a name known in advance (before it is used) and thus only needs to specify the return type, function name, parameter types, and parameter names (parameter names are optional). In the following program segment, for example, function **bar** calls function **foo** and function **foo** calls function **bar**. In such a case, we cannot satisfy the declare-before-use require-ment without using forward declaration.

```
void bar(float, char);          // forward declaration to satisfy scope rule
int foo(void);                  // forward declare all functions

...

int foo(void) {                 // genuine declaration

    . . .

    bar(2.5, '+');              // call function bar()

    . . .

}
void bar(float f, char c) {     // genuine declaration

    . . .

    k = foo();                  // call function foo()

    . . .

}
```

Most C/C++ compilers today use multi-scan technique and thus forward declaration is not necessary for mutually recursive functions. However, forward declaration is still frequently used for two reasons:

■ Make the program independent of compiler
■ Better readability: The forward declarations serve as an index to (overview of) all functions

2.3.3 BASIC DATA TYPES

C defines five basic data types, or called value types. They are:

■ Character (char)
■ Integer (int)
■ Floating-point (float)
■ Double precision floating-point (double)
■ Valueless (void)

C++ adds two more basic data types:

■ Boolean (bool)
■ Wide-character (wchar_t)

There is no Boolean type in C. The logic values are represented by integer: 0 for **false** and any other value will be interpreted as **true**. The character type in C is based on the 7-bit ASCII code, which allows 128 characters. The C++'s wide-character type is based on the 16-bit Unicode, which allows $2^{16} = 65,536$ characters. Java's character type is also based on the Unicode.

Several of these basic types can be modified using one or more of these modifiers:

signed, unsigned, short, long, register

The type modifiers **signed** and **unsigned** explicitly specify that the integer type is signed and unsigned, respectively, although by default an integer type is signed without any modifier. For a signed integer, a "1" at the most significant bit indicates a negative number, while for an unsigned integer, no bit is used for the sign and only non-negative numbers can be represented. Thus a "1" at the most significant bit indicates a large positive number. The type modifiers **short** and **long** indicate the data ranges of the integers of these types. It is more efficient to specify a short integer if you know your integer won't be very large. The type modifier **register** suggests to the compiler that the programmer wants to access the variable as fast as possible. Obviously, a variable can be accessed in the fastest way if it is put in a register. Since a processor has a very limited number of registers, you should use **register** modifier sparingly. The **register** modifier is normally used for variables that need to be accessed frequently in a short period of time such as loop variables. Please note that the **register** modifier is only a suggestion to the compiler. The compiler will take it into consideration where it is possible. However, there is no guarantee that the compiler can put the variable into a register longer than any other variables.

Table 2.2 summarizes the basic data types available in C/C++. Since C/C++ can be implemented on machines of different sizes, e.g., word length = 8, 16, 32 and 64, the number of bits used to implement a particular data type can vary. However, the language requires that a minimum number of bits must be guaranteed for each data type. The larger machines can use more bits to provide extra data range and/or higher precision. The second and third columns of the table list the guaranteed minimum number of bits and the minimum data range for each of the data types.

Table 2.2 Basic data types in C/C++

Type	Minimum bits	Minimum range
bool (C++ only)	1	true/false
char	8	from -127 to 127
signed char	8	from -127 to 127
unsigned char	8	from 0 to 255
wchar_t (C++ only)	16	from 0 to 65 535
int	16	from -32 768 to 32 768
signed int	16	same as int
unsigned int	16	from 0 to 65 535
short int	16	from -32 768 to 32 768
signed short int	16	same as short int
unsigned short int	16	same as unsigned int
long int	32	±2 147 483 647
signed long int	32	same as long int
unsigned long int	32	from 0 to 4 294 967 295
float	32	6 decimal digits of precision
double	64	10 decimal digits of precision

To find the exact size of each type on a particular machine, you can call the sizeof function using the type name as the parameter sizeof (type_name). For example:

```
printf("size of long type = %d\n", sizeof(long));
```

will print the "size of long type = 4" if the machine uses 4 bytes to store a long integer. If we call

```
printf("bool-size = %d, true = %d, false = %d\n", sizeof(bool), true, false);
```

the output would be

```
bool-size = 1, true = 1, false = 0
```

which means C++ uses one byte to store a bool type variable, the internal value of true is 1 and the internal value of false is 0.

To see the relationship between the types, we can classify the data types into four categories: scalar, function, aggregate, and valueless (void) types, as shown in figure 2.7. The scalar types can be further divided into pointer, arithmetic and enumeration types. In the diagram, boldfaced words are keywords, italic words are optional keywords. Other names are generic terms. The basic data types we discuss in this section belong to arithmetic types. Functions are considered a special data type. In the following sections, we will discuss pointer, enumeration, and aggregated types.

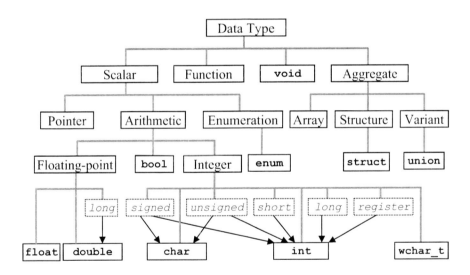

Figure 2.7 Classification of data types

2.4 COMPLEX TYPES

In the previous section, we discussed basic data types. In this section, we discuss more complex data types including array, string as array of characters, pointer, constant, and enumeration.

2.4.1 ARRAY

Array is a homogeneous collection of data elements that are stored in a consecutive block of memory locations. At the assembly language level, we use the initial address of the block plus the offset (index) of the element to access a particular element. At the high-level language level, we use the array variable name and the index to access an array element. An array is declared by

typename variablename[length] = {v_0, v_1, v_2, ..., $v_{length-1}$};

The **length** and the initialization part, = {v_0, v_1, v_2, ..., $v_{length-1}$}, are optional, which produces four possible combinations:

1. typename variablename[length];
2. typename variablename[ ] = {v_0, v_1, v_2, ..., $v_{length-1}$};
3. typename variablename[ ];
4. typename variablename[length] = {v_0, v_1, v_2, ..., $v_{length-1}$};

The first two array declarations are correct and are most frequently used. In the first declaration, the array variable and its length are declared. However, array elements are not initialized. In the second declaration, the length of the array is implied by the number of elements in the initialization list.

The third array declaration will immediately cause a compilation error because the compiler needs to know the size of the array to allocate the right amount of memory space for the array, which is missing in the declaration.

The fourth declaration is syntactically correct, but one can easily make a contextual error in using this declaration! There are three possible cases when we use both explicit and implicit mechanisms to specify the length of the array:

■ If length = n (the number of elements given in the initialization list), no problem would occur. However, this case is exactly same as the second way of declaration.

■ If length < n, a compilation (contextual) error will occur: there are not enough places to hold the elements given in the list.

■ If length > n, no compilation error will occur. The n elements in the initialization list will be put in the first n places 0, 1, 2, ..., n-1. This is a case that is not covered by the first two ways of array declaration. Maybe this is the only case where we really need to use the fourth way of array declaration.

In the declarations of arrays, the **length** must be an integer value or a simple expression with integer operations like 20+5-1. It cannot contain a variable, even if the variable has been initialized.

The following piece of code illustrates the different ways of array declaration.

```
void main() {
    int a[3], sa, sb, sc, sd;  // a is correctly declared without initialization
    int b[] = {2, 3, 9, 4};    // b is correctly declared and initialized
    int c[2] = {15, 14};       // c is correct, but the length is unnecessary
    int d[5] = {15, 14, 18};   // the first 3 elements of d are initialized
//  int d1[2] = {15, 14, 18};  // incorrect: not enough places
//  int e[];                   // incorrect: no length indication
    a[0] = 20;                 // array index always starts from 0
    a[1] = 30;
    a[2] = 90;
    sa = sizeof(a);            // number of bytes used by a is 12
    sb = sizeof(b);            // number of bytes used by b is 16
```

```
    sc = sizeof(c);              // number of bytes used by c is 8
    sd = sizeof(d);              // number of bytes used by d is 20
    printf("sa = %d\t sb = %d\t sc = %d\t sd = %d\n", sa, sb, sc, sd);
    printf("d0 = %d\t d1 = %d\t d2 = %d\t d3 = %d\t d4 = %d\n", d[0], d[1], d[2], d[3], d[4]);}
```

The output of the program is

sa = 12	sb = 16	sc = 8	sd = 20	
d0 = 15	d1 = 14	d2 = 18	d3 = 0	d4 = 0

The first four lines of comments explain the different ways of declarations. The two incorrect declarations are commented out so that the program can be compiled and executed.

In the program, the system function **sizeof** returns the number of bytes (a byte = 8 bits) of the variable. The program is compiled on a 32-bit PC, an integer type variable takes 32 bits (four bytes). If you compile the same program on a different machine, e.g., a 16-bit or 64 –bit machine, the **sizeof** function will return different integer sizes. In table 2.2, the minimum integer size given is 16 bits (2 bytes). When you write C/C++ program, you need to handle the word length of the machine on which your program runs. You can use the **sizeof** function to find the word length of your computer and use the **sizeof** function to make your program independent of the word length. More uses of the **sizeof** function will be seen later in the text.

In Java, array declaration is different: We can declare an array without indicating its size and later give the size when we create the array object during the execution. This way of memory allocation is called **dynamic memory allocation**. The array declaration we discussed in this section is based on the **static memory allocation** by the compiler. However, C/C++ does provide the dynamic memory allocation mechanism for array and other structured data types. This will be discussed in conjunction with the pointer type.

We can define an array of int, char, and float, etc. Can we have an **array of arrays**? The answer is yes. C and C++ use array of arrays to represent multidimensional arrays. Arrays of arrays are declared and initialized like this:

```
char mac[5][7];
int mai[2][3] = {{4, 2, 3}, {7, 8, 9}};
```

Conceptually, array **mai** is stored in a matrix of 2 by 3, and its elements are accessed using the array name and the two indices **mai[i][j]**. Structurally, array **mai** is stored in a block of consecutive memory locations like this:

4	2	3	7	8	9

The following program illustrates the use of multidimensional arrays. Please note that **maxrow** and **maxcolumn** are defined as macros. The compiler would not accept the declaration of the maze[maxrow][maxcolumn+1] if they were defined as constant variables by using "**const**".

```
#define maxrow 50
#define maxcolumn 100
#include <stdio.h>
//const int maxrow = 100, maxcolumn = 100;
```

```
char ma[maxrow][maxcolumn+1];
void main(void) {
    int i, j;
    for (i=0; i < maxrow; i++)
            for (j = 0; j < maxcolumn + 1; j++)
                    ma[i][j] = 'x';
}
```

2.4.2 Pointer

Pointer type is the most demanding and challenging data type in C/C++. This is especially true for Java programmers. Pointers provide programmers the flexibility in accessing memory locations and modifying their values. On the other hand, the flexibility can easily create incorrect programs due to the lack in understanding of computer organization and the relationship between different data types. This section will explain the principle of pointer type and correct ways of using pointer variables.

Let's start by exploring different aspects of a **variable**:

- **Value**. A variable will hold a single value or a set of values. For example, an integer variable holds a single value and an array variable holds a set of values. A value can appear on the right-hand side of an assignment statement only and thus is called an **r-value** (for right-hand-side value).
- **Location**. A variable will be associated with a location or a set of memory locations. The value of a variable is stored in the location.
- **Address**. Address of a variable is a natural number directly associated with a memory location by the hardware. Address provides a direct way for programmers to access (read or write) a memory location or variable. Address refers to the literal number and thus is also an r-value.
- **Name**. Name of a variable is a mnemonic symbol that provides a convenient way for programmers to access a memory location or variable. A name is associated with a memory location (or translated into the address of the location) by the compiler. Some languages only use names to access memory locations, e.g., Java. Some languages allow using both names and addresses to access memory locations, e.g., C/C++. A variable name can appear in the left-hand side and right-hand side of an assignment statement and is called **l-value** (for left-hand-side value). A variable name has two faces: If it is used on the left-hand side of an assignment, it refers to the memory location. If it is used on the right-hand side of an assignment, it refers to the value stored in the memory location.

We can use an analogy to understand these aspects. Let's consider the soccer teams attending the World Cup. Each team consists of a number of members, corresponding to the set of values stored in a variable. Each team member will stay in a location, e.g., a hotel room. Each location will have a unique address (e.g., street address of the hotel plus room number). The team and each team member can be accessed by the address. In computer memory, the set of values related to a variable is normally stored in a consecutive block of memory locations, and thus, we can use the initial address of the block to access the values starting at that address. The hotel and rooms may also have names. If the context (scope) is clear, we can also use the name of the hotel and the name of a room to access a team member stayed in the room. Read appendix section A.2 for a more detailed example.

Why do we need the name if we have the address of a memory location? Humans are better in reading, understanding, and remembering names than long tedious numbers.

Why do we need addresses in high-level language programming if we have names? The reasons are twofold. First, every memory location in a computer has an address, but not every memory location has a name. We can use addresses to access unnamed variables. Second, memory addresses are numbers and can be manipulated. For example, we can easily increment the address of the current location to obtain the address of the next location, or compare the two addresses to determine which address is smaller. As a result, it is more powerful and more flexible to access memory locations using addresses than using names.

What is a pointer? To take advantage of names (easy for humans to remember) and addresses (flexible in programming), we give a name to an address. The name of an address is a **pointer**. In other words, a pointer variable contains the address of another variable. Like any variable, a pointer variable is a l-value and the address stored in the pointer variable is a r-value.

Pointer as a data type is common in most imperative languages. The data range is the address space of the programming language. In C/C++, the data range is same as an unsigned integer. The operations on pointers include the following:

- Assignment operation: An address value can be assigned to a pointer variable.

- Integer operations: A pointer variable can be operated like an integer variable.

- Referencing operation: Obtain the address of a variable x from the variable name: &x. The ampersand & is called **address-of** operator that returns the address value of the variable it precedes. For example, if integer x is allocated at memory address = 2000, then &x will return 2000. Please note that &x returns the address value, not a pointer variable containing that address value, and thus &x is a r-value and can never appear on the left-hand side of an assignment statement.

- Dereferencing operation: To access the variable pointed to by a pointer variable y, we can use the **dereferencing** operator *y. In other words, the dereferencing operator * creates a new name for the variable pointed to by the pointer variable y. Please note that *y is a new name of the variable pointed to by the pointer variable that * precedes. *y is a l-value and can appear on both sides of an assignment statement.

Although C/C++ has a pointer type, there is no type name for pointers. A pointer is declared by the type that it points to. For example:

```
int i = 137, *j;
j = &i;
```

Variable i is an integer and j is a pointer variable pointing to the integer variable i or *j, which becomes an alias (another name) of the variable. In other words, variable i has two names: i and *j. Assume that the compiler has associated the variable i to the address 100, then the statement "j = &i;" will assign 100 to j.

A pointer variable is a variable too. We can define another pointer variable to point to a pointer variable. For example, we can extend the above example to

```
int i = 137, *j = 0, **k = 1;          // 1
j = &i;                                 // 2
k= &j;                                  // 3
*j = 0;                                 // 4
**k = 1;                                // 5
```

In the example, k is a pointer variable pointing to the pointer variable j. Assume the compiler has allocated address 100 to i, 160 to j and 120 to k. Initially, the three variables are independent, as shown in figure 2.8. Please note, the initializations "*j = 0, **k = 1;" in line 1 put the value 0 in variable j and put the value 1 in variable k. This is different from the assignment statements in lines 4 and 5, where 0 and 1 are put into the variable *j and **k, respectively! Here you can see again that static semantics (context) and dynamic semantics are different!

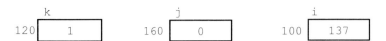

Figure 2.8 Variables i, j, and k are declared as independent variables at line 1 of the code

After the execution of statement at line 2, the address of variable i is put in j, resulting in j pointing to i (holding i's address); and after the execution of the statement at line 3, the address of variable j is put in k, resulting in k pointing to j (holding j's address). The new relationship between the three variables i, j, and k after statements at lines 2 and 3, is illustrated in figure 2.9.

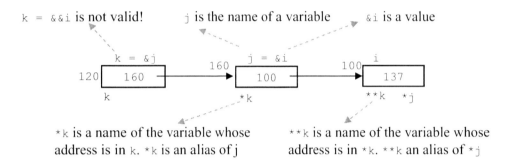

Figure 2.9 Relationship between variables and their pointers after lines 2 and 3

Variable i is initialized to value 137. Using the address-of operator, statement "j = &i;" puts the address of i, 100, into pointer variable j. Statement "k = &j;" put the address of j, 160, into pointer variable k. On the other hand, we use the dereferencing operator to access the variable pointed to by the pointers. Since k holds the address of j, we can use *k to access j, or *k becomes an alias of j. Similarly, since j holds the address of i, we can use *j to access i, or *j becomes an alias of i. Furthermore, since *k is an alias of j, **k is an alias of i too, that is, i has two aliases: *j and **k. However, since &i is a r-value (not a variable), we cannot perform &&i operation.

At lines 4 and 5, both assignment statements modify variable i (*j and **k are aliases of i), resulting in the variable i being first changed from 137 to 0, and then changed from 0 to 1. If we compare the effect of these two statements with the initialization at line 1, we can see that similar assignment operations in the initialization part (contextual structure) and in the execution part (semantic structure) have different effects.

In this section, we only discussed the concept, the declaration, and the assignment of pointer variables. We will discuss more applications of pointers in the following sections. It will make a lot more sense when we combine pointer type with other complex data types.

2.4.3 STRING

There is no specific string type in C/C++. Any array of characters can be considered a string, and thus string variable can be declared as an array of characters, for example:

```
char str1[ ] = {'a', 'l', 'p', 'h', 'a'};        // initialized as an array
char str2[ ] = "alpha";                          // initialized as a string
char str3[5];                                     // without initialization
```

As can be seen from the example, there are two different ways to **initialize** an array of characters in the declaration. The effect of these two initializations is slightly different.

The first declaration and initialization uses exactly the same method that declares and initializes any array, and thus **str1** is 100% an array of characters. On the other hand, we can also consider and use **str1** as a string. It has all features that an array of characters should have. For example, we can modify the string in the following code and print the modified string

```
char str1[] = {'a', 'l', 'p', 'h', 'a'};
for (i = 0; i < sizeof(str1); i++) {
    str1[i] += 1;      // same as str1[i] = str1[i]+1;
    printf("%c", str1[i]);
}
printf("\t sizeof(str1) = %d\n", sizeof(str1));
```

As expected, the output of the code is

```
bmqib       sizeof(str1) = 5
```

The second initialization indicates to the compiler that the array of characters is considered a string. In this case, the compiler will append a null character '\0' to the end of the string. In ASCII table, the code for the null character is 0 (seven binary zeros). Please notice that code for the digit '0' is 48. Appending the null character to the end of a string increases the size of the string by one, as shown in the following code.

```
char str2[] = "alpha";
for (i = 0; i < sizeof(str2); i++) {
    str2[i] += 1;
    printf("%c", str2[i]);
}
printf("\t sizeof(str2) = %d\n", sizeof(str2));
```

The output of the code is.

```
bmqib⊛      sizeof(str2) = 6 // '\0'is not a printable character
```

To have the same effect, one can use the following initialization to append the '\0' to the end of the string:

```
char str4[] = {'a', 'l', 'p', 'h', 'a', '\0'};
```

As we discussed in the array section, we can specify the size in the declaration. If the size of the array is specified and the size is smaller than "string_length+1", the '\0' character and possibly some characters of the string cannot be stored in the variable. This is called **truncated initialization**. For example:

```
char str5[5] = "alpha";
char str6[4] = "alpha";
```

In this example, the null character '\0' will not be stored in **str5**; furthermore, the last 'a' and the null character are not stored in **str6**. Figure 2.10 shows the memory map and initialization of **str1** through **str6**.

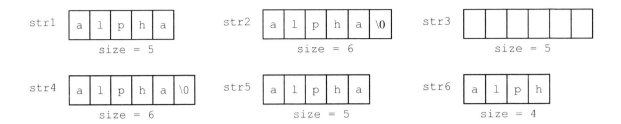

Figure 2.10 memory allocation and initialization of six strings

A number of string functions have been defined in the string package **<string.h>** and related library packages. A list of useful string and character manipulation functions are given in table 2.3.

Having introduced the string functions, we can use the **strlen(str)** to replace the **sizeof(str)** in the previous example. In fact, **sizeof(str)** worked in that example because each character takes exactly one byte and **sizeof(str)** returns the number of bytes. The program would not work if we had used the **wchar_t** (two bytes per character) type instead. However, **strlen(str)** will work in both cases. Another difference, **sizeof** will include the byte used to store the null character '**\0**', while **strlen** does not.

So far, we discussed the string as an array of characters. A string can also be defined by a pointer to a character, more accurately, a pointer to the first character of a string. For example, the declaration

char *p = "hello, ", *q = "world", *s;

declares three pointer variables **p**, **q**, and **s**, each pointing to a character type variable. Pointer variables **p** and **q** are initialized to values that point to a string, while **s** is not initialized. Now the question is, what is the difference between the array-based strings and the pointer-based strings?

Let's examine the following example and see in detail the differences and similarities between array-based strings and pointer-based strings.

Table 2.3 Useful string and character manipulation functions

Library	Function	Description	Example
stdlib.h	atoi(str)	Convert a numeric string into an integer	atoi("356") returns 356 as an integer
	itoa(i, str, base)	Converts an integer **i** to a string using the specified **base** and link the result to pointer *str*	itoa (356, str, 10) results in pointer str point to string "356".
stdio.h	getc(stdin)	Reads a character from keyboard	ch = getc(stdin);
	gets(str)	Reads a string from keyboard	gets(s); strcpy(str, s);
	putc(ch, stdout)	Print a character onto screen	ch = 'a'; putc(ch, stdout);
string.h	strcat(str1, str2)	Concatenate str2 to the end of str1	strcat (str, "hello world");
	strncat(str1, str2, n)	Concatenate the first n characters (sub string) of str2 to the end of str1	strcat (str, "hello world", 3);

Table 2.3 Useful string and character manipulation functions (continued)

Library	Function	Description	Example
	strcmp(str1, str2)	Return 0 if str1 == str2, Return <0 if str1 < str2, Return >0 if str1 > str2,	if (strcmp(s1, s2)) y = x+1;
	strncmp (str1, str2, n)	Same as strcmp, except only compare the first n characters	if (strncmp (s1, s2, 3)) y = x + 1;
	stricmp (str1, str2)	Same as strcmp, except letter comparisons are case insensitive	if (stricmp (s1, s2)) y = x + 1;
	strcpy(str1, str2)	Copy str2 into str1	strcpy(str, "hello world");
	strlen(str)	Return the length of str	L = strlen(str)
ctype.h	tolower(ch)	Return the lower case equivalent	tolower('D') returns 'd'
	toupper(ch)	Return the upper case equivalent	toupper('b') returns 'B'

```
#include <stdio.h>
#include <string.h>
void main (void) {
      char p1[] = "hello", q1[] = "this is an array-string", s1[6];        //1
      char *p2 = "Hi", *q2 = "this is a pointer-string", *s2=0;            //2
      char *temp;                                                          //3
//    s1 = p1;              // Array name cannot be a L-value              //4
//    s1 = "hi";            // Array name cannot be a L-value              //5
      strcpy(s1, p1);       // We must use string-copy function            //6
      printf("s1 = %s\t len-s1 = %d\n", s1, strlen(s1));                   //7
      strcpy(s1, q1);                                                      //8
      printf("s1 = %s\t len-s1 = %d\n", s1, strlen(s1));                   //9
      printf("s1 = %s\t size-s1 = %d\n", s1, sizeof(s1));                  //10
      for (temp = s1; temp < s1+strlen(s1); temp++)                        //11
            *temp += 1;                                                    //12
      printf("s1 = %s\n", s1);                                             //13
      for (temp = &s1[0]; temp < &s1[0] + strlen(s1); temp++)             //14
            *temp -= 1;                                                    //15
      printf("s1 = %s\n", s1);                                             //16
//    strcpy(s2, p2);                                                      //17
      s2 = q2;                                                             //18
      printf("s2 = %s\t len-s2 = %d\n", s2, strlen(s2));                   //19
      printf("s2 = %s\t size-s2 = %d\n", s2, sizeof(s2));                  //20
      for (temp = s2; temp < s2+strlen(s2); temp++){                       //21
//          *temp += 1;                                                    //22
```

```
    }
    strcpy(s1, q2);                                                      //23
    for (temp = s1; temp < s1+strlen(s1); temp++)                        //24
        *temp += 1;                                                      //25
    printf("s1 = %s\t len-s1 = %d\n", s1, strlen(s1));                   //26
}
```

All incorrect statements are commented out so that the program can be compiled and executed. The output of the program is

s1 = hello   len-s1 = 5

s1 = this is an array-string   len-s1 = 23

s1 = this is an array-string   size-s1 = 6

s1 = uijt!jt!bo!bssbz.tusjoh

s1 = this is an array-string

s2 = this is a pointer-string   len-s2 = 24

s2 = this is a pointer-string   size-s2 = 4

s1 = uijt!jt!b!qpjoufs.tusjoh len-s1 = 24

Now we explain each statement in the program.

Statement 1 declares three array-based strings p1, q1 and s1. Variables p1 and ?1 are initialized to a string while s1 is not initialized.

Statement 2 declares three pointer variables p2, q2, and s2, each pointing to a character type variable. Variables p2 and q2 are initialized to values pointing to a string while s2 is not initialized.

Statement 3 declares a pointer variable "temp", to be used as a temporary pointer variable.

Statement 4 tries to assign the string variable p1 to string variable s1. A compilation error occurs, because s1 is in fact an array name. We cannot assign anything to an array name. We can only assign a value to an element of an array, e.g., "s1[0] = 'a';" is a valid assignment.

Statement 5 tries to assign a string literal (value) to s1. For the same reason stated above, the statement causes a compilation error.

The correct way to assign a string variable or a string literal to an array-based string is to use the library function strcpy(s1, p1). In statement 6, string p1 is copied into string s1 correctly and printed correctly in statement 7.

Statement 8 copies q1 into s1. String s1 and its length strlen(s1) are correctly printed in statement 9 (see output of the program). Please note that the length of s1 is declared to be 6. How can the program put 24 characters in 6 places? This is in fact a semantic error that the compiler does not check. The runtime system could handle the error by checking the sizes and lengths of the two arrays in strcpy and prevent a longer array to be string-copied into a shorter array. However, these kinds of checks will slow down the execution of the program, and the designers of C decided to leave the responsibility to the programmer! As a programmer, you should know the lengths of the two arrays. If you really do not, you can always use the strlen function to find the lengths; for example, you can use the following statement to replace statement 6:

```
if (sizeof(s1) >= strlen(p1)) strcpy(s1, p1); else printf("error\n");
```

We still haven't answered the question of how to put 24 characters in 6 places. What has happened is that the 18 extra characters are appended to the 6 declared memory locations, as shown in figure 2.11.

Before we perform the strcpy, s1 contains 5 characters and the size of s1 is 6 as specified in the declaration. After we have performed the strcpy, a 23-character string is copied to the memory location starting from address s1. Obviously, the string goes beyond the limit of the size of s1. That's why we can still print the string s1 with all characters, because the printf function starts from s1 and stops when the character '\0' is detected.

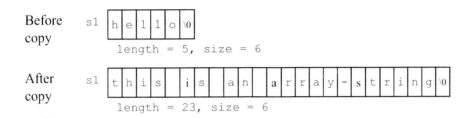

Figure 2.11 A strcpy operation may illegally use more space than what is declared

The problem is that the use of memory beyond the declared boundary is unknown to the compiler and the runtime system. Please note that in the output of print-statement 10, size of s1 is still 6, even if a 23-character long string has been copied into s1. There are three possibilities:

■ the locations are not allocated to any variable and you are lucky;

■ the locations are allocated to other variables and you have overwritten the values of those variables;

■ the locations are allocated to other variables and your values will be overwritten later.

In cases (2) and (3), your program may crash or, even worse, still behave normally but produce incorrect results that go undetected and cause much more damaging consequences. We explained in chapter one that C/C++ use weak type checking. As you can see here, C/C++ are also weak in runtime checking, which leaves bigger responsibility to the programmers.

Now let's continue to discuss the example. In statement 11, "temp = s1;" means to assign the address of s1 (or the address of the first element s1[0]) to a pointer variable temp. Note that we use &x to obtain the address of a simple variable x, and we simply use the array name s1 to obtain the address of an array s1 (or the address of the first element of the array). In some C compilers, you can use either &s1 or s1 to obtain the address of array s1. However, in C++, you can only use the array name to obtain the address of the array: Please also note that "temp = s1;" is same as "temp = &s1[0];" because s1[0] is a simple variable of character type, not an array (see the use in statement 14). In the next part of the for-loop, we use "temp < s1+strlen(s1);" to test if the value (address) of temp is less than the initial address of s1 plus the length of s1. And then we increment temp in the next part.

In statement 12, we do "*temp += 1;", which means we increment the value pointed to by the pointer variable temp. The statement is same as "(*temp)++;", but not same as "*(temp++);", which increments the pointer value, instead of the pointed value. Please note that "*temp++;" is same as "*(temp++);", because the unary operators * and ++ operate at the same precedence level. However, they associate from RIGHT to LEFT! Therefore, in "*temp++;", temp associates with ++ before *, and hence "*(temp++);" gets evaluated as "*temp++;".

Statement 13 will print the string in which every character is changed to the next character in the ASCII code. For example, s is changed to t, h is changed to i, and i is changed to j, etc.

Statement 14 is equivalent to statement 11, and statement 12 is equivalent to statement 13 in structure, and it reverses (decrypts) the encryption in statement 12. Statement 16 prints the decrypted string that is same as the string before encryption.

We have discussed array-based strings so far, and now we turn to discuss pointer-based strings.

In statement 17, we try to do what we did in statement 6; string-copy p2 to s2. However, the attempt will cause a compilation error. Thus, we commented the statement out so that we can continue with the other statements. The reason of this compilation error is that s2 is a pointer variable and there is no memory allocated for a string. In the declaration in line 2, "char ... *s2=0;" means that s2 is declared as a pointer variable to char and the pointer is initialized to 0. It does not mean that the pointer is initialized to the address of the string "0". However, should we use "char ... *s2="0";", it does mean that the pointer is initialized to the address of string "0".

In statement 18, we assign q2 to s2. We assign the value of q2 (a pointer value) to pointer s2. Both pointers point to the same string. Here only pointer manipulation is involved. No string duplication is performed, as shown in figure 2.12.

Statement 19 prints the string pointed to by s2 and its length. Statement 20 does not print the size of the string; instead, it prints the size of the pointer variable, which is 4 bytes (same as the size of an integer).

Statement 21 is similar to statements 11 and 14. Statement 22 tries to modify the character pointed to by temp, as we did in statements 12 and 15. However, we will have a runtime error. In C/C++, if a string is assigned to a pointer-based string variable, the string is a string literal and cannot be modified. If we try to modify it, we will encounter a runtime error. Thus, we commented out this statement so that we can continue to compile other statements.

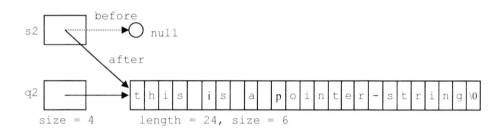

Figure 2.12 Both pointers q2 and s2 point to the same string

Although we cannot modify a string initialized as a pointer-based string, we can modify the string if it is copied into an array. Statement 23 copies pointer-based string q2 into s1 and then we can modify the string in s1 in statements 24 and 25. Statement 26 prints the modified string.

Through this example, we explained the following aspects of a string in C/C++.

■ We can use array of characters to declare a string variable and initialize the string variable to a string literal. We can access (read and write) the characters in the string as array elements. We can assign the initial address of the array (string) to a pointer variable and use this pointer to access (read and write) the characters in the string.

■ We can declare a string variable using a pointer to character type and initialize the string to a string literal. We can read the characters in the string, but we cannot modify the characters.

■ We can copy a pointer-based string into an array and we can modify the characters in the array.

2.4.4 CONSTANTS

Most programming languages allow constants to be declared. However, their implementations depend on the language definition and the compiler technologies.

C/C++ provides three different ways to introduce constants:

- Macro: As discussed in section 1.4.2, we can use a macro definition to introduce a constant. The constant will substitute for the name at the pre-processing time. The advantage of a macro constant is its efficiency. A small constant may fit in an immediate-type of a machine instruction and thus save a memory access. The disadvantage is that the way a macro is defined is different from the way a variable is declared and initialized (non-orthogonal).

- const qualifier: A constant is a "variable" that a program cannot modify. The advantage is that the constant is declared and initialized in the same way as a variable is declared and initialized (orthogonal). However, a memory access is needed in order to access the constant (slower). We will discuss this kind of constant in this section.

- Enumeration constant: We can introduce constants by defining an enumeration type variable. This topic will be discussed in the following section.

The simplest way to introduce constants in C/C++ is to use the qualifier const before the variable declaration. For example:

```
const int min = 5, max = 100, pi = 3.14159265358979;
const char x = 'a', y = 's';
```

Constants increase the readability of programs. For example, the statement

```
if (x >= min and x <= max) x = x*x*pi;
```

is easier to understand than the statement

```
if (x >= 5 and x <= 100) x = x*x*3.14159265358979;
```

Constants also prevent us from making semantic errors. For example, if we try to modify a constant, e.g., in a statement like

```
max = max + 10;
```

the compiler will raise a compilation error because **max** is a constant.

A constant defined by qualifier **const** is actually a "constant variable" and thus have a memory address. We can apply the dereferencing operator on the constant. For example, the statement

```
temp = &max;
```

will put the memory address of constant **max** into the pointer variable **temp**.

In the following example, we demonstrate that we can even modify a constant variable if we can get around the compiler's check.

```
void main( ) {
    const int max = 100;
    int *temp;                  // temp is a pointer to an integer
//  max = max + 10;             // Compilation error would occur
    temp = &max;                // assign the address of max to temp
    *temp = *temp + 10;         // max is modified through pointer temp
    printf("max = %d\n", max);  // The output is: max = 110
}
```

Self-checking question: What would happen if we use "#define max 100" to define the constant? Will the statement "temp = &max;" work?

Through this example, we can see that a constant defined by **const** qualifier is in fact a variable:

- It has memory location and memory address and we can use & operator to obtain its address.
- Compiler protection is used. A compilation error will occur if you try to modify a const variable. In some version of compiler, warning, instead of error, will be given.
- It can be modified if you can get around the compiler, e.g., using an alias, you can modify a const variable.

2.4.5 ENUMERATION TYPE

We have discussed data types predefined in C/C++. Most modern programming languages also provide mechanisms (type constructors) to allow programmers to define more complex data types. We will discuss the enumeration type in this section and other complex data types in the following sections.

Enumeration type is usually used for variables that can take an enumerable ordered set of values. Each of these values is given a name and we use the name to access the corresponding value. These names are associated with integer values starting from 0. Each enumeration type is a distinct data type.

Enumeration types in C/C++ are defined using the keyword **enum**. For example:

```
#include <stdio.h>
typedef enum {
            Sun, Mon, Tue, Wed, Thu, Fri, Sat
    } Days;
Days x = Sun, y = Sat;
void main (void) {
    while (x <= y) {
            printf("x = %d\t", x);
            x++;
    }
    printf("\n");
}
```

The names (constants) in the **Days** are not initialized and integers starting from 0 will be associated with each name in the given order. Thus, the type definition above defines seven constants equivalent to:

```
const int Sun   = 0;
const int Mon   = 1;
const int Tue   = 2;
const int Wed   = 3;
const int Thu   = 4;
const int Fri   = 5;
const int Sat   = 6;
```

The output of the program is

x = 0   x = 1   x = 2   x = 3   x = 4   x = 5   x = 6

We can also initialize the names in the definition. For example, if we define Days as follows

```
typedef enum {
        Sun = 1, Mon = 2, Tue = 3, Wed = 4, Thu = 5, Fri = 6, Sat = 7
    } Days;
```

then the output of the program will be

x = 1   x = 2   x = 3   x = 4   x = 5   x = 6   x = 7

We now show a longer example demonstrating the use of enumeration types.

```
#include <stdio.h>
#include <time.h>
typedef enum {
        red, amber, green
    } traffic_light;
void sleep( clock_t wait );   // forward declaration

main() {
traffic_light x = red;
printf("Red:\tStop!\n");
while (1)
    switch (x) {
        case amber:
            sleep(1);              //sleep 1 second
            x = red;
            printf("Red:\tStop!\n");
            break;
        case red:
            sleep(6);              //sleep 6 second
            x = green;
            printf("Green:\tGo>>>\n");
            break;
        case green:
            sleep(12);             //sleep 12 second
            x = amber;
            printf("Amber:\tBrake...\n");
    }
}
// Sleep for a specified number of seconds.
void sleep( clock_t wait ) {
    clock_t goal;                          // clock_t defined in <time.h>
```

```
        goal = wait * CLOCKS_PER_SEC + clock();
        while( goal > clock() )

                ;

}
```

In this program, we defined an enumeration type called **traffic_light** with three possible values: **red**, **amber**, and **green**. We could use an **int** type instead. However, the program would be less readable and prone to error. A snapshot of the output is given as follows.

```
Red:        Stop!
Green:      Go>>>
Amber:      Brake...
Red:        Stop!
Green:      Go>>>
Amber:      Brake...
...
```

In this example, the time function **clock()** in <time.h> is used to obtain the number of clock cycles from a given point. This function can be used to measure the time between any two points. For example, the following piece of code can measure the time used by a function **foo()**.

```
c1 = clock();                                      // time stamp 1
foo();
c2 = clock();                                      // time stamp 2
interval = (double) (c2 - c1) / CLOCKS_PER_SEC; // time difference
```

The time difference computed in this example is in seconds. The precision of this method is 0.001 second.

There is another time function **time()** that can be used to measure the time in second. The following code show the use of the time function and other related function functions.

```
#include <stdio.h>
#include <time.h>
main() {
    int n; time_t start, finish; double result, duration;
    time( &start );  // get the initial time
    for( n = 0; n < 900000000; n++ )
            result = 3.1415 * 2.23;
    time( &finish ); // get the end time
    duration = difftime( finish, start);       // compute difference
    printf( "\nThe program takes %2.4f seconds\n", duration );
}
```

2.5 COMPOUND DATA TYPES

In this section, we discuss data types that are composed of several data types, including structure, union, array of structures, linked list of structures connected by pointers, and file types.

2.5.1 STRUCTURE TYPES

A structure is created using the keyword **struct**. The general way to define a structure type is

```
struct type_name {
        type    field1;
        type    field2;
        . . .
        type    fieldn;
    } struct_variable_name;
```

For example:

```
struct stype {
    char    ch;
    int     x;
} u, v;                 // We can declare variables of the type here.
void main() {
    struct stype s, t;      // We can use the type to declare variables here too.
    ...                     // The keyword struct must be used before type name.
}
```

Now let's study an example with a structure type.

```
struct Contact {      // define a type that can hold a person's detail
    char    name[30];
    long    phone;
    char    email[30];
};
void main() {
    struct Contact x, y, z;
    strcpy(x.name, "Mike Smith");
    x.phone = 9650022;
    strcpy(x.email, "mike.smith@asu.edu");
    strcpy(y.name, "Jane Miller");
    y.phone = 9650055;
    strcpy(y.email, "jane.miller@asu.edu");
}
```

As you can see from the example, we use x.name notation to access the name field of the variable x. We will see more examples of structures in the following sections, where we will combine the structure types with the array and pointer types.

2.5.2 Union

A **union** type variable is a region of shared memory that, over time, can contain different types of value. At any moment, a union can contain only one value. Programmers must make sure the proper type is used at the proper time. The general way to define a union type is

```
union union_name {
    type    field1;
    type    field2;
    . . .
    type    fieldn;
} union_variable_name;
```

For example:

```
union utype {
    char    ch;
    int     x;
} v;
void main(){
    union utype s, t;       //We can use the type to declare variables here too.
    ...                     // The keyword union must be used before type name.
}
```

In this example, we define a union type called **utype** and declare a variable **v** of **utype**. Similar to a structure type, we can have multiple data fields in the type definition. In this example, there are two data fields. The field variable **x** belongs to **int** type and takes 32 bits or 4 bytes (in a 32-bit machine) and **ch** takes 8 bits or 1 byte. If the union type is defined as a structure type, the variable **v** will have 4+1 bytes of memory allocated. However, in the union type, all data fields share the same memory. If these data fields require different sizes of memory, the largest size among the data fields will be allocated and the smaller-sized fields will occupy a part of the memory. In this example, four bytes of memory will be allocated and the smaller field ch will share the first byte of x.

The way we access a union type variable is similar to that of the structure type variable. For example,

```
v.x = 124000;       // put an integer value into the data field x
v.ch = 'C';  // put a character value into the data field ch.
```

Since the two data fields share a part of the memory, the second assignment will overwrite the first byte of **v.x**, destroying the integer value in **v.x**. Obviously, if we do not use the data fields carefully, we may easily make mistakes in programming.

The question is, why do we need such an unsafe data structure? The reason is that it could be useful in certain situations. The following example depicts such a situation where union type variables make the program more elegant.

Assume we want to define a data type to store personnel information for both faculty members and students in a university. The faculty and students have ID numbers with different lengths. A person in a university has either a faculty ID or a student ID. If we use two separate data fields for faculty ID and student ID, we will only use one of the two data fields for every record. If we only use one data field and leave the extra bytes free when an ID number does not have enough characters to fill all bytes, we could lose our view of whether we are dealing with a student record or a faculty record. A union type will solve the problem as shown in the following program.

```c
#include <stdio.h>
#include <string.h>
struct Personnel {  // Define a structure type called Personnel
    char    name[30];
    long    phone;
    union identity { // Define a union type inside the structure type
        char facultyid[8];        // Two alternative data fields are defined here
        char studentid[12];
    } id;    // We declare a variable of the union type here.
};
main(){
    struct Personnel x, *p;  // Declare a Personnel type variable and a pointer
    strcpy(x.name, "Mike Lee");     // Copy a name into the name field
    x.phone = 21400000;                    // Assign a number to phone field
    strcpy(x.id.studentid, "1999eas1234"); // Copy student ID
    printf("x.id.studentid = %s\n", x.id.studentid);
    strcpy(x.name, "Jane Smid");   // Use the same x for a faculty record
    x.phone = 9659876;
    strcpy(x.id.facultyid, "cse1234");
    printf("x.id.facultyid = %s\n", x.id.facultyid);
    p = &x;
    printf("p->id.studentid = %s\n", p->id.studentid);
    printf("p->id.facultyid = %s\n", p->id.facultyid);
}
```

In this example, the same variable is used for a student record and a faculty record. The different ID field names allow us to differentiate which record we are handling.

2.5.3 Array of Structures Using Static Memory Allocation

Structure types will make more sense if we combine them with array and pointer types to form collections of structures. In the following example, we define an array of structures to form a database.

```c
/* This program demonstrates how to define an array of structures.
    It statically allocates memory for the variables of structure type */
#include <stdio.h>
#include <string.h>
#define max 100
struct Contact {      // define a node that can hold a person's detail
    char    name[30];
```

```
        long     phone;
        char     email[30];
};
struct Contact ContactBook[max];  // an array of structures, 100 entries
int tail = 0;                     // tail is defined here as a global variable
void branching(char c);           // forward declaration of a function
int insertion();                  // forward declaration of a function
int search();                     // forward declaration of a function
// void deletion();               // not implemented in this example
// void printall();               // not implemented in this example
void main() {                     // main() first prints a menu for selection
    char ch = 'a';
    while (ch != 'q') {
            printf("enter your selection\n");
            printf("          i: insert a new entry\n");
            printf("          s: search an entry\n");
            printf("          d: delete an entry\n");   // not implemented
            printf("          p: print all entries\n"); // not implemented
            printf("          q: quit\n");
            fflush(stdin);                    // flush input buffer to make sure getc reads correctly
            ch = getc(stdin);
            branching(ch);
    }
}
void branching(char c) {     // branch to different tasks
    switch(c) {
            case 'i': insertion(); break;
            case 's': search(); break;
            case 'q': printf("You exit the program\n"); break;
            default:  printf("Invalid input\n");
    }
}
int insertion() {     // insert a new entry
    if (tail == max) {
            printf("There is no more place to insert\n");
            return -1;
    }
    else {
            printf("Enter name, phone, email\n");
            scanf("%s", ContactBook[tail].name);
            scanf("%d", &ContactBook[tail].phone);
```

```
                scanf("%s", ContactBook[tail].email);
                tail++;
                printf("The number of entries = %d\n", tail);
                return 0;
        }
}
int search() {          // search and print phone and email via name
        char sname[30];
        int  i;
        printf("please enter the name to be searched\n");
        scanf("%s", sname);
        for (i=0; i<tail; i++)
                if (strcmp(sname, ContactBook[i].name)== 0) {
                        printf("phone = %d\n", ContactBook[i].phone);
                        printf("email = %s\n", ContactBook[i].email);
                        return 0;
                }
        printf("The name does not exist\n");
        return -1;
}
```

In the program, **Contact** is a structure type with three data fields. The declaration

struct Contact ContactBook[max];

declares an array of structures with 100 entries. Then we use the **tail** variable as the index to access the next unused element of the array: **ContactBook[tail]**. Figure 2.13 shows the structure of the array.

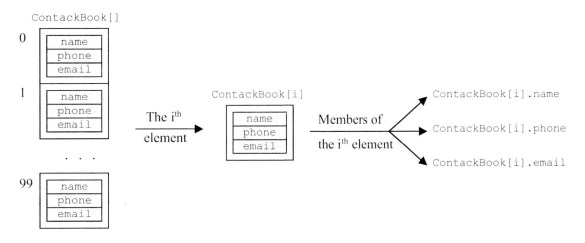

Figure 2.13 Array of structures, its element, and the members of the element

Since the element of the array is of the **struct contact** type with three data fields, we use the dot-notation to access the data fields of the ith element:

ContactBook[tail].name

ContactBook[tail].phone

ContactBook[tail].email

The array variable **ContactBook[max]** is a **global variable**, that is, a variable that is outside all functions. The memory locations for global variables are statically allocated by the compiler during compilation time. We call this kind of memory allocation **static memory allocation**. In this example, the compiler will allocate an array of 100 (**max**) elements before the program starts. Assume a **long** integer takes 4 bytes, and the name and email take 30 bytes each. The total number of bytes needed for one array element is then 64 bytes. The array of 100 elements will take 6400 bytes.

In the next chapter, we will discuss in detail the three different memory areas: static, stack and heap, the mechanisms for allocating memory from these three areas, as well as how memory is de-allocated (garbage collection).

2.5.4 LINKED LIST USING DYNAMIC MEMORY ALLOCATION

The advantage with static memory allocation is that the memory for the variables is already available when we want to store data in them. The problem is that we need to know the maximum number of elements in advance, which is possible in some cases and not possible in some other cases. If we overestimate the data amount, we waste memory. If we underestimate the data amount, we have to stop the program, modify the **max** value and recompile the program. To solve this problem, we can use **dynamic memory allocation** that allocates memory to variables during the execution by a function call.

In C, the function that dynamically allocates memory is

void *malloc(size_t size);

The function takes one parameter that is of type **size_t**. The type **size_t** is usually **unsigned int**. The parameter specifies the number of bytes to be allocated. For example, if you need memory location for an integer variable, then you can call

p = malloc(4);

However, this statement will work only on a machine that uses 4 bytes for an integer. If you run your program on another machine with a different word-length, the statement will cause a problem. A better way to allocate memory for a given type of variable is to call **malloc (sizeof(type_name))**. For example, if you need memory for an integer variable, it is better to do

p = malloc(sizeof(int));

The function **malloc** returns a pointer to the initial address of the memory. If the runtime system runs out of memory, it returns **null**.

Please notice that the notation "**void ***" means here that the **malloc** function returns a generic pointer that can point to a variable of any data type. This is possible because all pointer types are structurally equivalent and C mainly uses structural type equivalence in its type checking. Of course, you can also make an explicit type casting to convert the generic pointer type to the specific type, for the purpose of readability, for example:

p = (int *) malloc(sizeof(int));

casts the return value to an integer type pointer.

In C++, a new dynamic memory allocation operator has been introduced:

```
class_name p = new class_name;
```

The new operator allocates the right amount of memory for a variable (object) of the given class and returns a pointer of that class. Java uses a similar operator to dynamically allocate memory. The new operator will be explained in more detail in the next chapter.

Since the malloc function returns a generic pointer, we often combine dynamic memory allocation with pointers to define a collection of structures. The following example re-implements the array of structures using dynamic memory allocation.

```
/* This program demonstrates how to define a linked list of structures.
    It dynamically allocates memory for the variables of structure type.
    Only the parts that are different from the array of structure example
    are given here. */
#include <stdio.h>
#include <stdlib.h>              // used for malloc
struct Contact {                 // define a node holding a person's detail
    char name[30];
    long phone;
    char email[30];
    struct Contact *next;    // pointer to Contact structure
} *head = NULL;                  //head is a global pointer to first entry
void branching(char c);      // function forward declaration
int insertion();
int search();
// void deletion();
// void printall();

int insertion() {                 // insert a new entry
    struct Contact *p;
    p = (struct Contact *) malloc(sizeof(struct Contact));
    if (p == 0) {
            printf("out of memory\n");  return -1;
    }
    printf("Enter name, phone, email \n");
    scanf("%s", p->name);
    scanf("%d", &p->phone);
    scanf("%s", p->email);
    p->next = head;
    head = p;
    return 0;
}
int search() {          // print phone and email via name
```

```
char sname[30];
struct Contact *p = head;
printf("please enter the name to be searched\n");
scanf("%s", sname);
while (p != 0)
        if (strcmp(sname, p->name)== 0) {
                printf("phone = %d\n", p->phone);
                printf("email = %s\n", p->email);
                return 0;
        }
        else p = p->next;
printf("The name does not exist\n");
return -1;
}
```

In the example, the Contact type is redefined with an extra field next:

struct Contact *next;   // pointer to Contact structure

The next field is a pointer to a Contact type variable. We use it to form a linked list. Please note that we need to use the keyword **struct** whenever we refer to a structure type.

In the insertion function, we use

p = (struct Contact *) malloc(sizeof(struct Contact));

to allocate the right amount of memory for a variable of Contact type, and we link the initial address of this memory chunk to a pointer variable **p**. The type casting makes it clearer that the memory is allocated for a Contact type variable.

Figure 2.14 illustrates the insertion process. Assume that the linked list has already two nodes and a new node is being inserted.

This insertion function inserts the new node at the beginning of the linked list. You can also insert the new node to the end (or at any required position). In this case, you can use a temporary pointer, say **temp**, and move temp to the last node before performing insertion, as shown in the following code.

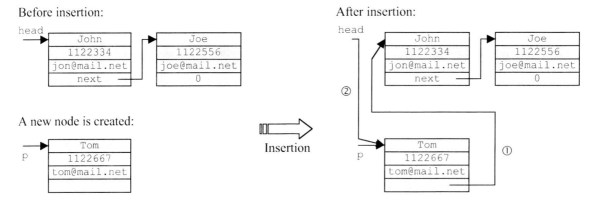

Figure 2.14 Insert a new node at the beginning of a linked list

```
int insertion_at_end() {                    // insert a new entry at the end
    struct Contact *p, *temp;
    p = (struct Contact *) malloc(sizeof(struct Contact));
    if (p == 0) {
            printf("out of memory\n"); return -1;
    }
    printf("Enter name, phone, email \n");
    scanf("%s", p->name); scanf("%d", &p->phone); scanf("%s", p->email);
    p->next = 0;
    if (head == 0) head = p;
    else {
            while (temp->next != null)
                    temp = temp->next;          // Find the last node
            temp->next = p;                     // Link the new node
    }
}
```

Generally, a node can be inserted in any position in a linked list. Figure 2.15 illustrates the insertion process. It consists of three steps: (1) Find the position where the new node is to be inserted. Use a temporary pointer variable **temp** to point to this position. (2) Set the new node's next pointer to the node next to the node pointed to by **temp**. (3) Set the next pointer of the node pointed to by **temp** to the new node.

In the earlier example of the array of structures, we used the dot-notation to access the data field of a structure variable. It is different when referring to a data field of a structure pointed to by a pointer variable. We use the **arrow operator** (or called pointer-to-member operator) instead, that is, we use

p->name
p->phone
p->email
p->next

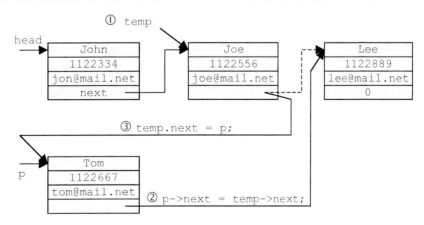

Figure 2.15 Insert a new node in the middle of a linked list

to access the four fields of a Contact structure variable pointed to by p. The differentiation is necessary because their meanings are different. Let's examine the piece of code:

```
struct Contact *p, q;
p = (struct Contact *) malloc(sizeof(struct Contact));
strcpy(p->name, "smith");   // or strcpy(*p.name, "smith");
strcpy(q.name, "miller");
free(p);       // return the memory allocated by malloc to the memory heap
p = &q;        // p is now pointing to variable q.
```

In the example, p is a pointer to a Contact structure variable and p only has 4 bytes of memory allocated, while q is the name of a variable of Contact type, as shown in figure 2.16. The compiler has allocated the entire memory that can hold all four data fields to q. Thus, we can directly copy a name "miller" into the name field of q. Before we can copy anything into the variable pointed to by p, we must first use malloc to obtain the memory for that variable.

The last statement in the example assigns the address of q to p. Now p is pointing to the variable q. In other words, now q has another name which is *p. If we do not free (delete) the Contact variable pointed to by p before we assign the address of q to p, the variable will be completely inaccessible and becomes a piece of **garbage**. The "free" function is, in fact, doing the job of garbage collection.

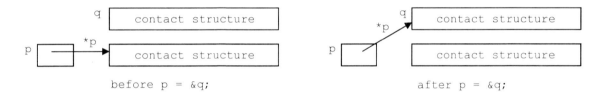

Figure 2.16 Variable q is statically allocated,
while the variable pointed to by p is dynamically allocated

The function free(p) is the opposite of the function p = malloc(size), in that it returns the memory linked to p to the **heap**, the pool of free memory. If we keep using malloc to get memory from the heap, but do not collect the garbage, the heap will eventually be empty and we thus run out of memory. Not collecting garbage is also called a **memory leak**. More detail on garbage collection and memory leak will be discussed in the next chapter.

2.5.5 STACK

A **stack** is a data structure that can contain a set of ordered items. The items are ordered in such a way that an item can be inserted into the stack or removed from the stack at the same end. This end is called the top of the stack.

The stack is one of the most important data structures in computer hardware and software design. This section introduces the basic concept of stack through an example. More applications of the stack will be further discussed in Chapter 3 when we study the memory management, in section A.2 in Appendix A when we introduce basic computer architectures, and in A.3 when we discussed the implementation of function calls at the assembly language level.

Like any structured data type or a data structure, a stack is defined on simpler data types and the new operations on the data types.

Typically, a stack is defined on an array type. The basic operations defined on the stack are push (add an element onto the stack top) and pop (remove the top element from the stack). The code below shows the definition of a stack.

```
elementType stack[stackSize];
int top = 0;
void push(elementType Element) {
    if (top < stackSize) {
            stack[top] = Element;
            top++;
    }
    Printf("Error: stack full\n");
}
elementType pop() {
    if (top > 0) {
            top--;
            return stack[top];
    }
    Printf("Error: stack empty\n");
}
```

Now we use the stack to implement a four-function calculator that supports addition, subtraction, multiplication, and division operations on floating point numbers. The basic part of the implementation is same as the code above, except that the **elementType** is now **float**, and four extra arithmetic functions are included. To perform operations, data are first pushed onto the stack. Every time an operation is performed, the two data on the stack top are popped out for operation and the result is pushed back onto the stack.

```
#define stackSize 8         // a sample value
#include <stdio.h>
float stack[stackSize];
int top = 0;
void push(float Element) {
    if (top < stackSize) {
            stack[top] = Element;
            top++;
    } else
    printf("Error: stack full\n");
}
float pop() {
    if (top > 0) {
            top--;
            return stack[top];
```

```
        } else
            printf("Error: stack empty\n");
    }
    float add() {
        float y;
        y = pop() + pop(); push(y);
    }
    float sub() {
        float y;
        y = pop() - pop(); push(y);
    }
    float mul() {
        float y;
        y = pop() * pop(); push(y);
    }
    float div() {
        float y;
        y = pop() / pop(); push(y);
    }
    void main() {
        float x1 = 1.5, x2 = 2.5, x3 = 3.5, x4 = 4.5, x5 = 5.5, x6 = 6.5;
        push(x1); push(x2); push(x3);
        push(x4); push(x5); push(x6);
        add(); sub(); mul(); div(); add();
        printf("final value = %f\n", pop());
    }
```

What is computed in the main program by the sequence of operations add(), sub(), mul(), div(), and add()? Figure 2.17 shows the stack status after each push operation and after each arithmetic operation. Initially, stack top = 0. It increments after each push operation. In each arithmetic operation, two pop operations and one push operation are performed, resulting in the top decreased by one. The final value computed is 12.0. After the pop operation is performed in the printf statement, the top returns to zero.

2.5.6 FILE AND FILE OPERATIONS

So far, we have discussed using memory (variables) to store data. However, memory is only a temporary place to store data. When we quit a program, all memory allocated to the program is taken back by the operating system for reuse. If our program has data that need to be stored for future use, we need to store the data into the permanent storage of a computer—the disk.

Data stored on disk are organized in **files**. We consider a file as a structured data type and we access data in a file using a pointer to an object of type FILE, which records whatever information is necessary to control the stream of data.

As we know that disk operations are extremely slow, million times slower than memory operations. The challenge is to make file operations faster. The solution is to use a buffer in the memory to hold a

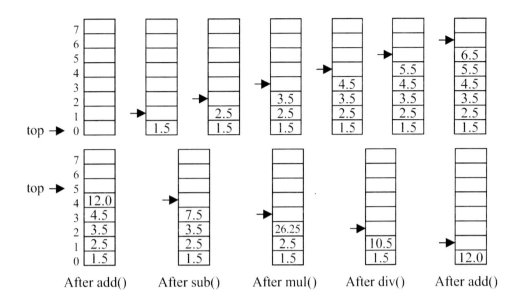

Figure 2.17 Stack status after each operation

large block (e.g., 1024 bytes) of data. Each disk operation will transfer a block of data, instead of a byte or a word of data. Figure 2.18 shows how read and write operations are implemented.

For the read operations, the process is as follows:

■ Declare a pointer f of a FILE type;

■ Open a file for read: Create a buffer that can hold a block of bytes (e.g., 1024 bytes);

■ Copy the first block of a file into buffer;

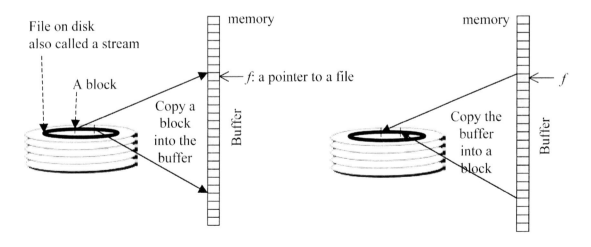

Figure 2.18 File read and write operations

■ A program uses the pointer to read the data in the buffer;

■ When the pointer moves down to the end of the buffer, copy the next block into buffer

For the write operation, the process is as follows:

■ Declare a pointer f of a FILE type;

■ Open a file for write: Create a buffer that can hold a block of bytes (e.g., 1024 bytes);

■ A program uses the pointer to write the data in the buffer;

■ When the buffer is full, copy the block into the disk;

■ Move the pointer to the beginning for more write-operations

The following example demonstrates basic file operations including opening, reading, writing, and closing a file.

```
// demonstrate the use of fopen, fclose, feof,  fgetc and fputc operations
#include <stdio.h>
#include <string.h>
// This function reads all characters in the file and puts them in string str
void file_read(char *filename, char *str) {
    FILE *p;
    int index=0;
    p=fopen(filename, "r");        // Open the file for "read".
                                   // Other options are "w" (write), "a" (append),
                                   // and "rw" (read and write).
    while(!feof(p)) // while not reaching the end-of-file character
            *(str+index++)=fgetc(p); //read a character from file and put it
                                   // in str. p is incremented automatically.
    str[index]='\0';               // add the null terminator
    puts(str);                     // print str. You can use printf too.
    fclose(p);                     // close the file
}
// This function creates a new file (or opens an existing file), and then
// stores (puts) all characters in the string str into the file.
void file_write(char *filename, char *str) {
    int i, l;
    FILE *p;                            // declare a pointer to file type
    p=fopen(filename, "w");             // open/create a file for "write".
    l = strlen(str);                    // get string-length
    for(i=0;i<l;i++)
            fputc(*(str+i),p);          // write a character to the file pointed
                                        // by p. p is incremented automatically.
```

```
        fclose(p);                              // Close the file.
}
// This function encrypts the string in str.
void encrypt(int offset, char *str) {
        int i,l;
        l=strlen(str);
        printf("original str = \n%s\n", str);
        for(i=0;i<l;i++)
                str[i] = str[i]+offset;
        printf("encrypted str = \n%s \nlength = %d\n", str, l);
}
void main() {
        char filename[25];
        char strtext[1024];
        printf("Please enter the name of the file to be read\n");
        // you should enter the name of an existing text file, e.g., letter1.txt
        scanf("%[^\n]s", &filename);         // Read a line till the end-of-line "\n"
        file_read(filename, strtext);        // read text from file and put it in strtext
        encrypt(5, strtext);                 // manipulate the string strtext
        printf("Please enter the name of the file to be written\n");
        scanf("%[^\n]s", &filename);         // Read a line till the end-of-line "\n"
        file_write(filename, strtext);       // write the text into the given file
}
```

The program first takes a file name from the keyboard, reads the file (we assume the file exists), put the entire content of the file in a string variable **strtext**. Then we call the encrypt function to encrypt the string. Finally we write the encrypted string into another text file.

In the program, we use the following basic file open operation

```
p = fopen(filename, "r");
```

to open the file in "read" mode. The pointer **p** points to the first character in the text file. Other mode options are "w" for "write" and "a" for "append" data at the end of the file. In addition to these modes, the following characters can be included in mode to specify the translation mode for newline characters: "t": Open in text (translated) mode. In this mode, CTRL+Z is interpreted as an end-of-file character on input. "b": Open in binary (untranslated) mode; translations involving carriage-return and linefeed characters are suppressed.

Having opened a file, we can use the function

```
ch = fgetc(p);
```

to read the first character from the file. After each **fgetc** call, the pointer is automatically moved to the next position, ready for reading the next character. Another function is

```
fputc(ch, p);
```

that puts the character in parameter **ch** into the file at the position pointed to by **p**.

After we have completed file operations (read or write), we must close a file by using the file close operation

```
fclose(p);
```

If a file is not closed, the file descriptor that is used by the operating system to identify the file will not be freed. The total number of file descriptors that an operating system can issue is usually very limited. For example, in Unix operating system, the file descriptor must be between 0 and 20. File descriptors 0, 1, and 2 are reserved for three system files: standard input, standard output, and standard error output, leaving only 18 file descriptors for all users concurrently using the operating system. If no file descriptors are available, the operating system will not be able to open any file for any user applications.

In the statement scanf("%[^\n]s", &filename) in the program example above, the control sequence [^\n] ensures that the scanf reads till the newline symbol "\n", including the spaces in the line.

In the program above, we used fflush(stdin) to remove the delimiter (a space, a newline, etc) before using getc(stdin). The reason is, the formatted input function scanf will only read up to the delimiter and leave the delimiter in the input buffer. If we do not call fflush(stdin), the left delimiter will be read by an unformatted input function such as getc(stdin) and gets(stdin). Thus, we must call function fflush(stdin) to flush the buffer of the standard input file stdin. It is not a problem if two consecutive scanf functions are called because formatted input function can automatically remove the delimiter. The C++ function equivalent to fflush is cin.ignore, which will be discussed later in this section.

The other file operations include

- scanf(control sequence, parameter list); // formatted input from keyboard
- fscanf(filename, control sequence, parameter list); // this function is same as scanf except it inputs from a file
- printf(control sequence, parameter list); // formatted output to screen
- fprintf(filename, control sequence, parameter list); // this function is same as print except it outputs to a file
- fread(buffer, size, count, fileName); // unformatted read
- fwrite(buffer, size, count, fileName); // unformatted write

The definitions of the functions fread and fwrite are:

```
size_t fread(void *buffer, size_t size, size_t count, FILE *fileName );
size_t fwrite(const void *buffer, size_t size, size_t count, FILE *fileName );
// Using these two functions require to include <stdio.h> header
```

The functions are defined in the standard library stdio.h. The function fread returns the number of full items actually read, which may be less than count if an error occurs or if the end of the file is encountered before reaching count. You can use the feof or ferror function to distinguish a read error from an end-of-file condition. If size or count is 0, fread returns 0 and the buffer contents are unchanged.

The function fwrite returns the number of full items actually written, which may be less than count if an error occurs. Also, if an error occurs, the file-position indicator cannot be determined.

The parameters in the functions are specified as follows:

buffer: pointer to the source variable (for fwrite) or to the destination variable (for fread)

size: item size in bytes

count: maximum number of items to be read or written

fileName: pointer to FILE structure

The following segment of code consists of two functions. The **save_file** function saves a linked list of node into a file called **fileName**, and the **load_file** function reads the file called **fileName**, and rebuild the linked list according to the save data. The segment of code demonstrates how to write and read strings and integers to and from a file.

```
// demonstrate the use of fopen, fclose fread and fwrite operations
void save_file() {
    FILE *fileName;
    personnel *node;
    char ch;
    long sid;

    fileName = fopen(file_name, "wb");      //b for binary mode
    if(fileName != NULL) {
            node = head;
            while(node != NULL) {
                    fwrite(node->getName(), 30, 1, fileName);
                    fwrite(node->getBirthday(), 11, 1, fileName);
                    sid = node->getId();
                    fwrite(&sid, sizeof(long), 1, fileName);
                    node = node->getNext();
            }
    }
    else {
            printf ("ERROR - Couldnot open file for saving data !"\n);
    }
}

void load_file() {
    FILE *fileName;
    personnel *node, *temp;
    char sname[30];
    char sbirthday[11];
    long sid;

    fileName = fopen(file_name, "rb");
    if(fileName != NULL) {
            while(fread(sname, 30, 1, fileName) == 1) {
                    fread(sbirthday, 11, 1, fileName);
                    fread(&sid, sizeof(long), 1, fileName);
                    node = new personnel(sname, sbirthday);
                    node->setId(sid);
                    if(head != NULL)
```

```
                    temp->setNext(node);
            else
                    head = node;
            temp = node;
        }
        fclose(fileName);
    }
}
```

We have used **scanf** and **printf** to read from the keyboard and print to the monitor. In fact, in C/C++, the keyboard is considered to be a read-only file (standard input file) and the screen is considered to be a write only file (standard output file). Their file names are **stdin** and **stdout**, respectively.

The functions **fscanf** and **fprintf** are more general forms of file operations in which we can specify what file we want to read and write. The standard input and output functions **scanf** and **printf** are special case of them and are equivalent to

```
fscanf(stdin, control sequence, parameter list);
fprintf(stdout, control sequence, parameter list);
```

The following example shows the application of **fprintf** and **fscanf**. First, an integer number and a float number are written in the file named **PersonData**. Then the file is closed and reopened for read. An integer number and a float number are read into two variables **len** and **hei**, respectively

```
#include <stdio.h>
void main() {
    FILE *fileID;
    int length = 35429, len;
    float height = 5.8, hei;
    fileID = fopen("PersonData", "wb");       // open for write
    if(fileID != NULL) {
            fprintf(fileID, "%d\n", length);   // write an integer into a file
            fprintf(fileID, "%f\n", height);   // write a float into a file
    }
    else
            printf ("ERROR - Couldnot open file for saving data !\n");
    fclose(fileID);
    fileID = fopen("PersonData", "rb");       // open for read
    if(fileID != NULL) {
            fscanf(fileID, "%d", &len);                // read an integer from a file
            fscanf(fileID, "%f", &hei);                // read a float from a file
            printf("length = %d, height = %f\n", len, hei);
    }
    fclose(fileID);
}
```

In C++ styled I/O, similar operations are defined:

```
cin>>
cout<<
cin.ignore();
cin.get(strvar, strlength, achar);
cin.getline(strvar, strlength, achar);
```

The function **cin.ignore()** is similar to but more powerful than the C-styled **fflush(stdin)** function that flushes the input buffer to remove the remaining delimiter in the buffer of the standard input file **stdin** after a **scanf** operation. In C++, you must use **cin.ignore()** if you switch from the formatted input function **cin >>** to an unformatted input functions such as **cin.get** or **cin.getline**, and etc. Similar to **scanf**, **cin >>** will only read up to a space or newline and leave the space or newline in the buffer. The function **cin.ignore()** will remove the space or newline. The function **cin.ignore()** is more powerful than simply remove one character from the input buffer. There are three overloaded functions. (1) **cin.ignore()**: discard one character from the input buffer; (2) **cin.ignore(int n)**: discard **n** characters from the input buffer; and (3) **cin.ignore(int n, char term)**: discard **n** characters or stop when the character in the parameter **term** is encountered. For example, .

```
#include <iostream>
using namespace std;
void main(void) {
    char strvar[12];
    cin >> strvar;                 // Enter: Hi
    cout << "Please enter the string: Hello world" << endl;
    // cin.ignore();               // option 1
    // cin.ignore(10);             // option 2
    // cin.ignore(10, 'w' );       // option 3
    cin.getline(strvar, 12, '\n'); // Enter: Hello world
    cout << strvar << endl;
}
```

Figure 2.19 illustrates the states of the input variable **strvar** and the input buffer in the execution process of the program above. Notice that the newline character '\n' is left in the buffer after the **cin >>** operation is completed and thus the next input string "**Hello world**" is appended to the character. The **cin.getline** function reads the input buffer till a newline character. Since a newline character already exists in the buffer, the **cin.getline** function will not wait for the user to enter a newline. As the result, no input is needed and an empty string is read into the input variable **strvar**. The print statement **cout <<** will then print nothing. It creates an illusion that the last two statements in the program are skipped.

To solve the problem, we can use the function **cin.ignore()** to discard the newline character (option 1 in the program). To illustrate the effects of the three **cin.ignore** functions, we apply the three options one by one. The outputs of the statement "**cout << strvar << endl;**" in the three executions will be, respectively:

```
Hello world      // correctly printed
ld               // 10 characters are discarded
orld             // It stops after the character 'w' is read
```

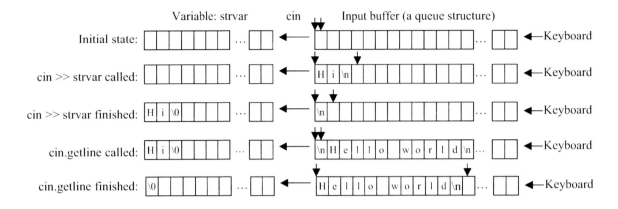

Figure 2.19 The input buffer between the keyboard and the input variable

Option 1 removes a single character. Option 2 removes 10 characters. Option 3 removes 10 characters or stops when a character 'w' is encountered, whichever comes first, and thus one 8 characters are removed. Please notice that **cin.ignore** removes the characters left in the input buffer. If there is no character in the buffer, it will remove the character entered after the **cin.ignore** statement!

The **cin.get** and **cin.getline** functions work like the **>>** operator except that they will read **space** characters and are less likely to cause a tied output stream that needs to be flushed, where the parameter **aline** is a string variable that will hold the entered string; parameters **alength** and **achar** are optional. **alength** is an integer that limits the maximum number of characters to be passed to parameter **aline**. Parameter **achar** is an character that serves as the terminator. The input functions stop reading when the terminator character is read. By default, the terminator is the **newline** character '\n'. Both **get** and **getline** will reserve one character for the terminator, that is, you can only enter **alength-1** characters. The only difference between **get** and **getline** are that the **getline** function will remove the terminator from the **aline** variable, while **get** will keep the terminator in the **aline** variable. The following code shows a simple example where the character '**@**' is used as the terminator.

```
#include <iostream.h>
void main() {
    char line[25];
    cout << "Please enter a line terminated by '@'" << endl;
    cin.getline(line, 25, '@');
    cout << line;
}
```

2.6 FUNCTIONS AND PARAMETER PASSING

Functions, also called procedures or subroutines in some other programming languages, are named blocks of code that must be explicitly called. The purpose of functions is twofold:

- Abstraction: statements in a function form a conceptual unit.
- Reuse: statements in a function can be executed multiple times in the program.

As part of a program, a function must communicate with the rest of the program. To pass values into a function (**in-passing**), we usually have two methods: global variable and parameter passing. To pass values out of a function (**out-passing**), we usually have three methods: global variable, parameter passing, and return value. Different programming languages have different value passing policies and mechanisms.

- In imperative and object oriented programming languages like C/C++ and Java, all combinations of the in-passing and out-passing methods are allowed.
- In functional programming languages like Scheme or Lisp, parameter passing is the only in-passing method and return value is the only out-passing method allowed.
- In logic programming language like Prolog, parameter passing is the only in-passing and the only out-passing method allowed.

It has side effects to use a global variable to pass a value in or out of a function and thus it is generally not recommended to use global variables for passing values. It is conceptually simple to use a return value to pass a value out of a function. We will thus focus on the parameter passing mechanisms that pass values in and out of functions.

When we discuss parameter passing, we need to differentiate two kinds of parameters: formal parameters and actual parameters.

Formal parameters are the parameters we use when we declare (define) a function. Formal parameters are local variables of the function.

Actual parameters are the values or variables we use to substitute for the formal parameters when we call a function. Actual parameters are variables/values of the caller before we enter the function, but become the variables/values of the function after we enter the function.

Now the question is, what would happen if we modify the formal parameters in the function? Will the modification have an impact on the actual parameters? The answer to the question depends on what kind of parameter passing mechanisms we use. The most frequently used parameter passing mechanisms are call-by-value, call-by-reference, and called-by-address.

Call-by-value: The formal parameter is a local variable in the function. It is initialized to the value of the actual parameter. It is a copy of the actual parameter. The modification of formal parameters has no impact on the actual parameters. In other words, call-by-value can only pass values into a function, but cannot pass values outside the function. Functions using call-by-value must use return-value to pass a value to the outside. The advantage of call-by-value is that it has no side effects and is considered to be the reliable programming practice. The drawback is that it is not convenient to handle structured data types.

The following piece of code demonstrates value in-passing by global variable and call-by-value mechanisms.

```
#include <stdio.h>
int i = 1;                       // i is outside any function and is a global variable
foo(int m, int n) {              // m and n are formal parameters
    printf("i = %d m = %d n = %d\n", i, m, n);
    i = 5; m = 3; n = 4;         // Modify i, m and n.
    printf("i = %d m = %d n = %d\n", i, m, n);
}
main() {
    int j = 2;                   // j is a local variable, local to main() function
    foo(i, j);                   // i and j are actual parameters of function foo
    printf("i = %d j = %d\n", i, j);
}
```

The output of the program is

```
i = 1       m = 1       n = 2
i = 5       m = 3       n = 4
i = 5       j = 2
```

As you can see, the global variable i is changed in the function and i remains changed after leaving the function. On the other hand, j is passed to formal parameter n and n is modified in the function. The modification to n has no impact on j.

Please read chapter three for more detail on stack management and its impact on parameter passing.

Call-by-reference: It is also called call-by-alias. The formal parameter is an alias name of the actual parameter. Call-by-reference can pass a value into and out of a function. However, it has the side effect, that is, a variable outside a function can be changed by an action in a function.

For call-by-reference, there is only one variable (memory location) with two names for the formal and actual parameters, respectively. Changing the formal parameter immediately changes the actual parameter. The actual parameter must be a variable. It cannot be a literal value because a value cannot have an alias. This mechanism is supported by C++, but not by C.

To declare a formal parameter x in call-by-reference, an ampersand symbol is prefixed to the parameter: &x. The following code demonstrates parameter passing by call-by-reference mechanism, where the second parameter of **foo** function is an alias to the corresponding actual parameter.

```
#include <iostream>
void foo(int, int &);                   // forward declaration
int i = 1;
void main() {
    int j = 2;                          // j is a local variable, local to main() function
    foo(i, j);                          // i and j are actual parameters of function foo
    printf("i = %d j = %d\n", i, j);
    foo(j, i);                          // i and j are swapped
    printf("i = %d j = %d\n", i, j);
}
void foo(int m, int &n) {               // call-by-reference is applied to parameter n
    printf("i = %d m = %d n = %d\n", i, m, n);
    i = 5; m = 3; n = 4;                // Modify i, m and n.
    printf("i = %d m = %d n = %d\n", i, m, n);
}
```

The output of the program is

```
i = 1       m = 1       n = 2
i = 5       m = 3       n = 4
i = 5       j = 4                   // notice that j is changed
i = 5       m = 4       n = 5
i = 4       m = 3       n = 4       // notice that i is changed immediately
i = 4       j = 4
```

This program is basically same as the call-by-value example, except that the modification to the variable n in the foo function is passed to the variable j in the main program, in the first call, and is immediately passed to i in the second call to foo.

Call-by-address: It is also called call-by-pointer. The address of the actual parameter is passed into a local variable of the function. The actual parameter can be an address value or a pointer variable. You can use the address to directly modify the actual parameter pointed to by the address. You can also modify the address value stored in the formal parameter. This modification will not modify the actual parameter though. In fact, for the pointer variable itself, call-by-value is applied. In the next example, we demonstrate parameter-passing by call-by-address.

```c
#include <stdio.h>
void foo(int *n) {
    printf("n = %d\n", *n);    // print the variable value pointed to by n
    *n = 30;                   // modify the variable value pointed to by n
    printf("n = %d\n", *n);    // print the variable value pointed to by n again
    n = 0;                     // Modify the pointer itself.
}
void main() {
    int i = 15;
    foo(&i);
    printf("i = %d\n", i);
    i = 10;
    foo(&i);
    printf("i = %d\n", i);
}
```

In the main program, we have a local variable i, initialized to 15. We, then, call function foo using &i, the address of variable i. The actual parameter is the address value (a pointer) of i, not the variable i itself.

In the function definition, the formal parameter is a pointer to an integer type. We use the pointer n to modify the variable *n pointed to by n, which is in fact i. Thus, we have indirectly modified variable i in the main() function. When the control exits the function, i remains modified. As the last statement in the function, we modify n itself. However, this modification will not have an impact on the address value passed to n when the control exits the function. As you can see here, call-by-address and call-by-value are relative. When we use call-by-address, if our intention is to pass the variable pointed to by the pointer (address value) to the function, we are doing real call-by-reference. If we change the variable through its address, the variable remains changed after exiting the function. On the other hand, if the address value is what we really want to pass into the function, instead of the variable pointed to by the address, we are actually doing call-by-value.

Another application of call-by-address is in the situation where we want to pass a structure variable (an array, a string, or a structure) to a function. It is more convenient to pass the pointer of the structure variable, instead of passing the structure itself.

In Java, parameter passing is limited in such a way that

- if the parameter is primitive type, only call-by-value is allowed;
- if the parameter is of a class-based type, only call-by-address is allowed. Some books say that Java only supports call-by-value. They are referring to the pointer variable (reference) itself passed to a function. However, since the intention of passing the reference variable is to access the object pointed

to by the reference, it is better to say that it supports call-by-address, instead of call-by-value. Notice that the pointer in Java is called "reference". However, Java's parameter passing for objects is not call-by-reference, according to the definition of call-by-reference.

In C/C++, all combinations of parameter passing are allowed. You can pass a pointer (call-by-address) or an alias (call-by-reference) to a simple variable, e.g., of integer type, or pass a complex type of variable using call-by-value, call-by-reference, or call-by-address.

The following program shows how to pass a string into and out of a function using call-by-address.

```
// file name: strop.c
#include <stdio.h>
#include <string.h>
char *getString(char *str){   //The function returns a pointer to its parameter.
    return str;               // returns a pointer.
}
void setString(char *str1, char *str2) {          // Copy str2 into str1
    strcpy(str1, str2);
}
void main() {
    char *p, q[8] = "morning", *s = "hello";
    printf("s = %s\n", s);
    p = getString(s);
    printf("p = %s\n", p);
    setString(q, p); // q is the address of the array-based string
    printf("q = %s\n", q);
}
```

The output of the program is

```
s = hello
p = hello
q = hello
```

2.7 RECURSIVE STRUCTURES

Section 2 discussed basic control structures in C/C++. This section studies the complex recursive structures. We first compare recursive structures with the iterative structures. Then we formulate the generic steps of writing recursive functions. Finally, we use a longer example as a case study to go through the design steps. More examples of recursion will be studied in chapters 4 and 5.

2.7.1 LOOP STRUCTURES VERSUS RECURSIVE STRUCTURES

A function (or procedure) is said to be **recursive**, if the function calls itself. A recursive function can call itself anywhere, except the first statement, and once or multiple times, in the body of the function. If a recursive function calls itself only once and in the last statement, the function is said to be **tail-recursive**. Tail-recursion has the simplest structure.

Figure 2.20 compares three different repetition structures: (a) while-do-loop, (b) non-tail-recursion, and (c) tail-recursion.

Although there exist other loop structures, like for-loop and do-while-loop, while-do-loop is sufficient to implement other possible loop structures. The non-tail-recursion breaks its loop-body down into two parts, separated by the recursive call. Part 1 is first repeatedly executed n times, and then, part 2 is executed n times. It is important to recognize that part 2 is executed the same number of times as part 1. The partially completed computations are stored on the stack. When part 1 is eventually repeated the sufficient number of times, or the stopping condition is satisfied, the control exits part 1 and enters part 2. Then part 2 will be executed the same number of times, and finally exit at the end of part 2.

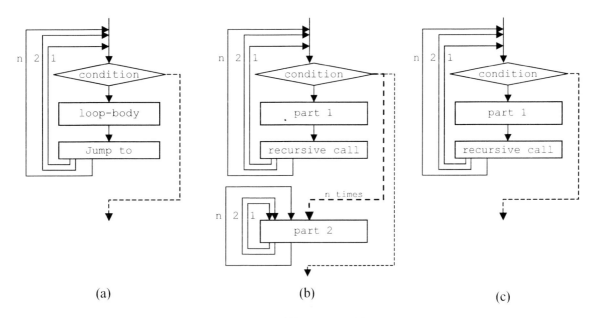

Figure 2.20 Three different repetition structures

In the case of tail-recursion, the recursive call is the last statement, and, thus, there is no part 2. As we can see, the general recursive structure is very different from the iterative loop structure. However, the tail-recursive structure has exactly the same control structure as the while-do-loop. In other words, the while-do-loop structure is a special case of the recursive structure. We will see in chapter 4 that functional program languages can use recursion as their only repetition structure, completely removing loop structures from the languages.

Here we are taking a glass-box approach to understand the recursive function; that is, we try to study recursion by trying to understand the structure and the control flow of the function. This approach is taken by many programmers. It works fine for simple recursive functions. However, if a recursive function has multiple recursive calls in its body, the structure will be far too complex to understand. We will take an innovative approach in this book to study the recursive function: the black-box approach or called **abstract approach**. This approach works fine for both simple and complex recursive functions. We will see soon that this approach is far easier to understand and to apply to solve all kinds of recursive problems in all possible programming languages.

2.7.2 The Fantastic Four Abstract Approach of Writing Recursive Functions

The idea of recursion may not be as straightforward as iterative looping. However, writing recursive function can be as simple as writing iterative functions, as long as we strictly follow the **fantastic four abstract approach**. The approach was first proposed by the author in the first edition of this book and was called "simple steps of writing recursive procedures". The approach has been rated by all students who learn it to be the most efficient method of teaching and learning recursion and was called by the students "fantastic four". This edition formally names it the fantastic four abstract approach, which consists of the following steps:

1. **Formulate the size-n problem.** Recursion is necessary only if we want to solve a problem that needs to repeat the same operations for a number of times. We assume the number of repetition is n. In most cases, n is obvious. For example, if we want to compute factorial n!, the size n is already given. Formulating size-n problem is merely choosing a function name, using n as the parameter, and defining the return type (not the return value) of the function. It is similar to writing the forward declaration in C. Thus, the size-n problem for factorial problem is

       int factorial(int n);

   The return value of the size-n is what the function is supposed to compute, or the value we are looking for. In this step, we do not need to design the solution for the size-n problem.

2. **Find the stopping condition and the corresponding return value.** The body of a recursive function should begin with checking the stopping condition. If the stopping condition is true, the function returns the corresponding value and exits. Otherwise, it performs certain operations, including calling the function itself. In most cases, identifying the stopping condition and corresponding value is trivial or given. For example, the stopping condition of factorial(n) is n = 0, and the corresponding value is 1.

3. **Select m and formulate the size-m problem.** Since we have formulated the size-n problem, the size-m problem is easy: We simply replace parameter n by m in the size-n problem, where m < n. Size m is determined by how much we can reduce the size of the problem in one iteration. If we can only reduce the problem size by one, m is n-1, and thus our task in this step is formulating a size-(n-1) problem. For example, the size-(n-1) factorial problem is simply factorial(n-1). Some times, we may need to find an m that is not n-1. How to find a proper m is application-specific. We will use several examples to illustrate this point in this section and study many more examples in chapter 4. Most students who have difficulty to comprehend recursion misunderstand this step: they try to define a solution, or the return value, of size-m problem here in this step! It is not possible and it is not necessary to produce the return value in this step. All we need to do about the return value here is exactly the same as what we did in step 1. We simply assume the size-m problem will return a value and use this value in step 4. For example, the return value of size-(n-1) factorial problem is factorial(n - 1).

4. **Construct the solution of size-n problem.** In this step, we will use the assumed solution or return value for size-m or size-(n-1) problem to construct the solution of the size-n problem. Again, this is application-specific. In the case of factorial problem, the solution of the size-n problem is n*factorial(n-1).

Sometimes, we may need to use the return values of multiple size-m problems, where $0 \leq m < n$ (assume size-0 is the stopping condition), to construct the solution of size-n problem.

Strictly following these steps, we can define the complete factorial function as follows:

```
int factorial(int n) {            // size-n problem
    if      (n == 0)              // Stopping condition
            return 1;             // Return value at the stopping condition
    else
            return n * factorial(n - 1); //use size-(n-1) problem's assumed
            // solution to construct of size-n problem's solution
}
```

2.7.3 CASE STUDY 1: THE TOWER OF HANOI

The Tower of Hanoi is a famous puzzle game and is a popular example used for explaining recursion. As shown in figure 2.21, the rules of playing the game are:

- There are three pegs, and n successively smaller disks are initially placed on the left peg. n = 4 in figure 2.21. The objective is to move all disks to the right peg. The center peg can be used as an auxiliary holding peg.

- Disks may only be moved from one peg to another. Only one disk may be moved at a time.

- The only disks that may be moved are the top disks on one of the three pegs.

- At no time may a larger disk be placed on a smaller disk.

Now we follow the fantastic four abstract approach to define a solution for the Hanoi Towers problem.

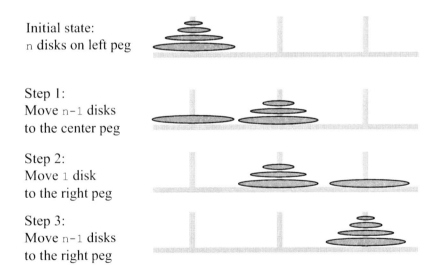

Initial state:
n disks on left peg

Step 1:
Move n−1 disks
to the center peg

Step 2:
Move 1 disk
to the right peg

Step 3:
Move n−1 disks
to the right peg

Figure 2.21 Solving Hanoi Towers problem

1. Formulate the size-n problem

We can simply formulate the size-n problem as **void hanoi(int n)**. However, in the return value (solution), we need to print how to move one disk from one peg to another in each step, and we need to name these three pegs. We could hard code the names as, for example, p1, p2, and p3; or left, center, and right, etc. To increase the flexibility of the code, we add three parameters to the function, so that the user can pass different names into the function. Thus, we formulate the problem as

```
void hanoitowers(int n, char *left, char *center, char *right);
```

Notice that the function does not return a value, instead, it prints instructions (steps) how to move n disk from the left peg, using center peg as the auxiliary, to the right peg.

2. Find the stopping condition and the corresponding return value

The stopping condition is n = 1. In this case, the size-1 problem is hanoitowers(1, left, center, right), and the solution is to print "move the disk from the left peg to the right peg".

3. Select m and formulate the size-m problem

Since we can only move one disk at a time, it is obvious that we can only reduce the size by one in one iteration. Furthermore, since we have multiple parameters in the function, we could have multiple size-(n-1) problems. The following are six possible size-(n-1) problems:

(1) move n-1 disks from left to right, using center as auxiliary:

hanoitowers(n-1, left, center, right)

(2) move n-1 disks from left to center, using right as auxiliary:

hanoitowers(n-1, left, right, center)

(3) move n-1 disks from center to left, using right as auxiliary:

hanoitowers(n-1, center, right, left)

(4) move n-1 disks from center to right, using left as auxiliary:

hanoitowers(n-1, center, left, right)

(5) move n-1 disks from right to left, using center as auxiliary:

hanoitowers(n-1, right, center, left)

(6) move n-1 disks from right to center, using left as auxiliary:

hanoitowers(n-1, right, left, center)

4. Construct the solution of size-n problem

Use the solutions for size-(n-1) problems to construct the solution for the size-n problem.

Figure 2.21 and the text on the left-hand side showed how we construct the solution for the size-n problem based on the solutions for size-(n-1) and size-1 problems, that is,

```
hanoitowers(n-1, left, right, center)      // move n-1 disks left -> center
hanoitowers(1, left, center, right)        // move 1 disk left -> right
hanoitowers(n-1, center, left, right)      // move n-1 disks left -> center
```

In words, the solution for the size-n problem is: (1) Move **n-1** disks from **left** peg to the **center** peg. We simply assume that we can do it, because it is a size-(n-1) problem. (2) Move the remaining disk from **left** to **right**. (3) Move **n-1** disks from **center** to the **right**.

Once we have designed the solution, we can easily obtain the C program that solves the Hanoi Towers problem as follows.

```c
#include <stdio.h>
void hanoitowers(int n, char *S, char *M, char *D) {
    if (n == 1) {                        // stopping condition
        printf("move top from %s to %s\n", S, D);
        // output at stopping condition
    } else {                             // from size-(n-1) to size-n problem
        hanoitowers(n-1, S, D, M);
        hanoitowers(1, S, M, D);
        hanoitowers(n-1, M, S, D);
    }
}
void hanoi(int n) {                      // define a simpler human-interface
    hanoitowers(n, "Left", "Center", "Right");
}
void main() {
    hanoitowers(3, "Source", "Spare", "Destination");
    printf("—————————————————————————————————\n");
    hanoi(4);
}
```

In the program, we defined a one-parameter function **hanoi(n)** as a simpler user interface, in case the user wants the hard-coded peg names. The function with more parameters is defined as a recursive function. When the **main()** function is executed, the functions **hanoitowers(3, "Source", "Spare", "Destination")** and **hanoi(4)** will be called, resulting in the following output describing how to solve the size-3 and size-4 Hanoi Towers problems.

```
move top from Source to Destination
move top from Source to Spare
move top from Destination to Spare
move top from Source to Destination
move top from Spare to Source
move top from Spare to Destination
move top from Source to Destination
_____

move top from Left to Center
move top from Left to Right
move top from Center to Right
```

```
move top from Left to Center
move top from Right to Left
move top from Right to Center
move top from Left to Center
move top from Left to Right
move top from Center to Right
move top from Center to Left
move top from Right to Left
move top from Center to Right
move top from Left to Center
move top from Left to Right
move top from Center to Right
```

As you can see from the example, the most important idea of recursive functions is that we simply assume that we have the solution for size-(n-1) problem and we do not need to solve it. Why does it work? Because the recursive mechanism will actually solve the problem from size-1 upwards automatically; that is, it will solve size-1 problem, then use the solution of size-1 problem to construct the solution of size-2 problem, and so on. Since we have given the solution of size-1 problem and we have defined how to find the solution of size-n problem based on the solution of size-(n-1), we basically have given solutions to the problem of all sizes!

2.7.4 CASE STUDY 2: SORTING AN ARRAY

Now let's follow the fantastic four abstract approach to solve a **sorting problem**. Assume we have an array containing n integers: A[n]. The task is to sort the n numbers in ascending order.

1. Formulate the size-n problem

We can simply formulate the size-n problem as

```
int* sorting(int *A, int n);
```

where A is the initial address of the array to be sorted and n is the size of the array. The function will return the initial address of the sorted array.

2. Find the stopping condition and the corresponding return value

The stopping condition is $n = 1$. In this case, the size-1 problem is sorting(int *A, 1), and the solution or return value is the address of A. A is not changed, because A has only one element and is already sorted.

3. Select m and formulate the size-m problem

Here we take a simple approach by reducing the size of the problem by one. Thus, $m = n - 1$ and the size-(n-1) problem is

```
sorting(B, n-1);
```

where B is the address of an array of size-(n-1). We **assume** B will be sorted if we call this function. This is very important!

4. Construct the solution of size-n problem

Since step 3 can solve the size-(n-1) problem, it is then easy to solve the size-n problem:

(1) We split array A into two parts: the sub array of the first n-1 elements is B, and the remaining element is x.

(2) We call the function in step 3 to sort the size-(n-1) array B.

(3) We find the right position p for inserting x into B.

(4) We make space for x by shifting the elements after position p one place right;

(5) We insert x at the position p.

The following program implements the four-steps in the abstract approach. The comments in the program associate the statements with the five steps described above.

```c
#include <stdio.h>
int* sorting(int *A, int n) {
    int *B, i, j, p = n-1, x;
    if (n==1) return A;              // stopping condition and return value
    else {
        x = A[n-1];                  // Store the last element in x
        B = sorting(A, n-1);         // size-(n-1) problem
        i = 0;
        while (i < n-1) {            // Start to construct size-n solution
            if (x < B[i]) {
                p = i;    // locate the position p for x
                i = n;    // exit the loop
            }
            else i++;
        }                            // x should be inserted at position p
        for (j = p; j < n-1; j++)  // make space
            B[n-1-(j-p)] = B[n-1-(j-p)-1];
        B[p] = x;                    // put x in the right place
        return B;
    } // end of else branch
}
void main() {
    int *SA, i, k, A[] = {3, 2, 4, 2, 9, 7, 1, 6}; // sample array
    k = (int)sizeof(A)/sizeof(int);            // get the length of the array
    SA = sorting(A, k);
    for (i = 0; i < k; i++)
        printf("%d, ", SA[i]);
}
```

Figure 2.22 illustrates the execution process and the changes of the array. In the part 1 of the recursive function (before the recursive call), the array size is reduced by one every time the recursive function is called, till n = 0. Since the array index starts from 0, the array has one element when n = 0, as shown on the left side of the figure. On the right hand side, corresponding to the part 2 (after the recursive call), the last element is inserted into the right position to form the size-n problem's solution at each level of recursion.

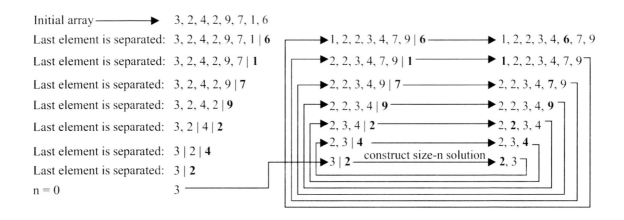

Initial array ⟶ 3, 2, 4, 2, 9, 7, 1, 6
Last element is separated: 3, 2, 4, 2, 9, 7, 1 | **6**   ⟶ 1, 2, 2, 3, 4, 7, 9 | **6** ⟶ 1, 2, 2, 3, 4, **6**, 7, 9
Last element is separated: 3, 2, 4, 2, 9, 7 | **1**   ⟶ 2, 2, 3, 4, 7, 9 | **1** ⟶ **1**, 2, 2, 3, 4, 7, 9
Last element is separated: 3, 2, 4, 2, 9 | **7**   ⟶ 2, 2, 3, 4, 9 | **7** ⟶ 2, 2, 3, 4, **7**, 9
Last element is separated: 3, 2, 4, 2 | **9**   ⟶ 2, 2, 3, 4 | **9** ⟶ 2, 2, 3, 4, **9**
Last element is separated: 3, 2 | 4 | **2**   ⟶ 2, 3, 4 | **2** ⟶ 2, **2**, 3, 4
Last element is separated: 3 | 2 | **4**   ⟶ 2, 3 | **4** ⟶ 2, 3, **4**
Last element is separated: 3 | **2**   ⟶ 3 | **2** — construct size-n solution ⟶ 2, 3
n = 0   3

Figure 2.22 Three different repetition structures

For some problems, it is possible to reduce the size by more than one, resulting in a more efficient solution. For example, in step 3 of the above sorting example, we could select $m = \lfloor n/2 \rfloor$ (floor of n/2). In other words, we divide the size-n problem into two proximately equal-sized problems by dividing the array **A** into two half-sized arrays **B1** and **B2**. Then we call

```
sorting(B1, ⌊n/2⌋); // floor of n/2
sorting(B2, ⌊n/2⌋); // ceiling of n/2
```

respectively and have both **B1** and **B2** sorted. Then we merge **B1** and **B2** into an array **B** by comparing the elements of the two sub arrays sequentially. This sorting algorithm is called **merge sort**, which is one of the most efficient sorting algorithms.

Figure 2.23 shows the sorting process through an example, illustrating how each sub array is split, sorted, and merged.

2.8 MODULAR DESIGN

Functions bring a level of abstraction into our programs. The abstraction makes our program easier to understand and to manage. However, the programming task can still become too large to understand. We need to introduce another level of abstraction, that is, modular design. Other advantages of modular design include

■ **Sharing**: We can group some frequently used functions and data into a module for being shared with other programmers, e.g., library functions.

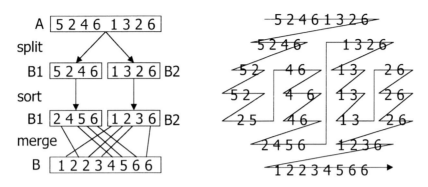

Figure 2.23 Merge sort and its sorting process

- **Separate compilation**: This is a maintenance issue. If we find a programming error or we need to make functional modification in a part of the program, we do not have to recompile the entire program.
- **Expandability**: We can easily add new modules into the system.

So far, we have been focusing on designing a program to solve relatively small problems. This is called programming-in-the-small. We need the skill of programming-in-the-small before we can do programming-in-the-large, which combines programming modules into a large program.

To design a module in a large system, we need to separate the specification from the implementation. The specification part tells what the module does and gives external view of the module, while the implementation part gives code that implements the specification. Variable and function names given in the specification part are available to users inside the module as well as outside the module.

All programming languages provide mechanisms to support modular design. In C, specifications of programs are stored in .h files, while implementations are stored in .c files. In order to use functions defined in another module named, say, **modulename.c**, we need to use

```
#include "modulename.h"   // user-defined header files are quoted by "..."
```

Let's consider the traffic light example in section 2.4. Since the **sleep** function may be used by other programs, we want to put this function and possibly other frequently used functions into a module, say, called **mylib.c**, which contains the following code:

```
// file name: mylib.c
#include<time.h>
const float pi = 3.14159265;
// Sleep for a specified number of seconds.
void sleep(int wait) {
    clock_t goal;                       // clock_t defined in <time.h>
    goal = wait * CLOCKS_PER_SEC + clock();
    while( goal > clock() )
        ;
}
// This function computes the volume of a cylinder:
```

```
double cylinder (int h, int r) {        //h: height, r: radius
    const double pi = 3.14159265;
    return pi*r*r*h;
}
```

Notice that a module does not need to have a **main()** function.

Then, we can put the headers of all functions, the type definitions, as well as the global variables to be shared among different modules, in the header file called **mylib.h**. In this example, we only have two functions and one type definition. Thus, the header file should look like:

```
typedef enum {red, amber, green} traffic_light;
void sleep(int wait);
double cylinder (int h, int r);
```

In the main program of the traffic light example, we do not need the function **sleep**, nor the type definition.

In .Net programming environment, all modules (.c files) should be placed in the folder "Source Files" and all the user-defined header files should be placed in the folder "Header Files", as shown in figure 2.24,

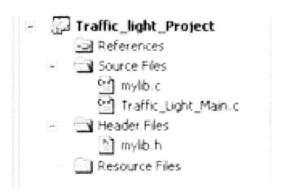

Figure 2.24 Organizing the modules and header files

2.9 SUMMARY

In this chapter, we started from very basic issues in writing imperative C/C++ programs and went through important and advanced topics in the languages. The major topics we discussed include

■ getting started with writing simple C/C++ programs;

■ control structures in C/C++ using syntax graphs;

■ relationship between memory locations, memory addresses, variable names, and variable addresses;

■ pointers and pointer variables, referencing, and dereferencing;

■ array-based and pointer-based strings;

- three different ways of introducing constants: macro, const, and enumeration type;
- structure types and compound data types;
- file type and file operations;
- two major parameter passing mechanisms: call-by-value and call-by-reference;
- recursive structures; and
- a brief introduction to the modular design.

2.10 Homework, Programming Exercises, and Projects

1.   Multiple Choice. Choose only one answer in each question. Choose the best answer if more than one answer is acceptable.

1.1   Forward declaration in modern programming practice
      ❏ provides a level of abstraction.   ❏ is never necessary.
      ❏ is not required if <iostream> is included.   ❏ is useless.

1.2   C language does not have a Boolean type because
      ❏ C is not designed to handle logic operations.
      ❏ C uses strong type checking.
      ❏ Boolean values can be represented as integers.
      ❏ C++ already defined a Boolean type.

1.3   Two functions are called mutually recursive functions if
      ❏ one function is defined within the other function.
      ❏ they call each other.
      ❏ each function calls itself.
      ❏ they are independent of each other.

1.4   Assume that a string is declared as char str[] = "alpha", what is the return value of sizeof (str)?
      ❏ 1   ❏ 5   ❏ 6   ❏ 7   ❏ 40

1.5   Assume that two pointers are declared as: char *str1 = "alpha", *str2;
      Which assignment statement below will lead to a runtime error?
      ❏ str2 = str1;   ❏ str2 = 0;
      ❏ str1 = str1+1;   ❏ *str2 = "world";

1.6   Which of the following declarations will cause a compilation error?
      ❏ char s[5];   ❏ char s[3] = "hello";
      ❏ char s[];   ❏ char s[] = {'s', 't', 'r'};

1.7   Given a declaration: int i = 25, *j = &i, **k = &j;
      which of the following operations will change the value of variable i?
      ❏ j++;   ❏ k++;   ❏ (*k)++;   ❏ (**k)++;

1.8   Given a declaration: int i = 25, *j = &i, **k = &j;
      Which of the following operations will cause a compilation error?
      ❏ i++;   ❏ (&i)++;   ❏ (*j)++;   ❏ (**k)++;

2.   What is a byte and what is a word in memory? What is the name of a variable? What is the address of a memory location? What is the content of a memory location?

3.   What is the difference between a memory location and a register? How do we access a memory location and a register?

4.   A variable has several aspects (name, address, value, location), and different aspects are used in different places.

4.1   If a variable is used on the left-hand side of an assignment statement, which aspect is actually used?

4.2   If a variable is used on the right-hand side of an assignment statement, which aspect is actually used?

4.3   If we apply the address-of operator "&" to the name, i.e., &name, which aspect is returned?

5.   Given a piece of C code

```
1       #include <stdio.h>
2       void main() {
3               char str[] = "hello", *p;
4               p = str;
5               while (*p != '\0')
6                       (*(p++))++;
7               printf("str = %s, p = %s\n", str, p);
8       }
```

5.1   What is the exact output of the printf statement?

5.2   At line 3, if we replace char str[] = "hello" by char *str = "hello", it will cause
      ❏ compilation error.   ❏ runtime error.   ❏ no error at all.   ❏ incorrect output.

5.3 At line 3, if we replace *p; by char *p = str; it will cause
   ❏ compilation error.   ❏ runtime error.   ❏ no error at all.   ❏ incorrect output.

5.4 In lines 5 and 6, the string is accessed using a pointer and pointer operations. Rewrite the program from line 3 to line 6, so that only array operations are used to access the string.

6. What are the three different methods of defining constants in C/C++? What are the differences of the constants defined in these methods?

6.1 Can a constant defined by const ever be modified? If yes, how and why? If no, why?

6.2 Can a constant defined by #define ever be modified? If yes, how and why? If no, why?

6.3 What are advantages of defining an enumeration type instead of using an integer type directly?

7. What is the difference between a structure type and a union type? In what circumstances union type is useful?

8. Parameter passing

8.1 What is a formal parameter and what is an actual parameter?

8.2 What is the difference between call-by-value and call-by-reference?

8.3   Where do you need to use call-by-value and where do you need to use call-by-reference?

8.4   How do you use call-by-value and call-by-reference?

9.   Structure type

9.1   How do you define a structure type? How do you declare a variable of a structure type? How do you declare a pointer to a structure type variable?

9.2   How do you obtain memory statically for a structure type variable? How do you create dynamic memory and link it to a pointer?

9.3   How do you use the name of a structure and a pointer to a structure to access the fields in the structure?

10.   Programming exercise. This question exercises declarations, forward declarations and scopes of functions and variables, and type checking in C and C++.
       Given the C program below, answer the following questions.

```
// This program shows function and variable declarations and their scopes.
#include <stdio.h>
int keven = 0, kodd = 0;
long evennumber(short);
long oddnumber(short);
int even(int);
int evennumber(int a) {          // genuine declaration
    if (a == 2) {
            printf("keven = %d, kodd = %d\n", keven, kodd);
            return keven;
    }
```

```c
    else {
            a = (int)a/2;
            if (even(a)) {     // Is a even?
                    keven++;
                    return evennumber(a);
            }
            else {
                    kodd++;
                    return oddnumber(a);
            }
    }
    // return a;
}
int oddnumber(int b) {         // genuine declaration
    if (b == 1) {
            printf("keven = %d, kodd = %d\n", keven, kodd);
            return kodd;
    }
    else {
            b = 3*b+1;
            if (!even(b)) {     // Is a odd?
                    kodd++;
                    return oddnumber(b);
            }
            else {
                    keven++;
                    return evennumber(b);
            }
    }
    // return b;
}
int even(int x) {       // % is modulo operator.
    return ( (x%2 == 0) ? 1 : 0);
}
void main() {
    register short r = 0;       // a register type variable is faster,
    int i = r;                  // it is often used for loop variable
    float f;
    for (r = 0; r < 3; r++) {
            printf("Please enter an integer number that is >= 2\n");
            scanf("%d", &i);
```

```
            if (even(i))
                    f = evennumber(i);
            else
                    f = oddnumber(i);
    }
}
```

10.1 Save the file as **declaration.c.** (consider the program as a C program). Choose the commands under the menu "**Build**":

Compile declaration.c

Build declaration.exe

Execute declaration.exe

What errors or warning messages are displayed?

10.2 Save the file as **declaration.cpp** Repeat question 1.

10.3 Analyze the type requirement of functions and variables in the given program. Make minimum changes to **declaration.cpp** to remove all compilation errors and warnings.

10.4 Explain global variables and local variables. List global variables and local variables in the program. The parameters of a function are local variables too.

10.5 Can we swap the order of the two variable declarations: "**register short r = 0;**" and "**int i = r;**"? Explain your answer according to C/C++'s scope rule.

10.6 Explain the forward declaration. If the forward declarations in the program are removed, what would happen?

10.7 Explain type casting and type coercion. List all type castings and type coercions used in the program.

10.8 According to the analysis above and the definition of strong type checking, are C and C++ strongly typed? Which language's typing system is stronger, C or C++?

10.9 Program correctness/reliability issue. A correct program must terminate for all valid inputs. The given program has been tested by many people. It has always terminated for the inputs used. However, nobody so far can prove that this program can terminate for any integer input. Thus, this program is often used as an example of improperly designed loop structure or recursive procedure. A good programming practice in writing loop or recursive procedure is to guarantee that the loop variable or the size-related-parameter (they control the number of iterations) is defined on an enumerable set (e.g., integer), has a lower bound (e.g., 0), and decrease strictly (e.g., 9, 6, 5, 3, 2, 1). Add a print-statement in functions **evennumber** and **oddnumber** to print the size-related parameter value and use input values i = 3, 4 and 7, respectively, to test the program. Give the three sequences of values printed by the added print-statements.

10.10 Compare questions 10 with homework question 17 in chapter one and explain why it is difficult to prove that the program can terminate for any integer input.

11. The following program will open and read an existing text file called **file1.txt**, add a number between 1 and 25 to each and every character, and then write the modified text into a new file called **file2.txt**. Read this program carefully and answer the questions following the program.

```
#include <stdio.h>
#include <string.h>

// Read all characters in the file and put them in a string str
void file_read(char *filename, char *str) {
    FILE *p;                // p is declared as a pointer to the FILE type.
    int index=0;
    p=fopen(filename, "r"); // Open the file for "read".
                            // Other options incl. "w" (write) and "a" (append)
    while(!feof(p))  // while not reaching the end-of-file character
        *(str+index++)=fgetc(p); //read a character from file and put it
```

```c
                                      // in str. Then p is increased automatically.
    str[index-1]='\0';                // add the string terminator
    puts(str);                        // print str. You can use printf too.
    fclose(p);                        // close the file
}
void encrypt(int offset, char *str) {
    int i,l;
    l=strlen(str);
    printf("unencrypted str = \n%s\n", str);
    for(i=0;i<l;i++)
            str[i] = str[i]+offset;
    printf("encrypted str = \n%s \nlength = %d\n", str, l);
}
void file_write(char *filename, char *str) {
    int i, l;
    FILE *p;
    p=fopen(filename, "w");           // open the file for "write".
    l = strlen(str);                  // string-length
    for(i=0;i<l;i++)
            fputc(*(str+i),p);        // write a character in the file pointed
                                      // by p. p is increased automatically
    fclose(p);                        // close the file
}
void main(void) {
    char filename[25];
    char string[1024];
    strcpy(filename, "file1.txt");
    file_read(filename, string);
    encrypt(7, string);
    strcpy(filename, "file2.txt");
    file_write(filename, string);
}
```

11.1   Enter the following text in a text file named file1.txt.

Politician A said "Politician B is a liar, because he promised in last year's election that he would give every homeless person a home".

Politician B said "Politician A is a liar, because he promised in last year's election that he would give every jobless person a job". Are these functions mutually recursive?

Enter the following text in a text file named **file4.txt**.

Politician B said "Politician A is a liar, because he promised in last year's election that he would give every homeless person a home".

Politician A said "Politician B is a liar, because he promised in last year's election that he would give every jobless person a job". These quotations are not mutually recursive.

Use **file1.txt** file and the **key** = 7 as the test case for the program **encrytion0.c**. Load the program into Visual Studio C++ and execute the program. The program should generate a file called **file2.txt**. Hint: **file1.txt** must be in the same directory as the program.

11.2 Rewrite the **void encrypt(int offset, char *str)** function in the given program using pointer operations to replace array operations, e.g., replace **str[i] by *(str+i)**. Replace the for-loop by a while-loop, where you must use a terminator to detect the end of the string. Comment the code where changes have been made.

11.3 Write a function called **int difference(char *filename1, char *filename2)** that compares two files. The file's names must be passed to the parameters **filename1** and **filename2**, respectively. The program should return the number of characters that are different (mismatches). For example, if the two files are exactly the same, the function returns 0. If the program detects 10 mismatches, it returns 10. If one file is longer than the other, the extra characters count as differences. This function must use string and pointer operations and compare each character one after another. You may not use the library function for string comparison. Write at least two lines of comment at the beginning of the function, describing what this function does and how it is implemented.

11.4 Write a function **void faultinjection(char *filename1, char *filename2, int n)** that injects n character faults into the file specified by the parameter **filename1**. Each character fault is a modification to a character by adding a random number between -10 and 10. The positions of the n faults are chosen randomly between the first character and the last character in the file. The modified file is stored in the file specified by the parameter **filename2**.
Note, to generate a random number, you can call library function, e.g., **rand()**. For a simple example, the following code prints 20 pseudo random numbers between 0 and 99.

```
#define size 100
#include <stdio.h>
#include <stdlib.h> // function rand() is defined in this library
main() {
    int i, rdm;
    for (i = 0; i<20; i++) {
        rdm = rand() % size;
        printf("random = %d\n", rdm);
    }
}
```

11.5   Rewrite the **main()** function to perform the following operations described in the pseudo code.

```
encrypt file1.txt into file2.txt
decrypt file2.txt into file3.txt        // use a negative key
Find the differences between file1.txt and file3.txt
Find the differences between file1.txt and file4.txt
Call faultinjection (file4.txt, file5.txt, n); // choose n = 5
Find the differences between file4.txt and file5.txt
```

12.   The following program generates maps representing mazes, where blank (space) characters represent open rooms through which a path may pass, while 'X' characters represent closed rooms that cannot be used on any path. The starting position is marked by a character 'S' and the goal position is marked by a character 'G'. For a given maze, one can write a program to check if there is path from 'S' to 'G', and print the paths if they exist. In this exercise, we only generate the mazes and do not attempt to write a program to find the paths.

```
// This program exercises the operations on multidimensional array and the
// the problem with using static memory for storing dynamic sets.
#define maxrow 100
#define maxcolumn 100
#include <stdio.h>
#include <stdlib.h>
//const int maxrow = 100, maxcolumn = 100;
char maze[maxrow][maxcolumn+1];
int lastrow = 0;

// Forward Declarations
int even(int);
void initialization(void);
void randommaze (void);
void printmaze(void);

int even(int x) {                    // % is modulo operator.
    return ( (x%2 == 0) ? 1 : 0);
}
void initialization(void) {
    int i, j;
    for (i=0; i<maxrow; i++)
            for (j = 0; j <= maxcolumn; j++)
                    maze[i][j] = ' ';
}
```

```c
void randommaze () {
    int i, j, i1, j1, d, row, column;
    printf("Please enter the size of the maze: two integers\n");
    scanf("%d\n%d", &row, &column);
    while ((row < 1) || (column < 1)) {
        printf("both integers must be greater than 0. Please reenter\n");
        scanf("%d\n%d", &row, &column);
    }
    for (i=lastrow; i < row+lastrow; i++) {
        for (j = 0; j < column; j++) {
            d = rand();
            if (even(d))
                maze[i][j] = ' ';
            else
                maze[i][j] = 'X';
        }
        maze[i][column] = '\0';          // add terminator
    }
    i = rand() % row;
    j = rand() % column;
    maze[i+lastrow][j] = 'S';            // define Starting point
    i1 = rand() % row;
    j1 = rand() % column;
    while ((i1 == i) && (j1 == j) && ((row > 1) || (column > 1))) {
        i1 = rand() % row;
        j1 = rand() % column;
    }
    maze[i1+lastrow][j1] = 'G';          // define Goal point
    lastrow = lastrow + row + 1;
    for (j = 0; j < column; j++)         // print separator
        maze[lastrow-1][j]='-';          // add separators
    maze[lastrow-1][column]='\0';  // add terminator
}
void printmaze() {
    int i;
    for (i=0; i < lastrow; i++) {
        printf("%s\n", maze[i]);         // A 2-dimensional array
    }                                    // is an array of array
}
void main() {
    initialization();
```

```
    // loadmaze();
    randommaze();
    randommaze();
    randommaze();
    printmaze();
    // savemaze();
}
```

12.1   Carefully go through the program and answer the following questions.

(1)   The multidimensional array **maze** is defined as a global variable. Can it be moved into the **main()** as a local variable in **main()**? What is the difference between a global variable and a local variable in the **main()** function?

(2)   The variable lastrow is defined as global variables. Can it be moved into the **main()** function? Explain your answer.

(3)   What are the purposes of using subroutines (procedures/functions) in writing large programs?

12.2   Rewrite the procedure **int even(int)** using macro definition.

12.3   Try to change the macro definitions **maxraw** and **maxcolumn** into constants defined using "**const**". Explain why macros work and constants defined using "**const**" do not.

12.4   Rewrite the function **randommaze** by substituting pointer operations for array operations.

12.5   Write a function called **loadmaze()**: If there exists a text file called **maze.txt**, use the text file to reinitialize the array **maze** and the global variable **lastrow**. The function must be called in the **main()** function after calling the function **initialization**.

12.6 Write a function called **savemaze()**: Save the mazes that you created through the function **randommaze** into a text file called **maze.txt**. The function **savemaze** must be called in **main()** function before exiting. You should only save the area that is printed in function **printmaze**.

12.7 Test the program using these three sets of inputs: (i, j) = (4, 3), (8, 4), (15, 4).

12.8 Write a function called **menu()**. The function prints the following options for the user to select:

i   insert a new maze into the maze array by calling randommaze();

d   delete a maze from the maze array by calling **deletemaze(i)**;

p   print all mazes in the array by calling **printmaze()**;

q   quit the program

The function then takes a character input and calls corresponding functions. If an invalid input is entered, the function must prompt user to re-enter a character. You could split this function into two or more functions. After the selected function is completed, it returns to the menu for taking another input.

12.9 Write the function **void deletemaze(int i)** that deletes the ith maze, where i ≥ 1, from the maze array. This function must call the following functions (you must write these functions):

(1)   **int startline(int i)**: Return the index of the first line of the ith maze;

(2)   **int endline(int i)**: Return the index of the last line of the ith maze;

(3)   **void shift (int s, int e)**: Shift the following mazes up, so that the maze to be deleted is overwritten.

12.10 Modify the randommaze() function: It returns -1 if the array maze does not have enough space to hold the maze to be inserted. Otherwise, it returns 0. Test the function by inserting two mazes (i, j) = (14, 8), (87, 12). It should return -1.

12.11 Test the program by inserting four mazes (i, j) = (4, 3), (15, 4), (18, 14), (12, 6), deleting maze 3, and then printing the mazes. Submit the mazes saved in maze.txt.

13.   You are given a program below. Save the given program under the name contactbook.c. The program takes a command line parameter: the database's name in which contact records are to be saved, assuming the database name is person.dbms.

To run a program with command line parameters under Visual Studio, you can use one of these two methods:

I.   You can pass command line parameters within Visual Studio .Net environment as follows:

1.   Use Visual Studio .Net to compile and to build the program contactbook.c.

2.   Choose menu "Project" and "properties...".

3.   Under the item "configuration Properties" click on "Debugging", and enter the file name person.dbms right to the field "Command Arguments".

4.   Click OK to return.

5.   Now you can execute the program.

II.   You can also pass command line parameters using following method for both Visual Studio C++ and Visual Studio .Net programming environments:

1.   Compile and build the program.

2.   Choose MS Windows "Start" Menu.

3.   Choose "Run ...".

4.   Click on "Browse ...".

5.   Browse to the folder where your contactbook.c is stored.

6.   Go into the folder "Debug". This folder should have been created by the compile and build commands in step 1).

7.   Choose the executable program called contactbook and then click "open".

8.   You should see the path "...\Debug\contactbook.exe".

9.   Append the file name **person.dbms** to the end of the path, with a space in between. The entire command sequence should looks like: "...\Debug\ contactbook.exe" person.dbms.

10. Click "OK". The program should start to run.

The tasks of this assignment are as follows.

13.1 Read the program carefully and make sure you understand the program and each function in the program. Then add at least two lines of comments below each function's forward declaration to explain what the function does.

13.2 Write a function called **sort()**. The function should sort the existing linked list by the name field in dictionary order. Use the simplest sorting algorithm. For example, the selection sort: find the name with smallest dictionary value and place it in the first place in the linked list, and then find the name with the next smallest dictionary value and put it in the second place, and so on.

13.3 Add your **sort()** function into the program and modify the program to offer users an extra option "sort" in the menu.

13.4 Test each function of the program: insert, delete, search, and sort. You can quit the program and restart the program. The records stored in the linked list should be saved and reloaded into the list. To copy the output in Visual Studio: Highlight the text you want to copy, click on the small icon "c:\" at the top-left corner of the output window. Choose Edit-Copy. And then you can paste the output into a text file.

```
// Manipulation of files and singly linked list
// Command line parameter inputs

#include <stdio.h>
#include <stdlib.h> // malloc is defined in this library
#include <string.h>// string operations are defined in this library

struct contact {
  char name[30];
  char phone[20];
  char email[30];
  struct contact *next;
}*head = NULL;

char *file_name;

// forward declaration
void menu();
void branchinq(char c);
```

```c
struct contact* find_node(char *str, int *position);
void display_node(struct contact *node, int index);
int insert();
int deletion();
int modify();
int search();
void display_all();
void load_file();
void save_file();

int main(int argc, char *argv[]) {
    char ch;
    if(argc != 2)    {       // Two command line parameters required
            printf("Command Line Parameters Required !\n");
            printf("Try again......\n");
            getchar();       // enter any character to return
            return -1;
    }

    printf("SINGLY LINKED LIST\n");
    printf("*******************");
    file_name = argv[1];
    load_file();

    do {
            menu();
            fflush(stdin);                     // Flush the standard input buffer
            ch = tolower(getchar()); // read a char, convert to lower case
            branching(ch);
    } while (ch != 'q');
    return 0;
}

void menu() {
    printf("\n\nMENU\n");
    printf("——\n");
    printf("i: Insert a new entry.\n");
    printf("d: Delete an entry.\n");
    printf("m: Modify an entry.\n");
    printf("s: Search for an entry.\n");
    printf("p: Print all entries.\n");
```

```c
        printf("q: Quit the program.\n");
        printf("Please enter your choice (i, d, m, s, p, or q) —> ");
}


void branching(char c) {
    switch(c) {
            case 'i':if(insert() != 0)
                                printf("INSERTION OPERATION FAILED.\n");
                        else
                                printf("INSERTED NODE IN THE LIST SUCCESSFULLY.\n");
                        break;
            case 'd':   if(deletion() != 0)
                                printf("DELETION OPERATION FAILED.\n");
                        else
                                printf("DELETED THE ABOVE NODE SUCCESSFULLY.\n");
                        break;
            case 'm':   if(modify() != 0)
                                printf("MODIFY OPERATION FAILED.\n");
                        else
                                printf("MODIFIED THE ABOVE NODE SUCCESSFULLY.\n");
                        break;
            case 's':   if(search() != 0)
                                printf("SEARCH FAILED.\n");
                        else
                                printf("SEARCH FOR THE NODE SUCCESSFUL.\n");
                        break;
            case 'p':   display_all();
                        break;
            case 'q':   save_file();
                        break;
            default:printf("ERROR - Invalid input.\n");
                        printf("Try again.....\n");
                        break;
    }
    return;
}

int insert() {
    struct contact *node;
    char sname[30];
    int index = 1;
```

```c
        printf("\nInsertion module...............\n");
        printf("Enter the name of the person to be inserted: ");
        scanf("%s", sname);
        node = find_node(sname, &index);     // find duplicates
        if(node != NULL) {
                printf("ERROR - Duplicate entry not allowed.\n");
                printf("A entry is found in the list at index %d.\n", index);
                display_node(node, index);
                return -1;
        }
        else {
                node = (struct contact*) malloc(sizeof(struct contact));
                if (node == NULL) {
                        printf("ERROR - Could not allocate memory !\n");
                        return -1;
                }
                strcpy(node->name, sname);
                printf("Enter his telephone number: ");
                scanf("%s", node->phone);
                printf("Enter his email address: ");
                scanf("%s", node->email);
                node->next = head;
                head = node;
                return 0;
        }
}

int deletion() {
    char sname[30];
    struct contact *temp, *prev;
    int index = 1;
    printf("\nDeletion module...............\n");
    printf("Please enter the name of the person to be deleted: ");
    scanf("%s", sname);
    temp = head;
    while (temp != NULL)
            if (stricmp(sname, temp->name) != 0) {          //case insensitive comparation
                    prev = temp;
                    temp = temp->next;
                    index++;
            }
```

```
        else {
                printf("Person to be deleted is found at index %d.", index);
                display_node(temp, index);
                if(temp != head)
                        prev->next = temp->next;
                else
                        head = head->next;
                free(temp);
                return 0;
        }

    printf("The person with name '%s' does not exist.\n", sname);
    return -1;
}


int modify() {
    struct contact *node;
    char sname[30];
    int index = 1;

    printf("\nModification module...............\n");
    printf("Enter the name whose record is to be modified in the\n");
    printf("database: ");
    scanf("%s", sname);
    node = find_node(sname, &index);
    if(node != NULL) {
            printf("Person to be modified is found at index %d.", index);
            display_node(node, index);
            printf("\nEnter the new telephone number of this person: ");
            scanf("%s", node->phone);
            printf("Enter the new email address of this person: ");
            scanf("%s", node->email);
            return 0;
    }
    else {
            printf("The person with name '%s' does not exist \n", sname);
            printf("database.\n");
            return -1;
    }
}
```

```c
int search() {
    struct contact *node;
    char sname[30];
    int index = 1;
    printf("\nSearch module...............\n");
    printf("Please enter the name to be searched in the database: ");
    scanf("%s", sname);
    node = find_node(sname, &index);
    if(node != NULL) {
        printf("Person searched is found at index %d.", index);
        display_node(node, index);
        return 0;
    }
    else {
        printf("The person '%s' does not exist.\n", sname);
        return -1;
    }
}
void display_all() {
    struct contact *node;
    int counter = 0;

    printf("\nDisplay module...............");
    node = head;
    while(node != NULL) {
        display_node(node, ++counter);
        node = node->next;
    }
    printf("\nNo more records.\n");
}

void load_file() {
    FILE *file_descriptor;
    struct contact *node, *temp;
    char str[30];

    file_descriptor = fopen(file_name, "rb");
    if(file_descriptor != NULL) {
        while(fread(str, 30, 1, file_descriptor) == 1) {
            node = (struct contact*) malloc(sizeof(struct contact));
            strcpy(node->name, str);
```

```
                    fread(node->phone, 20, 1, file_descriptor);
                    fread(node->email, 30, 1, file_descriptor);
                    if(head != NULL)
                            temp->next = node;
                    else
                            head = node;
                    node->next = NULL;
                    temp = node;
            }
            fclose(file_descriptor);
    }
}

void save_file() {
    FILE *file_descriptor;
    struct contact *node;

    file_descriptor = fopen(file_name, "w");
    if(file_descriptor != NULL) {
            node = head;
            while(node != NULL) {
                    fwrite(node->name, 30, 1, file_descriptor);
                    fwrite(node->phone, 20, 1, file_descriptor);
                    fwrite(node->email, 30, 1, file_descriptor);
                    node = node->next;
            }
    }
    else {
            printf("\nERROR - Could not open file for saving data !\n");
            getchar();
            exit(-1);
    }
}

struct contact* find_node(char *str, int *position) {
    struct contact *temp = head;

    while (temp != NULL) {
            if (stricmp(str, temp->name) != 0) {
                    temp = temp->next;
                    (*position)++;
```

```
                }
            else
                    return temp;
        }
        return NULL;
    }


    void display_node(struct contact *node, int index) {
        printf("\nRECORD %d:\n", index);
        printf("\t\tName:\t\t%s\n", node->name);
        printf("\t\tTelephone:\t%s\n", node->phone);
        printf("\t\tEmail Address:\t%s\n", node->email);
```

14.   Follow the fantastic four abstract approach to write a recursive function to find the largest number in a given array of integers.

15.   In section 2.7, an array is sorted by a simple recursive function. In step 3 of the fantastic four abstract approach, the **m** is selected to be n-1. Rewrite the sorting program, but select m to be **n/2** (merge sort). You can assume that the initial size **n** is a power of 2 to simplify the problem.

16.   Fibonacci numbers are defined by

$$fib(n) = \begin{cases} 0 & n = 0 \\ 1 & n = 1 \\ fib(n-1) + fib(n-2) & n \geq 2 \end{cases}$$

   Follow the fantastic four abstract approach to implement the function in C.

16.1   Define the size-n problem.

16.2   Define the stopping conditions and the return values.

16.3   Define the size-m problems.

16.4   Construct the size-n solution from the size-m solutions.

16.5   Give the program that can be used to compute Fibonacci numbers for any given integer $n \geq 0$.

The Object-Oriented Programming Language, C++

3

We discussed C/C++ as an imperative programming language in chapter two. Although we mainly discussed C, we used the notion C/C++. The reason is that C is part of C++, or C is the imperative part of C++. In this chapter, we study C++ as an object-oriented programming language, or we will focus on the object-oriented features of the language.

The main idea of object-oriented programming is to use abstract and extendable data types as the building blocks of programs. The principle of object-oriented paradigm consists of a number of programming concepts including the following:

■ Abstract data type (class): Encapsulate related information in a class. A class (type) is used to declare objects (variables) that consist of data and operations (functions). Access to data members can be accurately controlled through operations defined on the data.

■ Inheritance: Derive a new class (derived class) based on an existing class (base class). Inheritance allows us to reuse and extend the data structures and functions that we or others have defined.

■ Class hierarchy: Link all related classes together using inheritance.

■ Late binding and polymorphism: Support virtual functions that use late binding. Allow pointers to objects in the class hierarchy to move downwards, and allow the same function call to bind to different implementations of the function.

In this chapter we will describe all these object-oriented features of C++. By the end of the chapter, you should

■ have a good understanding of object-oriented programming paradigm;

■ be able to define classes with data members (also called member variables) and member functions (also called methods) in C++;

■ understand the differences and similarities between data types and classes;

■ understand memory allocation mechanism in programming languages and the three memory allocation mechanisms: static, stack, and dynamic memory;

■ be able to apply major object-oriented features in program design, including inheritance, class hierarchy, polymorphism, dynamic memory allocation, and late binding.

The chapter is organized as follows. In section 3.1, a complete example of a C++ program is presented. The program will be used and explained in the following sections. In section 3.2, the composition and definition of classes are discussed. The static and dynamic memory allocation and de-allocation are studied in section 3.3. Section 3.4 discusses the main features of object-oriented programming paradigm, including class inheritance, inheritance-based class hierarchy, polymorphic pointer, virtual functions, and late binding. In section 3.5, C++ exceptions and exception handling are discussed.

3.1 A Long Program Example: A Queue and A Priority Queue

In this section, I present a complete C++ program that illustrates various features we will discuss in the next two sections:

- class definition;
- the in-class implementation of member functions and the out-class implementation of member functions using scope resolution operator;
- constructor and destructor;
- overloading of member functions;
- creation of stack and heap objects;
- access of class members using dot-operator and pointer-to-member operators.

The program is only explained through comments embedded in the program in this section. Different parts of the program will be further explained and studied in the following sections.

```
#include <iostream.h>
class Queue {                    // Class definition
private:                         // private members can only be accessed in the class
    int queue_size;
protected:        // protected members can also be accessed in derived classes
    int *buffer;                 // pointer to first element of array
    int front;                   // used for removing an element from the queue
    int rear;                    // used for adding an element into the queue
public:     // public members can be accessed by all functions in the program
    Queue(void) {                // constructor with no parameters
        front = 0;
        rear = 0;
        queue_size = 10;
        buffer = new int[queue_size]; // create a heap object of integer array
    }
    Queue(int n) {               // overloaded constructor with one parameter
        front = 0;
        rear = 0;
        queue_size = n;
        buffer = new int[queue_size]; // create a heap object of array
    }
```

```
        ~Queue(void) {                      // destructor
                delete buffer;
                buffer = NULL;
        }
        void enqueue(int v) {     // add an element at the end of the queue
                if (rear < queue_size)
                        buffer[rear++] = v;
                else
                        if (compact())
                                buffer[rear++] = v;
        }
        int dequeue(void){        // return and remove the 1st element from the queue
                if (front < rear)
                        return buffer[front++];
                else {
                        cout<< "Error: Queue empty"<<endl;
                        return -1;
                }
        }
private:
        bool compact(void);                   // implementation outside class
};                                            // End of the class definition
class PriQueue : public Queue {               //PriQueue is derived from Queue
public:
        int getMax(void); // return and remove the max value from priority queue
        PriQueue(int n) : Queue(n) { };
        // base class constructor may not be inherited. It has to be explicitly
        // called. PriQueue's constructor simply calls Queue's constructor;
        ~PriQueue() {                         // base class destructor may not be called here or
                delete buffer;                // inherited. We must explicitly use delete.
                buffer = NULL;
        }
};
bool Queue::compact(void){                    // out-class using scope resolution operator
        if (front == 0) {
                cout<<"Error: Queue overflow"<<endl;
                return false;
        }
        else {
                for (int i=0;i<rear-front;i++)
                        buffer[i]=buffer[i+front];
```

```
                    rear = rear - front;
                    front = 0;
                    return true;
            }
    }
int PriQueue::getMax(void) { // get and remove max value from priority queue
        int i, max, imax;
        if (front < rear) {
                    max = buffer[front];
                    imax = front;      // imax holds the index of current max value
                    for (i=front;i<rear;i++){
                            if (max < buffer[i]) {
                                        max = buffer[i];
                                        imax = i;
                            }
                    }
                    for (i=imax;i<rear-1;i++)
                            buffer[i]=buffer[i+1];      // remove the max value
                    rear = rear - 1;
                    return max;
            }
        else {
                    cout<< "Error: Queue empty"<<endl;
                    return -1;
            }
    }
void main() {                               // main function must be outside any class
        Queue Q1(5);                        // will call constructor Queue(int)
        Q1.enqueue(2);                      // insert 2 into Q1
        Q1.enqueue(8);                      // insert 8 into Q1
        int x = Q1.dequeue();
        int y = Q1.dequeue();
        cout << "x = " << x << endl << "y = " << y << endl;

        Queue *Q2 = new Queue(4);           // will call constructor Queue(int)
        Q2->enqueue(12);                    // insert 12 into Q2
        Q2->enqueue(18);                    // insert 18 into Q2
        x = Q2->dequeue();
        y = Q2->dequeue();
        cout << "x = " << x << endl << "y = " << y << endl;
        PriQueue *Q3 = new PriQueue(4);     // will call constructor Queue(int)
```

```
        Q3->enqueue(12);              // insert 12 into Q3
        Q3->enqueue(18);              // insert 18 into Q3
        Q3->enqueue(14);              // insert 14 into Q3
        x = Q3->getMax();
        y = Q3->getMax();
        cout << "x = " << x << endl << "y = " << y << endl;

        delete Q2; Q2 = NULL;
        delete Q3; Q3 = NULL;
}
```

3.2 CLASS DEFINITION AND COMPOSITION

The class is the fundamental building block of C++ programs. A **class** consists of a number of **class members**. A member can be a data member or a function member (also called member function or method).

3.2.1 CLASS DEFINITION

The syntax of the class definition is given in figure 3.1. The access privilege of a member has three levels. If a member is prefixed with the **public** access privilege, the member can be accessed by any functions inside or outside the class. If a member is prefixed with no access privilege (default access privilege) or the **private** access privilege, the member can only be accessed by member functions within the same class. If a member is prefixed with the **protected** access privilege, the member can only be accessed by member functions within the same class and the inherited classes (derived classes).

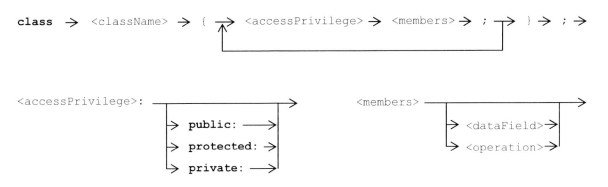

Figure 3.1 Syntax graphs of class definition

Now let's examine the class definition in the **Queue** example given in section 3.1. In this example, we define a **Queue** class that has several data and function members. There is one data member that is private. There are three data members that are protected. All function members are declared as public so that they can be accessed by all functions in the program.

In the previous chapter, we discussed that a C structure consists of a number of data members. As you can see in the definition of a C++ class, the C structure is a special case of a class when

■ there are only data members and no member functions;

■ all members are public members.

If you are familiar with Java, you can see that the class definitions in the two languages are similar. However, C++ allows you to put the implementation part of a member function outside the class to separate the specification (function declaration) from the implementation (the body of the function) by using a scope resolution operator.

3.2.2 SCOPE RESOLUTION OPERATOR

In Java, implementations of member functions (methods) are always within the class definition. In C++, they can be inside the class definition (for short functions) or outside the class definition (for longer functions). It is more efficient to have function implementations in the class because we save the time needed to jump to another memory area to access the implementations. However, it is structurally clearer to separate the implementation from the specification.

If the implementation of a function is outside the class, we must specify which class the implementation belongs to. The **scope resolution operator** in C++ serves this purpose. It consists of the class name and two consecutive colons. Generally, the format is

```
return_type class_name::function_name(parameters){implementation};
```

For the Queue example we discussed above, we put the shorter functions enqueue and dequeue in the class, while putting the longer function's implementation outside the class using the scope resolution operator, that is "Queue::", as shown in the code below.

```
bool Queue::compact(void){        // Queue:: is the scope resolution operator
    if (front == 0) {
            cout<<"Error: Queue overflow"<<endl;
            return false;
    }
    else {
            for (int i=0;i<rear-front;i++)
                    buffer[i]=buffer[i+front];
            rear = rear - front;
            front = 0;
            return true;
    }
}
```

For much longer implementation, it makes the structure better to put the body of a member function outside the class definition, if the implementation is very long, e.g., over a hundred lines.

3.2.3 OBJECTS FROM A CLASS

Like a structure in C, a class in C++ can be used to declare variables. The variable declared by a class is called an **object** of the class. For example:

```
Queue r;                    // r is a variable (object) of Queue class.
Queue *s;                   // s is a pointer to a Queue variable.
r.enqueue(25);              // push/add a number into the Queue variable
```

```
x = r.dequeue();              // pop/remove the front element from the Queue
s = new Queue;                // create a heap object of Queue and link it to s
s->enqueue(25);               // push a number into the object pointed to by s
y = s->dequeue();             // pop the front element from the Queue object.
```

As can be seen in this example, we can allocate memory for a variable (object) from the stack or from the heap. In this example, we declare r as a variable of Queue class. The variable obtains memory (or the object is created) from the stack during the compilation. We can immediately push an integer into the r object by r.enqueue(int) operation.

On the other hand, variable s is not an object of the Queue class. It is a pointer to a Queue object from the heap. The object is dynamically created by a **new** operation:

```
s = new Queue();
```

Having created the object, we push an integer into the object linked to s by a s->enqueue(int) operation.

3.2.4 DEFINITION OF CONSTRUCTOR AND DESTRUCTOR

A **constructor** in a class is a special member function whose name is same as the class name. A constructor is used to automatically initialize objects when an object is created. We can also define multiple constructors with different number of parameters or different types of parameters. Defining two or more functions with the same name is called **overloading**. As long as these functions have different parameter lists or different return types, they are considered to be different functions.

A **destructor** is a special member function whose name is same as the class name but prefixed by the tilde character "~". The tilde character is often used for complement operation, suggesting that the destructor is the complement operation of the constructor. A destructor is used to delete objects (collect garbage) created within the class, normally within the constructors. A destructor cannot have any parameters or a return value, and thus it cannot be overloaded. The definition and the use of constructors are basically same as that in Java. However, there are no destructors in Java. Instead, Java uses a built-in garbage collector to automatically collect all objects that have no references.

There are two constructors and a destructor defined in the Queue class in the example program. The first constructor has no parameters and it creates an object of array with 10 elements. The second constructor takes a parameter and creates an object of array with the given number of elements. Both constructors initialize the front and rear pointer to zeros, indicating an empty queue.

```
Queue(void) {                 // constructor with no parameters
        front = 0;
        rear = 0;
        queue_size = 10;
        buffer = new int[queue_size]; // create a heap object of array
}
Queue(int n) {                // overloaded constructor with one parameter
        front = 0;
        rear = 0;
        queue_size = n;
        buffer = new int[queue_size]; // create a heap object of array
}
```

```
~Queue(void) {                    // destructor
        delete buffer;
        buffer = NULL;
}
```

The definitions of constructors and the destructor are relatively simple. However, understanding how memory is allocated by the constructor and de-allocated by the destructor is not trivial. We will devote the entire next section to discuss the general memory management in imperative and object-oriented programming languages like C, C++, and Java.

3.3 MEMORY MANAGEMENT AND GARBAGE COLLECTION

When a program is started, the operating system will allocate a segment of memory to the program. The segment of memory is divided into two sections: the code section used to store instructions (program) and the data section used to store data that are being processed by the program, as shown in figure 3.2. In this section, we will only discuss the data section allocated to a program.

The memory (data section) allocated to a program is managed by the programming language environment (runtime system) and it is divided into three areas: **static**, **stack**, and **heap** areas.

The programmers can choose from which area to obtain memory by declaring their variables in different ways. In C/C++:

■ All **static** local variables in functions obtain memory from static memory. In other words, if we want to have memory from the static area for any variable, we can add the qualifier static before the variable declaration, for example, "static int s;" will declare a static integer variable. All global variables (variables declared outside any functions) obtain memory from static memory, whether the qualifier static is used or not.

■ All non static local variables obtain memory from the stack. This stack is also called **program runtime stack** to differentiate from other possible stacks used in the computer system.

■ All dynamically allocated variables obtain memory from the heap. In C, the memory allocated by the function **malloc**, and in C++, the memory allocated by using **new**, are from the heap area.

Now the question is, what difference will it make to a programmer by using these different memory areas? This question will be answered in the following subsections.

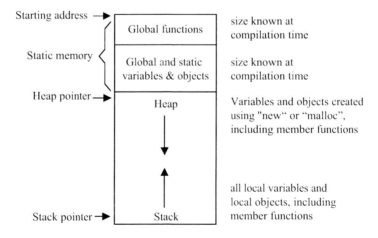

Figure 3.2 Partition of the memory allocated to a program

3.3.1 Static: Global Variables and Static Local Variables

Static memory is allocated statically, i.e., during the compilation stage (before the program is executed). There is only one copy of the static memory. Changes made to a static variable will have an impact on all other functions that use the variable. A static variable will go out of scope only if the program gets terminated. Why do we need a static local variable? The following function shows a situation where using a static local variable is better than using a global variable.

```
void login() {
    static int counter = 0;        // will be initialized only once
    readId_pwd( );
    if (verified( ))
            counter++;             // count the # of users logged in
}
```

The function allows users (callers) to login to a secure resource and keeps track of the number of users who entered the resource. If the **counter** variable is not declared as static, the variable will be reallocated and initialized every time the function is called. As a static variable, **counter** will be allocated and initialized only once. Thus, the variable can keep the history of the logins.

If a static local variable is declared as a class member, it may not be initialized when it is declared. It must be initialized outside the class using scope resolution operator. In the **Queue** class example, a static local variable **counter** is declared in the class. It has to be initialized outside the class using the scope resolution operator:

```
class Queue {

    ...

    static int counter;     // declaration is inside the class

    ...

}
int Queue::counter = 0;     // initialization is outside the class
```

The variable **counter** is incremented in the constructors and decremented in the destructor. The variable can keep track of how many objects of the **Queue** class exist.

Generally, a static local variable could be declared as a global variable. The advantages, however, of using a static local variable are twofold:

- It puts the variable declaration in the same place where the variable is actually used. It makes the program easier to read and to understand.
- It prevents other functions from accessing the variable. As a global variable, all other functions can read and modify it.

Although a static local variable exists all the time, it is invisible outside the function. In the following program example, we define a static local variable **counter** in the **login()** function and a global variable also called **counter**. Although both variables obtain their memory from static area, there is no name conflict. There are two independent variables.

```
#include <stdio.h>
int counter = 0;
void login() {
    static int counter = 0;
            counter++;
            printf("login counter = %d\n", counter);
}
void main() {
            int i;
            for (i=0;i<5;i++) {
                    counter = counter + 2;
                    login();
            }
    printf("main counter = %d\n", counter);
}
```

The output of the program is as follows. It can be seen that, within the function login(), only the static local variable counter is visible. Outside the function, only the global variable is visible.

```
login counter = 1
login counter = 2
login counter = 3
login counter = 4
login counter = 5
main counter = 10
```

3.3.2 RUNTIME STACK FOR LOCAL VARIABLES

Local variables are variables declared within a function. When the control enters a function, a block of memory (called a **stack frame**) is created on the stack. All non-static local variables obtain memory from the stack frame. When the control leaves the function, all these local variables are freed and the contents of these variables are no longer valid (no longer accessible). More detail on stack frames used to accommodate local variables and to support re-entrant and recursive function calls are discussed in Appendix A.

The stack memory allocation is illustrated in the example in figure 3.3. As shown in the left part of figure 3.3, the program consists of two functions. The main function has one local variable i. The function bar has two local variables j and k. Please note that the formal parameter of a function is a local variable to the function.

The state (0) shows the initial state of the stack before the main function is executed. When the control enters the main function, the local variable i obtains the memory on the top of the stack, as shown in stack state (1). The value of i is initialized to 0 and then incremented to 1. Then i is passed as the actual parameter to function bar. When the control enters the function bar, the two local variables j and k obtain memory on the top of the stack, as shown in state (2). The value of i is passed to the formal parameter j. Please note that j and i have different memory locations. j has a copy of i's value. When j is modified in the function bar, the modification has no impact on variable i.

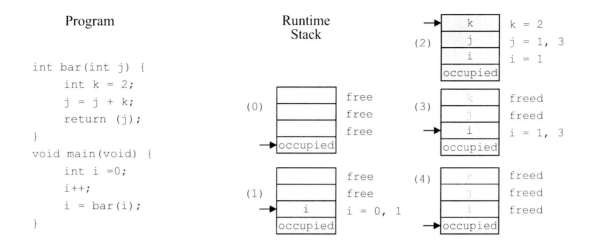

Program   Runtime Stack

```
int bar(int j) {
    int k = 2;
    j = j + k;
    return (j);
}
void main(void) {
    int i =0;
    i++;
    i = bar(i);
}
```

Figure 3.3 A simple program and its runtime stack

When the control exits function **bar**, variables **j** and **k** go out of scope. The stack pointer returns to its original position before it entered the function. The memory used for variables **j** and **k** is thus freed, as shown in stack state (3). Therefore, we cannot access **j** and **k** outside the function. Finally, when the control exits the **main** function, variable **i** is also freed and stack pointer returns to its position before it entered the main function, as shown in state (4) in figure 3.3.

Since local variables are automatically garbage-collected by the runtime stack when they go out of scope, there is no need for programmers to explicitly return the memory to the system.

Having understood the stack used to allocate memory for local variables, we can easily understand how recursive functions are implemented. In fact, no special mechanism is needed. The stack that handles all local variables handles the variables in recursive functions, too.

Let's examine the following recursive function. There are two local variables in the function: the formal parameter **n** and a temporary variable **fac** that holds the return value from $(n-1)^{th}$ iteration. Figure 3.4 shows the runtime stack before and during the execution of the recursive function **fac(3)**.

```
int fac(int n) {
    if (n <= 1)
            return 1;
    else
            return n* fac(n - 1);
}
```

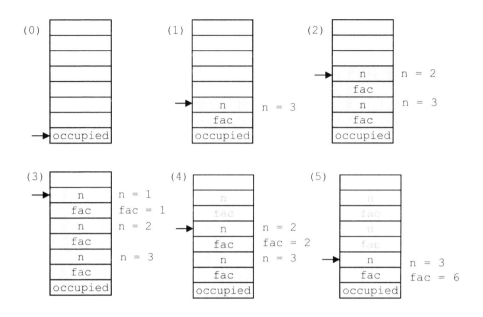

Figure 3.4 The runtime stack of a recursive program

State (0) is the state before the function fac(3) is called. When the control enters the function fac(n) for the first time, the two local variables n and fac obtained memory on the stack, as shown in state (1). Formal parameter n is initialized to the actual parameter 3, but variable fac is not given a value yet. Within the first iteration, fac(n-1) is called and the function is re-entered. Again the two local variables obtain memory from the stack. Now, n is initialized to the actual parameter value 2 and fac is not given a value, as shown in state (2) in figure 3.4. The variables n and fac in the second iteration are different from n and fac in the first iteration, although they happen to have the same names. Since they have different scopes, they are considered to be different variables.

Within the second iteration, fac(n-1) is called again. In this iteration, n is initialized to 1 and the condition (n <= 1) is true. Now the function fac(n-1) is actually completed. It did not complete before. Now a value is then returned to fac in this iteration, as shown in state (3). The return of iteration 3 completed the function call fac(n-1) in iteration 2 and the return value fac = 1 is passed into iteration 2. The operation n*fac(1) then will produce a value 2, as shown in state (4). The return value 2 will, in turn, be passed to iteration 1 and produces a value 6, as shown in state (5) in figure 3.4. When the final iteration is completed, the fac(n) function exits and the stack pointer will return to its original state (0).

If you compare the recursive function call here and the ordinary function call in the previous example, you can see that the processes of variable allocation on the stack are handled exactly in the same way. In fact, the temporary variable fac may not be stored on the stack. It can be stored in a register. I put variable fac on the stack here to make the value passing visible on the stack

In fact, at the assembly language (or machine code) level, the variable fac used to hold the return value is not on the stack. Instead, a register is used. A register can be considered a global variable used by the compiler, which is invisible to the high-level language programmers. Since the concept of register is not a part of high-level language programming, we use a stack variable fac here to make the value passing visible on the stack.

3.3.3 HEAP: DYNAMIC MEMORY ALLOCATION

The third area in the data section is the heap. Heap is used for dynamic memory allocation requested by operations like **malloc(size)** in C and **new class_name** in C++. For example, in C,

```
struct Contact { // define a structure
    char name[30];
    int phone;
} *p;
p = (struct Contact *) malloc(sizeof(struct Contact));
```

The function **malloc** will acquire a memory block from the heap. The size of the memory block should be the size of the **Contact** type variable, and we cast the address of the piece of memory to the **Contact** pointer type. In C++, we use the **new** operator to acquire the memory for an object of **Contact** class, as shown in the code below.

```
class Contact { // define a class
    char name[30];
    int phone;
};
Contact *p = new Contact();
```

The data types that acquire memory from heap are called **reference types** because their variables take memory addresses (references) as their values.

3.3.4 SCOPE AND GARBAGE COLLECTION

So far we explained when we should use static, stack, and heap memory. We also explained how we acquire memory from static, stack, and heap areas. The last question we need to answer is, do we need to worry about garbage collection? In other words, do we need to de-allocate memory that we allocated? The answer to the question depends on where we acquire the memory.

According to the definitions, global and static variables should exist in the entire lifetime of the program (even when they are invisible), and thus they should never be garbage-collected by the programmer or by the runtime system. When the **main** function exits, the operating system that starts the program will reclaim the entire memory segment allocated to the program. Thus, if a variable or an object is static or global, we do not need to worry about collecting its memory.

If a variable or an object obtains its memory from the stack, the memory will be de-allocated automatically by the system. As we explained in section 3.3.2, when the control enters a function, local variables or objects obtain memory from the stack. When the control exits the function, the stack pointer moves back to the original position when it entered the function; that is, the memory allocated to the local variables is returned back to the stack. This memory de-allocation is basically managed by the scope rule of the language: the scope of a variable starts from the declaration and ends at the end of the block. When a variable goes out of scope, the memory allocated to the variable returns to the system.

However, if variables or objects acquire their memory from the heap, it will **not** be automatically de-allocated or freed. We will have to explicitly use **free** and **delete** operations to return the memory allocated by **malloc** in C and by **new** in C++, respectively.

Now let's go back to the **Queue** example we discussed earlier in this chapter. We now focus on the constructor and the instantiation of objects in another function, as shown in the following segment of code.

```
Queue(int n) {                          // overloaded constructor with one parameter
    front = 0;
    rear = 0;
    queue_size = n;
    buffer = new int[queue_size]; // create a heap object of array
}
void foo() {
    Queue Q1(5);                        // will call constructor Queue(int)
    Q1.enqueue(2);                      // insert 2 into Q1
    Q1.enqueue(8);                      // insert 8 into Q1
    int x = Q1.dequeue();
    int y = Q1.dequeue();
    cout << "x = " << x << endl << "y = " << y << endl;

    Queue *Q2 = new Queue(4);    // will call constructor Queue(int)
    Q2->enqueue(12);                    // insert 12 into Q2
    Q2->enqueue(18);                    // insert 18 into Q2
    x = Q2->dequeue();
    y = Q2->dequeue();
    cout << "x = " << x << endl << "y = " << y << endl;

    delete Q2; Q2 = NULL;
    delete Q3; Q3 = NULL;
}
```

The declaration "**Queue Q1(5);**" will create a stack object **Q1** shown in the left part of the diagram in figure 3.5. Object **Q1** has four data members: **queue_size, front, rear,** and a pointer variable ***buffer**. When **Q1** is created, the constructor **Queue(int n)** will be called and a heap object **int[5]** will be created and linked to the pointer ***buffer**, as shown in the right part of the diagram in figure 3.5.

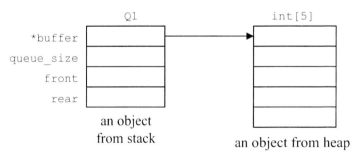

Figure 3.5 A stack object is first created and then a heap object is created

On the other hand, the declaration with the **new** operator "**Queue *Q2 = new Queue(5);**" will create a pointer variable **Q2** on the stack, and then create a **Queue** object with four data members from the heap. The constructor **Queue(int n)** will create a further object **int[5]** from the heap and link it to the pointer ***buffer**, as shown in figure 3.6.

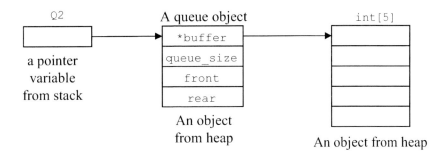

Figure 3.6 A pointer variable is created from the stack;
a **Queue** object and an **int[5]** object are created from the heap

Since any program will only be allocated limited amount of memory, garbage collection is extremely important, especially for those programs that continuously add and delete data. In Java, an automatic and expensive garbage collection mechanism is implemented to collect unused memory. It is expensive because the system has to maintain a reference counter associated with each object created. When the reference counter drops to zero, the object is no long accessible and thus can be collected. C++ does not have an automatic garbage collection mechanism. The garbage is partially collected by the system and partially the responsibility of the programmers. Table 3.1 summarizes the memory allocation, de-allocation mechanisms, and the applications of static, stack, and heap memory.

As we can see from the table, the heap is the only memory that programmers need to garbage-collect. If you write a constructor and create an object in the constructor, you must write a destructor and call the **delete** operation in the destructor to delete the object. If you are using a class defined by somebody else, you should not worry about garbage-collecting the objects created in the constructor. The destructor should collect the object automatically.

If you create an object in your program, you must call the **delete** operation in an appropriate place to delete the object. For example, assume you are writing a program to maintain a database. You create an object in a function called **insertion()** that adds a new data item into your database. Then you should have a function called **deletion()** that removes an unwanted data item from the database. In the deletion function, you should not only remove the links to the data item, but also use the **delete** operation to

Table 3.1 Allocation and de-allocation of different kinds of memory

Memory	Allocation	De-allocation	Application
Static	Global variables: declared outside any class or function; local variables with **static** prefix.	De-allocated by the system when the main function exits	Unique copy in global or local context
Stack	Local variables declared in a function.	De-allocated by the system when the function exits.	Temporary variable used in a function
Heap	Use **malloc** in C; or use **new** in C++.	The programmer must explicitly use **free** in C; or use **delete** in C++.	Variables that should never go out of scope unless explicitly deleted

garbage-collect the memory that holds the data item. If you fail to do so, you have a memory leak that will eventually lead to failure (out of memory) of the entire system.

Now let's consider memory de-allocation in the foo() function in the Queue example. We created a stack object Q1 and a heap object is created in the constructor and linked to the buffer pointer in Q1, as shown in figure 3.5. When the Q1 goes out of scope, Q1 is returned to the stack. Now what happens to the heap (integer array) object linked to Q1? If Q1 is simply de-allocated, the object from the heap will hang up and can never be accessed or garbage collected. To avoid this situation, C++ runtime system will call the destructor whenever a function exits, to delete any objects that are created in a constructor and are linked to an object that is going out of scope.

In the foo() function in the Queue example, we also created a heap object and linked it to Q2. Since this object is not created in a constructor, we must call the delete operation outside the destructor to delete the object. We call the delete operation before exiting the foo() function. When the object linked to Q2 is de-allocated, what happens to the heap (integer array) object linked to the object, as shown in figure 3.6? Again, to garbage collect the heap object created in the constructor, the delete operation will call the destructor to delete any objects that are created in a constructor and are linked to an object that is being deleted.

In summary, the destructor will be called in the following situations:

1. When a function exists and local object (from stack) goes out of scope. The destructor will be called to garbage-collect any objects linked to the local object before the memory of the local object goes out of scope.

2. When a program (the **main** function) ends and global or static objects exist. Since the **main** function should be treated like any other functions, the destructor will be called. However, when the **main** function exits, the entire program exits, the operating system will take back the entire memory segment allocated to the program.

3. When the **delete** function is called. An object allocated using the new operator (from heap) outside the class must be explicitly de-allocated using the **delete** operator. The destructor will be called to garbage-collect any objects linked to the object to be deleted.

4. When the destructor is explicitly called. The destructor is simply a function. A user can call the destructor function like calling any other functions.

3.4 INHERITANCE

3.4.1 CLASS CONTAINMENT AND INHERITANCE

C language does not support the inheritance from one structure to another. However, we can still share the structures defined before. The way we reuse the existing structures is through **class containment** mechanism, that is, we can use a structure to declare a variable within another structure, and, thus, we do not have to redefine the existing structure. Such a containment mechanism is also available in C++. For example, assume that we have defined a class Employee as follows:

```
class Employee {
    char        name[30];
    long        id;
    char        department[50];
    int         salary(int base, int bonus) { ... };
    int         tax(int thisMonth, int thisYear) { ... };
}
```

Now we want to define a linked list to hold the information of all the employees. We can then define an employee node class in the following two different ways:

```
// Definition 1:
class EmployeeNode1 {
    Employee     data;    // containing the class Employee
    EmployeeNode *next;
}
```

```
// Definition 2:
class EmployeeNode2 {
    char         name[30];
    long         id;
    char         department[50];
    int          salary(int base, int bonus) { ... };
    int          tax(int thisMonth, int thisYear) { ... };
    EmployeeNode *next;
}
```

In the definition of **EmployeeNode1**, we contain an **Employee** class in the **EmployeeNode1** class, while in the definition of **EmployeeNode2**, we copy (rewrite) all the data members and member functions into the new class. What are the advantages and disadvantages of these two definitions?

The advantages of using containment mechanism are:

- The new class is more concise;
- There is a level of abstraction in the **EmployeeNode1**. This class has only two members: a data member that contains employee information and a pointer that points to the next node. Normally, we do not need the detail of the data. However, if we do need to access the detail of the data member, it will be a bit less convenient. For example, if we declare a stack object by "**EmployeeNode x;**", then we will have to use **x.data.name** (three sections), **x.data.id**, **x.data.department**, **x.data.salary()**, and **x.data.tax()** to access the members; and use **x.next** (two sections only) to access the next member in **EmployeeNode1** object. Since the members from the **Employee** class are not semantically related to the next member in the **EmployeeNode1**, it makes sense to separate them in two different levels.

The second advantage could become a disadvantage if these members are semantically related and should not be separated. Now we define two new manager classes based on the employee class as follows.

```
// Definition 1:
class Manager1 {
    Employee     empl;   // containing the class Employee
    int          rank;
}
```

```
// Definition 2:
class Manager2 {
    char        name[30];
    long        id;
    char        department[50];
    int         salary(int base, int bonus) { ... };
    int         tax(int thisMonth, int thisYear) { ... };
    int         rank;
}
```

Here the extra member **rank** defined in the manager classes is related to the members in the **Employee** class. It should be put at the same level as the other members, so that members' **name**, **id**, **department**, **salary()**, and **tax()** can be access in the same way as the member rank. Thus, the class definition **Manager2** is better suitable than **Manager1**.

What's wrong with the definition of **Manager2** class? There are several problems associated with the approach of repeating the members in another class:

- It wastes time and space, especially, when the member functions **salary()** and **tax()** in the **Employee** class are very long.

- A more serious problem is data integrity: redundant structures exist in your program. When you change the **Employee** class, you must change the **Manager** class to preserve data integrity. If you have multiple redundant data in different places, it is very difficult to maintain the code.

Object-oriented programming languages introduced the inheritance mechanism to address the problem. The **inheritance mechanism** supports the definition of a new class based an existing class. In C++, the existing class is called the **base class** and the new class is called **derived class**. In Java, they are called parent (super) class and child (sub) class, respectively. The inheritance mechanism allows the derived class to

- inherit all members (data members and member functions) of the base class without having to repeat any of them;
- be able to add new members;
- be able to redefine members of the base class.

Using the inheritance mechanism, we can define a new manager class as follows.

```
class Manager3 : public Employee {
    int         rank;
}
```

The **Manager3** class can be used in the exactly same way as the **Manager2** class; that is, we can access the inherited members from the **Employee** class in the same way as using the new member rank. The only difference is that, when the members of the **Employee** class are modified, the inherited members of the **Manager3** class are automatically modified.

As we can see from above discussion, containment and inheritance mechanisms have different applications. Now the question is, how can we decide which mechanism is the right one for a particular situation? As we mentioned above, we can make the decision based on whether the new members are really related to the members in the base class. Another way to help you make the decision is to characterize the containment relation and the inheritance relation as "***has-a***" relation and "***is-a***" relation. For example, an employee node (in a linked list) has an employee as its data, a car *has-a* wheel, a university *has-a* student; and a manager *is-an* employee, pixel *is-a* point, etc. Whenever the *has-a* relation holds, we apply the containment mechanism, and whenever the *is-a* relation holds, we apply the inheritance mechanism. For example:

- Since it is better to consider that the employee node *has-an* (contains an) employee than to consider that the employee node *is-an* employee, we should apply the containment mechanism.

- Since it is better to consider that the manager *is-an* employee than to consider that the manager *has-an* (contains an) employee, we should apply the inheritance mechanism.

Now let's examine our Queue and PriQueue example at the beginning of the chapter. Obviously, it is better to consider that the **priority queue** PriQueue *is-a* Queue than to consider that the PriQueue *has-a* Queue. Thus, we used the inheritance mechanism to define the PriQueue.

```
class PriQueue : public Queue {
public:
    int getMax(void); // return and remove the max value from the queue
    PriQueue(int n) : Queue(n) { };
    // base class constructor may not be inherited. It has to be explicitly
    // called. PriQueue's constructor simply calls Queue's constructor;
    ~PriQueue() {                    // base class destructor may not be called here or
        delete buffer;               // inherited. We must explicitly use delete.
        buffer = 0;
    };
};
```

The third line defines a new member in the PriQueue class that returns and removes the element with the maximum value from the queue. The fourth line defines the constructor of the PriQueue class. Please note that the base class's constructor may not be inherited. It has to be explicitly called. PriQueue's constructor simply calls the Queue's constructor. The next member function is the destructor of the PriQueue class. The base class's destructor may not be inherited and may not be called in the derived class's destructor. Thus, we have to use the explicit delete operation to delete the objects created in the constructor of the PriQueue class.

3.4.2 INHERITANCE AND HIERARCHY

Inheritance is very useful in associating many related classes and organizing them into a hierarchy of classes. From this section and in the following sections, we will use a more complicated example to illustrate the major properties of object-oriented programming languages, including inheritance, class hierarchy, late binding, polymorphism, and type checking.

Assume that we are developing a database for a university to hold personnel information of students and employees. We break the information to be stored into multiple classes and organize the classes in a hierarchy using inheritance. As show in figure 3.7, the class Personnel is the root of the inheritance tree. Classes Student and Employee inherit Personnel. Classes Faculty, Staff and Consultant inherit Employee, etc. In each class, a number of members are defined. According to the inheritance principle, a child (derived) class will inherit the members of its parent (base) class and, in turn, its grandparent class, and great grandparent class, etc.

C++ also support **multiple inheritances**, that is, a class can inherit members from more than one class. The need for multiple inheritances arises when a class has an *is-a* relation with multiple classes. For example, the Consultant class inherit the Employees and ConsultingCo classes, as shown in figure 3.7. Syntactically, the use of multiple inheritances is simple, we simply list the classes from which the derived class wants to inherit. For example, using the multiple inheritances, we defined the Consultant class as follows:

```
class Consultant: public Employee, public ConsultingCo{ // inherit two classes
    ... // new members here
}
```

However, the semantics of multiple inheritances is complex and error prone. It must be used with caution. In this example, the Consultant class inherits from two classes that are not in the same inheritance hierarchy. If a class inherits two classes in the same hierarchy, we must use a **virtual base class** to avoid the duplication of members in the derived class. For example, assume we have a TA (teaching assistant) class that inherits from Employee and Student classes. We must define the Personnel class as a virtual base class. Then, when we derive the Employee and Student classes, the members in Personnel, i.e., name, id, etc., will not be doubly copied into the TA class through Employee and Student, as shown in the following piece of code.

```
class Personnel {
    // members
};
class Employee : virtual public Personnel {
    // members
};
class Student : virtual public Personnel {
// members
};
class TA : public Employee, public Student {
// Member list
};
void main() {
    ...
}
```

Please note that we defined two classes, Contact and PersonnelNode that do not have the inheritance or *is-a* relation with other classes. Containment relation is used to relate them to a class in the hierarchy. Class Contact is contained in the class Personnel, and class PersonnelNode contains a Personnel class.

We could put a particular member in different classes. The principle is to put a member in a class where all its derived classes share the member. For example, features like name, id, and birthday, that everyone shares should be in the Personnel class that is the root of the hierarchy.

If a member only shares the name with its base class and has a different data structure or functionality, we can redefine or override the member in the derived class. In figure 3.7, the display() function in each node will print each data member in the class. Since each class has different data members, we have

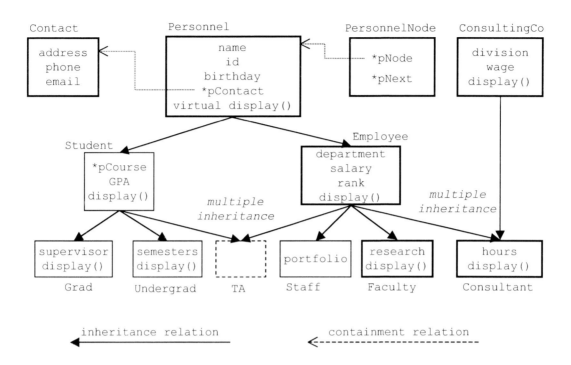

Figure 3.7 Organizing classes in a hierarchy

to write a different display function in each class. Of course, we could use different names in different classes. However, we will shortly see that it is a much better way to redefine the display function than to use different names. For any member of a class to be redefined, we must put the keyword **virtual** before the name. In the derived classes, we may, but we do not have to, use the keyword **virtual** before the member that has been declared as virtual. If a member is declared as **virtual**, all redefined members in the derived classes will be virtual, no matter whether the keyword **virtual** is used or not. The destructor of a class must be defined as **virtual** if the class is used as a base class and there are destructors defined in the derived classes.

You can also define an **abstract function**, or called **pure virtual function**, by assigning the virtual function to 0. An abstract function must be overridden in the derived classes. If a class contains an abstract function, the class is an **abstract class** and it cannot be used to instantiate an object. It can be used to derive new classes only. The code segment below shows the definition of an abstract class and an abstract function.

```
abstract class Student : public Personnel {          // abstract class
    Queue *course;
    public virtual float getGPA(char* name) = 0;     // abstract function
}
```

A C++ implementation of a part of the hierarchy in figure 3.7 is given below. The program includes the classes **Contact, Personnel, Employee, Faculty, ConsultingCo, Consultant, PersonnelNode**, and a list of global functions. In the global functions, the menu function allows users to select desired operations, e.g., insertion of new node and printing the node information. Different insertion functions are used to create a new object of different classes and insert it into the linked list. A single remove() function deletes an object of any class from the linked list and garbage-collect the memory allocated to the object using an explicit delete operation. The display_all() function display the object information stored in the linked list. The display_all() function will call the polymorphic member functions defined in each class to display class specific information. More details of the program are given as comments in the program.

The purpose of this program is to illustrate:

- **Class definition**: public, protected, and private members, and use public member functions to access private members.
- **Class inheritance and hierarchy**: Employee inherits Personnel and Faculty inherits Employee;
- **Multiple inheritance**: Consultant inherits Employee and ConsultingCo classes.
- **Class containment**: Personnel class contains Contact class, and PersonnelNode class contains Personnel class.
- **Constructor**: The constructor is defined in every class. The constructor of a derived class can call the constructor of the base class.
- **Destructor**: Destructors are defined in **Personnel**, **Employee**, and **Faculty** classes. The destructor of a derived class cannot call the destructor of the base class. It has to repeat the statements if it wants to perform the same operations.
- **Explicit garbage collection**: Objects created in the insertion functions have to be deleted (garbage-collected) explicitely. The program contains a remove() function. Heap objects created in the insertion functions are explicitly deleted using the delete operator.
- **Polymorphism**: Polymorphic pointer: use a pointer to Personnel class object to access objects of derived classes. Polymorphic function: display() function is defined as virtual and a different function is called when the polymorphic pointer points to a different class object.
- **Linked list**: In the PersonnelNode class, a pointer pNext to PersonnelNode (itself) is declared. The pointer forms the links of the linked list.
- **Global variable**: head is defined as a global variable that holds the starting address of the linked list, or called head pointer.
- **Static local variable**: In the constructor of the Personnel class, a static local variable ildCounter is declared to hold the current ID number that has been issued. The static qualifier ensures that the variable is initialized only once and incremented after each instantiation of a new object.
- **Global functions**: member functions in each class are associated with the object of the class. Global functions are not associated with any class and can be called anywhere in the program.

```
#include <iostream.h>
#include <stdlib.h>
#include <string.h>
#include <ctype.h>

class Contact {
private:
        char cAddress[75];
        char cPhone[25];
        char cEmail[75];
```

```cpp
public:
        void setAddress(char *cAddress) {strcpy(this->cAddress, cAddress);}
        void setPhone(char *cPhone) { strcpy(this->cPhone, cPhone); }
        void setEmail(char *cEmail) { strcpy(this->cEmail, cEmail); }
        char* getAddress() { return cAddress; }
        char* getPhone() { return cPhone; }
        char* getEmail() { return cEmail; }

        Contact(char *cAddress, char *cPhone, char *cEmail) { // constructor
                setAddress(cAddress);
                setPhone(cPhone);
                setEmail(cEmail);
        }
};
class Personnel {
    private:
        char cName[50];
        int iId;
        char cBirthday[11];
    protected:
        Contact *pContact;
    public:
        void setName(char *cName) { strcpy(this->cName, cName); }
        void setBirthday(char *cBirthday) {strcpy(this->cBirthday, cBirthday);}
        void setId(int iId) { this->iId = iId; }
        char* getName() { return cName; }
        int getId() { return iId;}
        char* getBirthday() { return cBirthday; }
        Contact * getContact() { return pContact; }
        virtual void display() {
                cout << "PERSONNEL" << endl;
                cout << "Name:\t" << getName() << endl;
                cout << "Id:\t" << getId() << endl;
                cout << "Birthday:\t" << getBirthday() << endl;
                cout << "Address:\t" << pContact->getAddress() << endl;
                cout << "Phone:\t" << pContact->getPhone() << endl;
                cout << "Email:\t" << pContact->getEmail() << endl;
        }

        Personnel(char *cName, char *cBirthday, char *cAddress, char *cPhone, char *cEmail)
                                // constructor
{
```

```cpp
            static int ildCounter = 0;
            setName(cName);              // set Name
            setId(ildCounter);           // set Id by a self-incremental counter
            ildCounter++;                // increment the ID generator;
            setBirthday(cBirthday);      // set Birthday
            pContact = new Contact(cAddress, cPhone, cEmail);
        }

        ~Personnel() {                   // destructor
            delete pContact;             // delete the object linked to pContact
            pContact = NULL;             // Make sure pContact not point to an object
        }
};

class Employee : public Personnel        {    // inherit from Personnel
    private:
            char cDepartment[75];
            float fSalary;
            char cRank[75];

    public:
            void setDepartment(char *cDepartment) {strcpy(this->cDepartment, cDepartment);}
            void setSalary(float fSalary) { this->fSalary = fSalary; }
            virtual void setRank(char *cRank) { strcpy(this->cRank, cRank); }
            char* getDepartment() { return cDepartment; }
            float getSalary() { return fSalary; }
            virtual char* getRank() { return cRank; }

            void display() {
                Personnel::display();
                cout << "EMPLOYEE" << endl;
                cout << "Department:\t" << getDepartment() << endl;
                cout << "Salary:\t" << getSalary() << endl;
                cout << "Rank:\t" << getRank() << endl;
            }

            Employee(char *cName, char *cBirthday, char *cAddress, char *cPhone, char *cEmail,
        char *cDepartment, float fSalary, char *cRank)
                : Personnel(cName, cBirthday, cAddress, cPhone, cEmail)
            {
                setDepartment(cDepartment);
```

```
                setSalary(fSalary);
                setRank(cRank);
        }

        ~Employee() {                   // destructor
                delete pContact;        // delete the object linked to pContact
                pContact = NULL;        // Make sure pContact does not point to
        }                               // any object
};


class Faculty : public Employee {  // inherit from Employee
    private:
                char cResearch[75];
    public:
                virtual void setResearch(char *cResearch) {
                        strcpy(this->cResearch, cResearch);
                }
                char* getResearch() { return cResearch; }
                virtual void display() {
                        Employee::display();
                        cout << "FACULTY" << endl;
                        cout << "Research\t" << getResearch() << endl;
                }


                Faculty(char *cName, char *cBirthday, char *cAddress, char *cPhone, char *cEmail,
        char *cDepartment, float fSalary, char *cRank, char *cResearch)
                        : Employee(cName, cBirthday, cAddress, cPhone, cEmail, cDepartment, fSalary,
        cRank)
                {
                        setResearch(cResearch);
                }

                ~Faculty() {                    // destructor
                        delete pContact;        // delete the object linked to pContact
                        pContact = NULL;        // Make sure pContact does not
                }                               // point to any object
};


class ConsultingCo {                    // not inherit from a class
private:
    char division[30];
    float wage;
```

```
public:
    virtual void display(){
            cout << "ConsultingCo" << endl;
            cout << "Division: " << getDivision() << endl;
            cout << "Wage: " << getWage() << endl;
    }
    char* getDivision(){
            return division;
    }
    void setDivision(char *division_){
            strcpy(this->division, division_);
    }
    float getWage(){
            return wage;
    }
    void setWage(float wage_){
            this->wage = wage_;
    }
    ConsultingCo(char *division_, float wage_) {
            setDivision(division_);
            setWage(wage_);
    }
};

// multiple inheritance: Consultant class inherit from two classes
class Consultant : public Employee, public ConsultingCo{
private:
    int hours;
public:
    virtual void display() {
            Employee::display();
            ConsultingCo::display();
            cout << "Consultant" << endl;
            cout << "Hours: " << getHours() << endl;
    }
    int getHours(){ return hours;}
    void setHours(int hours_) {this->hours = hours_;}
    Consultant(char *cName, char *cBirthday, char *cAddress, char *cPhone, char *cEmail, char
*cDepartment, float fSalary, char *cRank, char* division_, float wage_, int hours_)
                : Employee(cName, cBirthday, cAddress, cPhone, cEmail, cDepartment, fSalary,
cRank), ConsultingCo(division_, wage_)
    {
```

```cpp
                setHours(hours_);
        }

            ~Consultant() {                    // destructor
                delete pContact;               // delete the object linked to pContact
                pContact = NULL;               // Make sure pContact does not point to
            }                                  // any object
};

class PersonnelNode {                          // This is a container class
    private:
            Personnel *pNode;                  // It contains a Personnel class
            PersonnelNode*pNext;               // pointer used to form a linked list
    public:
            void setNode(Personnel *pNode) { this->pNode = pNode; }
            void setNext(PersonnelNode *pNext) { this->pNext = pNext; }
            Personnel* getNode() { return pNode; }
            PersonnelNode* getNext() { return pNext; }
            PersonnelNode() {                  // constructor
                    pNode = NULL;
                    pNext = NULL;
            }
} *head = NULL;    // declare a global pointer variable head

// Forward declaration of global functions outside any class
int main();                     // The main function
void menu();                    // display main choices
void branching(char);           // branch to the chosen function
void sub_menu();                // display different insertion options
void insert();                  // call sub_menu() and branch to chosen function
int insert_personnel();         // insert a personnel node
int insert_employee();          // insert an employee node
int insert_faculty(); // insert a faculty node
int insert_consultant();
void remove();                  // call remove function
void display_all();             // display members in all nodes in the linked list
void display_node(Personnel*, int);      // display the members in one node

int main() { // main function is the entry point of the program
    char ch;
    cout << "CLASSES INHERITANCE, HIERARCHY AND POLYMORPHISM" << endl;
    cout << "***************************************************" << endl;
```

```cpp
    do {
            menu();                     // display choices
            cin >> ch;                  // enter a choice from the keyboard
            ch = tolower(ch);           // convert to lower case
            branching(ch);              // branch to the chosen function
    }
    while (ch != 'q');                  // 'q' for quit
    return 0;
}


void menu() {
    cout <<endl << endl << "MENU" << endl;
    cout << "———" << endl;
    cout << "i: Insert a new entry." << endl;
    cout << "d: display all entries." << endl;
    cout << "r: remove an entry." << endl;
    cout << "q: Quit the program." << endl;
    cout << endl << "Please enter your choice (i, d, r, or q) —> ";
}


void branching(char c) {               // branch to chosen function
    switch(c) {
            case 'i':     insert();
                          break;
            case 'd':     display_all();
                          break;
            case 'r':     remove();
                          break;
            case 'q':     cout << endl << "@Exiting the program..............." << endl;
                          cin.get();         //type any key.
                          break;
            default:      cout << endl << "@ERROR - Invalid input." << endl;
                          cout << "@Try again....." << endl;
    }
}


void sub_menu() { // display insertion options
    cout <<endl << endl << "INSERTION SUB-MENU" << endl;
    cout << "————————————" << endl;
    cout << "p: insert a personnel entry." << endl;
    cout << "e: insert an employee entry." << endl;
```

```
        cout << "f: insert a faculty entry." << endl;
        cout << "c: insert a consultant entry." << endl;
        cout << "q: Quit insertion and back to main menu." << endl;
        cout << endl << "Please enter your choice (p, e, f, c, or q) —> ";
}

// insert() is the umbrella insertion function that calls different insertion
// functions according to the selection in the sub-menu.
void insert() {
        char ch;

        cout << endl << "@Insertion module...............";
        do {
                sub_menu();
                cin >> ch;
                ch = tolower(ch);
                switch(ch) {
                        case 'p':       if(insert_personnel() != 0)
                                                cout << "@INSERTION OPERATION FAILED." << endl;
                                        else
                                                cout << "@INSERTED SUCCESSFULLY." << endl;
                                        break;
                        case 'e':       if(insert_employee() != 0)
                                                cout << "@INSERTION OPERATION FAILED." << endl;
                                        else
                                                cout << "@INSERTED SUCCESSFULLY." << endl;
                                        break;
                        case 'f':       if(insert_faculty() != 0)
                                                cout << "@INSERTION OPERATION FAILED." << endl;
                                        else
                                                cout << "@INSERTED SUCCESSFULLY." << endl;
                                        break;
                        case 'c':       if(insert_consultant() != 0)
                                                cout << "@INSERTION OPERATION FAILED." << endl;
                                        else
                                                cout << "@INSERTED SUCCESSFULLY." << endl;
                                        break;
                        case 'q':       cout << endl << "@Exiting the insertion..." << endl;
                                        cin.get();
                                        break;
                        default:        cout << endl << "@ERROR - Invalid input." << endl;
```

```cpp
                            cout << "@Try again....." << endl;
            }
    }
    while (ch != 'q');
}


int insert_personnel() {                 // insert a Personnel node
    Personnel *person = NULL;
    PersonnelNode *node = NULL;
    char name[50], birthday[11], address[75], phone[25], email[75];
    cout << endl << "@Inserting personnel node.........." << endl;
    cout << "Enter the name: ";
    cin.ignore();      // fflush()
    cin.getline(name, 50);
    cout << "Enter the birthday, e.g., 05/24/1985: ";
    cin.getline(birthday, 11);
    cout << "Enter the address: ";
    cin.getline(address, 75);
    cout << "Enter the phone number: ";
    cin.getline(phone, 25);
    cout << "Enter the email: ";
    cin.getline(email, 75);
    person = new Personnel(name, birthday, address, phone, email);
    node = new PersonnelNode();

    if((person != NULL) && (node != NULL)) {
            node->setNode(person);
            node->setNext(head);
            head = node;
            return 0;
    }
    else {
            cout << endl << "@ERROR - Could not allocate enough memory!" << endl;
            return -1;
    }
}


int insert_employee() {                  // insert an Employee node
    Personnel *person = NULL;
    PersonnelNode *node = NULL;
    char name[50], birthday[11], address[75], phone[25], email[75], department[75], rank[75];
```

```cpp
      float salary;

      cout << endl << "@Inserting employee node.........." << endl;
      cout << "Enter the name: ";
      cin.ignore();
      cin.getline(name, 50);
      cout << "Enter the birthday, e.g., 05/24/1985: ";
      cin.getline(birthday, 11);
      cout << "Enter the address:";
      cin.getline(address, 75);
      cout << "Enter the phone number: ";
      cin.getline(phone, 25);
      cout << "Enter the email: ";
      cin.getline(email, 75);
      cout << "Enter the department: ";
      cin.getline(department, 75);
      cout << "Enter the salary. It must be a float number: ";
      cin >> salary;
      cout << "Enter the rank: ";
      cin.ignore();
      cin.getline(rank, 75);

      person = new Employee(name, birthday, address, phone, email, department, salary, rank);
      node = new PersonnelNode();

      if((person != NULL) && (node != NULL)) {
             node->setNode(person);
             node->setNext(head);
             head = node;
             return 0;
      }
      else {
             cout << endl << "@ERROR - Could not allocate enough memory!" << endl;
             return -1;
      }
}

int insert_faculty() {          // insert a Faculty node
      Personnel *person = NULL;
      PersonnelNode *node = NULL;
      char name[50], birthday[11], address[75], phone[25], email[75], department[75], rank[75],
```

```
    research[75];
        float salary;

        cout << endl << "@Inserting faculty node.........." << endl;
        cout << "Enter the name: ";
        cin.ignore();
        cin.getline(name, 50);
        cout << "Enter the birthday, e.g., 05/24/1985: ";
        cin.getline(birthday, 11);
        cout << "Enter the address: ";
        cin.getline(address, 75);
        cout << "Enter the phone number: ";
        cin.getline(phone, 25);
        cout << "Enter the email: ";
        cin.getline(email, 75);
        cout << "Enter the department: ";
        cin.getline(department, 75);
        cout << "Enter the salary. It must be a float number: ";
        cin >> salary;
        cout << "Enter the rank: ";
        cin.ignore();
        cin.getline(rank, 75);

        cout << "Enter the research: ";
        cin.getline(research, 75);

        person = new Faculty(name, birthday, address, phone, email, department, salary, rank,
    research);
        node = new PersonnelNode();
        if((person != NULL) && (node != NULL)) {
                node->setNode(person);
                node->setNext(head);
                head = node;
                return 0;
        }
        else {
                cout << endl << "@ERROR - Could not allocate enough memory!" << endl;
                return -1;
        }
    }
    int insert_consultant() {              // insert a Faculty node
```

```
Personnel *person = NULL;
PersonnelNode *node = NULL;
char name[50], birthday[11], address[75], phone[25], email[75], department[75], rank[75],
division[30];
float salary, wage;
int hours;

cout << endl << "@Inserting consultant node.........." << endl;
cout << "Enter the name: ";
cin.ignore();
cin.getline(name, 50);
cout << "Enter the birthday, e.g., 05/24/1985: ";
cin.getline(birthday, 11);
cout << "Enter the address: ";
cin.getline(address, 75);
cout << "Enter the phone number: ";
cin.getline(phone, 25);
cout << "Enter the email: ";
cin.getline(email, 75);
cout << "Enter the department: ";
cin.getline(department, 75);

cout << "Enter the salary. It must be a float number: ";
cin >> salary;
cout << "Enter the rank: ";
cin.ignore();
cin.getline(rank, 75);
cout << "Enter the division: ";
cin.getline(division, 30);
cout << "Enter the wage. It must be a float number: ";
cin >> wage;
cout << "Enter the hours. It must be an integer: ";
cin >> hours;

person = new Consultant(name, birthday, address, phone, email, department, salary, rank,
division, wage, hours);
node = new PersonnelNode();
if((person != NULL) && (node != NULL)) {
        node->setNode(person);
        node->setNext(head);
        head = node;
        return 0;
```

```
        }
    else {
            cout << endl << "@ERROR - Could not allocate enough memory!" << endl;
            return -1;
    }
}


/* void remove() function removes a node in the linked list. In the remove function, an id number will
be entered as the key. The node whose id field stored an id number that is equal to the entered id
number will be removed. */
void remove() {
    int id;
    PersonnelNode *temp, *prev;
    Personnel *person;
    int index = 1;
    cout<<"Remove module...............\n" << endl ;
    cout<<"Please enter the ID number of the person to be deleted: "<<endl;
    cin>> id;
    temp = head;
    while (temp != NULL) {
            person = temp->getNode();
                if (id != person->getId()){
                        prev = temp;
                        temp = temp->getNext();
                        index++;
                }
                else {
                        cout <<"Person to delete is found at index" << index<<endl;
                        display_node(person, index);
                        if(temp != head)
                        prev->setNext(temp->getNext());
                        else
                                head = head->getNext();
                        delete person; //explicit garbage-collection
                        person=NULL; //make it not to point to any object
                        delete temp;    // explicit garbage-collection
                        temp = NULL; // Make sure temp does not point to any object
                        return;
                }
            }
        cout <<"The person with ID = << id << does not exist."<< endl;
    }
```

```
void display_all() { // Display contents of all nodes in the linked list
    PersonnelNode *node;
    int node_count= 0;
    cout << endl << "@Display module...............";
    node = head;
    while(node != NULL) {
            display_node(node->getNode(), ++node_count);
            node = node->getNext();
    }
    cout << endl << "@No more records." << endl;
}
void display_node(Personnel *node, int index) {// Display contents of one node
    cout << endl << "Record " << index << "." << endl;
    node->display();         // Polymorphic call. Depending on the object pointed to
}                            // by node, a different display function will be invoked.
```

3.4.3 INHERITANCE AND POLYMORPHISM

Polymorphism is the ability of applying the same operation to different objects and to receive different forms of responses. Polymorphism in C++ is applied to different classes related by inheritance. It allows a pointer declared to point to an object of class *A* to point to an object of class *B* if *B* is a descendant class of *A*. Therefore, the pointer of a base class is polymorphic. Furthermore, a member function of a class can be defined as a virtual function and redefined in the derived classes. Then, the same call to a virtual function in different classes will cause different functions to be invoked. Thus, the calls are polymorphic.

Polymorphism has been illustrated in the long example in section 3.4.2, where the **display()** functions in different classes are virtual.

Now let's examine how polymorphism simplifies the design. In the program, we defined the linked list node to have two pointer variables.

```
class PersonnelNode {
        Personnel          *pNode;
        PersonnelNode      *pNext;
}
```

The first pointer variable points to an object of the **Personnel** class that is the data portion of the linked list. The second pointer variable points to an object of **PersonnelNode** that is the link portion of the linked list. Since the **pNode** is declared as a pointer to the root class's objects, it can be used to point to objects of all derived classes: **Personnel, Employee, Faculty, Staff,** and **Consultant,** etc. In other words, we can link different objects in the same linked list, as shown in figure 3.8.

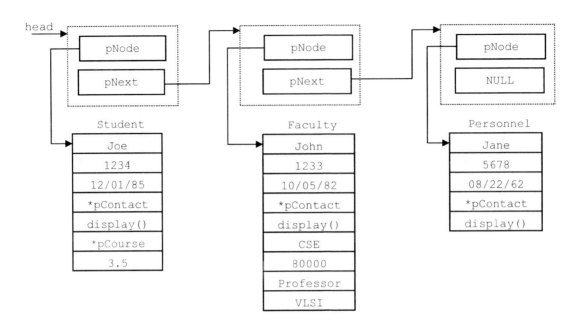

Figure 3.8 Different objects are linked into the same list

Having inserted different nodes into the linked list, we could use the following code to print members defined in the **Personnel** object (the root node) using a pointer **pl** to the **Personnel** object:

```
PersonnelNode *pn;
for (pn = head; pn != NULL; pn = pn->next) {// traverse the linked list
    Personnel *pl = pn->pNode;          // pl is a Personnel class pointer
    cout << "name = " << pl->cName << endl;
    cout << "id = " << pl->iId << endl;
    cout << "birthday = " << pl->cBirthday << endl;
    cout << "Contact->address = " << pl->pContact->cAddress << endl;
    cout << "Contact->phone = " << pl->pContact->cPhone << endl;
    cout << "Contact->email = " << pl->pContact->cEmail << endl;
}
```

Now the question is, can we add the following statements to print members defined in the **Student** class?

```
cout << "GPA = " << pl->GPA << endl;
cout << "department = " << pl->cBirthday << endl;
```

The answer is no, because the type checking mechanism in C++ will prevent us from using the **Personnel** pointer **pl** to access the members that do not exist in the base class **Personnel** (see next subsection). In order to print the complete information in different kinds of nodes in the linked list, we defined a virtual function **display()** in each class in the hierarchy. When pl points to a particular object, the display() function specifically defined in the class of the object is invoked, as shown in the following piece of code.

```
PersonnelNode *pn;
for (pn = head; pn !=0; pn = pn->pNext) {
    Personnel *pl = pn->pNode;    // pl can point to any object
    pl->display();                // the function defined in current class is invoked
}
```

Since the **Personnel** class has also the function **display()**, the compiler won't complain. However, since **display()** is redefined in the derived classes, polymorphism will cause the redefined **display()** function to be called, thus allowing the specific information to the node to be printed. For example, the **display()** function in the **Student** class could be defined as follows, in which the class specific members GPA and major can be printed.

```
Student::display() {
    cout << name = " << name << endl;
    cout << "id = " << id << endl;
    cout << "birthday = " << birthday << endl;
    cout << "Contact->address = " << Contact->address << endl;
    cout << "Contact->phone = " << Contact->phone << endl;
    cout << "Contact->email = " << Contact->email << endl;
    cout << "GPA = " << GPA << endl;
}
```

3.4.4 POLYMORPHISM AND TYPE CHECKING

As we have seen in the previous subsection, although polymorphism allows us to move a pointer from a base class object to a derived class object, it only allows us to access members inherited from the base class. It does not allow us to access the new members defined in the derived class. Let's observe a further example:

```
Personnel *p = new Personnel();   // link a Personnel object to p.
Employee *e = new Employee();     // link an Employee object to e.
Faculty *f = new Faculty();       // link a Faculty object to f.
```

then, according to polymorphism, we can use the pointer p to access the objects of the derived class:

```
p = e;            // p is now pointing to the object pointed by e.
p->id = 123;      // Now we use p to access members in Employee object.
p = f;            // p is now pointing to the object pointed by f.
p->id = 124;      // Now we use p to access members in Faculty object.
```

However, we cannot access the members that do not exist in the base class. For example, if we write the following statements in our program:

```
p = e;
strcpy(p->department, "computer science");
```

we will have a compilation error. The reason is: classes in C++ are essentially user-defined types. Static type checking is enforced by the compiler. After we have moved the **Personnel** class pointer to an **Employee** class's object and then access **p->id**, the compiler will consider that we are still accessing the **Personnel** class's member, and thus it won't complain. However, if we try to access **p->department**, the compiler will not be able to find the member **department** in the **Personnel** class and thus the compiler will report a compilation error.

3.4.5 POLYMORPHISM AND LATE BINDING

When a member function is declared as a virtual function, late binding will be used; that is, the function name will be bound to the actual memory locations that store the function's code not during the compilation, but during the execution of the program. Binding a name to its memory locations during the execution stage is called **late binding** or **dynamic binding**. If late binding is applied, the function can be redefined. On the other hand, binding a name to its memory locations during the compilation stage is called **early binding** or **static binding**. If early binding is applied, the member cannot be redefined. In C++, only member functions can be dynamically bound. Data members can only be bound statically. Early binding is considered a feature of imperative programming paradigm, while late binding is considered a feature of object-oriented programming paradigm. In Java, late binding is applied to all member functions of a class by default. If you specifically want to apply early binding to a member function, you must use the keyword "final" to enforce the early binding. Polymorphic function calls are possible only if late binding is applied.

Why do we need early binding? For example, if you write a password verification member function in a class and do not want anyone to redefine/override the function in a derived class, you can apply early binding to prevent overriding. Another advantage of early binding is its efficiency. Late binding during execution is less efficient than early binding. For efficiency reason, C++ applies early binding to all members of a class by default. If you specifically want to apply late binding to a member function, you must use the keyword "virtual" to enforce the late binding.

3.5 EXCEPTION HANDLING

An **exception** is a forced deviation caused by a known event, which represents an abnormal situation, from the normal execution sequence of the program. There are **internal exceptions** and **external exceptions**.

An internal exception is caused by a message to the CPU seeking attention from a source within the CPU itself, for example, when an operation performs a division by 0, causes an overflow, or executes an illegal (undefined) operation. Internal exceptions are called software related exceptions.

An external exception is caused by a message to the CPU seeking attention from a source outside the CPU, e.g., out-of-memory, memory access violation, bus error, and device busy, etc. External exceptions are also called **interrupts**.

Exceptions are difficult to handle and are normally handled at all levels of a computer system.

At hardware level, when an exception occurs, the hardware will identify the exception source, compute the exception handler's entry address, and load the address into the program counter of the CPU. Thus, CPU starts to execute the exception handler's code. A very limited number of exceptions can be handled at the hardware level. For example, Motorola 68000 processor can handle up to 256 exceptions and interrupts. At operating system level, more exceptions can be handled. For each exception, a simple exception handler will be provided. At the program language level, most programming languages provide exception handling mechanisms. For example, C++ provides several exception classes to facilitate programmers to handle exceptions more effectively. At the user program level, a programmer can write application-specific exception handlers to handle various semantics related exceptions. Only the programmers know the semantics of their programs.

At each level, exception handling can make use of the exception handlers below and can add extra exception handlers.

If an exception is not caught by the programmer's handlers, there are two possibilities. (1) The exception is caught by a lower level of exception handler and an error message will normally be shown. The programmer can either terminate the program or enter the debugging state to see what instruction or operation caused the exception. (2) If the exception is not caught by a lower level exception handler, the program will normally crash or freeze.

Visual Studio C++ provides an exception library <stdexcept> that includes the following exception classes.

exception Class (root class)
domain_error Class
invalid_argument Class
length_error Class
logic_error Class
out_of_range Class
overflow_error Class
range_error Class
runtime_error Class
underflow_error Class

C++ also provides several constructs for programmers to define their exception conditions and exception handlers. The syntax, which is similar to that of Java, is given in BNF notations as follows.

<exception-structure> ::= **try** <code-block> <handler-list>

<handler-list> ::= <empty> | <handler> | <handler-list> <handler>

<handler> ::= **catch** (<except-declaration>) <code-block>

<except-declaration> ::=   <type-name> | <type-name> <identifier> |
                           <type-name> *<identifier>

<throw-statement> ::= **throw** | **throw** <expression>

The code-block following the **try** keyword is the code that is a part of the code required by the semantics of the program. However, an exception condition may occur in this part of code. For example, there is a division operation on a variable whose value could be zero, or a memory request is made, which may or may not receive the required memory.

The handler-list may consist of zero, one, or multiple handlers, each of which handles a different type of exception variable. Each handler starts with the keyword **catch** and is followed by declaring an exception variable and a block of code. The variable will be used to receive the "return" value of a **throw** statement in the **try** statement. The code-block in the **catch** statement will handle the exception in a specific way, e.g., print an error message of the value of exception variable.

The **throw** statement is similar to a **return** statement. It is normally used in the **try** statement to exit (return from) the block and possibly to pass a value to an exception variable. Multiple **throw** statements can be used. If the types of the return values are different, different exception handlers (multiple **catch** statements) must be used. We can also consider that **catch** is a function and **throw** statement is a function call to the catch function. Since there can be multiple catch statements, catch is an overloaded function with different parameter types. The value in the throw statement will be parameter-passed to the catch function.

The following program illustrates the application of the exception statements.

```
#include <iostream>
using namespace std;        // It includes <stdexcept> library
int main() {
    int *queue, n;
    cout << "Enter queue-size >= 10: " << '\n';
    cin >> n;
    try {
            if (n < 10)
                    throw -1;         // return an integer value
            queue = new int[n];
                    if( queue == 0 )
                            throw "heap allocation failed!";
    }
    catch( char * se ) {
            cout << "Exception: " << se << '\n'; // return a string
    }
    catch( int ie ) {
            cout << "Exception: " << ie << " too small" << '\n';
    }
    // ...
    return 0;
}
```

In this program, there are two throw statements, handling two different exception situations, respectively. One returns an integer value and the other returns a string. Thus, two catch statements (two exception handlers) are necessary. The integer return value will be passed the integer exception variable ie and the string return value will be passed to the string variable se, respectively.

Although we can use the normal data types to declare exception variables, it is recommended, for the purpose of readability, to define an exception class (type) and use the class to declare exception variables. The following piece of code checks if a date entered is in a valid format and in the valid ranges. A class DataErr is defined and used to declare an exception variable derr. The variable is assigned values in the try statement. In the catch statement, another variable dateerr of DataErr type is declared. When a throw statement calls the catch function, the values in the variable derr are passed to the variable dateerr.

```
class DateErr {
    public:
            char *pdate;
            int idate;
} derr;
```

```
char birthday[11], atemp[11], *ptemp;
cout << "Enter birthday, eg, 05/24/1985";
try {          // handling incorrect date input
    cin.getline(birthday, 11);
    strcpy(atemp, birthday); // 05/24/1985
    ptemp = atemp;
    derr.pdate = birthday;
    atemp[2] = '\0'; //extract the month
    // handling incorrect date input
    derr.idate = atoi(ptemp); // extract month
    if ((derr.idate<1)||(derr.idate>12)) {
            throw derr;      // out of month range 1..12
    }
    atemp[5] = '\0';
    ptemp = ptemp + 3;
    derr.idate = atoi(ptemp);          //extract day
    if ((derr.idate<1)||(derr.idate>31))
            throw derr;      // out of day range 1..31
    ptemp = ptemp + 3;      //extract the year
    derr.idate = atoi(ptemp);
    if ((derr.idate<1800) || (derr.idate>2050))
            throw derr;
}
catch (DateErr dateerr) {
    cout << "Exception: "
            << dateerr.idate << "incorrect in"
            << dateerr.pdate << '\n';
}
```

3.6 SUMMARY

In this chapter, we first briefly reviewed the principles of object-oriented paradigm. We then discussed class composition and definition, including information hiding through defining public, protected and private members of a class. A large program example was used to explain the related concepts. Understanding memory management in a programming language is the key to understanding memory allocation and de-allocation of global/static, stack and heap variables. After the discussion of the memory management, we are in a much better position to understand the constructor and destructor of a class. Garbage collection in C++ is done jointly by stack management, destructor and explicit **delete** operations. In section 3.4, we studied the major features of object-oriented programming paradigm, including class inheritance, inheritance-based class hierarchy, polymorphic pointer, virtual functions and late binding that support polymorphic function calls. Again, we used a large example, the **Personnel** hierarchy, to illustrate the concepts and principles we studied in this section. Finally, section 3.5 briefly studied the exceptions in computer systems and how to write exception handlers in C++.

3.7 HOMEWORK, PROGRAMMING EXERCISES, AND PROJECTS

1. Multiple Choice. Choose only one answer in each question. Choose the best answer if more than one answer is acceptable.

1.1 In C++, if class B is derived from class A, then without casting,
   ❏ a pointer to a class A object can point to a class B object.
   ❏ a pointer to class B object can point to a class A object.
   ❏ a pointer to class A object can point to a class B object, and vice versa.
   ❏ a pointer to class A object can NOT point to a class B object, and vice versa.

1.2 If class B is derived from class A, and x is a **protected** member of A, in which classes can x be accessed?
   ❏ Only in A.   ❏ Only in B.   ❏ In A and B.   ❏ None of them.

1.3 A virtual member function in C++
   ❏ is an abstract interface that has no implementation.
   ❏ is an extendable function that allows programmer to add formal parameters to the function.
   ❏ implies early binding between the function name and the code.
   ❏ implies late binding between the function name and the code.

1.4 Type checking during compilation will prevent a base-class pointer from accessing
   ❏ any members of the derived class object.
   ❏ the inherited members of the derived class object.
   ❏ the additional members of the derived class object.
   ❏ public members in the derived class object.

1.5 What part of memory can be de-allocated by the destructor?
   ❏ heap object created in the constructor.   ❏ stack object created in constructor.
   ❏ heap object created in main() function.   ❏ stack object created in main() function.

1.6 What part of memory must be de-allocated by an explicit "delete" operation?
   ❏ heap object created in the constructor   ❏ stack object created in constructor
   ❏ heap object created in main() function   ❏ stack object created in main() function

1.7 If class B is derived from class A, and x is a *protected* member of A, in which classes can x be accessed?
   ❏ Only in A.   ❏ Only in B.   ❏ In A and B.   ❏ None of them.

1.8 If class B is derived from class A, and two pointers p and q are declared by

   A *p; B *q;

   which operation below is valid according to polymorphism?
   ❏ p = q;   ❏ q = p;   ❏ Both of them.   ❏ None of them.

1.9 If a member function in a class **A** is defined as a virtual function, then the member function
- ❏ cannot be defined in class **A**.
- ❏ cannot be re-defined in a derived class.
- ❏ can be re-defined in a derived class.
- ❏ none of them.

1.10 Type checking during compilation will prevent a base-class pointer to access
- ❏ any members of the derived class object.
- ❏ the inherited members of the derived class object.
- ❏ the new (extended) members of the derived class object.
- ❏ public members in the derived class object.

1.11 If the relationship between two classes can be best described as "*is-a*" relation, we should
- ❏ derive one class from the other (use inheritance).
- ❏ contain one class in the other.
- ❏ define them totally independent of each other.
- ❏ none of them.

1.12 The class hierarchy of a C++ program is formed according to the
- ❏ number of data fields in classes.
- ❏ number of member functions in classes.
- ❏ number of public members in classes.
- ❏ inheritance relationship among classes.

1.13 In the C++ exception structure, how many handlers can be defined following each try-block?
- ❏ zero or more.
- ❏ one only.
- ❏ one or more.
- ❏ at most two.

1.14 What is the function of throw statement?
- ❏ exit from try-block and pass a value to a catch-block
- ❏ same as try
- ❏ exit from catch-block and pass a value to the try-block
- ❏ None of them.

Given the C++ class definitions below, answer the following three questions.

```
class employee {char *name; long id; char *department;}
class manager1 {employee empl; short rank;}
class manager2: public employee {short rank;}
```

1.15 What class is defined using containment relationship?
- ❏ manager1
- ❏ manager2
- ❏ both of them
- ❏ none of them

1.16 How does an object **m** of manager1 class access the member **id**?
- ❏ m.id
- ❏ m.empl.id
- ❏ m.empl->id

1.17 How does an object **n** of manager2 class access the member **id**?
- ❏ n.id
- ❏ n.empl.id
- ❏ n.empl->id

2. Given the C++ code below, answer the following questions.

```
class Queue {
private:
    int queue_size;
protected:
    int *buffer; int front; int rear;
```

```
public:
    Queue(int n) {
        front = 0; rear = 0; queue_size = n;
        buffer = new int[queue_size];}
    virtual ~Queue(void) {delete buffer; buffer = NULL;}
    void enqueue(int v) {
        if (rear < queue_size) buffer[rear++] = v;
    }
    int dequeue(void){ // return and remove the 1st element
        if (front < rear)
            return buffer[front++];
    }
}
Queue InitialQueue(100);
void main() {
    Queue *myQueue = new Queue(50);
    myQueue->enqueue(23);
    InitialQueue->enqueue(25);
    delete myQueue;
}
```

2.1   What is the destructor of the Queue class?
       ❏ enqueue(int v)   ❏ dequeue(void)   ❏ Queue(int n)   ❏ ~Queue(void)

2.2   What variable must be destructed (garbage-collected) by the destructor in the Queue class?
       ❏ front   ❏ rear   ❏ queue_size   ❏ *buffer

2.3   Where does the variable (object) InitialQueue obtain memory from?
       ❏ static memory   ❏ stack   ❏ heap   ❏ queue

2.4   Where is the destructor called in the program above?
       ❏ in the constructor   ❏ in the destructor   ❏ in the enqueue function
       ❏ in the dequeue function   ❏ implicitly in delete myQueue;

2.5   Where does the pointer variable myQueue obtain memory from?
       ❏ static memory   ❏ stack   ❏ heap   ❏ queue

2.6   Where does the object pointed to by the pointer variable myQueue obtain memory from?
       ❏ static memory   ❏ stack   ❏ heap   ❏ queue

3.   What are the main differences between imperative paradigm and object-oriented paradigm?

4.   What is the purpose of scope resolution operator?

5.   What is the purpose of a constructor? Can we have more than one constructor?

6.   What is the purpose of a destructor? Can we have more than one destructor? When do we need a destructor?

7.   What are the main differences between **Queue r**, ***s**, where **Queue** is a class? How do we use them? Where do they obtain memory? Which of the following operations are valid?

r = s;

s = r;

s = &r;

r = &s;

r = *s;

s = *r;

8.   In the queue example in section 3.1, an enqueue operation will cause the queue elements to shift to make spaces (compact operation) if the rear pointer is pointing to the end of the queue. This will cause a longer delay than other enqueue operations. To smooth the performance, we can organize the queue into a "cyclic queue", as shown in figure 3.9. In other words, when **rear = n**, we set **rear = 0**, as long as the number of the entries in the queue is less than the queue size (or **front > 0**). Modify the given program to implement the cyclic queue. You can add a variable "entries" in the class to keep track of the number of entries in the queue.

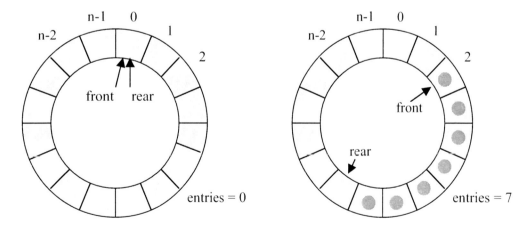

Figure 3.9 A cyclic queue, its initial state and the state with 7 entries

9.   Memory management.

9.1   What is a static variable? What is the difference between a static local variable and a global variable? Do we need to collect the memory allocated to static variables?

9.2   What is the programming language's stack? What variables obtain memory from stack? What mechanism is used to collect the memory allocated from the stack?

9.3   What is the programming language's heap? What variables obtain memory from heap? What mechanism is used to collect the memory allocated from the heap?

9.4   Compare and contrast variables from static memory, stack, and heap. What would happen if we declared a local variable as static local? What would happen if we declared a static local variable as a simple local variable? What would happen if we declared a static local as a global?

10.   What is inheritance? What is the "*is-a*" relation? What is a "*has-a*" relation? When do we use inheritance? What are the advantages of using inheritance?

11.   Consider the contactbook.c program given in question 13 in the section of homework, programming exercises, and projects in chapter two.

11.1 Read the program and try to understand what the program does. Set command line parameter and execute the programming following the instructions given in the question.

11.2   Save contactbook.c as contactclass.cpp (cpp for C++). The executable is then contactclass.exe and the database should be called contactclass.dbms.

11.3   Change the structure definition struct contact to a class definition class contact. All the four data members must be private.

11.4   Write public get- and set- member functions for each of the four data members, so that the data members can be accessed through member functions.

11.5   Write a constructor. The constructor takes three parameters (name, phone, email). The data members name, phone, email must be initialed by the parameter values, e.g. strcpy(this->name, name); The pointer next must be initialized to NULL.

11.6   Change malloc to new and change free(p) to delete p. Make minimum changes to the rest of the program to make the program executable.

11.7   Test the program by inserting five records, displaying all the records, searching for an existing record, searching for an non-existing record, deleting the record in the middle of the linked list, deleting the first and the last records, and displaying the remaining records.

12.   Memory management and garbage collection experiment.
       Close all other applications before you load the following C++ program into Visual Studio C++.

12.1   Build and run the program. It takes a few minutes to complete.

12.2   Modify the program: Call deletion1(); in the main() function, instead of deletion2();

12.3   Modify the program: Call deletion0(); in the main() function, instead of deletion2();

12.4   Explain the differences between deletion0(), deletion1(), and deletion2().

```
/* Warning: This program illustrates memory leak. The program has been tested in Visual C++ 6.0
and Visual Studio .Net on Windows 2000 and XP. Do not run the program on computers with
Windows 98 or older. If you don't see the memory leak problem, you can increase the number of
iterations for i in the main() function. */
#include <iostream>
#include <string.h>
using namespace std;
// forward declaration
int insert(void);
void deletion0(void);
void deletion1(void);
void deletion2(void);
int IDgenerator = 0;          // global variables
class contact {
    private:
            char name[30];
            char phone[20];
            char email[30];
            contact *next;
            int userId;
    public:
            contact() {}
            contact(char* name, char* phone, char* email){
                strcpy(this->name, name);
                strcpy(this->phone, phone);
                strcpy(this->email, email);
                userId = IDgenerator++;
                this->next = NULL;
            }
            contact* getNext() { return next; }
            void setNext(contact* nx) { next = nx; }
} *head = NULL; // declare head pointer as global
int main() {
    int i = 0, j = 0;
    while (i<10000) {
            for (j = 0 ; j<1000; j++) {
                insert();// insert 1 000 records
            }
            deletion2();
// What happens if you call deletion0() or deletion1() here?
            i++;
            cout << i << " - " << IDgenerator << endl;
```

```
            }
            return 0;
        }
    int insert() {
        contact *node;
        char sname[30] = "John", sphone[20] = "1234 567", semail[30] = "john@asu.edu";
        node = new contact(sname, sphone, semail);
                if (node == NULL) {
                        cout << "ERROR - Could not allocate memory !" << endl;
                        return -1;
                }
                node->setNext(head);
                head = node;
                return 0;
    }
    void deletion0() { head = NULL; }
    void deletion1() { delete head; head = NULL; }
    void deletion2() {
        contact *p;
        while (head != NULL) {
                p = head;
                head = head->getNext();
                delete p;
        }
    }
```

13. Complete the **Personnel** hierarchy program in section 3.4 by adding the following classes and functions into the program.

13.1 Add the classes **Student**, **Grad**, **Undergrad**, and **Staff**.

13.2 Add functions **save_file()**, and **load_file()**, so that the records stored in the linked list can be preserved onto the disk before the program quits and the linked list can be reloaded with the entries stored in the disk file when the program is restarted.

13.3 Add a menu item and related functions to delete all nodes in the **PersonnelNode** linked list. Make sure there is no memory leak for all dynamic memory.

13.4 Use C++ exception constructs to define and handle all possible exceptions in the program, for example, out of memory or file operation error exceptions.

13.5 Use **typeid(*ptr)** to identify the type of the object that the pointer **ptr** is pointing to. For example, the following code can be used to determine if the pointer **ptr** is pointing to an object of **Employee** Class.

```
#include<typeinfo>
...
if(typeid(*ptr) == typeid(Employee)) {...}
```

In VS .Net 2003 environment, you must enable the runtime type info setting, in order to use this feature, by following these steps:

Menu: Project->YourProjectName Properties... -> Configuration Properties -> C/C++ -> Language -> Enable Run-Time Type Info: Choose "Yes"

Modify the **display()** function in each class to print the class name of the current object using the **typeid** function.

14.   Define your own heap to replace the system heap used in the question above.

14.1 Declare a large block of memory (e.g., a global array) called **myheap** and use the block of memory as your own heap. Organize the memory as a linked list whose nodes can have different sizes. In each node, use the first word (e.g., an integer of four bytes) to store the size (number of bytes) of the node. Define two system functions

```
void insertion(void *p);
void *deletion(int m);
```

that can insert a new node and remove a node from the linked list (my heap), respectively.

14.2 Define a user function

```
void *GetMem(int n);
```

that takes n bytes of memory from **myheap** and returns the initial address. The function must call the **deletion** function to obtain the memory.

14.3 Define a user function

```
void ReleaseMem(void *p);
```

that returns the memory pointed to by **p** to **myheap**. The function must call the **insertion** function to return the memory.

14.4 Make a copy of the program you wrote. Modify the copy to use **myheap** for the objects of the Student class.

14.5 Test your program by adding and deleting Student nodes.

The Functional Programming Language, Scheme

4

When we moved from the imperative programming paradigm to the object-oriented paradigm, we did not really feel that we had a paradigm shift. Indeed, object-oriented paradigm is based on the imperative paradigm. Some texts categorize imperative and object-oriented paradigms as **procedural paradigm**. However, you will see in this chapter that it is a real paradigm shift when you switch from imperative and object-oriented programming to functional programming.

In this chapter, we will use Scheme as example to study the main features and programming techniques of functional programming languages. By the end of the chapter, you should

- have a good understanding of functional programming paradigm and its major differences with imperative and object-oriented programming paradigms;
- have a good understanding of data types and their operations;
- be able to define procedures and macros;
- understand the relationship between λ-calculus and the functional programming language;
- be able to define and use global and local variables;
- be able to write Scheme programs with multiple procedures;
- have a good understanding of the principles of recursion;
- be able to apply recursive procedures to solve different types of problems;
- understand higher order functions and use order functions to solve recursive problems.

The chapter is organized as follows. We first discuss the main differences between imperative and functional programming paradigms. In section 4.2, we briefly review the prefix notation used in Scheme and other functional programming languages. In section 4.3, we put together the terminology that will be used throughout the chapter. In section 4.4, we study the data types and the predefined Scheme functions that form the Scheme environment on which we can define our own programs. In section 4.5, we discuss the basic syntax and semantics of the general computing system λ-calculus. Scheme and many other programming languages can be simply considered to be an implementation of λ-calculus. From section 4.6, we study the important programming constructs of functional programming languages: named procedure, unnamed procedure, let-form that defines local variables, and the conversion between unnamed procedures and let-forms. We also start to write our own Scheme programs with multiple procedures. In section 4.7, we study the most important programming technique in functional programming languages:

recursion. We discuss structural (white-box) and functional (black-box) approaches of understanding a recursive procedure. We outline simple steps that can guide us to write recursive procedures. In section 4.8, we continue to study recursive procedures on different data types. Finally, in section 4.9, we present the unique feature of functional programming languages: the higher order functions, where they are used, and how they are implemented. A programming environment that supports the development of Scheme programs, DrScheme, is introduced in Appendix B.

4.1 FROM IMPERATIVE PROGRAMMING TO FUNCTIONAL PROGRAMMING

The idea of functional programming is to liberate programming from von Neumann-style (or stored program concept) based imperative programming paradigm. Imperative programming languages are more efficient to implement because they match the currently-used stored program concept-based computer architecture. However, they force programmers' attention to the detail of storing states and modifying states. The major problems of imperative programming paradigms are

- the lack of accurate definition of the semantics;
- the referential use of variables and its side effects;
- requirement of good understanding of computer architecture and memory organization;
- difficult to program the parallel-executable components.

Functional programming paradigm tries to address these problems by focusing on what is wanted rather than how it is implemented. An analogy is to compare ordering a pizza in a restaurant and making your own pizza at home. When you order a pizza, you focus on what you want. When you make your own pizza, you need not only know what you want, but also understand the underlying hardware, for example, at what temperature, how long the pizza needs to be baked, and how to control the temperature and set the timer of the oven.

The major advantages of functional programming paradigm are as follows.

- Higher level of abstraction that needs less attention to the details of the underlying computer architecture.
- Simpler and accurate definition of semantics. It is based on well-founded mathematics and thus easier to reason about.
- Side-effects-free or referential transparency. For example, in an imperative program, $f(x) + f(x)$ may or may not be equal to $2*f(x)$, depending on whether the function modifies any global variables or the parameter x. However, in a functional program, it is guaranteed that $f(x) + f(x)$ is always equal to $2*f(x)$.
- Easier for parallel processing. In functional programs, operations at the same level are independent of each other and can thus be processed in any order or in parallel.
- Powerful higher order functions. You can pass the operation (not only the return value) of another function as the parameter to a function.

Above differences are more at the conceptual level. What are the differences at programming level? That is, what different approaches do we have to take in writing functional programs? Understand that these differences are the main topics of this chapter. The following are an outline of these differences.

- Functional programming languages are not based on the stored program concept. You cannot declare a variable (a memory location) to store a value and later modify the value, or store another value in the same memory location. What you can do is to define a name and associate a value to the name (named value). This name then represents the value, not the container of the value, and thus you can never associate the name to another value nor modify the value. This approach is often considered by imperative programmers as a restriction that brings least convenience in programming. However, this approach is the milestone of the paradigm shift that gets rid of stored program concept of stepwise storing and manipulating data.

■ In functional programming languages, parameter passing is the major mechanism that passes values into a function. Only call-by-value is allowed. Call-by-reference is not allowed. In fact, parameter passing is used to replace most assignment statements in imperative programs.

■ Every function in a functional programming language will return a single value. Since intermediate values cannot be stored in memory and be used later, you must organize your program to use a return value immediately. In other words, a return value must be passed to another function immediately. If you want to return two or more values, you can

● split the function into multiple functions and each function return one value, or

● organize multiple values into a pair (or nested pair) structure, or

● organize multiple values into a list structure.

■ Functions are treated as **first-class** objects. In other words, a function can appear in any place where a value is expected. In this case, the function will be first evaluated, and its return value will be used as the value expected. This mechanism effectively supports immediately passing the return value to another function.

Now let's use an example to illustrate these differences. The following imperative program declares two global variables a and b and two functions foo and main.

```
int a = 5;                          // declare a global variable and initialize it to 5
float b = 2.4;                      // declare a global variable and initialize it to 2.4
float foo(int x, float y) {         // return value type, function name, parameters
    int f1;                         // declare a local variable and initialize it to 0
    float f2;                       // declare a local variable and initialize it to 0
    x = x + 5;                      // modify variable value
    y = y + 10.5;                   // modify variable value
    f1 = abs(x);                    // call a function and assign to return value f1
    f2 = square(y);                 // call a function and assign to return value f2
    f2 = max(f1, f2);               // call a function and assign return value to f2
    return f1 + f2;                 // return
}
void main() {                       // main function does not return any value
    float f;
    f = foo(a, b);                  // function call and parameter passing
    printf("%f\n", f);
}
```

As we can see, the program is written in a way that a typical imperative program is written:

■ stores values in variables;

■ manipulates (modifies) variable values;

■ returns a value.

How do we write a functional program to implement the same function? The following Scheme program does exactly the same job.

```
(define a 5)                            ; name value 5 as a
(define b 2.4)                          ; name value 2.4 as b
(define (foo x y)                       ; function name followed by parameters
    (+      (abs    (+ x 5))            ; the first operand of + is abs function
            (max    (abs (+ x 5))       ; the second operand of + is max function
                    (square (+ y 10.5)) ; the second operand of max is square
            )
    )
)
(print (foo a b)    )                   ; the main function will return a value
```

The syntax of the Scheme program is straightforward: Every operation or expression consists of strictly a list in prefix notation:

(operator operand ... operand)

where, the first element is always the operator, e.g., +, abs, square, max, followed by the list of operands. Each operand can be either a value, or a function that returns a value.

Now you are in a good position to understand the Scheme program. A careful comparison between the two programs will confirm the approaches used in the functional program: no memory is available to store the intermediate values; intermediate values must be passed to another function immediately; every function returns a value; a function can be placed in any place where a value is expected. Having understood these differences, your imperative programming experience could be positively used in writing functional programs.

4.2 PREFIX NOTATION

We can represent mathematical operations and expressions in three different notations: infix, prefix, and postfix. Table 4.1 shows examples of these notations:

Table 4.1 Different representations of mathematical expressions

Infix	Prefix	Prefix with parentheses	Postfix
3 + 4	+ 3 4	(+ 3 4)	3 4 +
(3 + 4) * 5 + 6	+ * + 3 4 5 6	(+ (* (+ 3 4) 5) 6)	3 4 + 5 * 6 +
45 max 29	max 45 29	(max 45 29)	45 29 max

Infix notation was invented in the 1920's by Polish mathematician Jan Lukasiewicz and it is thus also known as Polish notation. The postfix notation is also called Reverse Polish Notation. Although infix notation is easier for humans to use, Scheme language uses prefix notation with parentheses for all expressions. The reasons for this decision are:

- We can consistently use prefix notation to represent unary, binary, and multi-operand operations, for example, unary: (- 3), binary: (+ 3 4), and multi-operand: (max 3 4 5 6 7), while infix notation can only represent binary operations.

- Prefix notation is a parenthesis-free notation. Although parentheses in the expression help to understand the order of evaluation, they are not necessary for prefix notation to define the order of the evaluation. On the other hand, infix notation has to rely on the parentheses to define the order of evaluation.

- Expressions in prefix notation are easier to be executed on a stack-based computer architecture.

A mathematical expression can also be represented as a rooted tree. A **rooted tree** is a directed tree with a unique **root** node, and there is a **path** from the root to any other node. A **directed tree** is a **directed graph** in which there is at most one path between any pair of nodes. The prefix, infix, and postfix notations can be obtained via traversing the tree, which is the process of inspecting the nodes of the tree. There are three common ways of tree traversing: preorder, inorder, and postorder.

Preorder traversing: The root node of a (sub) tree is visited first, its leftmost subtree is then visited, and finally the rightmost tree is visited. Preorder traversing can be applied to any rooted tree.

Inorder traversing: The left subtree is visited first, then the root node of the (sub) tree, and finally, the right subtree is visited. Inorder traversing is defined only for binary trees.

A **binary tree** is a tree in which each node hàs at most two child nodes.

Postorder traversing: Starting from the leftmost subtree, then the rightmost subtree, and finally, the root node. Postorder traversing can be applied to any rooted tree.

Figure 4.1 shows a binary tree representing a mathematical expression with binary operations.

If we traverse the tree in the three orders: prefix, infix and postfix, and print the value of the node when we visit a node, the following expressions will be printed:

Preorder:

*x+*abc

The printed sequence is the prefix notation of the expression represented by the binary tree.

Inorder:

x*a*b + c {infix notation}

The printed sequence is an incorrect infix notation of the expression, because parentheses are necessary in infix notation. We have to apply a more complex algorithm to print the infix notation with correct parentheses. The correct infix notation of the expression represented in the tree should be

(x*(a*b + c))

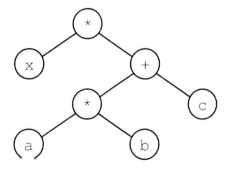

Figure 4.1 Tree representation of a mathematical expression

Postorder:

xab*c+*   {postfix notation}

The printed sequence is the postfix notation of the expression represented by the binary tree.

Note that expressions in prefix and postfix notations are free of parentheses: the order of computation is specified by the sequence of symbols only. They can be calculated easily on a stack-based processor. For example, one simple algorithm of calculating an expression in prefix is as follows:

(1) The expression is scanned (read) from right to left;

(2) If a parenthesis character "(" or ")" is scanned, simply ignore it and continue to scan the next character;

(3) If a variable or a value is scanned, push it onto the stack;

(4) If an operator (a symbol representing an operation) is scanned, the appropriate number (in the example above, the number is 2) of variables is popped out from the stack, and the operation applied to them;

(5) The result of the operation is pushed back onto the stack;

(6) The scan of the expression continued;

(7) After the expression has been completely scanned, the result is the only item left in the stack.

For example, if we evaluate expression (- 5 (+ a b) c)) on a stack-based processor, we start from the right most parenthesis and stop at the left most parenthesis, as shown in figure 4.2.

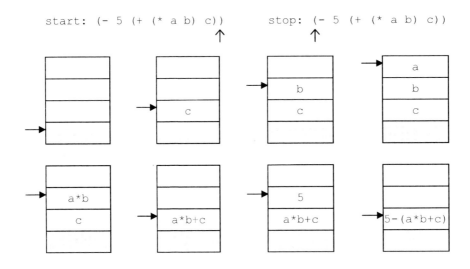

Figure 4.2 Expression processed and the stack maps during processing

The first stack map is the initial stack status. Following the algorithm above, parentheses are ignored and characters c, b, and a are pushed onto the stack (stack map 2 - 4). The operator * is scanned, a and b are popped out, multiplied and pushed back onto the stack (stack map 5). Then the operator + is scanned, the value of "a*b" and c are popped out, added and pushed back onto the stack (stack map 6). Next, 5 is pushed onto the stack (stack map 7), and, finally, operator - is scanned, the value of "a*b+c" and 5 are popped out, subtracted and pushed back onto the stack (stack map 8).

4.3 BASIC SCHEME TERMINOLOGY

This section introduces basic terminology used in this chapter.

Primitive: A primitive is a predefined operation in Scheme. These operations cannot or do not need to be defined in terms of anything simpler. When we use a Scheme environment, we, in fact, use the set of primitives to build our applications. For example, the following operations are examples of the primitives.

```
(+ 3 6)
(<= 2 5)
(sqrt 32)
(number? 45)
(symbol? "x")
(append "abc" "123")
```

In the rest of the chapter, we will see many more of DrScheme's primitives.

Form: Anything that you ask Scheme to evaluate is a **form**. The answer (return value) to a form is the **value** of the form. For example:

```
(+ 3 6)
(+ (* 4 6))
(twoscomplement '(1 0 0 1 1 0))
```

Procedure: Procedure is a user defined new "*primitive operation*" using the keyword *define*. A procedure always returns a value when it is evaluated.

Function: In Scheme, there is no function. The term **function** is only used in its general meaning, say, a mathematical function. A procedure in Scheme has the same meaning as the *function* in C/C++.

Keyword **define**: It is used to create a named form (named constant or **named procedure**). In other words, it associates a form to a name. A complete definition consists of parts: (1) the keyword **define**, (2) the name to be defined, (3) any form that gives a value. For example:

```
(define size 100)            ; named constant
(define x (* 5 6))           ; named operation
(define (add1 x) (+ x 1))    ; named procedure, where x is the parameter
```

Keyword **define-macro**: It is used in the same way as define is used, except that it introduces a macro, instead of a procedure. For example:

```
(define-macro (add1 x) (+ x 1))    ; define a macro, where x is the parameter
```

Keyword **lambda**: It is a keyword used to define an **unnamed procedure**. For example:

(define (add1 x) (+ x 1))	; named procedure, where x is the parameter
((lambda (x) (+ x 1)) 7)	; unnamed procedure performing x+1 = 7+1
((lambda (x y) (+ x y)) 4 5)	; unnamed procedure performing x+y = 4+5

Since unnamed procedure is a form, we can associate an unnamed procedure to a name, thus introducing another way of defining a named procedure as shown in the examples below.

(define (add1 x) (+ x 1))	; define named procedure without using lambda
(define (f x y) (+ x y))	; define named procedure without using lambda
(define add1(lambda (x) (+ x 1)))	; define named procedure using lambda
(define f (lambda (x y) (+ x y)))	; define named procedure using lambda

As we can see from these examples, we can define a named procedure using or without using lambda. The two ways of definition are equivalent.

Parameter: Variables used when we define a procedure. Parameters will be replaced by arguments when they are evaluated.

Argument: The input values that a procedure call needs for performing the evaluation. For example, when we call procedures (add1 x) and (f x y), we must substitute forms or values for the parameters. For example:

(add1 5)	; 5 is the argument. The procedure call will return 6
(f 6 (* 3 7))	; 6 and (* 3 7) are arguments. It will return 27.

Application: It applies an operation to the results of evaluating the other forms. In other words, a primitive applies a simple operation to values that do not need any further evaluation, while application involves nested evaluation, or complex operations like procedure calls or macro calls. For example:

(+ 5 1)	; is a primitive. It applies addition to simple values
(+ (2 3) 1)	; is an application. It involves nested operation.
(add1 5)	; is an application. It calls a procedure.

Figure 4.3 summarizes the terminology introduced and shows the relationship between the components of a Scheme program. Everything we ask Scheme to evaluate is a form. Definitions of a procedure or a macro are not forms, because they do not cause actual evaluation. Only when we use arguments to replace the parameters and call a procedure, it becomes a form, that is, procedure call is a form, not the procedure itself. A form can be a simple primitive, or a complex application.

A mathematical expression can be evaluated in different orders. For example, to evaluate 3 + 4 + (15 / 3), we can have the following orders:

(1) 3 + 4 = 7, 15 / 3 = 5, 7 + 5 = 12, or

(2) 15 / 3 = 5, 4 + 5 = 9, 3 + 9 = 12, or

(3) 15 / 3 = 5, 3 + 4 = 7, 7 + 5 = 12

Generally, there are two main methods that are used to determine the evaluation orders. Assume that an expression has multiple nested operations.

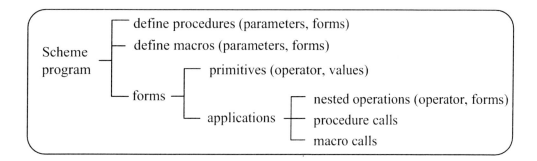

Figure 4.3 Summary of terminology and relationship between the components of a Scheme program

Eager evaluation: It tries to start from innermost operations first. At the same level, operations can be performed in any order. If there is a function with parameters, it always evaluates all parameters first before it attempts to evaluate the function.

Lazy evaluation: It tries to start from outermost operations first. At the same level, operations are performed from left to right sequentially. If there is a function with parameters, it will evaluate a parameter only if its value is needed.

For example, if the Scheme form to be evaluated is

(+ (+ 3 5) (* (+ 4 6) (- 5 3)))

then the eager and lazy evaluations will evaluate the form in the following orders, respectively.

Eager: (+ 4 6), (- 5 3), (+ 3 5), (* 10 2), (+ 8, 20)
Lazy: (+ 3 5), (+ 4 6), (- 5 3), (* 10 2), (+ 8, 20)

The orders of the evaluation for the conditional form (if a b c) are

Eager: a, b, c, if   // both b and c will be evaluated
Lazy: a, if, b; or a, if, c   // only one of b and c will be evaluated

For imperative languages, the order of evaluation must be strictly predefined, because different orders may produce different results. Most imperative languages, including C, C++, and Java, use lazy evaluation. For functional programming languages, the order of evaluation does not matter and thus, the languages do not have to predefine the order. As a result, parallel computing is possible. For example, a multi-processor computer can evaluate the function (if a b c) in two steps: (1) Evaluate a, b, and c simultaneously; (2) Choose the result from b or c according to the result of a. On the other hand, a multi-processor computer cannot speedup the evaluation of (if a b c) in an imperative language. It has to evaluate the function in three steps: (1) Evaluate a; (2) Choose to evaluate b or c according to the result of a; (3) evaluate b or c.

4.4 BASIC SCHEME DATA TYPES AND FUNCTIONS

This section introduces basic data types and primitive Scheme functions. The available primitive functions depend on the programming environment and the version of the environment. Our discussion is mainly based on DrScheme environment. Not all functions listed in this section will be explained here. Some of them will be explained in the later sections when we use these functions to define more complex functions.

A **data type** is defined by the range of the values and the operations defined in these values. Basic Scheme data types include number, boolean, character, string, symbol, pair, and list. This subsection will briefly introduce these data types and basic operations defined on these data types.

4.4.1 NUMBER

Different types of **number**s are included in this type: long, short, integer, float, and double, all belong to this type, e.g., 2, -5, 1.03, 2/5, 2.5e-3 are all numbers. Because numbers are represented internally as list, not stored in a "memory location", there is theoretically no limit on the length of the numbers. For example, there is no overflow when we compute very large numbers like 100! or (factorial 100). Within the number type, we can still differentiate integer and real. An incomplete set of operations defined on number type is listed in table 4.1.

Table 4.1 Operations defined on number type

Accessor functions	Meaning	Predicate functions	Meaning
(+ <num> ... <num>)	addition	(number? <num>)	Is it a number?
(- <num> ... <num>)	subtraction	(integer? <num>)	Is it an integer?
(* <num> ... <num>)	multiplication	(real? <num>)	Is it a real number?
(/ <num> ... <num>)	division	(negative? <num>)	Is it negative?
(- <number>)	negate	(positive? <num>)	Is it positive?
(add1 <num>)	add one	(even? <num>)	Is it even?
(sub1 <num>)	subtract one	(odd? <num>)	Is it odd?
(quotient <int> <int>)	quotient	(zero? <num>)	Is it zero?
(remainder <int> <int>)	remainder	(= <num> ... <num>)	Are they equal?
(round <num>)	round to nearest		
(truncate <num>)	integer part		
(abs <num>)	absolute value		
(sqrt <num>)	square root		
(expt x y)	returns x^y		
(max <num> ... <num>)	maximum		
(min <num> ... <num>)	minimum		
(random <int>)	random number between 0 & <int>		

4.4.2 BOOLEAN

Boolean is a simple type with two possible values: #t (true) or #f (false). An incomplete set of operations defined on boolean type is given in table 4.2.

Table 4.2 Operations defined on boolean type

Accessor functions	Meaning	Predicate functions	Meaning
(and <expr> ... <expr>) (or <expr> ... <expr>) (not <expr>)	logical and logical or logical not	(eq? <bool> <bool>)	Are they equal? Example: (define x #t) (define y #f) (eq? x y)

Boolean type variables can be used in conditional statements like

(if c a b)

In the conditional form, if the value of c is #t, the form returns a, otherwise, returns b. For example,

(if (= x 0) (+ a1 a2) (- b1 b2)))

the conditional form will evaluate (+ a1 a2) if (= x 0) is true, otherwise, it will evaluate (- b1 b2).
Another conditional form is the multiple conditional form cond:

(cond (c1 e1) (c2 e2) ... (cn en) (else ex))

In this form, the conditions c1, c2, ..., cn will be evaluated sequentially. When ci, i = 1, 2, ..., n, evaluates to #t, the corresponding expression ei will be evaluated. If all c1, c2, ..., cn evaluate to #f, the expression ex in the else part will be executed. If the else part is missing, no action will be taken.
The following example defines a procedure that converts a numerical grade into a symbolic grade.

```
(define grade (lambda(n)
    (cond   ((>= n 90) 'a)
            ((>= n 80) 'b)
            ((>= n 70) 'c)
            ((>= n 60) 'd)
            (else 'f)
    )
))
(grade 89)          ; procedure call, will return b
(grade 55)          ; procedure call, will return f
```

4.4.3 CHARACTER

The data values of **character type** are the set of ASCII characters. A complete set of ASCII characters is given in the Appendix C. An incomplete set of operations defined on character type is given in table 4.3. The comparisons between two characters are based on their integer values in the ASCII table.
To differentiate a character from other similar values of other types, e.g., number, symbol, or string, we use #\5 for character 5, #\A for upper case A, #\b for lower case b, and #\space for the character space.

Table 4.3 Operations defined on character type

Accessor functions	Meaning	Predicate functions	Meaning
(char->integer <char>) (integer->char <int>)	convert to int convert to char	(char? <expr>) (char-alphabetic? <expr>) (char=? <char> <char>) (char<? <char> <char>) (char>? <char> <char>) (char-ci=? <char> <char>)	Is it a character? Is it an alphabetic? Are they equal? Is char < char? Is char > char? case insensitive comparison

According to ASCII table, we can find the integral value of a character, or find the character for a given integer:

```
(char->integer #\A)        ; will return 65
(char->integer #\C)        ; will return 67
(char->integer #\5)        ; will return 53
(integer->char 97)         ; will return #\a
(integer->char 36)         ; will return #\$
(integer->char 57)         ; will return #\9
```

The comparison between characters is also based on their integral values. For example:

```
(char<? #\A #\a)           ; will return #t because 65 < 97
(char>? #\$ #\9)           ; will return #f because 57 > 36
```

4.4.4 STRING

A **string** is a sequence of characters in a pair of double quotation marks. For example, "hello world" is a string with length 11 (there are 11 characters in the string). An incomplete set of operations defined on string type is given in table 4.4.

A string can be indexed and the first character (leftmost) of a string has the index 0. Thus, the following two forms

```
(string-ref "hello world" 0)
(string-ref "hello world" 6)
```

will return characters #\h and #\w, respectively.

Table 4.4 Operations defined on string type

Accessor functions	Meaning	Predicate functions	Meaning
(string <char>)	convert char to string	(string? <str>)	Is it a string?
(string->symbol <str>)	convert string to symbol		
(symbol->string <sym>)	convert symbol to string	(string=?	Are they equal?
(string->number <str>)	convert string to number	<str> <str>)	
(number->string <num>)	convert number to string		
(string-length <str>)	get string length	(string-ci=?	Are they case-
(string-append <str> <str>)	append two strings	<str> <str>)	insensitively
(string-ref <str> <i>)	get char at position i		equal?
(substring <str> <i> <j>)	get substring between i and j		

4.4.5 SYMBOL

A **symbol** is a name prefixed with a single quote, e.g., 'James and '2t3w are symbols. Unlike a string, a symbol cannot contain a space. A space marks the end of a symbol. Literal values of number, boolean, character, and string cannot be a symbol. The quote prefixed to them will be simply ignored. For example, (+ '2 4) is same as (+ 2 4) and will return 6; (string-length '"hello") is same as (string-length "hello") and will return 5. An incomplete set of operations defined on symbol type is given in table 4.5.

Table 4.5 Operations defined on symbol type

Accessor functions	Meaning	Predicate functions	Meaning
(quote x)	same as 'x	(symbol? <sym>)	Is it a symbol?
(string->symbol <str>)	convert char to string		
(symbol->string <sym>)	convert string to symbol	(eq? <sym> <sym>)	Are they equal?

Please note that symbols are case-insensitive, that is 'A and 'a are considered to be the same symbol. The form (eq? 'ABC 'abc) will thus return true.

4.4.6 PAIR

Pair is a structured data type in Scheme. A pair is denoted by '(x . y), where x and y can be any literal values of any data type.

An incomplete set of operations defined on pair type is given in table 4.6.

Table 4.6 Operations defined on pair type

Accessor functions	Meaning	Predicate functions	Meaning
(cons <expr> <expr>)	form a new pair	(pair? <expr>)	Is it a pair?
(car <pair>)	return first element		
(cdr <pair>)	return second element	(equal? <pair> <pair>)	Are they equal?

The acronyms **car** and **cdr** originally meant "Contents of Address portion of Register" and "Contents of Decrement portion of Register", which are the first part and second part of a register in IBM 704 machine.

The following piece of code illustrates the pair-based functions and their return values.

(cons 1 2)	; will return a pair (1 . 2)
(cons 4 8)	; will return a pair (4 . 8)
(cons 1 (cons 4 8))	; will return a pair (1 . (4 . 8))
(car '(4 . 8))	; will return the first element that is 4
(cdr '(4 . 8))	; will return the second element that is 8
(car (cdr '(1 . (4 . 8))))	; will return 4
(pair? '((4 . 8) . 9))	; will return #t (true)

In the piece of code, we see nested pairs like '(1 . (4 . 8)) and '((4 . 8) . 9). In fact, we can nest any level of pairs to produce a very complex structure, for example, the following two forms

(cons (cons 2 (cons 8 7)) (cons 4 8))

(cons 12 (cons 2 (cons 8 (cons 4 (cons 3 7)))))

will produce the following pairs:

((2 . (8 . 7)) . (4 . 8))

(12 . (2 . (8 . (4 . (3 . 7)))))

To reduce the complex appearances of nested pairs, Scheme allows us to apply the following **pair simplification rule** to simplify the notation of pairs:

A dot and the left-parenthesis to the right of the dot can be omitted, if the item to the right of the dot is a pair. After the left-parenthesis is removed, that corresponding right-parenthesis must be removed.

For example, in the following pairs:

((2 . (8 . 7)) . (4 . 8))

(12 . (2 . (8 . (4 . (3 . 7)))))

The dots and parentheses that can be removed according to the rule are underlined. After the removal, the pairs become:

((2 8 . 7) 4 . 8)

(12 2 8 4 3 . 7)

DrScheme uses the simplified pair notation for any outputs of the pairs. However, you can use the simplified pair notation or the complete pair notation when you use pair in your program.

4.4.7 List

Although pairs are capable of representing collections of data, lists, which are almost special cases of pairs, will be more convenient in many situations.

Using BNF notation, a **list** can be recursively defined as follows:

<list> ::= null | '()

<list> ::= (cons x <list>), where x can be any Scheme form.

The recursive definition starts with the definition of an empty list, which can be represented as null or '(). The recursive part defines a new list based on an existing list: (cons x <list>) produces a new list, where operator cons is the same operator used to produce a new pair and x can be any Scheme form. Since lists, except the empty list '(), are constructed by the pair construction operator cons, all lists, except the empty list '(), are in fact pairs.

Based on the definition of lists, we can create the following lists.

'()	; is a list. It is the empty list.
(cons 4 '( ))	; returns list (4 . ())
(cons 7 '(4 . ()))	; returns list (7 . (4 . ())) = (7 4 . ())
(cons 9 '(7 4 . ()))	; returns list (9 . (7 4 . ())) = (9 7 4 . ())

According to the simplification rule of pair representation, the pair (7 . (4 . ())) can be simplified to (7 4 . ()) and pair (9 . (7 4 . ())) can be simplified to (9 7 4 . '()). Now the question is, can we simplify the pair (4 . ()) to the pair (4)? The answer is "no" according to the pair simplification rule, because the empty list is not at all a pair. However, we can introduce another **list simplification rule** to simplify the list notation:

In a list, if to the right of a dot is an empty list, then the dot and the pair of parentheses representing the empty list can be omitted.

By applying this list simplification rule, the list (4 . ()) is simplified to (4), (7 4 . ()) is simplified to (7 4), and (9 7 4 . ()) is simplified to (9 7 4).

An incomplete set of operations defined on list type is given in table 4.7.

Table 4.7 Operations defined on list type

Accessor functions	Meaning	Predicate functions	Meaning
(cons <expr> <list>)	form a new pair	(list? <expr>)	Is it a pair?
(car <list>)	return first element	(null? <list>)	Is list empty?
(cdr <list>)	return sub-list without the first element	(member x <list>	Is x a member of list?
(list <expr> ... <expr>)	return (<expr> ... <expr>)	(equal? <list> <list>)	Are they equal?
(append <list> <list>)	append two list into one		
(length <list>)	return the length if list		
(list-ref <list> <p>)	return the element at position p		
(list-tail <list> <k>)	return the list after removal of the first k elements		

Please note that accessor functions **car** and **cdr** in the table 4.7 are the same operations for pairs. They work for a list, if and only if the list is a pair. The only situation where a list is not a pair is when the list is an empty list. For all non-empty lists, **car** and **cdr** will work. When car and cdr are applied to list, (car x) will return the first element of the pair, which is the first element in the list. Similarly,(cdr x) will return the second element of the pair, which is the residual list when the first element is taken out.

4.4.8 QUOTES

We have seen that we use quotes in symbols, pairs, and lists, for example:

```
(symbol->string 'James)     ; the symbol must be quoted
(cdr (car '((2 . 4) . 5)))     ; the pair must be quoted at the outermost level
(cons '(2 (5 . 6) 9) '(3 7))   ; the list must be quoted at the outermost level
```

It is clear that we need to quote a symbol. But it is not so straightforward why and when we need to quote pairs and lists. As we can see from the example above, we only quote the outermost level of a pair or a list. Can we also quote the pairs or lists inside a pair or a list? Let's first see the following example:

```
(cdr (car '((2 . 4) . 5)))     ; only quote the outermost level
(cdr (car '('(2 . 4) . 5)))    ; quote the inner pair too
```

What is the difference between these forms? To see the difference, we must understand the way Scheme forms are evaluated.

Scheme uses the prefix notation. Every form to be evaluated starts with a left-parenthesis. The first element, or the element that immediately follows the left-parenthesis is always the operator. The operator will be compared with the operators stored in the operator-table. When a match is found, Scheme will perform the operation defined for the operator.

A list and a pair also start with a left-parenthesis. To let the language know that lists and pairs are not forms for evaluation and that their first elements should not be considered to be an operator, we use a quote prior to the left-parenthesis. When Scheme sees a quote and a left-parenthesis, it knows that the parenthesis does not start a form, but start a pair or a list. Scheme will then find the corresponding right-parenthesis to identify the end of the pair or the list. Obviously, it won't have any operators within a literal list or pair. Thus, there is no need to quote any list or pair within a list or a pair. Some version of Scheme will report an error if you quote a list or a pair within a list or a pair. The DrScheme will consider the quote character ' to be a separate element and thus

```
(cdr (car '('(2 . 4) . 5)))
(car (car '('(2 . 4) . 5)))
```

will return rather unexpected results:

```
(2 . 4)
quote
```

According to the orthogonality, if we are allowed to quote literals of pair and list, we should be allowed to quote other types' literals. Scheme indeed allows you to quote literals of any types. For example, you can write '55 (quote number literal), '#t (quote boolean literal), '"hello" (quote string literal). In these cases, Scheme will simply ignore the quotes. Note that a literal value of any type cannot be a symbol!

In summary, what can or must be quoted? What cannot or should not be quoted?

- You can quote a name to make it a symbol.
- You must quote pair and list literals at the outermost level to differentiate them from forms to be evaluated.
- You must not quote pairs or lists within a pair or a list.
- You must not quote forms that you want to evaluate. If you quote a form, the form simply becomes a list. The operator in the first place will be considered the first element of the list.
- You may quote number, string and boolean literals, but it makes no difference. Thus, do not quote them.

4.4.9 DEFINITION OF PROCEDURE AND PROCEDURE TYPE

Procedures are user-defined functions that extend the predefined primitives in the language system. The set of procedures can be considered to form a special data type: the **procedure type**. The data values of the procedure type are all possible procedures. The operations defined on the procedure type are the higher-order functions. A **higher-order function**, or **higher-order procedure**, is a procedure that can take the operation of another procedure as its parameter. Please note that a procedure that takes the return value of another procedure is not a higher-order procedure. In functional programming languages, functions (procedures) are first class objects. A procedure can be put in any place where a value is expected and the procedure's return value will be used as the value that is expected. Thus, every procedure in Scheme that has a parameter can take the return value of another procedure. The higher-order procedure must take the operation of another procedure as parameter. Higher-order procedures will be discussed later in the chapter.

The syntax graph of procedure definition is given in figure 4.4.

Using the syntax, we can define a procedure as follows.

```
(define maximum (lambda (x y)
    (if    (> x y)
           x
           y
    )
))
```

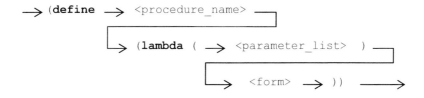

Figure 4.4 Syntax graph of procedure definition

The definition uses two keywords: define and lambda. There is a simplified definition that uses only one keyword. The syntax graph of the alternative procedure definition is given in figure 4.5.

Figure 4.5 Syntax graph of the simplified procedure definition

Using the simplified definition, the maximum procedure can be defined by

```
(define (maximum x y)
    (if     (> x y)
        x
        y
    )
)
```

We will use the two ways of definitions interchangeably in the text.

4.4.10 INPUT/OUTPUT AND NON-FUNCTIONAL FEATURES

Scheme has a simple input and output mechanism. The form (read) will wait for keyboard input and returns the input value. The inputted value will be interpreted as a symbol. You can convert the symbol to other types as required.

Output can be done by any one of these forms:

```
(display 3)
(write 3)
(print 3)
```

None of these forms print on a new line. You can use form (newline) to change to a new line.

The following Scheme program reads a symbol, converts it to a string, appends a space at the end, reads another symbol, converts it to string, and appends it to the first string. Finally, the string with a space is displayed.

```
(display
    (string-append
        (string-append (symbol->string (read)) " ")
            (symbol->string (read))
    )
)
```

The following is a more complex example that uses input and output. In this example, we implement the menu function and the branching function we implemented in C/C++.

The menu function takes input from the keyboard, and compares the entered selection with existing options. If a match is found, the program branches to the corresponding function.

```scheme
(define menu (lambda ()     ; no parameter
    (begin
            (newline) (newline)       ; print two newlines
            (display "enter your selection") (newline)
            (display "i: insert a new entry") (newline)
            (display "s: search an entry") (newline)
            (display "d: delete an entry") (newline)
            (display "p: print all entries") (newline)
            (display "q: quit") (newline)
            (let((c (read)))   ; read a symbol from keyboard and assign it to c
                    (if    (eq? c 'q)
                    (display "END.")
                    (begin
                            (branching c)          ; call branching below
                            (menu)                 ; recursive call to itself
                    )
                )
            )
        )
))
(define branching (lambda (sel)
    (begin
        (cond
                ((eq? sel 'i) (display "inserted ..."))
                ((eq? sel 's) (display "searched ..."))
                ((eq? sel 'd) (display "deleted ..."))
                ((eq? sel 'p) (display "printed ..."))
                (else (display "invalid input ..."))
        )
    )
))
(menu)
```

There are several forms in the program that we haven't discussed:

```scheme
(let (      (name value))
            body
)
```

The let-form assigns the **value** to the **name**, and then executes the **body** part of the code. The let-form will be discussed later in more detail.

In the procedure (**menu**), (**menu**) itself is called. A procedure that calls itself is a **recursive procedure**. Loops are features of imperative languages. Functional programming languages mainly use recursion to implement the functions of loops. Many more recursive procedures will be discussed in the rest of the chapter.

Now let's discuss some of the non-functional features in the program. The form

```
(begin
    form1
    ...
    formn
)
```

allows sequential execution of a sequence of independent forms. Sequential execution is really a feature of imperative programming paradigm. As you can see, Scheme does have some imperative features that make programming easier.

Another imperative feature is that the form (display x) does not return a value. For example, if you execute:

```
(+ (display 5) 7)
```

and expects the form returns 12, you will receive an error message instead:

```
Error: addition expects type <number> as 1st argument
```

The reason is that (display 5) only prints 5 on the screen, but it does not return any value.

However, we can define a function that performs output and returns a value, as shown in the following procedure definition.

```
(define writeln (lambda(x)
    (begin
            (display x)
            (newline)
            x
    )
))
```

For example, if we call the procedure:

```
(+ (writeln 5) 4)
```

it will print 5, and then pass the value 5 to the next form that adds it to 4 and returns 9.

Please note that in the implementation of the **writeln** procedure, we used the non-functional feature of sequential execution quoted by (**begin** ...) form.

*4.5 LAMBDA-CALCULUS

The λ-calculus (lambda-calculus) is a formal mathematical system devised by Alonzo Church in 1934 to investigate universal computing models, functions, function application, and recursion. It has influenced many computing systems and programming languages, especially the functional programming languages. Lisp was the first programming language based on λ-calculus. Scheme (a dialect of List), Haskell, Miranda, SML, and ML are more recent functional programming languages based on the mathematical system.

The λ-calculus is analogous to Turing machines. However, λ-calculus is much easier to understand and much simpler to use. Turing machines can be considered the most basic assembly language based on the simplest 1-bit computer architecture, whereas λ-calculus is a super high-level language that can be conveniently learned and applied to solve various kinds of complex problems.

In this section, we briefly discuss the structure (lexical, syntactic and semantic) of λ-calculus, so that we can better understand the Scheme programming language that is based on λ-calculus. You will shortly see that Scheme language is strictly based on λ-calculus. If you know λ-calculus, you know how to write Scheme programs.

4.5.1 LAMBDA-EXPRESSIONS

The structure of the λ-calculus is short and simple. At the lexical level, there are only three lexical units: λ, the parentheses "(" and ")", and an infinite list of variables (names), e.g., a, b, a1, a2, ... etc.

At the syntactic level, a λ-expression is a finite combination of lexical units and variables. Using BNF notation, a simplified λ-expression can be defined by

λ-expression ::=   <constant> | <variable> | <expression>

                     | λ<variable>(< λ-expression>)

                     | (<λ-expression> <λ-expression>)

In the definition, **constant** is a value of any data type. The definitions of the **variable (identifier)** and the **expression** have been discussed in chapter one. According to the definitions, the following expressions are λ-expressions.

5	; a constant is λ-expression
x	; a variable is λ-expression
x+y	; an expression is λ-expression
λx(x+y)	; λ<variable>(< λ-expression>) is λ-expression
λx(x+y) 5	; (<λ-expression> <λ-expression>) is λ-expression

4.5.2 λ-PROCEDURE AND PARAMETER SCOPE

One of the λ-expressions, λ<variable><λ-expression>, is called a λ-**procedure**. The variable prefixed by λ is called the **parameter** of the procedure and the λ-expression follows the parameter is called the **body** of the procedure. The **scope** of the parameter is body of the λ-procedure. For example, if we have a λ-expression

λx(x+y) (x+3)

the scope of the parameter x in λx is in and only in the body (x+y). It does not cover the x in (x+3).

An occurrence of a variable x in a λ-expression is **bound** if it is within the scope of a parameter in λx. An occurrence of a variable x in a λ-expression is **free** if it is not within the scope of a parameter in λx. An occurrence of a parameter x binds all free occurrences of x within its scope.

Given the following λ-expression

λx(+ (/ λx(* x 2) 8 λx(- x 1) 5) (* λx(+ x 2) 3 x)) 7

How many λ-procedures are contained in the λ-expression? What are the scopes of different parameters?

Each λx corresponds to a λ-procedure, and, thus, the λ-expression contains four λ-procedures. The scope of each parameter is underlined in the following expression.

λ<u>x</u>(+ (/ λ<u>x(* x 2)</u> 8 λ<u>x(- x 1) 5</u>) (* λ<u>x(+ x 2) 3 x</u>)) <u>7</u>

In the next subsection, we will discuss reduction rules that evaluate such complex expressions to a simple value, or the return value of the expression.

4.5.3 REDUCTION RULES

The process of evaluating a λ-expression is called a **reduction**. We will briefly discuss three reduction rules that transform a λ-expression into a simpler λ-expression. They are alpha (α) reduction, beta (β) reduction, and eta (η) reduction. Repeatedly applying these reduction rules transforms a λ-expression to a simple value, which is the return value of the expression. The reduction rules define the semantics of λ-calculus.

(1) The alpha (α) reduction

λx(E)   ⇔   λy([y/x]E)

The α-reduction rule says that for a λ-expression with a parameter x, we can substitute y for parameter x and all the occurrences of x in its scope.

The α-reduction rule allows us to freely choose and change parameter names for convenience.

For example, in the following expression, different parameters have the same name.

λx(+ (/ λx(* x 2) 8 λx(- x 1) 5) (* λx(+ x 2) 3 x)) 7

Although the expression is not ambiguous for the computer that evaluates it, it is simply easier for humans to understand if we choose different names for different parameters. Thus, we can apply α-reduction rule to rename the parameters in the λ-expression as follows.

λx1(+ (/ λx2(* x2 2) 8 λx3(- x3 1) 5) (* λx4(+ x4 2) 3 x1)) 7

(2) The beta (β) reduction

λx(E1) E2   ⇔   [E2/x]E1

The β-reduction rule says that we can remove the parameter x for E1 if we substitute the λ-expression E2 for all the occurrences of x in E1. λ-expression E2 is called argument to the λ-procedure λx(E1).

The β-reduction rule defines how to perform parameter passing in a λ-procedure to reduce the complexity of an λ-expression that contains λ-procedures.

Now let's repeatedly apply the β-reduction rule to the following λ-expression:

λ<u>x1</u>(+ (/ λx2(* x2 2) 8 λx3(- x3 1) 5) (* λx4(+ x4 2) 3 x1)) <u>7</u>

We assume we use lazy evaluation, that is, we proceed from outermost first (underlined part). Thus, the first step is to substitute argument 7 for **x1**, resulting in the following simplified λ-expression:

(+ (/ λx2(* x2 2) 8 λx3(- x3 1) 5) (* λx4(+ x4 2) 3 7))

Then the three λ-procedures are at the same level and we substitute their arguments for their parameters, respectively:

$$(+ (/ \ \underline{(*\ 8\ 2)} \ λx3(-\ x3\ 1)\ 5)) \ (*\ λx4(+\ x4\ 2)\ 3\ 7))$$

$\Rightarrow$ (+ (/ (* 8 2) <u>(- 5 1)</u>) (* λx4(+ x4 2) 3 7))

$\Rightarrow$ (+ (/ (* 8 2) (- 5 1)) (* <u>(+ 3 2) 7)</u>)

$\Rightarrow$ (+ (/ 16 4) (* 5 7))

$\Rightarrow$ (+ 4 35)

$\Rightarrow$ 39

Having completed the parameter passing, the λ-expression has become a simple mathematical expression that can be easily evaluated to 39.

(3) The eta (η) reduction

λx(E) $\Leftrightarrow$ E, if x does not appear in E.

For example, assume we have a λ-expression:

λx1(* λx2(+ x2 2) 3)

Parameter **x1** does not appear in the λ-expression in **x1**'s scope, we can then remove λx1 according to η-reduction. In words, η-reduction says that, if a parameter is not used in a procedure, it should be removed from the parameter list.

In fact, in beta reduction we have implicitly applied η-reduction: after we substitute the argument for the parameter **x**, there are no longer appearances of **x** in the expression and thus λx is removed.

4.6 DEFINE YOUR SCHEME PROCEDURES AND MACROS

Now we come back to Scheme. In this section we will discuss definition of procedures, scope of parameters, global, and local variable. We will also discuss the macro that is related to procedure.

4.6.1 UNNAMED PROCEDURES

Having studied λ-expressions, it is easy to write Scheme procedures and understand how procedures are evaluated. Let's consider the λ-expression:

λx(+ (/ λx(* x 2) 8 λx(- x 1) 5) (* λx(+ x 2) 3 x)) 7

To write a Scheme procedure that is equivalent to the expression, all we need to do is to use the Scheme keyword "lambda" to replace "λ" and add necessary parentheses. Thus we have

lambda x(+ (/lambda x(* x 2) 8 lambda x(- x 1) 5) (* lambda x(+ x 2) 3 x)) 7

After adding necessary parentheses we have a proper Scheme procedure that evaluates to 39.

```
((lambda (x)
    (+      (/      ((lambda (x)(* x 2)) 8)
                    ((lambda (x)(- x 1)) 5))
            (*      ((lambda (x)(+ x 2)) 3) x)
    )
 )
 7
 )
```

There are four procedures in code above. None of them are given a name. Such procedures are called **unnamed procedures**.

4.6.2 NAMED PROCEDURES

The problem with the unnamed procedures is that we cannot call the procedure multiple times to obtain the advantage of code reuse. Embedding one procedure in another procedure may compromise the readability of the code. The solution to these problems is to name the procedures and use the names to call the procedures. A **named procedure** is defined by using the keyword "define" to associate an unnamed procedure to a name. Using named procedures, we can rewrite the code as follows:

```
(define foo1 (lambda (x)(* x 2)))
(define foo2 (lambda (x)(- x 1)))
(define foo3 (lambda (x)(+ x 2)))
(define bar (lambda (x)
    (+      (/ (foo1 8) (foo2 5))
            (* (foo3 3) x))
))
(bar 7)
```

4.6.3 SCOPES OF VARIABLES AND PROCEDURES

In Scheme, any names defined by the keyword "define" are global. For example,

```
(define size 100)
(define foo (lambda (x)(* x 2)))
(define bar (lambda (x) ( ... ))
(define writeln (lambda (x) ( ... ))
```

A global name can be accessed in the entire program. For example, the value of global variable size can be used in any other procedures. Please note that, although we call size a variable, it is not a memory location that we can reassign a value to it. It is really a named value that we can use but cannot change.

As we have seen, a parameter of a procedure is local. Its scope is only within the body of the procedure. For example, the three procedures foo, bar, and writeln use the same parameter name, but they have different scope and thus won't cause name conflict. Now the question is, can we define a local variable?

Scheme offers a **let-form** to accommodate the needs of local variables. The syntax graph of let-form is given in figure 4.6.

A let-form consists of a list of (<name> <form>) pairs and a body part. In each pair, the name is associated to the form. The body is any form. For example:

(let ((a 3) (b 4)) (+ (* a a) (* 2 a b) (* b b)))

In this let-form, a is associated with 3, b is associated with 4. The body is the form:

(+ (* a a) (* 2 a b) (* b b))

The names defined by a let-form are called **local variables**. The scope of the local variables in the let-form is only within the body part of the form. It is different from imperative languages where the scope of a variable is from the declaration to the end of the block. Let's see the difference by the example below.

```
(let       ((x 5)
              (y (* x 4)))
     (+ x y)
)
```

What is the return value of the form? It is not 25, but the following error:

reference to undefined identifier: x

The problem is in the second local variable where we try to associate y to (* x 4). However, the scope of x does not start from the declaration (association). Its scope is only in the body part of the let-form. Thus, it is undefined.

To accommodate the expectation of some imperative programmers, some Scheme version added the let*-form to allow the scope of local variables to start from its association. Thus,

```
(let*      ((x 5)
              (y (* x 4)))
     (+ x y)
)
```

will return 25 as imperative programmers expected.

To build larger programs, a Scheme program can be divided into modules and further limit the scopes of global variables and procedures within a module. Names can be made visible outside a module using the **export** form. The following example shows the definition of a Scheme module and the export form.

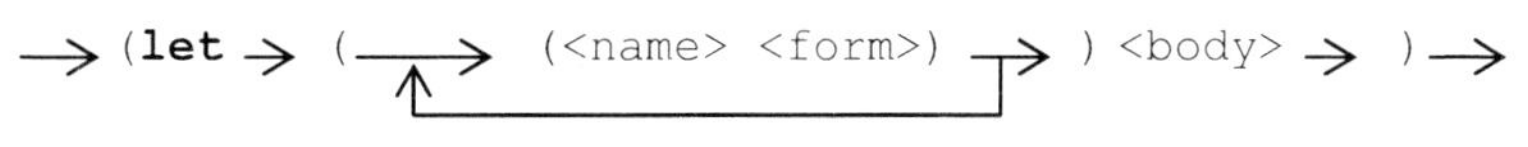

Figure 4.6 Syntax graph of let-form

```
(module module-name
    (export name1 name3 name5 … namen)          ; names visible outside the module
    (define name1 value1)                        ; define a global variable
    (define name2 (lambda (x) (…)))              ; define a global procedure
    (define name3 …)

    …
)
```

In the module definition, names **name1 name3 name5**, … are accessible outside the module, while names **name2 name4**, … are not accessible outside the module.

Now let's consider a secure email system that consists of several modules. In the encryption module, only the procedure string-encryption is exported and accessible from the outside.

```
(module encryption
    (export string-encryption)                              ; outside accessible
    (define character-rotation (lambda (ch)
    (define character-encryption (lambda (ch) (...)))
    (define string-encryption (lambda (str) (…)))
    (define encryption-helper (…))
    ( … )
)
```

Then, in another module, say, secure-email, the **string-encryption** can be called, as shown below.

```
(module secure-email
    (define load_file (lambda (str filename) (...)
    (string-encryption (load_file (str filetext)))

    …
)
```

4.6.4 Let-Form and Unnamed Procedure

Let-forms and unnamed procedures are, in fact, equivalent: they can be converted from one to the other. The general format of let-forms is

```
(let
    (        (name1  value1)
             (name2  value2)

             . . .

             (namen  valuen)
    )
    body
)
```

It can be mechanically translated into the unnamed procedure:

```
((lambda (name1 name2 ... namen)
    body)
    value1 value2 ... valuen)
```

For example, the let-form

```
(let
    (       (a 3)
            (b 4)
    )
    (+ (* a a) (* 2 a b) (* b b))
)
```

can be translated into the following unnamed procedure:

```
(   (lambda (a b)
    (+ (* a a) (* 2 a b) (* b b))
    )
    3 4
)
```

Now let's examine the let-form with incorrect scope

```
(let        ((x 5)
            (y (* x 4)))
    (+ x y)
)
```

If we translate it into unnamed procedure, we have

```
(   (lambda (x y)
    (+ x y)
    )
    5 (* x 4)              ; this x is unbound
)
```

From the unnamed procedure, we can see more clearly that the variable x in the argument (* x 4) is not initialized.

4.6.5 MACROS

Macros in Scheme have the same meaning as macros in other programming languages like C and C++. Macro introduces a name substitution instead of a control flow change.

The definition of Scheme macros is similar to the definition of procedures. All you need to do is to change the keyword **define** to the keyword **define-macro**.

The following definition defines a macro that computes the cube (the third power) of a number.

```
(define-macro cube (lambda (x) (* x x x)))
```

If we call the macro by (cube 5), it returns 125. It looks like that the macro works exactly like a procedure.

Now let's consider another use of the same macro in the following program:

```
(define i 5)
(cube i)                ; to be replaced by (* 'i 'i 'i)
```

If cube is defined as a procedure, the code should work fine. However, cube is defined as a macro. When we execute the code, we have the following error message:

```
expects type <number> as 1st argument, given: i;
```

To understand why this error happens, we need to review the idea of macro: name substitution instead of a control flow change. Before we call (cube i), the call has been replaced by the body of the macro definition, thus, what we really execute is:

```
(* 'i 'i 'i)
```

The system is smart enough to consider the first name is an operator and thus not consider it as symbol. Thus, what the macro is trying to do is to multiply three symbols.

Why does the call (cube 5) work? The call will be replaced by

```
(* '5 '5 '5)
```

Since numbers cannot be symbols, they will be evaluated to numbers. Thus, the form is same as

```
(* 5 5 5)
```

To make your macro also work for named values, you can use the list function in your definition.

```
(define-macro cube (lambda (x) (list * x x x)))
```

Using this definition, (cube i) will be replaced by

```
(list '* 'i 'i 'i)
```

which produces a list (* i i i). Since i has been defined to be 5, thus, (* i i i) will evaluate to 125.

4.6.6 COMPARE AND CONTRAST IMPERATIVE AND FUNCTIONAL PROGRAMMING PARADIGMS

Having covered the basic functional programming concepts, let's compare and contrast the imperative and functional programming paradigms again using an example.

In this example, we design a vehicle's Anti-lock Braking System (ABS). The requirement and specification of the ABS example are as follows:

Requirement:

To obtain the maximum braking effect

Specification:

    Define (or measure) the wheel diameter;

    Measure the wheel rotations per second rps;

    Compute the wheel velocity wv;

    Measure the body velocity bv;

    Error detection and action:

        if (bv > wv), reduce braking force

          else if (bv < wv), reduce acceleration force

            else "no action"

The following code is the C++ implementation using modular design, that is, we try to put the related code that performs a coherent job into a module or a function.

```cpp
#include <iostream>
using namespace std;
const float mile_inch = 63360.0;    // inches per mile
const float pi = 3.1416;
float wheel_diameter = 15;          // inches
float wheel_sensor() {
    float rps;
    cout << "get rotations per second: " << endl;
    cin >> rps;
    return rps;
}
float wheel_velocity(float rps) {
    float wv;
    wv = (pi * wheel_diameter * rps * 3600)/mile_inch;
    return wv;
}
float body_velocity() {
    float bv;
    cout << "get miles per hour: " << endl;
    cin >> bv; return bv;
}
void error_detection(float wv, float bv) {
    if      (abs(bv - wv) < 0.01)   // 0.01 is the tolerance
                cout << "no action" << endl;
    else
            if      (bv > wv)
                cout << "reduce brake force!" << endl;
            else
```

```
                cout << "reduce acceleration force!" << endl;
}
void start_engine () {
    float rps, wv, bv;
    rps = wheel_sensor();
    wv = wheel_velocity(rps);
    bv = body_velocity();
    error_detection (wv, bv);
}
void main() {
    start_engine();
}
```

A very similar Scheme program can be constructed using the modular design. For every C++ function, we define a global procedure.

```
(define mile-inch 63360.0)
(define pi 3.1416)
(define wheel-diameter 15)          ; inches
(define wheel-sensor (lambda ()
    (begin  (display "get rotations per second: ")
                (read)) ))
(define wheel-velocity (lambda (rps)        ; miles per hour
    (/      (* pi wheel-diameter rps 3600)
            mile-inch) ))
(define body-velocity (lambda ()
     (begin (display "get miles per hour: ")
            (read)) ))
(define error-detection (lambda(wv bv)
    (if     (< (abs (- bv wv)) 0.01) ; 0.01 is the tolerance
            (write "no action")
            (if     (> bv wv)
                    (write "reduce brake force!")
                    (write "reduce acceleration force!"))) ))
(define start-engine (lambda ()
    (error-detection (wheel-velocity (wheel-sensor))
            (body-velocity) )))
(define main (lambda ()
    (start-engine)))
(main)
```

Carefully examine and compare the two implementations, we can have the following observations. Both programs consist of functions (procedures). The programs and the functions are organized in the same way as much as possible. However, the two programs are still very different:

- Scheme program does not allow variables and there is no need to declare names.
- All Scheme procedures must return a value while C++ functions may or may not return a value.
- The return values of C++ functions have to be stored in temporary variables while Scheme procedures can be placed in the positions where the return values are needed. This difference can be seen clearly, for example, in the "start engine" functions in these two programs.
- The Scheme program is much more compact than the C++ program.

The Scheme program above used the global procedures, although those procedures are in fact local. In the following program, the four procedures wheel-sensor, wheel-velocity, body-velocity, and error-detection are defined as local procedures in let-forms.

```
(define start-engine (lambda ()
    (let (
            (wheel-sensor (lambda ()
                (begin  (display "get rotations per second: ")
                        (read)) ))
            (wheel-velocity (lambda (rps)   ; miles per hour
                (let    (       (pi 3.1416)
                                (mile-inch 63360)
                                (wheel-diameter 15))
                    (/ (* pi wheel-diameter rps 3600) mile-inch))))
            (body-velocity (lambda ()
                (begin (display "get miles per hour: ")
                        (read)) ))
            (error-detection (lambda(wv bv)
                (if     (< (abs (- bv wv)) 0.01)
                        (write "no action")
                    (if     (> bv wv)
                            (write "reduce brake force!")
                            (write "reduce acceleration force!")))))
        )
    (error-detection (wheel-velocity (wheel-sensor))
            (body-velocity) ))))
(define main (lambda ()
    (start-engine)))
(main)
```

4.7 RECURSIVE PROCEDURES

This section continues the discussion on this topic in chapter two and uses more examples to illustrate the fantastic tour abstract approach of understanding and writing recursive procedures:

1. Formulate the size-n problem;
2. Find the stopping condition and the corresponding return value;
3. Select **m** and formulate the size-m problem; and
4. Construct the solution of size-n problem from the assumed solution of size-m problems.

Please read section 2.7 before continuing with this section. The fantastic four abstract approach is generic. It can be applied in different programming paradigms. In this section, we use the sane example, the Tower of Hanoi problem, to illustrate the fantastic four abstract approach in functional programming paradigm.

1. Formulate the size-n problem

We can simply formulate the size-n problem as hanoi(n) or (hanoi n) in prefix notation. We can also formulate the problem as (hanoitowers n left center right), allowing the user to name the pegs. The solution of the return value of this function is to print instructions (steps) that move **n** disk from the **left** peg, using **center** peg as auxiliary, to the **right** peg.

2. Find the stopping condition and the corresponding return value

The stopping condition is **n = 1**. In this case, size-1 problem is (hanoitowers 1 left center right), and the solution or return value is "move the disk from the **left** peg to the **right** peg".

3. Select m and formulate the size-m problem

Since we can only move one disk at a time, it is obvious that we can only reduce the size by one in one iteration. Since we have multiple parameters in the problem, we have multiple size-(n-1) problems. As explained in section 2.7, we need the following two size-(n-1) problems:

(1) move **n-1** disks from **left** to **center**, using **right** as auxiliary:

hanoitowers(n-1, left, right, center)

(2) move **n-1** disks from **center** to **right**, using **left** as auxiliary:

hanoitowers(n-1, center, left, right)

4. Construct the solution of size-n problem

Use the solutions for size-(n-1) problems to construct the solution for the size-n problem.

The text on the left-hand side in figure 2.21 showed how we construct the solution for the size-n problem based on the solutions for size-(n-1) and size-1 problems, that is,

hanoitowers(n-1, left, right, center)	// move n-1 disks left -> center
hanoitowers(1, left, center, right)	// move 1 disk left -> right
hanoitowers(n-1, center, left, right)	// move n-1 disks left -> center

In words, the solution for the size-n problem is: (1) Move **n-1** disks from **left** peg to the **center** peg. We simply assume that we can do it, because it is a size-(n-1) problem. (2) Move the remaining disk from **left** to **right**. (3) Move **n-1** disks from **center** to the **right**.

Based on the discussion, we can directly obtain the Scheme program that solves the Hanoi Towers problem as follows. In the program, we defined a one-parameter procedure (hanoi n) as a simpler user interface. The procedure with more parameters is given as a helper procedure.

```
(define hanoi (lambda (n)   ; define a simpler human-interface
    (hanoi-pegs n "Left" "Center" "Right")
))
(define hanoi-pegs (lambda (n source spare destination)
    (if (= n 1)                        ; stopping condition
        (begin
            (display "move top from ")        ; return value at stopping condition
            (display source)
            (display " to ")
            (display destination)
            (newline)
        )
        (begin                            ; from size-(n-1) to size-n problem
            (hanoi-pegs (- n 1) source destination spare)
            (hanoi-pegs 1 source spare destination)
            (hanoi-pegs (- n 1) spare source destination)
        )
    )
))
```

If we call the procedure (hanoi 3), we will have the following output describing how to solve the size-3 Hanoi Towers problem.

```
move top from Left to Right
move top from Left to Center
move top from Right to Center
move top from Left to Right
move top from Center to Left
move top from Center to Right
move top from Left to Right
```

As you can see from the example, the most important idea of recursive procedure is that we simply assume that we have the solution for size-(n-1) problem and we do not need to solve it. Why does it work? Because the recursive mechanism will actually solve the problem from size-1 upwards; that is, it will solve size-1 problem, then use the solution of size-1 problem to construct the solution of size-2 problem, and so on. Since we have given the solution of size-1 problem, and we have defined how to find the solution from size-(n-1) to size-n problem, we basically have given solutions to the problem of all sizes!

4.8 DEFINE RECURSIVE PROCEDURES ON DATA TYPES

In this section, we continue to study recursion. We discuss recursive procedures that manipulate numbers, characters, strings, pairs, and lists. The purposes of this section are twofold: understand recursion and get familiar with data types on Scheme. In the discussion, we may or may not explicitly mention the four steps of writing recursive procedures. However, if you still do not fully understand the idea of writing recursive procedures, you should carefully go through these examples and try to identify the four steps and application-specific parts of the procedures.

4.8.1 NUMBER MANIPULATIONS

We will study several recursive procedures that manipulate decimal and binary numbers.

(1) Decimal-binary conversion

How do we convert a decimal number to a binary number? One of the algorithms frequently used is shown in figure 4.7. We divide the decimal number by 2, and keep dividing the quotient by 2, till the quotient becomes 0. The remainder in each step of division forms the binary number that equivalent to the decimal number.

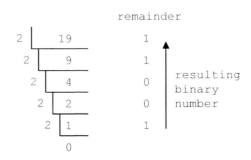

Figure 4.7 Converting a decimal number to a binary number

Following the same algorithm, we can devise a Scheme program to convert a decimal number in the list format, e.g., the list format of 354 is (3 5 4), into the equivalent binary number in list format.

```
(define dtob (lambda (n)
    (if    (= n 0)                            ; stopping conditions
           (list 0)                           ; return value at stopping
           (append    (dtob (quotient n 2))   ; size-m problem and from
                      (list (remainder n 2))  ; size-m to size-n solution
           )
    )
))
```

The output of the procedure call (dtob 19) is

(0 1 0 0 1 1)

The stopping condition is n = 0 and the corresponding return value is a list (0), because the binary number corresponding to decimal number 0 is also 0. The size-n problem is (dtob n) and the size-m problem is (dtob (quotient n 2)), where m = (quotient n 2), because the quotient of n/2 is smaller than n, and, thus, the size of the problem will eventually be reduced to the stopping condition.

Constructing the solution of the size-n problem is done by appending the current remainder of n/2 to the solution of size-(n-1) problem:

```
(append (dtob (quotient n 2)) (list (remainder n 2)))
```

(2) Binary addition

How do we add two binary numbers arithmetically? The algorithm that we use is shown in figure 4.8. We add from right to left. A carry will be generated if the result of addition at a position is greater than or equal to 2. The final result may have one more bit than the two numbers to be added.

The following Scheme program mimics the addition process. The program consists of multiple procedures, and all procedures are recursive.

```
(define binaryadd (lambda(L1 L2)
    (let ((len1 (length L1)) (len2 (length L2)))
        (if     (> len1 len2)
                (binaryadd L2 L1)
                (if  (< len1 len2)
                     (binaryadd (append '(0) L1) L2)
                     (bitadd (append '(0) L1) (append '(0) L2) 0)
)) )      ))
(define bitadd (lambda(L1 L2 carry)
    (if     (null? L1)
            '()
            (let     ((t (+ (tail L1) (tail L2) carry)))
                (append     (bitadd (rmtail L1)
                                    (rmtail L2)
                                    (quotient t 2))
                            (list (remainder t 2))
)) )      )      )
```

```
          1 0 0 1 1
    +     1 1 0 0 1
carry  1 0 0 1 1 0
result 1 0 1 1 0 0
       ◄───────────
```

Figure 4.8 Adding two binary numbers

In the main procedure, the procedure that is called first, we first define two local variables len1 and len2 to represent the lengths of the two binary numbers in list format. The size-n problem that the procedure is dealing with is (binaryadd L1 L2), where n is the absolute value |length(l 1)-length(L2))|, The procedure exits the recursive call (stopping condition) when len1=len2, or when n=0. If len1>len2, we recursively call (binaryadd L2 L1), which means we swap the position of L1 and L2. In other words, we always use the shorter number as the first argument. If len1<len2, we recursively call (binaryadd (append '(0) L1) L2 L1), which means we add one 0 to the left of the shorter number, attempting to make the two numbers to be added the same length. We keep adding 0 until the two numbers have same length in their list format.

When len1=len2, we exit the main procedure and call the bitadd procedure. We add a 0 to the left of both numbers to handle the situation when the addition result takes one extra bit. Again, the bitadd procedure is recursive. The size-n problem that bitadd is dealing with is (bitadd L1, L2, carry), where, n is the length of lists L1 and L2. The procedure stops when the lists become empty, or the length become 0. The size-(n-1) problem is (bitadd (rmtail L1) (rmtail L2) (quotient t 2)), where (rmtail L) returns the list with the last element of L removed. Thus, the size (length of the lists) of the problem becomes n-1. In the program, the addition of three binary bits is done in the definition of the local variable t: (let ((t (+ (tail L1) (tail L2) carry))) ...), where, procedure (tail L) returns the last element of the list L.

The implementation of (rmtail L) and (tail L) are not given here. You are asked to complete the recursive procedures as exercises.

(3) Two's complement

We can obtain two's complement of a binary by using its one's complement plus one at the end (the least significant bit). The addition is an arithmetic addition and may cause a carry to the higher bit. We can use the binaryadd procedure that we just defined for this purpose. The one's complement can be obtained by inverting each bit. Again, we assume the binary numbers we are dealing with are in their list format.

```
(define twoscomplement (lambda (x)
    (binaryadd '(1) (onescomplement x))
))
(define onescomplement (lambda (x)
    (if (null? x)
            '()
            (if (= (car x) 0)
                    (cons 1 (onescomplement (cdr x)))
                    (cons 0 (onescomplement (cdr x)))))))
```

The procedure onescomplement is recursive. The stopping condition is when the list is empty. The corresponding return value is empty list '(). The size-n problem is (onescomplement x), where x is a list with n elements. The size-(n-1) problem is (onescomplement (cdr x)), where (cdr x) is a list with n-1 elements.

4.8.2 CHARACTER AND STRING MANIPULATIONS

In chapter two, we wrote a C program to encrypt a string. Now we use Scheme to implement a similar string-encryption program.

Assuming str is a string of length n, we would like to add an integer k to the integer value of each character in the string. The integer value of each character is given in the ASCII table in the Appendix C.

The idea of the string-encryption is as follows:

■ If str is an empty string "" (stopping condition), then return empty string. There is no character to encrypt.

- The size-n problem is (string-encryption str), where str has n characters.
- We reduce the size-n problem to size-(n-1) problem by removing the first character from the string.
- We construct the solution of the size-n problem (string-encryption str) by encrypting the first character of str, append the solution of the size-(n-1) problem to the encrypted character.

Before we write the main procedure (string-encryption str), we need to write a few helper procedures:

(character-encryption ch) encrypts a character;

(string-car s) returns the first (left-most) character of string s;

(string-cdr s) returns the substring of s after removing the first character.

The Scheme program including all necessary procedures is given as follows. The basic operations defined on characters and strings have been given in tables 4.3 and 4.4.

```
(define string-encryption (lambda (str key)
    (if     (string=? str "")           ; stopping condition
            ""                          ; return empty string
            (string-append
                    (character-encryption (string-car str) key)
                    (string-encryption (string-cdr str) key)
            )
    )
))
(define character-encryption (lambda (ch k)
    (string (integer->char (+ (char->integer ch) k)))
))
(define string-car (lambda (s)
    (string-ref s 0)  ;return the element at position 0
))
(define string-cdr (lambda (s)
    (substring s 1 (string-length s)) ;return the element at position 0
))
```

To decrypt the string, we can use the following decryption program. The program calls the encryption program with a negative key value to reverse the encryption.

```
(define string-decryption (lambda (str key)
    (string-encryption str (- key))
))
```

We can add different features to the encryption program. The following procedure generates a random number between 3 and 9, uses it as the key to call (string-encryption str key), and append the key to the end of the encrypted string.

```
(define random-encryption (lambda (str)
    (let ((key (+ (random 7) 3)))
        (string-append (string-encryption str key)
                        (number->string key)
        )
    )
))
```

4.8.3 LIST MANIPULATIONS

List is the most important data type of functional programming languages. Since a list consists of a collection of elements, most list manipulations involve repetition or recursion.

The following program computes the sum of a list of numbers.

```
(define list-sum (lambda (lst)
    (if      (null? lst)
             (display "Error: the list is empty")
             (list-sum-helper lst)
    )
))
(define list-sum-helper (lambda (lst)
    (if      (null? lst)
             0
             (+ (car lst) (list-sum-helper (cdr lst)))
    )
))
(list-sum '(2 3 4 6)) ; call the procedure. It returns 15.
```

We split the program into two procedures. The first procedure checks if the initial list given is empty. If it is empty, the procedure returns error message. Note that if we call the second procedure using an empty list, it will return 0. This return value doesn't differentiate whether the sum is 0 or there is no element in the list.

The second procedure is recursive. The stopping condition is "the list is empty." The corresponding return value is 0. The size-(n-1) problem is (list-sum-helper (cdr lst)), because cdr returns the list without the first element. Thus, the size of (cdr lst) is one smaller than the size of lst. The construction of the solution of the size-n problem is by

(+ (car lst) (list-sum-helper (cdr lst)))

which add the first element to the sum of the remaining elements.

The next example we discuss is reversing a list. The size-n problem is (reverse-list lst). The stopping condition is empty list and the corresponding return value is empty list. To reduce the size-n problem to size-(n-1) problem, we take out the first element of the list using (cdr lst). To construct the solution from size-(n-1) problem to size-n problem, we append the first element of lst to the end of the solution of size-(n-1) problem. Thus, we obtain the following program.

```
(define reverse-list (lambda (lst)
    (if (null? lst)
            '()
            (append (reverse-list (cdr lst)) (list (car lst)))
    )
))
```

For example, the procedure call (reverse-list '(1 3 5 7 9)) will return: (9 7 5 3 1).

4.9 HIGHER ORDER FUNCTIONS

A **higher-order function** is a function that takes the operation of another function (not the return value) as an argument. All functional programming languages support higher-order functions. There are many different higher-order functions. We will discuss the two most useful higher-order functions defined on lists:

- Mapping: apply the same operation defined by another procedure to all elements of a list;
- Filtering: remove elements of a list that do not satisfy a predicate defined by another procedure.

4.9.1 MAPPING

The general form of mapping is

(map procedure-name list-parameter)

where, **list-parameter** is a list with the same type of elements; **procedure-name** is the name of any procedure that manipulates a single parameter that has the same type as the element of the **list-parameter**. The map procedure will call the procedure (**procedure-name list-element**) on each element of the list and return a list that consists of the return values of these procedure calls. For example, if we define a **foo** procedure on an integer and apply the procedure in a map procedure:

```
(define foo (lambda (x) (+ (* x x ) x)))
(map foo '(3 6 9 12 15 18))
```

The map procedure will apply **foo** on each and every element of the list (3 6 9 12 15 18), and, thus, the map procedure will return

```
    (3*3+3  6*6+6  9*9+9  12*12+12  15*15+15  18*18+18)
=   (12 42 90 156 240 342)
```

We can also embed the body of the **foo** into the map procedure to implement the same function:

```
(map (lambda (x) (+ (* x x ) x))'(3 6 9 12 15 18))
```

Now let's use map procedure to re-implement some procedures we wrote before, where the same operation is applied to each element of a list.

First, let's examine the one's complement. The same operation, the inversion operation, is applied on each element of the list. Thus, we can first define a bit-inversion procedure, and then apply the procedure to the list.

```
(define bitinvert (lambda(x) (if (= x 0) 1 0)))
(define onescomplement (lambda (x)
    (map bitinvert x)
))
```

Next, let's consider the string encryption, where an integer is added to each character in the string. Since map procedures only work on list, we need to convert the string to a list. The following is the program.

```
(define character-encryption (lambda (ch)
    (integer->char (+ (char->integer ch) 5))        ; key = 5
))
(define string-encryption (lambda (str)
    (list->string (map character-encryption (string->list str)))
))
```

As can be seen from these two examples, the previous implementations are recursive, involving repetition of operations. Using map higher-order function, no recursion is needed. The reason is that recursion is embedded in the map function and is thus transparent to the user of map higher-order function. If we look at the implementation of map, we will see the recursion.

```
(define map1 (lambda (procedure-name list-parameter)
        (if (null? list-parameter)
                '()
                (cons   (procedure-name (car list-parameter))
                        (map1 procedure-name (cdr list-parameter))
                )
        )
))
```

As can be seen from this program, procedure-name is an ordinary parameter of map1 procedure. However, in the body of the program, procedure-name is placed in the first place directly following a left parenthesis, where an operator is expected. Thus, the parameter procedure-name is considered an operator. This brings, in fact, a new type of parameter passing, known as **call-by-name**. Different from call-by-value or call-by-reference, call-by-name does not pass the value or address of the variable. It passes the name itself.

4.9.2 FILTERING

A filtering procedure or a filter is a higher-order function similar to a map procedure. It applies another procedure to all members of list:

```
(filter procedure-name list-parameter)
```

The difference is that the procedure that is the parameter of filter here is a **predicate** that returns either true or false. If the predicate (procedure-name list-element) returns true, the element will stay in the list that is to be returned by the filter procedure. If the predicate (procedure-name list-element) returns false, the element will be removed from the list.

For example

(filter (lambda (x) (> x 200)) '(50 300 500 65 800))

will return

(300 500 800)

which is the sub list of the list in the filter procedure with all elements that are less than or equal to 200 removed. Similar to map procedure, the predicate procedure in the filter procedure can be defined separately:

(define largerthan200? (lambda (x) (> x 200)))
(filter largerthan200? '(50 300 500 65 800))

The filter procedure can also be applied to the substructures with a list. For example, if we have list of (class-name class-size) pairs defined as follows:

(define class-list
    '(("CSE100" . 100) ("CSE200" . 80) ("CSE240" . 100) ("CSE310" . 70) ("CSE330" . 75) ("CSE310"
. 65) ("CSE420" . 50)))
(define large-class? (lambda (x) (>= (cdr x) 80)))
(define find-large-class (lambda (alist)
    (filter large-class? alist)
))

If we call the procedure that uses the filter procedure, the following sub list will be returned.

(("CSE100" . 100) ("CSE200" . 80) ("CSE240" . 100))

The filter procedure is not implemented in the current DrScheme version. We can define it as a user's procedure as follows:

(define filter (lambda (predicate-name alist)
    (if (null? alist)
        '()
        (if   (predicate-name (car alist))
                (cons (car alist) (filter predicate-name (cdr alist)))
                (filter predicate-name (cdr alist))
)
)
))

As we can see, the filter procedure is a recursive procedure. The stopping condition is "if the list is empty". The size-(n-1) problem is the problem when the first element is removed. To construct the solution of size-n, we use the predicate-procedure to test the current element of the list. If the return value of the predicate procedure is true, we include the element in the return list by performing cons operation on the element and the solution of the size-(n-1) problem. Otherwise, the solution of the size-n problem is simply the solution of the size-(n-1) problem: the current element is simply not included in the construction of size-n problem.

4.10 SUMMARY

In this chapter, we studied the major features of functional programming languages and important techniques of writing functional programs, including

- prefix notation;
- data types and predefined Scheme functions on the data types;
- the syntax and semantics of λ-calculus, and the relationship between λ-calculus and Scheme programming language;
- important programming constructs of functional programming languages: named procedure, unnamed procedure, let-form global and local variables, and the conversion between unnamed procedures and let-forms;
- writing Scheme programs with multiple procedures;
- the principle of recursion, and the techniques of writing recursive procedures;
- the higher-order functions that can be used to solve recursive problems in a much simpler way.

4.11 HOMEWORK, PROGRAMMING EXERCISES, AND PROJECTS

1. Multiple Choice. Choose only one answer in each question. Choose the best answer if more than one answer is acceptable.

1.1 In Scheme, the primitive (char? "#\A") will return
   ❏ #t   ❏ #f   ❏ A   ❏ error message

1.2 (member '2 '(3 4 2 1)) will return
   ❏ #f   ❏ (3 5 2 9)   ❏ (4 2 1)   ❏ (2 1)

1.3 (caddr '(2 4 6 8 10)) will return
   ❏ (6 8 10)   ❏ (6)   ❏ 6   ❏ (D) error message

1.4 The most efficient way, in terms of the execution time, to check whether a list L is empty is by
   ❏ (NULL? L)   ❏ (= (length L) 0)
   ❏ (< (length L) 1)   ❏ (= L 0)

1.5 Which of the following forms is an unnamed procedure?
   ❏ (+ z 3)   ❏ ((lambda (z) (+ z 3)) 4)
   ❏ (define foo (lambda (z) (+ z 3)))   ❏ (define bar 25)
   ❏ none of them

1.6 Eager evaluation evaluates
   ❏ all parameters of a function first.
   ❏ a parameter of a function only if it is necessary.
   ❏ no parameters at all.
   ❏ outermost first.

1.7 Lazy evaluation evaluates
   ❏ all parameters of a function first.
   ❏ a parameter of a function only if it is necessary.
   ❏ no parameters at all.
   ❏ innermost first.

1.8 In imperative programming languages, different orders of evaluations (eager or lazy)
   ❏ may produce different results.   ❏ always produce different results.
   ❏ never produce different results.   ❏ None of them are correct.

1.9 In functional programming languages, different orders of evaluations (eager or lazy)
   ❏ may produce different results.   ❏ always produce different results.
   ❏ never produce different results.   ❏ None of them are correct.

1.10 Each let-form in Scheme can be converted into
   ❏ an unnamed procedure.   ❏ a named procedure.
   ❏ a list of local variables.   ❏ a list of global variables.

1.11   Assume that you have (**define** x '(5)) and (**define** y '(8 9)). What operation will return a list (5 8 9)?

❏ (cons x y)   ❏ (list x y)   ❏ (append x y)   ❏ None of them

1.12   Which of the followings is NOT a Scheme pair?

❏ '()   ❏ '(x . y)   ❏ '(x)   ❏ '(())

1.13   What is the return value of the following form?

(filter <u>(lambda (x) (> x 20))</u> '(10 30 15 10 80))

❏ (30 80)   ❏ (10 15 10)   ❏ (10 15)   ❏ (10 10 15)

1.14   What is the return value of the following form?

(map (lambda (x) (+ x 10)) '(10 30 15))

❏ 20   ❏ 40   ❏ 25   ❏ (20 40 25)

1.15   In Scheme, an empty list is

❏ a pair.   ❏ not a pair.   ❏ a string.   ❏ 0

1.16   What mechanism cannot be used to pass a value into a Scheme procedure?

❏ call-by-value   ❏ call-by-reference   ❏ return value   ❏ global name

1.17   If you want to return multiple values from a Scheme procedure, which of these methods is invalid?
❏ Use multiple return-statements.   ❏ Split the procedure into multiple procedures.
❏ Put the values in a pair and return the pair.   ❏ Put the values in a list and return the list.

1.18   Normally, a recursive procedure can be written by following these steps: Define the size-n problem, find the solution for the base case or the stopping condition, and then,
❏ find the solutions of size-1, size-2, ..., size-n problems.
❏ find a loop variable that is incremented in each iteration.
❏ find the solutions of size-n, size-(n-1), size-(n-2), ..., size-1 problems.
❏ find the solution of size-(n-1) problem, and finally find the solution of size-n problem.
❏ find the solution of size-n problem based on the hypothetical solution of size-(n-1) problem.

2.   What is the major difference between the imperative and functional programming paradigms? How does an imperative program typically pass values from one function to another function? How does a functional program pass values from one function to another function?

3.   How does a Scheme program pass parameters into a procedure? Does Scheme support call-by-value? Does Scheme support call-by-reference?

4.   What is the difference between a Scheme procedure and a Scheme macro? Write a macro that returns the absolute value of a number.

5.   What is an unnamed procedure? Why do we need an unnamed procedure? How do we define and call an unnamed procedure?

6.   What are bound and free variables in λ-calculus?

7.   What are global and local variables in Scheme?

8.   What is eager evaluation? What is lazy evaluation? Is the order of evaluation (eager or lazy) important in a functional programming language like Scheme? Is the order of evaluation important in imperative programming languages like C/C++? Assume we have a multi-processor computer that can evaluate 10 independent operations simultaneously and each arithmetic operation takes a unit of time. How many units of time are necessary to evaluate the following form:

    (+ (+ (- 6 2) (* 5 7)) (* (+ 4 6) (- 5 3)))

8.1   if the form is evaluated in an imperative language like C?

8.2   if the form is evaluated in Scheme?

9.   According to the BNF definition of the λ-expression, if E1 and E2 are λ-expressions, E1 E2 is also a λ-expression. If E1, E2 and E3 are λ-expressions, Is E1 E2 E3 also a λ-expression? When do we need a λ-expression of the form E1 E2 E3?

10.   What is a λ-procedure? What reduction rule evaluates a λ-procedure?

11. What is the relationship between a λ-expression and a Scheme form? How do we convert a λ-expression into a Scheme form?

12. How do we convert a let-form into an unnamed procedure? How do we convert an unnamed procedure into a let-form?

13. Given a λ-expression: λx{+ λx[- x 1] 3 (* λx[+ x 2] 3 x) } 9

13.1 Indicate the scope of each variable by underlining the variable and the expression associated with it.

13.2 Use the α-conversion rule to convert the expression, so that different parameters have different names.

13.3 Use the β- and η-conversion rules to convert (using lazy evaluation) the expression. Show each step of conversion.

13.4 Give the Scheme unnamed procedure corresponding to the λ-expression.

14. How do we introduce a global variable/procedure? How do we define a local variable/procedure?

15. What kinds of data structures does Scheme support?

16. What is a character type in Scheme? Is a character treated as a string with only one element?

17. What is a pair? How do we represent a pair?

18. What is a list? How do we represent a list? Is a pair a list? Is a list a pair?

19. When do we need a quote and when not?

20. Convert the following expressions into prefix notations and use DrScheme to evaluate them.

20.1 (2 + (4 + (6 + (8 + (10 + 12)))))

20.2 (((((2 + 4) + 6) + 8) + 10) + 12)

20.3 ((2 + 4) + (6 + 8) + (10 + 12))

20.4 (2 + 4 + 6 + 8 + 10 + 12)

20.5 (2 + 4 * 6 + 8 * 10 + 12)

20.6 125^{187}

20.7 Input two integers and add them: (read) + (read)

20.8 Print ((2 + 4) + (6 + 8) + (10 + 12))

21. Write Scheme programs/forms to perform the following functions.

21.1 Find the second element of the list, e.g., '(2 4 6 8 10 12). Your form should work for any list containing two or more elements.

21.2 Find the last element of the list '(2 4 6 8 10 12). Your form only needs to work for lists of six elements.

21.3 What is the return value of the form (caddddr '(3 1 8 9 2))? 2 or '(2)?

21.4 Merge the two lists '(1 2 3 4) and '(5 7 9) into a single list '(1 2 3 4 5 7 9).

21.5 Obtain the length of the list '(a b x y 10 12).

21.6 Check whether '(+ 2 4) is a symbol.

21.7 Check whether '+ is a member of the list '(+ 3 4 6).

21.8 Check whether "+", '(+ 3 5), "(* 4 6)" are strings.

21.9 Check whether (* 3 5), '(/ 3 7), (1 2 3 4), "(+ 2 8)" and "(1 2 3)" are strings.

22.   Show how the form (/ (+ 5 4) (- 8 (* 2 3))) is executed on a stack machine, a computer architecture that is based on a stack instead of registers.

23.   Given the following Scheme program/procedure:

```
(define myabs
    (lambda (x)
        (if      (negative? x)
                 (- x)
                 x
        )
    )
)
```

23.1 What does this program do?

23.2 Find 3 test cases to test the program in DrScheme environment.

24.   Given the following Scheme program:

```
(define foo
    (lambda (n)
        (if      (= n 0)
                 1
                 (* n (foo (- n 1)))
        )
    )
)
```

24.1 What does this program do?

24.2 Test the program with n = 0, n = 5, n = 150, n = -5.

24.3 The program does not terminate for some inputs. Find and fix the bug and re-execute the program.

25.   Define a Scheme procedure with two parameters.

25.1 Define a procedure (mymax x y) that returns the larger value between x and y.

25.2 Test your program with inputs (0 0), (-2 0), (0 -2), (10 0), (0 12), (1000 10), (20 8000).

25.3 Find the largest value among (48, 6, 120, 35, 12) by repeatedly calling the procedure (mymax x y).

26. Given the following Scheme procedure:

```scheme
(define dtod (lambda (N)
    (if     (= N 0)
            (list 0)
            (append     (dtod (quotient N 10))
                        (list (remainder N 10)))
    )
))
```

26.1 What does this program do?

26.2 Modify the program to remove the leading zero in the output list.

26.3 Find 3 test cases to test program under DrScheme.

27. Write a Scheme program (**dtoh N**) that converts a decimal number into the list of its hexadecimal digits, where, you must use letter 'a for **10**, 'b for **11**, ..., and 'f for **15**, for example,

```
(dtoh 18)  → (1 2)
(dtoh 26)  → (1 a)
(dtoh 225) → (e 1)
```

28. What do the following Scheme procedures do?

```
(define dtoh (lambda (N)
    (if (= N 0)
            '(0)
            (dtoh0 N)
    )
))
(define dtoh0 (lambda (N)
    (if     (= N 0)
            '()
            (append     (dtoh0 (quotient N 16))
                        (list (remainder N 16))))
    )
))
```

29. Write a Scheme program to convert a decimal number into a decimal in list format.

30. Given a λ-expression:

λ(x, y){+ λx[- x 2] 4 (* λx[+ x 2] 3 x) (/λx[/ x 2] 4) y} 8 λx(+ x 2) 4

30.1 Indicate the scope of each variable by underlining the variable and the expression associated with it.

30.2 Use the α-conversion rule to convert the expression, so that different parameters have different names.

30.3 Use the β- and η-conversion rules to convert (using lazy evaluation) the expression. Show each step of conversion.

30.4 Give the Scheme program corresponding to the λ-expression. The program should consist of un-named procedures only.

30.5 Rewrite the Scheme program using let-forms instead of unnamed Scheme procedures.

31. Write a recursive program to implement (tail x): return the last element of list x. If x is empty, the program should return "error". For example, (tail '( )) ⇒ "error", (tail '(a 3 b)) ⇒ b and (tail '(1 2 w 5 7)) ⇒ 7. You may NOT call (reverse x) procedure in your program. Use the following procedure calls as test cases:

(tail '())
(tail '(2 3 4 ab 4 5 cd))
(tail '(2 (3 5)))
(tail '(7))

Hint: To handle the empty list, you can write a separate procedure to check if x is null. If it is, you return "error", otherwise, you call the procedure that handles a non-empty list.

32. Write a recursive program to implement (rmtail x): remove the last element of list x and return the resulting list. If x is empty, the program must return "error". For example, (rmtail '( )) ⇒ "error", (rmtail '(a 3 b)) ⇒ '(a 3) and (tail '(1 2 w 5 7)) ⇒ '(1 2 w 5). You must write a recursive program to do the job. You may NOT call (reverse x) procedure in your program. Use the following test cases to test your program:

(rmtail '())
(rmtail '(2 3 4 ab 4 5 cd))
(rmtail '(2 (3 5)))
(rmtail '(7))

33. Use C or C++ to write a recursive program to solve the Hanoi Town problem.

34. Given the following Scheme program:

```
(define mymax (lambda (lst)
    (if     (null? (cdr lst))
            (car lst)
            (let ((m (mymax (cdr lst))))
                    (if     (> (car lst) m)
                            (car lst)
                            m)))
))
```

34.1 Add a procedure to handle the case of empty list, that is, if the given list is empty, the program should return "error: list empty".

34.2 Consider that the four design steps for recursive programs are used to solve the problem. Describe each step and the solution obtained in each step.

34.3 Compare and contrast the algorithm used in this program and the divide-and-conquer algorithm used in the next question.

34.4 Use C to reimplement the program. Compare and contrast the C and Scheme programs.

35. Use the divide-and-conquer algorithm to implement a procedure (maxdac lst) that finds the largest number in the given list lst. A divide-and-conquer algorithm divides a size-n problem into two half-sized problems, solve each of them recursively, and combine the solutions of the two half-sized problems.

35.1 Define two procedures to find the first and the second halves of a given list: (firsthalf lst) and (secondhalf lst), where their lengths are $\lceil n/2 \rceil$ (ceiling) and $\lfloor n/2 \rfloor$ (floor), respectively.

35.2 Write an umbrella procedure to handle the empty list, that is, if the list is initially empty, the procedure should "error: list empty".

35.3 Use the divide-and-conquer algorithm and follow the four design steps to devise the solution of the size-n problem (maxdac lst). In each step the list is divided into two sub-lists of length $\lceil n/2 \rceil$ and $\lfloor n/2 \rfloor$, respectively. You cannot call any library function that can find the max-value. You can only use <, >, <=, or >= operators to perform comparison operations in your program.

Hint: You can use a let-form to assign the largest number from the first half to m1 and the largest number from the second half to m2, and then choose the larger one between m1 and m2.

35.4 Test the program using following test cases:

```
(define lst '(5))
(firsthalf lst)
(secondhalf lst)
(maxdac lst)
(define lst '(5 2))
(firsthalf lst)
(secondhalf lst)
(maxdac lst)
(define lst '(2 8 6 5 28 2 9))
(firsthalf lst)
(secondhalf lst)
(maxdac lst)
```

36. A computer system consists of hardware and software. Before we physically make a piece of hardware, we normally simulate the hardware by a program, so that we can verify its correctness and evaluate its performance. As we know, all complex hardware components can be implemented by the basic gates AND, OR, NOT, and XOR as shown in figure 4.9:

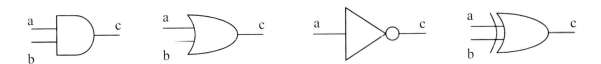

Figure 4.9 Basic gates

36.1 Write four Scheme procedures to simulate these four gates.

36.2 Define a Scheme procedure (fulladder x y d) to simulate the following logic in figure 4.10. The procedure must return a list with two elements '(s c), where s is the sum of x and y and c is the carry-out. Hint: You can use two procedures to produce the two results, respectively, and then write a main procedure to call the two sub procedures.

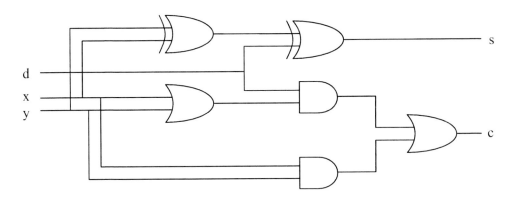

Figure 4.10 The logic of a full adder

36.3 Verify your procedure by exhaustive testing: use all valid inputs to test the procedure. There are eight valid inputs:

(fulladder 0 0 0)
(fulladder 0 0 1)
(fulladder 0 1 0)
(fulladder 0 1 1)
(fulladder 1 0 0)
(fulladder 1 0 1)
(fulladder 1 1 0)
(fulladder 1 1 1)

36.4 Figure 4.11 shows the design of an n-bit (n = 32 in the figure) adder using n one-bit adders. The carry-out of bit-i is the carry-in of bit i+1, where carry-in of bit 0 is 0. Write a recursive procedure to implement the n-bit adder, and design test plan to test the program.

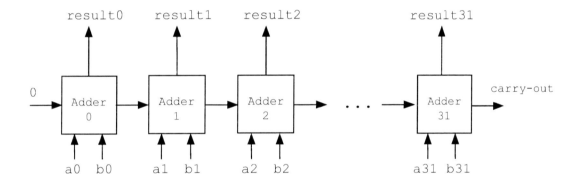

Figure 4.11 Design of a n-bit adder, where n = 32

5

The Logic Programming Language, Prolog

Functional programming languages are considered higher level programming languages that focus more on what is wanted rather than how it is implemented. Logic programming language takes a step further towards getting rid of programming altogether. It tries to describe what the problem is and let the computer find a way to solve the problem.

In this chapter, we will use Prolog as example to study the main features and programming techniques of logic programming languages. By the end of the chapter, you should

- have a good understanding of logic programming paradigm and its major differences with imperative and functional programming paradigms;
- have a good understanding of variables in Prolog and their differences with variables in imperative and functional programming languages;
- be able to define database consists of multiple facts and rules;
- be able to write recursive rules;
- be able to write goals (questions) that inquire a database;
- have understood the execution model of Prolog facts, rules, and goals.

The major part of this chapter, sections 5.1 through 5.7, is reprinted, arranged by the publisher, from Tom Hankins and Thom Luce's book Prolog Minimanual.

5.1 A First Look at Prolog

Prolog is easy to learn and fun to use. This section introduces the language, and begins with some comments about its development. A look at a simple Prolog program follows, while later sections discuss syntax and ways of getting information from a Prolog program.

5.1.1 Brief Background

The word Prolog is from the phrase *"programming in logic"* Alain Colmeraurer first developed the language in France in 1970 to use in natural language parsing. David H. D. Warren and others at the

From *Prolog Minimanual* by T. Hankins and L. Thom. Reproduced with permission of The McGraw Hill Companies.

University of Edinburgh constructed a Prolog compiler called Prolog-10 later in the 1970s. In 1981, William Clocksin and Christopher Mellish, of the Department of Artificial Intelligence of the University of Edinburgh, published *Programming in Prolog*. The book quickly became the *de facto* standard for the language. Today the terms Edinburgh Prolog, Clocksin and Mellish (or C&M) Prolog, standard Prolog, and classic Prolog all refer to Prolog as described in that book.

Prolog might have remained one of the many obscure languages if the Japanese had not announced in 1981 that logic programming would play a major role in the development of their fifth-generation computer. Prolog has since flourished with the arrival of many new texts, interpreters, and compilers including those oriented to microcomputer use. Prolog and Lisp are now the two main languages for developing artificial intelligence applications.

The original Prolog compiler was written in Fortran. However, most subsequent Prolog systems have been written in C on Unix systems, which is why many predefined Prolog terms resemble Unix commands. There are several characteristics that differentiate Prolog from other languages, especially procedural languages:

- Prolog does not distinguish between program code and program data.

- Prolog systems use few, if any, reserved words.

- Prolog does not execute code sequentially.

- Prolog allows the user to define new operators with a single line of code.

- Prolog is a conversational language, i.e., it allows the user to carry on a kind of conversation with the computer.

5.1.2 Arity Prolog

There are many implementations of Prolog available. One of the best is Arity Prolog from Arity Corporation. This is the version we will use for all of the examples in this chapter.

5.1.3 A Prolog Program

A Prolog program is often called a database or, sometimes, simply a base. It is appropriate to think of a Prolog program as a database because it contains lists of facts and rules about objects and relationships among those objects. Rather than a list of instructions, as in a procedural language program, the Prolog program is a collection of information describing a particular situation.

Three types of statements may be used in a Prolog program. One type declares **facts** about objects and their relationships. A second type defines **rules** about objects and their relationships. The third type asks **questions** about the objects and their relationships. As you can see, Prolog is well suited to problems that can be expressed in the form of objects and their relationships. The objective of the programmer is to provide information about the limited world on which the Prolog system will operate.

Prolog is not so well suited to some other types of tasks. You will see later that procedural tasks such as input and output, arithmetic, and matrix manipulation, can be performed in Prolog, but they are often awkward.

The Prolog term for a statement in a database is clause. First, we will consider programs consisting of clauses that represent facts but not rules; Listing 5.1 is such a program. In it, the clauses describe kinship relations in a family. These familiar relations lend themselves to illustrating many characteristics of a Prolog database; therefore, you will see this example expanded in later sections.

Prolog Syntax

Syntax refers to rules for writing clauses. The rules in Prolog are rigid, but they are also very simple and easy to learn. The general form of the statements in the Listing 5.1 is:

```
relationship(person_1, person_2).
```

The relationship is written first and always begins with a lower-case letter. The names of the persons who are related are enclosed in parentheses and separated by a comma. The statement ends with a period. The names of the related persons also begin with lower-case letters; this indicates that the persons are specific individuals, constant values which will not change. Whenever multiword names are necessary, underscores connect the words.

Read the facts in Listing 5.1 with the first person having the indicated relationship with me second person. For example, read **mother_of(edith, dick)** so that its English equivalent is: "Edith is the mother of Dick." The other relations in the program follow the same structure. If you preferred, you could reverse the persons to **mother_of(dick, edith)**. The new statement would translate to "The mother of Dick is Edith." Either way is acceptable and will work fine as long as you are consistent and do not mix the two in a program.

You can insert comments into a Prolog program by enclosing them with a beginning /* and an ending */. The first line of Listing 5.1 is a comment. Another way to add a comment is to precede it with the percent sign (%). Any text on a line following the % is interpreted as a comment. Note that if you comment with the %, you must repeat it on each line.

Prolog Terms

Facts are the simplest kind of Prolog statement. To this point, the examples have illustrated facts which describe a relationship among objects. However, a fact can also describe the character or condition of a single object. For example, the family database might well include facts describing gender:

```
male(luke).
female(sarah).
```

It is easy to think of many other examples such as **tall(kareem)**, **dirty(my_car)**, and **lovely(meryl)**.

The words indicating the relationships in facts are also known as **predicates**. The terms enclosed in parentheses are called **arguments** to the predicate. The number of arguments that a predicate has is the **arity** of the predicate.

If a predicate appears in a program with different numbers of arguments, Prolog will recognize the two as separate relationships. Thus, it is perfectly fine to include both of these facts in a database:

```
shoe(loafer).        /* shoe/1 */
shoe(trigger, Wednesday). /* shoe/2 */
```

The first fact could report that a loafer is a kind of shoe while the other might say that Trigger is to be shod on Wednesday. The comments following the predicates show the customary way of indicating a predicate and its arity. We will use this predicate-name/arity notation throughout the chapter.

Predicates can have any number of arguments, as these examples with arity of 3, 4, and 7 respectively indicate:

```
weather(new_orleans, summer, hot).
president(lincoln, kentucky, 1861, 1865).
class(is590, prolog, thursday, 6, 9, sullivan_hall, 511).
```

5.1.4 PUTTING PROLOG TO WORK BY QUERYING THE DATABASE

You retrieve information from a Prolog database by asking questions, often called **goals**. A goal is attained (or, as Prolog programmers say, it **succeeds**) if there are facts that **match** or **unify** the clauses in the goal. A clause and a fact **unify** if

1. their predicates are the same,
2. their arity is the same, and
3. their corresponding arguments are identical.

If there is no match for the clauses in a goal, the goal **fails**.

The simplest queries are ones that require a yes or no answer. Using the family database of Listing 5.1 we can ask questions, and Prolog will respond. The first two questions in Figure 5.1 are of this type. To answer them, Prolog searches the database for a fact that matches the goal. If it finds a match, it responds with "yes"; if it does not find a match, it answers "no."

Listing 5.1 Family Relationship Database

```
/* General form: relationship(person1, person2). */
    mother_of(edith, dick).
    mother_of(edith, tom).
    mother_of(sadie, calvin).
    mother_of(sadie, alice).
    mother_of(sadie, floyd).
    mother_of(gertie, john_benford).
    mother_of(gertie, edith).
    mother_of(gertie, vivian).
    mother_of(jane, luke).
    mother_of(jane, sarah).
    mother_of(jane, rachel).
    mother_of(marcy, heidi).
    mother_of(marcy, gretchen).
    mother_of(linda, andrew).

    step_father_of(tom, heidi).
    step_father_of(tom. gretchen).

    father_of(floyd, tom).
    father_of(floyd, dick).
    father_of(john_h, floyd).
    father_of(john_h, calvin).
    father_of(john_h, alice).
    father_of(john_r, vivian).
    father_of(john_r, edith).
    father_of(john_r, john_benford).
    father_of(john_benford, terri).
```

```
father_of(tom, luke).
father_of(tom, sarah).
father_of(tom, rachel).
father_of(tom, andrew).
```

Prolog Variables

You can ask more useful questions of Prolog by placing **variables** in your queries. Prolog variables function as placeholders in an argument list, and they always begin with an upper-case letter. For example. Child is a variable in the relationship mother_of(gertie, Child); it represents no specific person, but in a search, Prolog will match mother_of(gertie, Child) with all three of these facts in Listing 5.1:

```
mother_of(gertie, john_benford).
mother_of(gertie, edith).
mother_of(gertie, vivian).
```

By using variables, you can ask "who" questions of the database, as in questions 3 through 7 in Figure 5.1. Keep in mind that while Prolog reports Jane as the only argument in the database that matches with mother_of(X, sarah), it has no idea that Sarah is Jane's daughter.

Notice, too, that when there is more than one match of the variable X with an argument, Prolog finds them all. However, after the first match is reported, you must tap the semicolon key to see the next one. When there are no more matches to report, Prolog responds with "no."

To see how Prolog finds its answers to these queries, consider question 4 in Figure 5.1. Prolog reads through the database until it comes to a father_of relationship with tom as the first argument, matches the listing in the database with father_of(tom, luke), and gives X the value luke. The Prolog term for associating a variable with a specific constant is **instantiation**; in this case, Prolog instantiates X to luke. It then proceeds to find sarah, rachel, and andrew in the same way. When it runs out of father_of relationships, Prolog quits searching.

Queries 6, 7, and 11 introduce a special Prolog variable called the **anonymous** variable, which is indicated by a single underscore. The anonymous variable matches with anything, but Prolog does not report the matches. In the example of query 6, Prolog reports all 14 of the first arguments in the mother_of relationship, regardless of the name in the second argument. Question 7 is similar except that the anonymous variable is used as the first argument.

Prolog allows you to use the comma (,) as an *and* operator to combine clauses into compound questions. Question 8 is a query with no variables. To respond to it, Prolog searches for a match for father_of(john_h, floyd) and, after finding a match, finds the match for mother_of(sadie, floyd) and reports "yes" to indicate its successful search.

Questions 9, 10, and 11 have shared variables, i.e., variables that occur in two or more goals of the query. Shared variables provide a means of constraining a request by restricting the range of the variables. For example, question 9 asks Prolog to return only persons who are children of both John R and Gertie, and question 10 asks for any persons who are children of Marcy and Tom.

Query 11 introduces another Prolog operator. Prolog reads the vertical bar (|) and the semicolon (;) as a logical *or*. This goal asks for the names of persons in the database who are Gertie's children and who also are either a mother or a father. Notice the parentheses, which are necessary to identify the OR[ed] items.

Prolog Query and Response	An English Equivalent
1. father_of(john_r, vivian). yes	Is John R. the father of Vivian?
2. mother_of(jane, gretchen). no	Is Jane the mother of Gretchen?
3. mother_of(X, sarah). X = jane ->; no	Who is the mother of Sarah?
4. father_of(tom, X). X = luke ->; X = sarah ->; X = rachel ->; X = andrew ->; no	Who are Tom's children?
5. father_of(X, gretchen). no	Who is the father of Gretchen?
6. mother_of(X, _). X = edith ->; X = linda ->; no	Who is a mother?
7. step_father_of(_, X). X = heidi ->; X = gretchen ->; no	Who has a step_father?
8. father_of(john_h, floyd), mother_of(sadie, floyd). yes	Are John H. and Sadie the parents of Floyd?
9. mother_of(gertie, X), father_of(john_r, X). X = john_benford ->; X = edith ->; X = vivian ->; no	Who are the children of Gertie and John R.?
10. mother_of(marcy, X), father_of(tom, X). no	Do any children have Marcy and Tom as parents?
11. mother_of (gertie, X), (mother_of(X, _) | father_of(X, _)). X = john_benford ->; X = edith ->; X = edith ->; no	Which of Gertie's children are parents?

Figure 5.1 Queries to Prolog

In response to the query Prolog searches the list until it finds a **mother_of(gertie...)** relationship and notes the name of the child in that match (**edith**). It then searches **mother_of** or **father_of** relationship with the first argument edith. It finds two of these and so will report **edith** as an answer to the query twice. Failing in its search for more **edith** relationship, Prolog returns to **mother_of(gertie...)** and looks for other second arguments. It finds **john_benford** and continues as it had for **edith**. After exhausting the possibilities for **john_benford**, Prolog looks for other children of Gertie, and, finding none, quits the search.

Variables in Facts

Variables are also occasionally useful for stating facts in a database. As an example, **times(0, X, 0)** could indicate that anything times zero is zero. You could write the relationship **breathes(_)** to say that everyone breathes; but beware, it also will tell Prolog that anything breathes.

5.2 Rules, Structured Data and The Scope of Variables

This section introduces two extensions to the Prolog database. **Rules** allow Prolog to infer new facts from existing facts. **Structures** allow Prolog to manipulate a complex set of data as though it were a single item. The section concludes with an explanation of the scope of Prolog variables.

5.2.1 Rules and How They Work

A Prolog rule states a general relationship that may be used to conclude a specific fact. A synonym is an example of a simple rule. In English we use dad as a synonym for father and recognize that any person who is a father is a dad. To be more specific, one might say: Person A is person B's dad, if person A is the father of person B.

Prolog is much more succinct. To define dad as a synonym for father, just write

```
dad(X, Y) :- father_of(X, Y).
```

In this statement **dad(X, Y)** is known as the **conclusion** of the rule; it is also called the **head** of the rule. The right side, **father_of(X, Y)**, is the requirement or **condition** for finding a successful conclusion to the rule; this part of the rule is also referred to as the **body**. Between the head and body of the rule is the two-character symbol :- sometimes called the **neck**; you can read this as **if**. Note that the rule ends with a period.

A Prolog fact is nothing more than a rule without a body. Prolog will accept facts written as **father_of(floyd, dick) :-.**, but adding the if-operator is not necessary.

Another example of a simple rule is the fact that a person is a parent if she is a mother. In Prolog we could write

```
parent_of(X, Y) :- mother_of(X, Y).
```

If we add this rule to the family database of Program 1.1, we can ask who is a parent with this query

```
?- parent_of(Who, _).
```

and Prolog will respond with

```
Who = edith ->
```

What does Prolog do to obtain this response? It begins by finding **parent_of** as the head of a rule. It then examines the conditions of the rule. In this case, **mother_of** is the first and only condition, so Prolog begins to examine that list of facts. The first one is **mother_of (edith, dick)**. Prolog uses those two variables to instantiate the corresponding variables in the rule head: **parent_of(edith, dick)**. Our query only requested the value of the first variable, so Prolog reports **Who = edith**. If asked for another response (which is done by pressing the semicolon key), Prolog examines the next **mother_of** fact and repeats the process. If it finds no more **mother_of** facts to examine, it gives up the search.

Compound Rules

Compound rules are those with more than one requirement. As an example consider a grandmother. One sufficient condition for being a grandmother is to be the mother of a child who is also a mother. We can write this in Prolog as

```
grandmother_of(X, Z) :- mother_of(X, Y), mother_of(Y, Z).
```

If you read the comma in this statement as "*and*," the statement says that X is the grandmother of Z if X is the mother of Y *and* Y is the mother of Z.

If we query the database with **grandmother_of(X, Z)**, Prolog finds the grandmother rule and looks at the first condition. Next, it goes to the list of **mother_of** facts and instantiates X and Y to the corresponding arguments of the first fact in the list X = edith and Y = dick. Its next step is to look at the second condition. Because that condition has a Y in it, Prolog begins again at the top of the **mother_of** list looking for a match for **mother_of(dick, _)**.

After finding no match for **dick** as the first argument of **mother_of**, Prolog returns to the first condition and instantiates its arguments to those of the second fact in the **mother_of** list, **edith** and **tom**. It proceeds again to the second condition, this time with Y instantiated to **tom**. Again it finds no match for the second condition.

It is not until the first condition is instantiated to **mother_of(gertie, edith)** and the second condition becomes **mother_of(edith, _)** that Prolog finds a match. The first one it discovers is **mother_of(edith, dick)** and then, at the next fact in the list, **mother_of(edith, tom)**. After returning

```
X = gertie
Z = dick ->;

X = gertie
Z = tom ->;
```

for the two matches, Prolog continues its exhaustive search of the database. When it has examined all the possibilities, Prolog quits.

Another type of compound rule is that in which only one condition or another, or one condition out of several, need be true for the conclusion to hold. The **parent_of** relationship illustrates this nicely One person is the parent of another if the first person is either the mother or the father of the second person.

There are two ways to write this in Prolog. One is to use the semicolon (;) to write

```
parent_of(X, Y) :- mother_of(X, Y); father_of(X, Y).
```

Alternatively, we can write

```
parent_of(X, Y) :- mother_of(X, Y).
parent_of(X, Y) :- father_of(X, Y).
```

The latter version is used most often because it is easier to read, especially if the conditions are long. It is the form used for the programs in this book.

While the semicolon is not recommended in rules, it is necessary for queries. For example, to ask about the father or step father of Heidi, you must write father_of(X, heidi); step_father_of(X, heidi)

Returning to our **grandmother_of** rule, what is necessary to have it include all the possibilities for being a grandmother? The existing rule need not be changed. All that needs to be done is to add this second **grandmother_of** rule:

grandmother_of(X, Z) :- mother_of(X, Y), father_of(Y, Z).

Complex Rules

Rules are not limited to having only facts as their conditions; they also may have other rules as a part of their requirements. For example, let's make use of our **parent_of** rule in defining a grandmother. A person is a grandmother if she is the mother of a person who is the parent of someone. We can write

grandmother_of(X, Z) :-   mother_of(X, Y),
                          parent_of(Y, Z).

Given this definition of **grandmother_of**, look at how Prolog responds to the query

grandmother_of(Grandmother, Grandchild).

The first step is to find the **grandmother_of** rule and then examine its first condition, in this case, **mother_of(X, Y)**. X and Z in the rule's head are uninstantiated at this point, and so the X in **mother_of** is also uninstantiated. Prolog goes to the **mother_of** list and begins by instantiating X to **edith** and Y to **dick**. After that, it finds the next (and last) condition in the rule, **parent_of**.

Y is now instantiated to **dick**. Prolog looks at the first **parent_of** rule (remember, there are two) and finds its first and only condition is **mother_of(X, Y)**. Prolog now searches the list of **mother_of facts** trying to find one with **dick** as the first argument.

After failing in that attempt, Prolog examines the next **parent_of** rule. Its condition is father_of(X, Y) so Prolog goes off looking for a **father_of** relationship with **dick** as the first argument.

Failing again, Prolog returns to the **mother_of** portion of the **grandmother_of** rule and instantiates X and Y to **edith** and **tom**, respectively. This produces no success as Prolog examines the first **parent_of** rule, but when it goes to the second one, Prolog finds four sets of matches:

Grandmother = edith
Grandchild = luke ->;

Grandmother = edith
Grandchild = sarah ->;

Grandmother = edith
Grandchild = rachel ->;

Grandmother = edith
Grandchild = andrew ->;

Continuing in the same fashion, Prolog finds an additional five sets of matches before it completes its exhaustive search:

Grandmother = sadie
Grandchild = tom ->;

```
Grandmother = sadie
Grandchild = dick ->;

Grandmother = gertie
Grandchild = terri ->;

Grandmother = gertie
Grandchild = dick ->;

Grandmother = gertie
Grandchild = tom ->;
```

5.2.2 STRUCTURES

Prolog allows you to nest relationships. At times this is very convenient. As an example consider this long relationship:

```
class(prolog, thursday, 6, 9, jeanne, reid, sullivan, 517).
```

It defines a class relationship among eight separate items. Alternatively, we could give Prolog the same information with this statement:

```
class(prolog,
      time(thursday, 6, 9),
      instructor(jeanne, reid),
      location(sullivan, 517)).
```

Relationships like these are called **structures**. Although they may take a little longer to type than the first version, they make it much easier for a reader to understand the meaning of the arguments. They also have a related advantage of allowing meaningful rules like these:

```
teaches(Instructor, Day) :-
                              class(  Classname,
                                      time(Day, Start, Finish),
                                      Instructor,
                                      Location).
instructor(Instructor, Class) :-
                              class(  Class,
                                      Time,
                                      Instructor,
                                      Location).
```

Pay particular attention to the second of these two rules. The English word "instructor" appears there three times, once as the name of the rule and twice as a variable. The variable, Instructor, represents the same entity in both occurrences. In this case that entity is the clause instructor(X, Y). Prolog can instantiate a variable to a clause.

Listing 5.2 contains a list of class relationships and these two rules. Figure 5.2 presents some queries to that database and the results of the queries. The results show that Prolog avoids confusing the instructor rule with the instructor clause used in defining class. However, were we to add to the database facts of the form instructor(linda, maier), Prolog would not know which instructor we meant. In response to the query instructor(A, B), Prolog would list all of the instructors and the classes they teach as listed in the class definitions, and it would also list all of the instructors in the list of instructor facts.

Listing 5.2 A database with structures

```
class( prolog,
        time(thursday, 6, 9),
        instructor(jeanne, reid),
        location(sullivan, 517)).
class( micro_applications,
        time(tuesday, 6, 9),
        instructor(bill, kroesser),
        location(sullivan, 511)).
class( database,
        time(wednesday, 1, 4),
        instructor(bob, button),
        location(administration, 312)).
class( data_structures,
        time(monday, 6, 9),
        instructor(dave, mader),
        location(Wallace, 718)).
class( intro,
        time(monday, 5, 6),
        instructor(linda, maier),
        location(sullivan, 529)).
class( project,
        time(tuesday, 5, 6),
        instructor(bill, kroesser),
        location(sullivan, 301)).
class(pascal,
        time(thursday, 6, 9),
        instructor(polly, cushman),
        location(sullivan, 511)).
teaches(instructor, Day) :- class(   Classname,
                                     time(Day, Start, Finish),
                                     Instructor,
                                     Location ).
instructor(instructor, Class) :- class(Class,
                                       Time,
                                       Instructor,
                                       Location).
```

What instructors teach on Thursday?

```
?- teaches(Instructor, thursday).
Instructor = instructor(jeanne, reid)
Instructor = instructor(polly, cushman)
```

What classes does Bill Kroesser teach?

```
?- instructor(instructor(bill, kroesser), Class).
Class = micro_applications
Class = project
```

What days does Jeanne Reid teach?

```
?- teaches(instructor(jeanne, reid), Day).
Day = thursday
```

Who teaches the Prolog class?

```
?- instructor(Instructor, prolog).
Instructor = instructor(jeanne, reid)
```

or

```
?- instructor(instructor(Fname, Lname), prolog).
Fname = jeanne
Lname = reid
```

Who teaches classes that run from 6 to 9 on Mondays?

```
?- class(_, time(Monday, 6, 9), Instructor, _).
Instructor = instructor(dave, mader)
```

What classes are held in room 511 of Sullivan Hall?

```
?- class(Class, _, _, location(sullivan, 511)).
Class = micro_applications
Class = pascal
```

Figure 5.2 Some queries to Listing 5.2

Suppose you needed to ask frequent questions about the location of classes. You could avoid the need to query with the class rule and the anonymous variables it requires by adding a rule like this to the database:

```
room(Class, Building, Room) :- class(Class,
                                      Time,
                                      Teacher,
                                      location(Building, Room)).
```

Using this rule, you can find out the classes in room 511 of Sullivan with the query

```
room(Class, sullivan, 511).
```

Similarly,

```
room(prolog, Building, Room).
```

would cause Prolog to report the location of the Prolog class.

Those of you who are familiar with other programming languages may recognize these nested relations as Prolog's equivalent of records. Each relationship is a field in the record. This structured data type is useful in Prolog as elsewhere because of its ability to reflect the characteristics of a situation.

5.2.3 THE SCOPE OF PROLOG VARIABLES

The scope of a variable is the portion of a program that can refer to the variable. While this can be complicated to define in some languages, it is simple in Prolog. The scope of a Prolog variable is just the fact, rule, or query that contains it.

To illustrate this, consider this rule:

```
likes(Person, shish_kebab) :-
            likes(Person, grilled_vegetables),
            likes(Person, grilled_meat).
```

The scope of the variable Person is the entire rule. This means that, if we give Prolog a goal of the form

```
?- likes(john, shish_kebab).
```

then Person will be instantiated to john as Prolog determines the answer. Similarly, in responding to the query

```
?- likes(Person, shish_kebab) .
```

Prolog will instantiate **Person** to each name it finds in the list of relationships in the database with the form **likes(Name, Something)**. In every instance, **Person** will be instantiated to one constant at a time.

If **Person** is used in other relationships in the database, those instances have no relationship to the **Person** variable in this rule.

5.3 OPERATORS AND FUNCTIONS

Prolog was not designed to manipulate numbers. Nevertheless, numeric operations are a part of many Prolog programs that are not really numeric. These are some examples.

- Incrementing and decrementing coordinates to move a chess piece
- Counting items in a list
- Sorting or otherwise comparing items by size or order

This section begins by explaining the use of Prolog's two groups of operators, the comparison operators and the arithmetic operators. These are built-in Prolog predicates, set up so that they can be used without the normal predicate syntax. Next is a short section describing the arithmetic operator, followed by one on built-in math functions. The section concludes with examples that use some of the operators and functions.

5.3.1 OPERATORS

The normal syntax for Prolog predicates is to list the name of the predicate followed by its list of arguments in parentheses followed by a period. An example is

greater_than(Item1, Item2).

Operators that follow this syntax are called **prefix** operators. An alternative syntax is to put the predicate between the items being compared; these are infix operators. Substituting the symbol ">" for greater_than, we can write the above statement in **infix** form as

Item1 > Item2.

Because this syntax is used so often for arithmetic and comparison operations, most Prolog systems allow its use. Remember that both forms mean the same thing to Prolog: a data structure that can be evaluated true or false.

Comparison Operators

Arity Prolog's comparison operators compare two terms and evaluate their alphanumeric values. The == operator determines if two terms are equivalent, and the \== operator determines if two terms are not equivalent. For example the expression cat == cat would be true and cat \== cat would be false. The relative order operators are @<, @>, @=<, and @>=. Use these to determine less-than, greater-than, less-than-or-equal-to, and greater-than or equal-to, relationships respectively. You can use *not* in an expression with any operators.

Be careful not to confuse the = unification operator with the == comparison operator. The unification predicate combines the two terms if possible. The comparison predicate determines if the two terms are equivalent but has no other effect on them. As an example, consider the following statements:

X = 'Zooey'.
X == 'Zooey'.

The first statement gives X the value Zooey, and the statement succeeds. The second case will succeed if X has already been instantiated to Zooey; otherwise, it will fail.

Arity Prolog provides a prefix operator that either tests for or returns a comparison value. The operator is compare, and its form is

compare(Relationship, Term1, Term2)

If Relationship is an uninstantiated variable, compare returns the symbol (=, > or <) which describes the relationship between Term1 and Term2. Otherwise, it returns a true or false value.

Arithmetic Operators

Prolog implementations vary in arithmetic operators they provide. Arity Prolog offers the usual (+), subtraction (-), multiplication (*), and division (/) operators. In addition it includes operators to raise a number to a power (^), a modulo operator (mod), and a predicate to round a number.

Figure 5.3 lists Arity Prolog's arithmetic operators for common arithmetic operations and provide examples of their use. It also includes two built-in real number constants provided in Arity Prolog, pi and random. Each is replaced in the expression in which it appears by a real number; pi is replaced by the value of pi and random is replaced by a random number with a value between 0 and 1.

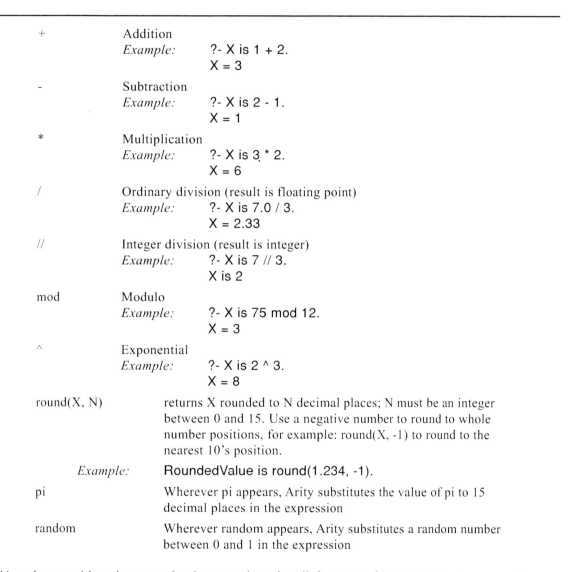

+	Addition	
	Example:	?- X is 1 + 2.
		X = 3
-	Subtraction	
	Example:	?- X is 2 - 1.
		X = 1
*	Multiplication	
	Example:	?- X is 3 * 2.
		X = 6
/	Ordinary division (result is floating point)	
	Example:	?- X is 7.0 / 3.
		X = 2.33
//	Integer division (result is integer)	
	Example:	?- X is 7 // 3.
		X is 2
mod	Modulo	
	Example:	?- X is 75 mod 12.
		X = 3
^	Exponential	
	Example:	?- X is 2 ^ 3.
		X = 8
round(X, N)	returns X rounded to N decimal places; N must be an integer between 0 and 15. Use a negative number to round to whole number positions, for example: round(X, -1) to round to the nearest 10's position.	
	Example:	RoundedValue is round(1.234, -1).
pi	Wherever pi appears, Arity substitutes the value of pi to 15 decimal places in the expression	
random	Wherever random appears, Arity substitutes a random number between 0 and 1 in the expression	

Note that an arithmetic expression is not evaluated until the expression appears as an argument to an arithmetic evaluable predicate.

Figure 5.3 The common arithmetic operators

To compare arithmetic expressions, Arity Prolog allows you to use the standard inequality operators ($>$, $<$, $>=$, $<=$). To test the equality of two arithmetic expressions use $=:=$ and use $=\=$ to test for their inequality.

5.3.2 ARITHMETIC

The word is tells Prolog to perform the calculations for a following arithmetic expression. It is another of Prolog's infix operators that does not require the normal predicate syntax. The general form for using it is

<variable> is <arithmetic_expression>

The following example illustrates its use.

bonus(Number) :- Number is 2 + 3.
?- bonus (3).
no
?- bonus(5).
yes
?- bonus(X).
X = 5 ->

Prolog evaluates the arithmetic expression first and then does one of two things:

1. If the variable is not instantiated, Prolog instantiates it to the value of the expression.
2. If the variable is already instantiated, Prolog compares the variable's value and the expression's value; only if the two are the same, does the goal succeed.

Prolog implementations traditionally provided only integer numbers but newer ones, including Arity Prolog, can manipulate both integer and real numbers. Arity Prolog integers range from -2,147,483,648 to 2,147,438,647. Be certain to use a space to separate integers from the periods that end clauses; in some Prolog implementations, numbers with a period are always interpreted as real.

Real numbers in Arity Prolog may range in magnitude from $-1.7e^{308}$ to $1.7e^{308}$. You may write real numbers either with exponents as in scientific notation or in the standard way with decimal points, although you must include a digit both before and after the decimal point. *Caution*: Because floating-point operations are inexact, an attempt to unify two apparently equal floating-point numbers may not succeed.

Real numbers can be used in is clauses.

Example: X is 0.1 * Y (as a condition in a rule)

Real numbers also can be used in a clause that unifies them with a variable.

Example: X = 3.14

Notice the difference in how Prolog evaluates the following two expressions.

?- X is 5 + 2.   ?- X = 5 + 2.
X = 7 ->   X = 5 + 2 ->

In the first example, Prolog evaluates the arithmetic expression and unifies X with the result, 7. In the second example, Prolog instantiates the variable X to 5 + 2.

When integers and real numbers are both in an arithmetic expression, the integers are converted to real numbers before Prolog performs the calculation. The result is a real number. You can explicitly convert real numbers to integers with the predicate integer(X). Similarly you can convert an integer to a real number with the predicate float(X).

If the result of a calculation is a number that is too large or too small to be expressed, Arity Prolog returns the atom err.

Math Functions

The Arity Prolog math functions work with integers, real numbers, and with both types used together, but all of the functions return real numbers. Prolog assumes that angles are measured in radians. The general syntax for all the functions is

X is function(Y)

where X is an unbound variable and Y is a bound variable or a number. Figure 5.4 lists the math functions available in Arity Prolog.

abs()	absolute value
sqrt()	square root
exp()	natural log base e raised to the value's power
ln()	natural log of the value
log()	decimal log of the value
sin()	sine
cos()	cosine
tan()	tangent
asin()	arc sine
acos()	arc cosine
atan()	arctangent

Figure 5.4 Math functions

5.3.3 USING THE OPERATORS

One entry in the database of a wholesale liquor distributor contains the brand name and the proof of the liquor. These are some of the entries:

proof(jims_beam, 160).
proof(old_logger, 177).
proof(johnny_runner, 130).
proof(some_times, 180).

The company found that they sometimes needed to report the percentage of the alcohol in liquors instead of the proof. To facilitate the reporting, they added this rule to the database.

```
percent(Liquor, Percent_alcohol) :-
        proof(Liquor, Proof),
        Percent_alcohol is Proof / 2.
```

This rule allows queries like this:

```
?- percent(old_logger. Percent_alcohol).
Percent_alcohol =88.5
```

They can also get reports on all items by asking

```
?- percent(Liquor, Percent_alcohol).
Liquor = jims_beam
Percent = 80.0
Liquor = old_logger
Percent = 88.5
Liquor = johnny_runner
Percent = 65.0
Liquor = some_times
Percent = 90.0
```

An example in which the arithmetic is a little more complex is a database containing the average annual temperature of cities. The climatologist who first set up the database entered all of the temperatures in degrees Fahrenheit. Here are some of the entries.

```
ave_temp(addis_ababa, 62).
ave_temp(berlin, 49).
ave_temp(calgary, 38).
ave_temp(belgrade, 52).
ave_temp(chicago, 50).
ave_temp(boston, 48).
ave_temp(washington_dc, 55).
ave_temp(jerusalem, 61).
ave_temp(khartoum, 84).
ave_temp(san_diego, 61).
```

These worked fine several years ago, but now she needs to use Celsius temperatures most of the time. Rather than reenter all of her data, she added this rule to her database.

```
ave_temp_celsius(Location, C_temp) :-
        ave_temp(Location, F_temp),
        C_temp is round((F_temp - 32) * 5 // 9, 0).
```

This lets her obtain the Celsius temperature with queries like this:

```
?- ave_temp_celsius(berlin, C_temp).
C_temp =9.0
```

She can also check the database to find all locations with a particular Celsius temperature with this query:

```
?- ave_temp_celsius(Location, 16.0).
Location = jerusalem ->;
Location = san_diego ->;
```

A final example uses the greater-than comparison operator. As an exercise, a high school geography teacher requires his students to compare pairs of cities and determine from their latitudes and longitudes which of the pair is further north and which is further west. How would an enterprising student get Prolog to figure this out?

The only problem in creating the fact base would be selecting the name for the relationship. Let's assume that it is called "location" and the order of arguments are city, latitude, and longitude. Assume also that the programmer chooses to enter south latitudes and east longitudes as negative numbers.

```
location(tokyo, 35, -139).
location(rome, 41, -12).
location(london, 51, 0) .
location(canberra, -35, -149).
location(madrid, 48, 3).
```

Now, to find out if one city is north of another, Prolog needs only to get the latitude of both cities and then compare their sizes. One city will be north of another if the latitude of the first city is greater than the latitude of the second. Our students Prolog rule to do that looks like this:

```
north_of(X, Y) :-
            location(X, Lat1, _),
            location(Y, Lat2, _).
            Lat1 > Lat2.
```

To learn if Madrid is north of Tokyo one can enter **north_of(Madrid, Tokyo)**, and Prolog will respond with a "yes." The query **north_of(City, tokyo)** will cause Prolog to report all cities north of Tokyo. The rule to determine if a city is west of another is quite similar:

```
west_of(X, Y) :-
    location(X, _, Long1),
    location(Y, _, Long2),
    Long1 > Long2.
```

Queries to Prolog using west_of are left to you.

Prolog's arithmetic capabilities become more useful when they are applied to iterative processes. These are discussed in sections 5.4 and 5.5.

5.4 RECURSION AND RECURSIVE RULES

Once upon a time there was a story that went like this:

    Once upon a time there was a story that went like this:

        Once upon a time there was story that went like this:

          *   *   *   *

        And everyone lived happily ever after.

    And everyone lived happily ever after.

And everyone lived happily ever after.

A process or definition (or story) is recursive if it uses or calls itself. The objective of a recursive process in a program is to repeatedly reduce the complexity of the problem until the solution is trivial. A popular example is the recursive solution to the towers of Hanoi problem. In that problem there are three pegs, one of which has a stack of successively smaller disks on it (see Figure 5.5). The objective is to move the stack from peg A to peg C subject to these rules:

1. Disks may only be moved from peg to peg.
2. Only one disk may be moved at a time.
3. The only disks that may be moved are the top disks on the pegs.
4. A disk may be placed only on the base level or on a larger disk.

You can solve the towers problem with this recursive algorithm: If n is the number of disks,

1. Move n-1 disks from the source peg to the spare peg.
2. Move the bottom disk from the source peg to the destination peg.
3. Finally, move the n-1 disks from the spare peg to the destination peg.

What part of this procedure is recursive? When does the solution become trivial? How does one know when to stop moving the disks?

Recursion is the main repetitive control structure available in Prolog. This section presents examples to illustrate its use. The final example is a Prolog program that solves the towers of Hanoi puzzle using the algorithm from the previous paragraph.

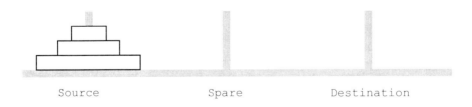

Figure 5.5 The Towers of Hanoi puzzle

5.4.1 RECURSION AS A GENERALIZATION OF NON-RECURSIVE RULES

One way to look at recursion is to consider it a generalization of a set of non-recursive rules. As an example, consider the set of rules that would define grandparent, great-grandparents, great-great-grandparents, and so on in our family database. Those rules might look like this:

```
grandparent(Ancestor, Descendant) :-
        parent(Ancestor, Person), parent(Person, Descendant),
greatgrandparent(Ancestor, Descendant) :-
        parent(Ancestor, Person), grandparent(Person, Descendant).
greatgreatgrandparent(Ancestor, Descendant) :-
        parent(Ancestor, Person), greatgrandparent(Person, Descendant).
```

Notice the pattern in the rules: The next ancestor in the sequence is the parent of the current ancestor. This recursive rule for ancestor captures that pattern:

```
ancestor (Ancestor, Descendant) :-
        parent(Ancestor, Person),
        ancestor(Person, Descendant).
```

This rule gives Prolog all of the information it needs to find ancestors except for telling it that parents are ancestors. For that, we need an additional rule:

```
ancestor(Ancestor, Descendant) :-
        parent(Ancestor, Descendant).
```

A non-recursive rule such as this one is necessary to allow Prolog to stop the repetitive calls and find solutions to the goal, if any exist.

Listing 5.3 contains the family database of Listing 5.1 together with the ancestor and parent rules. If we address this query to Prolog,

```
ancestor(sadie, sarah)
```

prolog will respond with "yes."

Listing 5.3 A family relationship database with an ancestor rule

```
ancestor(Ancestor, Descendant) :-
        parent(Ancestor, Descendant).

ancestor(Ancestor, Descendant) :-
        parent(Ancestor, Person),
        ancestor(Person, Descendant).

parent(Parent, Child) :- mother_of(Parent, Child).
parent(Parent, Child) :- father_of(Parent, Child).

mother_of(edith, dick)
mother_of(edith, tom).
```

mother_of(sadie, calvin).

mother_of(sadie, alice).

mother_of(sadie, floyd).

mother_of(gertie, john_benford).

mother_of(gertie, edith).

mother_of(gertie, vivian).

mother_of(jane, luke).

mother_of(jane, sarah).

mother_of(jane, rachel).

mother_of(marcy, heidi).

mother_of(marcy, gretchen).

mother_of(linda, andrew).

step_father_of(tom, heidi).

step_father_of(tom, gretchen).

father_of(floyd, tom).

father_of(floyd, dick).

father_of(john_h, floyd).

father_of(john_h, calvin).

father_of(john_h, alice).

father_of(john_r, vivian).

father_of(john_r, edith).

father_of(john_r, john_benford).

father_of(john_benford, terri).

father_of(tom, luke).

father_of(tom, sarah).

father_of(tom, rachel).

father_of(tom, andrew).

Prolog follows these steps to determine the truth of the query:

1. Try the first ancestor rule instantiating arguments to sadie and sarah, respectively
   2. Call parent(sadie, sarah).
      3. Check for mother_of(sadie, sarah) and fail.
      4. Check for father_of(sadie, sarah) and fail.
5. Try the second ancestor rule with the same arguments
   6. Call parent(sadie, —)
      7. Check mother_of list with sadie as first argument.
      8. Instantiate the second argument to the first of Sadie's children in the mother_of list = calvin
         9. Try the first ancestor rule with Calvin as Sarah's ancestor, ancestor(calvin, sarah)
            10. fail

11.   Try the second ancestor rule with Calvin as Sarah's ancestor, ancestor(calvin, sarah)

12.   fail

13. Instantiate the second argument to Sadie's next child = alice

14.   fail (as with calvin)

15. Instantiate the second argument to Sadie's next child = floyd

16. Call ancestor(floyd, sarah) with first rule

17.   fail

18. Call ancestor(floyd, sarah) with second rule

19.   Call parent(floyd. --).

20.   Call mother_of(floyd, --).

21.   fail

22.   Call father_of(floyd, --).

23.   Instantiate second argument to tom

24.   Call ancestor (tom, sarah) with first rule

25.   Call parent(tom, sarah)

26.   Call mother_of(tom, sarah)

27.   fail

28.   Call father_of(tom, sarah).

At that point, Prolog has confirmed that Sadie is Sarah's ancestor and will report "yes." If we were to ask it to (by pressing the semicolon key), Prolog would continue to search for other ways in which to confirm the relationship, but, for this database, would find none.

You can use the ancestor rules to find either ancestors or descendants or all possible combinations of the two. (Section 5.7 discusses the ordering of the clauses in the body of the rule to make it most efficient depending on whether it is finding descendants or ancestors.)

Stream Networks

The database in Listing 5.4 provides another example of a set of relationships that can be described recursively. The streams and the body of water into which they empty are identified with me relationship

    tributary(Stream, Body_of_water).

Two rules called drains_to define the relationship that specifies all the bodies of water receiving the waters of a given stream:

    drains_to(Stream, Body_of_water) :-
            tributary(Stream, Body_of_water).
    drains_to(Stream, Body_of_water) :-
            tributary(Stream, Intermediate),
            drains_to(Intermediate, Body_of_water).

The second drains_to contains the recursive call and allows Prolog to find the indirect tributaries.
The first drains_to lets Prolog find all of the situations listed in the tributary fact list and thus serves as a stopping condition for the recursion.

5.4.2 Suggestions for Writing Recursive Rule Sets

When writing recursive rules, put the stopping condition first. This ensures that Prolog will evaluate the non-recursive rule before generating another recursive call. Also, in the recursive rule, put the recursive predicate at the end of the body of the recursive rule. Recursion with the recursive call at the end of the rule is called **tail recursion**.

Following these suggestions will improve the efficiency of the rules and will, in some cases, prevent errors. To see how alternate arrangements can lead to errors, try switching the order of the two predicates in the body of the recursive drains_to rule in Listing 5.4. When you do that, Prolog responds to the query

Listing 5.4 Stream networks

```
?- drains_to(hurricane_ck, Where).
drains_to(X, Y) :- tributary(X, Y).
drains_to(X, Z) :-
            tributary(X, Y),
            drains_to(Y, Z).

tributary(mississippi, gulf_of_mexico).
tributary(missouri, mississippi).
tributary(ohio, mississippi).
tributary(kanawha, ohio).
tributary(hurricane_ck, kanawha).
tributary(poplar_fork_ck, hurricane_ck).
tributary(eighteen_mile_ck, kanawha).
tributary(long_branch, poplar_fork_ck).
tributary(jakes_branch, eighteen_mile_ck).
tributary(sandusky, lake_erie).
```

with the correct responses (kanawha, ohio, mississippi, and gulf_of_mexico) but continues in an endless loop. The loop never ends because as Prolog evaluates the drains_to condition in the second drains_to rule, both arguments are uninstantiated, and Prolog matches them with values from the database over and over.

Along with this advice on how to write recursive rules, we caution you to take care to avoid inadvertent recursion. You do this when you define a pair of rules in terms of one another. For example, one could define

```
brother(Boy, Girl) :- sister(Girl, Boy).
sister(Girl, Boy) :-brother(Boy, Girl).
```

You probably would never make such an obvious mistake, but this type of error becomes harder to recognize when there are more than two definitions in the cycle.

5.4.3 Finding Factorial Values

Mathematicians define the factorial of an integer as the product of the integer and all the integers less than it Five factorial is

5 * 4 * 3 * 2 * 1 = 120

They also define 1 factorial to be (1 * zero factorial) and zero factorial to be 1. While you may seldom want to know the factorial of a number, the process of determining the value provides a classic illustration of the way recursion works in Prolog.

This rule will return the correct value for zero factorial:

factorial(0, 1) :- !.

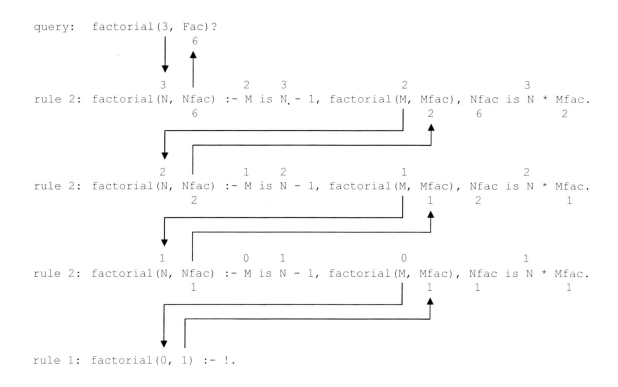

Figure 5.6 A query to factorial

Read it as saying that 0 factorial is 1. The body of the rule consists of just an exclamation point. The ! is a standard Prolog symbol called the **cut**. In this instance, it instructs Prolog to stop looking for other ways to satisfy the factorial rule.

By now, you may have an idea for a recursive algorithm for finding the other factorial values: For a number N, find the factorial of N-1 and multiply that value by N. In Prolog we can write the rule this way:

```
factorial(N, Nfac):-
              M is N - 1,
              factorial(M, Mfac),
              Nfac is N * Mfac.
```

Consider this interaction with Prolog:

```
?- factorial(3, Factorial)
Factorial = 6
```

Figure 5.6 shows the steps that Prolog followed to determine the value 6 for Nfac. The downward-pointing arrows show how values are passed for each recursive invocation of a rule, and the upward-pointing ones show the route of values passed back up the recursive chain.

5.4.4 THE TOWERS OF HANOI

The predicates defined in Listing 5.5 will solve the towers of Hanoi puzzle for whatever number of disks (N) you assign as an argument to the hand predicate. There are two built-in predicates in the report rule that need some explanation. The write predicate sends the item enclosed in parentheses to the output stream. The other new term is nl. Inserted into the body of a rule, nl puts a carriage return in the output stream. The report rule produced the statements shown in the lower portion of Listing 5.5

Listing 5.5 The Towers of Hanoi

```
hanoi(N) :- move(N, source, destination, spare).

report(X, Y) :-
              write('Move top disk from the '),
              write(X),
              write(' peg to the '),
              write(Y),
              write(' peg.'),
              nl.
move(0, _, _, _) :- !.
move(N, Source, Destination, Spare) :-
              M is N - 1,
              move(              ),  ; Algorithm   step 1
              report (           ),  ;             step 2
              move(              ),  ;             step 3

?- hanoi(3).
Move top disk from the source peg to the destination peg.
Move top disk from the source peg to the spare peg.
Move top disk from the destination peg to the spare peg.
Move top disk from the source peg to the destination peg.
```

Move top disk from the spare peg to the source peg.

Move top disk from the spare peg to the destination peg.

Move top disk from the source peg to the destination peg.

As with the previous examples, the recursive move procedure requires two rules. The first is the stopping condition that applies only when the number of disks to move is zero. The cut in this rule indicates that Prolog should allow no more recursive calls now that the number of disks to move is zero.

The second move rule contains two recursive calls. These, together with the report rule, implement the algorithm in the introduction to this section The algorithm's steps are:

1. Move n-1 disks from the source peg to the spare peg.

2. Move the bottom disk from the source peg to the destination peg.

3. Finally, move the n-1 disks from the spare peg to the destination peg.

Listing 5.5 does not list the arguments for the recursive calls; filling those in is left to you.

5.5 Lists

Often you will want to work with a group of data items all at once. Examples of data to consider as a group are the children of Edith, the streams that flow into the Kanawha River, and cities with an average annual temperature of 14-16° C. In Prolog you can manipulate data sets like these in lists.

A list is a data structure used especially for non-numeric processing and common to many programming languages. Consider a Prolog list as having the same characteristics as a shopping list with one exception: A Prolog list is an ordered, sequence of elements while in our every day lists order is seldom important.

A list may contain constants, variables (which are used as placeholders to be replaced with data later), structures, other lists, or a mixture of these. To write a list in Prolog, name the elements in order and enclose them in square brackets, as in these examples:

[tom, dick, harry]

[Father, Mother, [Kids]]

[father_of(luke), mother_of(andrew)]

This section contains a general discussion of using Prolog lists including an explanation of several Prolog predicates for manipulating and evaluating lists.

5.5.1 Referencing Lists

The procedures we have discussed so far do not allow you to reference the items in a Prolog list. To illustrate the problem, consider this example of a data entry and query:

child_of(sadie, [alice, floyd, calvin]).

?- child_of(sadie, alice).

no

Prolog responds to the query with no because it does not match alice in the query with the list in the fact. We begin this discussion of using lists with a description of the procedures for referencing the elements of a list.

Consider lists to have two parts: the first element, called the **head**, and the rest of the list, called the **tail**. The head of a list is not a list. The tail is a list containing every element of the original list except the first element. Figure 5.7 shows several examples of lists and identifies the head and tail of each.

Notice the empty brackets shown as the tail of the last list in Figure 5.7. The symbol [] represents a special list called the **empty list**. It is a part of all lists, and it differs from all other lists in that it has no head and no tail.

LIST	HEAD	TAIL
[alice, floyd, calvin]	alice	[floyd. calvin]
[soap, chips, [pop, beer, milk]	soap	[chips,[pop, beer, milk]]
[[chips, dip], [pop, beer]]	[chips, dip]	[[pop, beer]]
[milk]	milk	[]
[]	none	none
[a, b]	a	[b]
[a	b]	a	b

Figure 5.7 Lists, heads and tails

Prolog syntax recognizes the vertical bar (|) as a separator of the head and tail of lists. To illustrate its use, look at this query about child_of relationships with sadie as the first argument:

```
?- child_of(sadie, [H | T]).
H = alice
T = [floyd, calvin]
```

Prolog finds the fact in the database with sadie as the first argument and instantiates the second argument in the query to the second argument of the fact, [alice, floyd, calvin]. It then instantiates H to the first element in the list and T to the remainder of the list.

Figure 5.8 provides several examples of queries referencing a list. The last three reference both the head and tail of the list. Queries 4 and 5 reference the head of the tail of the list with the notation [H | [M | . . .] where M indicates the element that is the head of the tail, or the second element in the list.

Notice that the fourth query causes Prolog to respond with no. The response is negative because no list of children in the database of child_of relationships has the element rachel remaining after the first two elements are removed. What does remain after the first two elements are removed is the list [rachel] as query 5 confirms.

There is one Prolog list that differs from all the others, the list referenced by [element1 | element2]. When this notation is used, with a constant following the vertical bar, the tail of the list is an element, not a list.

If the database contains grocery_list([bread, beans]), Prolog will respond as follows:

```
?- grocery_list([Head | Tail]).
Head = bread
Tail = [beans]
```

These queries and responses are based on the following list of facts:

child_of(sadie, [alice, floyd, calvin]).

child_of(jane, [luke, sarah, rachel]).

child_of(edith, [dick, tom]).

child_of(linda, [butch, erica, elizabeth, eliot, andrew]).

1. ?- child_of(X, [luke, sarah, rachel]).

   X = jane

2. ?- child_of(X, [_, _, _]).

   X = sadie

   X = jane

3. ?- child_of(X, [H | T]).

   X = sadie

   H = alice

   T = (floyd, calvin]

   X = jane

   H = luke

   T = [sarah, rachel]

   X = edith

   H = dick

   T = [tom]

   X = linda

   H = butch

   T = [erica, elizabeth, eliot, andrew]

4. ?- child_of(X, [H | [M | [rachel]]]).

   no

5. ?-child_of(X, [H | [M | [rachel]]]).

   X = jane

   H = luke

   M = sarah

Figure 5.8 Queries referencing a list

This is the response we have seen before; the tail of the list is itself a list. However, look closely at this response to the query when the database fact is changed to **grocery_list ([bread I beans])**:

?- grocery_list([Head | Tail]).

Head = bread

Tail = beans

For this case, the tail is not a list. The last list in Figure 5.7 is another example of this special list.

Referencing all of the items in a list is typically a recursive operation; queries 4 and 5 in Figure 5.8 exhibit the nested structure that lends itself to recursion. The process is to consider first the head of the list and then the head of the rest of the list. Most predicates that manipulate lists operate in this way We consider several of these predicates, the first being one that confirms membership in a list.

5.5.2 Examining the Elements of a List

It is often helpful to know a particular element is a member of a list. Is Vivian a child of Gertie? Does Hurricane Creek flow into the Kanawha River? Is IS 530 a core course for IS majors? Prolog has a standard (but not usually built-in) predicate to answer questions like these. It is called member.

The Member Predicate

The **member** predicate determines if an element is in a list by first checking if that element is the head of the list and then checking if it is a member of the tail of the list. The Prolog predicates to perform these two checks can be written like this:

```
member(X, [X|_]).
member(X, [_ | Tail]) :- member(X, Tail).
```

The first member predicate confirms those cases of membership when the element is the head of the list. The second strips the head from the list and calls member again with the shortened list.

Notice how the notation causes Prolog to remove the head for the recursive call. When you enter the query **member(cat, [dog, cat])**, what does Prolog do? Figure 5.9 traces the calls and the instantiation of the variables as Prolog tries to satisfy the query.

What happens after Prolog finds a solution to satisfy the query goal? It keeps searching for more solutions. If the list were **[dog, cat, cow, cat]**, Prolog would report yes twice, once for each cat in the list. The process continues until the tail of the list becomes the empty list. When that happens, the recursive call is **member (X, [ ])**. The set of arguments in this call does not match the arguments in either of the two member predicates so the attempt to satisfy the goal fails (again) and Prolog gives up the search.

Why does **member(X, [ ])** not match with the member predicates and thus stop the recursion? Remember the characteristics of the empty set. It has neither a head nor a tail and consequently cannot be divided into a head and a tail This means the second arguments of both member predicates have a structure different from the second argument of the recursive call and a match is impossible.

Another question to consider is the effect of the member determination process on the original list. The original list remains unchanged; only the value to which the tail variable is instantiated changes.

Although we have defined member to be a predicate for determining membership in a list, you can use it in other ways. Suppose you wanted to show all the members of a list. Just query member like this:

```
?-member (X, [sue, sally, sid]).
X = sue ->;
X = sally ->;
X = sid ->;
```

To satisfy the query member (cat. [dog, cat]), PROLOG begins by matching the query arguments with the arguments in the first member predicate:

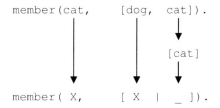

This fails because cat and dog do not match. PROLOG then tries the second member predicate:

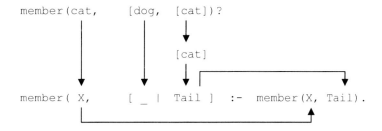

Now PROLOG matches the arguments in the recursive call against the first predicate:

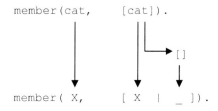

Because cat matches with cat the goal succeeds, and PROLOG reports yes indicating that cat is a member of [dog, cat].

Figure 5.9 How member works

Another, less obvious, but quite useful way you can use member is to find items common to more than one list. This compound query illustrates how to do that:

```
?- member(X, [sue, sally, sid]),
    member(X, [bill, coo, sue, sally, jack]).
X = sue ->;
X = sally ->;
no
```

In this case, the only X's reported are the ones that satisfy the membership test in both portions of the query.

Finding Elements in Specific Positions in a List

The First

What is a simple definition for a predicate that will return the first element in a list? Knowing that the first element is the head of the list and knowing how to reference the head of the list makes this definition simple:

```
first(X, [X | _]).
```

This query and response demonstrate the predicate:

```
?- first(First, [x, y, z]).
First = x
```

The Second

Finding the second element is only slightly more complicated. We need to return the head of the tail. This predicate does that:

```
second(X, [_, [X | _]).
```

This is an illustration of its use:

```
?- second(Second, [x, y, z]).  Second = y
```

The Last

The technique we have been using makes it easy to find the third, fourth, and so on elements in a list, but what happens when we need the last element in a list and don't know ahead of time how many elements are in the list? If this problem sounds to you like it requires some recursion in the solution, you are right.

If there is only one element in the list, this predicate will return the answer:

```
last(X, [X]).
```

This will serve as the stopping condition. When there is more than one element in the list, we need only remove the head of the list repeatedly until just one element remains. This predicate will remove the heads, eventually making a list that matches the arguments in the first last predicate:

```
last(X, [_ | Tail]) :- last(X, Tail).
```

If we apply it to the x, y, z list it returns the last element:

```
?- last(Last, [x, y, z]).
Last = z
```

Counting List Elements

Counting the elements in a list requires Prolog to remove successive heads just as it must do to find the last element in the list. In addition, there must be a clause to increment a counter each time a head is removed. This modification of the last/2 predicate does that:

```
count(Num, [_ | Tail]) :-
        count(Num2, Tail),
        Num is Num2 + 1.
```

There must also be a stopping condition. Since this predicate removes the heads from the list until there are no elements remaining, the empty list is an appropriate place to end the process. Enter this count rule before the recursive one:

```
count(0, []) :- !.
```

This illustrates a query to the count predicate and Prolog's response:

```
?- count(Num_elements, [49, 17, 4]).
Num_elements = 3
```

Arity Prolog provides a built-in predicate to count the elements in a list. It is **length(List, Length)**. It works just like count/2.

```
?- length(Num_elements, [a, b, [c, d, e]]).
Num_elements = 3
```

Summing a List

Summing a list differs from counting it only in that the accumulator sums the elements of the list This modified version of count, called sum_list, will find the sum of a lists elements:

```
sum_list(0, []):- !.
sum_list(Sum, [Head | Tail]) :-
        sum_list(Sum2, Tail),
        Sum is Head + Sum2.
```

5.5.3 FORMING NEW LISTS

Prolog's list syntax makes it easy to add a new element to the head to a list. This predicate does that:

```
addhead(List, Element, [Element | List]).
```

A query to addhead/3 can get the new list:

```
?- addhead([a, b, c], x, Newlist).
Newlist = [x, a, b, c]
```

or it can get the old list:

```
?- addhead(Oldlist, x, [x, a, b, c]).
Oldlist = [a, b, c]
```

or it can get the element added to the old list to get the new list:

```
?- addhead([a, b, c], Element, [x, a, b, c]).
Element = x
```

The Append Predicate

The process of adding one list to the back of another is called appending. For example, suppose we had these two lists:

```
List1 = ['RI', 'WV', 'OR']
List2 = ['OH', 'MO']
```

Appending List2 to List1 will produce new List3:

```
List3 = ['RI', 'WV', 'OR', 'OH', 'MO']
```

The standard Prolog predicate known as append/3 performs this operation:

```
append([], List2, List2).
append([Head | Tail1], List2, [Head | Tail3]) :-
        append(Tail1, List2, Tail3).
```

The first statement says that if the first list is empty, the result is just the second list. The second append/3 statement says that to append List2 to List1 to form List3, put the head of List1 at the head of List3 and append the two tails.

Figure 5.10 traces the instantiation of the variables in the recursive process of appending the list [c, d] to the list [a, b] to form the new list [a, b, c, d].

Append/3, like addhead/3, can be used in different ways. You already know how to use it to form a new list. You can also use it to determine what needs to be added to the front of a list to give a particular result, as in this example:

```
?- append(Front, [c, d], [a, b, c, d]).
Front = [a, b]
```

Another possibility is to use it to truncate a list of a specified front portion:

```
?- append([a, b], Truncated_list, (a, b, c, d]).
Truncated_list = [c, d]
```

Still another way to use it is to find all the possible combinations of List1 and List2 that will produce List3:

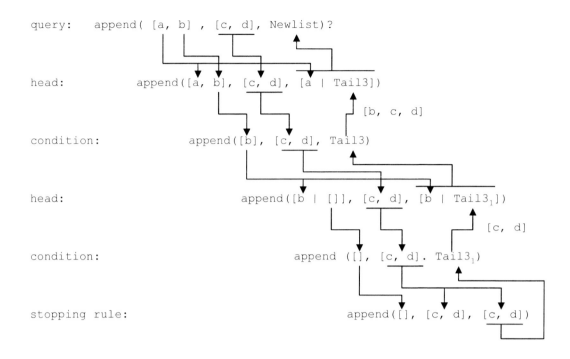

Figure 5.10 An example of appending

```
?- append(List1, List2, [a, b, c, d]).
List1 = []
List2 = [a, b, c, d]

List1 = [a]
List2 = [b, c, d] and so on.
```

5.5.4 OTHER LIST PREDICATES

There are many possible list manipulations for which built-in predicates exist or for which you can write a predicate. This section describes just two, one which determines if an object is a list and one which allows conversion between lists and Prolog facts.

Recognizing a List

How can Prolog recognize a list? The problem is not complicated, but it is perhaps not so simple as it appears at first thought. As a first try, isa_list([List]) might seem to work. It does, but only for a one-element list. The empty list and lists with more than one-element are not recognized as lists.

One way to recognize all lists is to use a recursive procedure that removes the head successively until only the empty list remains:

```
is_list([]).
is_list([Head | Tail]) :- is_list(Tail).
```

This will recognize lists including the empty list. It will also reject lists with the special form [head | tail] because the tail is not a list. One problem with this set of rules is that the query is_list(X) will cause it to loop infinitely.

Infinite loops can be prevented by adding the following clause before the other two:

```
is_list(X) :- var(X), !, fail.
```

This tells Prolog that an uninstantiated variable is not a list.

The Univ Predicate

Many versions of Prolog, including Arity, have a built-in predicate called univ that is represented in Prolog syntax with the symbol =.. This predicate forms lists from Prolog clauses and creates Prolog clauses out of lists. This is an example of turning a list into a clause:

```
?- Clause =.. [likes, jack, peanut_butter].
Clause = likes(jack, peanut_butter)
```

In response to this query Prolog returns a list:

```
?- likes(jack, peanut_butter) =.. List.
List = [likes, jack, peanut_butter]
```

You will find univ useful when you begin writing Prolog programs that modify themselves.

5.6 INPUT AND OUTPUT

This section explains the most often used built-in predicates for input and output. I/O predicates vary greatly among Prolog implementations, so be sure to test them on the system you will use to run your application. Because Prolog programs often must report lists of information found in a database, the standard Prolog predicates for forming and printing such lists are also explained in this section. The section concludes with an introduction to Arity Prolog's database-manipulation predicates.

Three short applications programs illustrate the use of the built-in predicates. Listing 5.6 creates a simple interactive menu system. Listing 5.7 reads a sentence from the keyboard and creates a list of each word and punctuation mark entered by the user. Listing 5.8, reads a text file and displays it on the screen.

Listing 5.6 A family database query menu

```
go :-
    cls,
    display_menu,
    read_inquiry_type(Type),
    find_goal(Type, Goal),
    call(Goal), nl, nl, nl,
    write('Do you want to query the family database again? (y/n) '),
```

```
        read_string(3, StringResponse),
        string_term(StringResponse, Response),
        continue(Response).

find_goal(1, one).
find_goal(2, two).
find_goal(3, three).
find-goal(4, four).
find_goal(5, five).

continue(Response) : -
        member(Response, ['Y', y, 'YES', 'Yes', yes]),
        go, !.

continue(Response) :-
        cls,
        nl, nl, nl,
        write(' Thanks for using the family database inquiry program.').

display_menu :-
        nl,
        write('      FAMILY DATABASE INQUIRIES'), nl, nl,
        write('Enter the number of the type of inquiry you wish to make.').
        nl, nl, nl,
        write('      1. Find the children of a person'), nl,
        write('      2. Find the parents of a person'), nl,
        write('      3. Find the grandparents of a person'), nl,
        write('      4. Find the grandchildren of a person'), nl,
        write('      5. Quit this program'), nl, nl,
        write('The type of inquiry you wish to make is number: ').

read_inquiry_type(Type) :-
        read_string(1, StringType),
        string_term(StringType, Type).

one :-
        nl,
        write('For what person do you want a list of children? '), nl,
        read_string(20, StringPerson),
        string_term(StringPerson, Person), nl,
        write('This is a list of the children of '),
        write(Person),
        write('; '), nl,
        find_children(Person).
```

```prolog
find_children(Person) :-
    find_it(Child, parent(Person, Child), Childlist),
    printlist(Childlist).

printlist( [] ).
printlist( (Head | Tail] ) :-
    tab(5),
    write(Head),
    printlist(Tail).
```

Listing 5.7 Reading a sentence

```prolog
read_sentence([Word | Word_list]) :-
    write('Enter a sentence.'), nl,
    get0(Ch),
    name(Char1, [Ch]),
    readword(Char1, Word, Char2),
    restsent(Word, Char2, Word_list).

restsent(Word, _, []) :- lastword(Word), !.

restsent(Word, Char1, [Word1 | Word_list]) :-
    readword(Char1, Word1, Char2),
    restsent(Word1, Char2, Word_list).

readword(Ch, Word, Ch1) :-
    one_char_word(Ch), !,
    Word = Ch,
    get0(C),
    name(Ch1, [C]).

readword(Ch, Word, Ch2) :-
    inword(Ch, NewChar), !,
    get0(C),
    name(Ch1, [C]),
    restword(Ch1, Char_list, Ch2),
    Word = [NewChar | Char_list].

readword(Ch, Word, Ch2) :-
    get0(C),
    name(Ch1, [C]),
    readword(Ch1, Word, Ch2).
```

```prolog
restword(Ch, [NewCh | Char_list], Ch2) ;-
    inword(Ch, NewCh), !,
    get0(C),
    name(Ch1, [C]),
    restword(Ch1, Char_list, Ch2).

restword(Ch, [], Ch).

inword(Char, NewChar) :-
    "Char" = [26],
    NewChar = ''.

inword(Char, Char) :-
    Char @>= 'a', Char @=< 'z'.

inword(Char, LCChar) :-
    Char @>= 'A', Char @=< 'Z',
    name(Char, [Ascii]),
    NewAscii is Ascii + 32,
    name(LCChar, [NewAscii]).

inword(Char, Char) :-
    Char @>= '0', Char @=< '9'.

inword(Char, Char) :-
    Char = "".

inword(Char, Char) :-
    Char = '-'.

lastword('.').
lastword('!').
lastword('?').

one_char_word('.').
one_char_word(',').
one_char_word(';').
one_char_word(' ').
one_char_word(':').
one_char_word('?').
one_char_word('!').
one_char_word("").
```

Listing 5.8 A program to display a text file

```
go :-
    write('Enter the name of the file to display: '),
    read_string(12, FileName),
    open(H, FileName, r),
    read_file(H, Line),
    close(H).

read_file(H, Line) :-
    read_line(H, Line),
    nonvar(Line),
    write(Line), nl,
    read_file(H, NextLine).

read_file(H, Line).
```

5.6.1 READING AND WRITING

Figure 5.11 contains four input predicates: read/1, get0/1, get/1, and read_string/2. The read/1 predicate reads a term from the standard input device (usually the keyboard). Prolog recognizes the end of the term when it reads a period followed by the Enter key, although it does not include the period as a part of the term. This is an example using read/1:

```
?- read(X).
butterfly.
X = butterfly
```

Reading and Writing Terms

read(X) Reads X from the current input stream; if the current input stream is the console, X must terminate with a period and a carriage return.

write(X) Writes X to the current output stream. X can be a term, string, list, or structure. Must be a separate write predicate for each item.

writeq(X) Writes X to the current output stream, quoting it when it begins with an upper-case letter or contains spaces.

Reading and Writing Characters

get0(X) Gets the next character from the current input stream.

get(X) Gets the next printable character from the current input stream; non-printable characters are ignored.

put(X) Puts the character X into the current output stream.

Reading and Writing Strings

read_string/2 read_string(MaxStrLength, String) reads a string of maximum length = MaxStrLength from the current input stream.

Miscellaneous Predicates

nl Puts a line feed into the output stream.

tab(N) If N is an integer, tab(N) puts N spaces into the output stream.

Figure 5.11 Input/output predicates

The get0/1 predicate reads one character at a time. It is especially useful for reading and parsing sentences, because a parsing program must examine each individual character including spaces and punctuation to know what to do. Also, get0/1 is useful for reading the scan codes from function and arrow keys. If the argument to get0/1 is instantiated, get0/1 will return true if the argument and the character match; otherwise it will return false. Because get0/1 reads a single character, it is not necessary (or possible) to enter a period before Prolog reads the character. The following code illustrates the use of get0/1:

```
?- get0(X).
a
X = 97 ->
```

The get/1 predicate also reads one character from the standard input device, but it skips any non-printing characters (ASCII codes < 32) like the form feed, the bell, and a space. When a printing character is entered, get/1 will produce the same results as get0/1; compare this example with the previous one:

```
?- get(X).
a
X = 97 ->
```

In the next example you can count the number of non-printing characters entered before the letter by noting the position on the line where the letter is echoed:

```
?- get(X).
     a
X = 97 ->
```

In Arity Prolog you can read strings with the built-in predicate read_string/2. This predicate's first argument is the maximum length of the string to be read, and its second argument represents the string. The following example illustrates its use; note that the string can include the carriage return and line feed symbols.

```
?- read_string(40, X).
One, Two, Three, Go!
X = $One, Two, Three, Go!$ ->
```

Notice how, in the previous example, Arity Prolog surrounded the string with dollar signs. The dollar sign is the symbol that Arity uses to denote the beginning and end of string. An empty string is indicated by $$. To include a dollar sign in a string, enter two dollar signs as in $The cost is $$4.98.$.

Figure 5.11 also contains three output predicates. The write/1 predicate writes a term, a string, a list, or a structure to the output stream as does writeq/1. For example:

```
?-write([butch, erica, elizabeth, eliot, andrew]).
[butch, erica, elizabeth, eliot, andrew]
```

The difference between the two write predicates is that writeq/1 places the item in quotes if it begins with an upper-case letter or contains spaces. You must use a separate write or writeq for each item being written.

The put/1 predicate writes a single character into the output stream.

Two other terms in Figure 5.11 help format output. Use nl/0 to put a carriage return and line feed into the output stream, and use tab/1 to put spaces into the output stream. Both are used as separate goals and not as arguments to the output predicates. For example, the following code will indent five spaces, write "Hello, Eliot!," skip a line, and write "How are you?"

```
?- tab(5), writeq('Hello, Eliot!'), nl, write('How are you?').
    'Hello, Eliot!'
How are you?
```

5.6.2 DATABASE MANIPULATION PREDICATES

Prolog differs from most programming languages in that Prolog programs can change themselves. Figure 5.12 lists single-argument Arity Prolog predicates that can change the contents of a database.

The first two read the contents of a file of Prolog clauses and append them to any clauses already in the database. Sometimes you may have clauses in the file with the same name and arity as are already in the database. To avoid placing duplicates of the clauses into the database, use reconsult/1 rather than consult/1; reconsult/1 will replace any duplicate definitions with the definition being read from the file.

consult(FName)	Reads clauses from the file and places the clauses in the database.
reconsult(FName)	Performs the same process as consult/1 except it replaces any duplicate definitions with the definition from the file.
asserta(clause)	Adds the clause to the beginning of the list of clauses of the same name.
assertz(clause)	Adds the clause to the end of the list of clauses of the same name.
assert(clause)	Performs the same function as assertz.
retract(clause)	Removes a single clause from the database; the predicate name must be specified.
abolish(Name/Arity)	Removes all clauses from the database with the specified name and arity.

Figure 5.12 Database manipulation predicates

To write a rule that adds clauses to the database, use one of the assert predicates. Two of them, assert/1 and assertz/1, add the clause to the end of the list of clauses of the same name in the database; asserta/1 adds the clause to the beginning of the list of clauses of the same name. The find_it/3 rule in Figure 5.13 uses asserta/1 to insert a list of facts into the database.

The last two predicates remove clauses from a database. Use retract/1 to remove one clause. To remove all clauses with the same name and arity, use abolish/1. The list_it/2 predicate in Figure 5.13 uses retract/1 to remove a clause from the database as it inserts the clause's argument into a list of items.

Rule	Function

find_it(X, G, _) :-
    call(G),
    asserta(found(X)),
    fail.
	Creates a list of facts in the database of the form:
	found(X). Each X satisfies the goal G.

find_it(_, , L) :-
    list_it([], L),
    !.
	Call list_it/2 to form the list, L.

list_it(s, L) :-
    retract(found (X)),
    list_it([X | S], L).
	Retracts the found(X) facts from the database as it adds the X's to the head of the list. Fails when there are no more found(X)'s to retract.

list_it(L, L).	The stopping condition for list_it; tried and succeeds when the first rule fails.

Figure 5.13 Building lists from the database

5.6.3 INPUT AND OUTPUT EXAMPLES

This section discusses some common input and output tasks and demonstrates built-in predicates from Figure 5.11.

Forming a List From Information in a Database

The most convenient way to report information found in a database is first to put the items in a list and then to print the list. The-children-of-Edith and streams-that-flow-into-the-Ohio-River as found in the family (Listing 5.3) and stream (Listing 5.4) databases respectively, are examples of items that might go into such a list.

The Clocksin and Mellish names for the predicates that form a list this way are findall/3 and collect_found/2. Figure 5.13 contains a slightly modified pair of rules, find_it/3 and list_it/2. Figure 5.13 also describes what each rule does. You could use find_it/3 to query the family database to get a list of a person's children this way:

```
?- find_it(Child, parent(sadie, Child), Childlist).
Childlist = [calvin. alice, floyd]
```

Printing a List

You can always write a list in list form with the brackets, but users are likely to prefer having elements printed individually. This set of rules will do that:

```
printlist( [] ).
printlist( [Head | Tail] ) :-
            tab(5),
            write(Head), nl,
            printlist(Tail).
```

This query shows how it works:

```
?- printlist([jim, bob, jones]).
   jim
   bob
   jones
```

This rule set is easy to tailor to your specific needs. To cause the list to print in reverse order, just reverse the order of the last two conditions of the second rule. This example illustrates what happens when you make that change:

```
?-printlist2([jim, bob, jones]).
   jones
   bob
   jim
```

In addition, you might need to add some end-of-list punctuation to the first rule or omit the nl/0 predicate so that all elements of the list are on a single line.

Creating a Menu

Menus are an easy way for users to select among program options. Listing 5.6 illustrates the structure of a program that allows people unfamiliar with Prolog to query a family database. In addition to the rules shown there, the program uses the member/2, printlist/1, find_it/3, and list_it/2 predicates.

The first rule, go, starts the program and directs it: The built-in predicate cls clears the screen. Successive predicates print the menu on the screen (display_menu), read the user's choice of query type (read_inquiry_type (Type)), translate the type number into a word that can be a Prolog predicate (find_goal(Type, Goal)), perform the appropriate query (call (Goal)), prompt the user about another query (write/1) and read the response (read_string(3, StringResponse)), and, finally, evaluate that response (continue(Response)).

Only one of me query types is implemented in this example. one/0 asks the user the name of the person whose children are sought (print) and reads the name (read_string(20, String Person)). After printing a title (write/1), it calls find_children(Person), to get and print the list of children. Find_children/1 uses the find_it/3 and printlist/1 rules discussed above.

Once the program displays the response to the query, it asks if the user wants answers to other questions. The first continue/1 rule determines if the user's response to the prompt is a member of the set of continue responses. If it is, this rule begins the program again by calling go/0. If it is not, the first continue/1 rule fails and the second one succeeds, clears the screen, prints a farewell message, and turns on the prompt.

Listing 5.6 needs a lot of work before it would be very useful, and it can be enhanced in many ways. Predicates to implement inquiry types 2-5 are missing, and additional inquiry types would make the program more useful. People unfamiliar with Prolog are likely to enter names with an upper-case first letter; converting to lower-case would avoid problems. Also, the list of names printed by the program would look more natural if the first letter of each name were in upper-case. Finally, a query category that would allow direct Prolog queries to the database would add a nice touch.

Reading Sentences

Listing 5.7 contains a program to form a list of the words and punctuation that comprise a sentence entered from the keyboard.

The inword/2 predicate screens all characters that can come from the keyboard and accepts for the program only those that are allowed in a sentence. The first inword/2 reads the end of file character and converts it to a null character. The third inword/2 predicate converts all upper-case characters to their lower-case equivalent.

The one_char_word/1 facts screen incoming characters and identify those that are words in themselves, the comma, period, and so on. The lastword/1 facts identify the three one-character words that signal the end of a sentence, the period, exclamation point, and question mark.

Read_sentence/1 is the driving predicate. It obtains the list of words and punctuation that make up the sentence. It gets the first character in the input stream, reads the first word, and men gets me rest of me sentence.

There are three readword/3 predicates. The first is for one-character words; it converts the character from a list to a word and then gets the next character. The second one does most of the work in ordinary sentences. It checks to see if a character is usable. If it is usable, this readword/3 performs the necessary character conversions, gets the next character, obtains the rest of the word, puts the new character at the head of the character list, and converts the character list to a word string. The final readword is for characters that are not allowable in a sentence. It simply ignores the current character and continues by getting the next character and then the rest of the word.

The first restword/3 predicate checks to see if a character is acceptable, and, if it is, puts it at the head of the character list, and gets the next character and the rest of the word. The second restword is for lastword characters. It returns a second character that is the same as the first and an empty character list.

The first restsent/3 predicate is also for lastword characters. When these characters are detected, this restsent/3 predicate stops looking for more of the sentence. The second restsent/3 predicate reads a word and then reads the rest of the sentence.

5.6.4 FILE I/O

The predicates for writing to files are similar to those I/O predicates discussed previously. The only difference is an additional first argument that instantiates to the system assigned number (called a handle) associated with the file. Figure 5.14 lists the file I/O versions of the predicates. You can use the file I/O predicates with the standard I/O devices by specifying a handle = 0.

Before you can read from or write to a file you must open it. The predicate open/3 opens a file. The first argument to open/3 is the file handle. The second argument represents the file name and should be instantiated to a valid DOS file name. The third argument denotes the mode in which the file is to be accessed. Figure 5.14 lists the five possible access modes.

If the file you are going to use does not exist, you must create it. The create/2 predicate will create a file, open it for writing, and assign a handle.

A third predicate for opening files is p_open/3. It will open a file just like open/3, but, in addition to searching the current directory for the file, it will look for the filename in the directory of the .exe file of the current application and then in the directories listed in the path command of the autoexec.bat file.

After your program is finished using a file, the file should be closed. This is important so that your programs do not attempt to have more files open at one time than your system allows. To close a file, use close/1. It will close the file with the specified handle.

Predicates for Input/Output

All of the I/O predicates in Figure 5.11 are available with an additional argument (the first) that indicates a file handle. In mat form, they read from or write to the file with the specified handle. The predicates in this form are listed below. Also listed is the read_line/2 predicate which reads a full line of text from a text file. As with the other file I/O predicates, you can use it to read from the keyboard by using 0 for the handle argument.

read(H, Term)	get0(H, Char)	read_string(H, MaxL, S)	tab(H, N)
write(H, Term)	get(H, Char)	read_line(H, Line)	nl(H)
writeq(H, Term)	put(H, Char)		

File Manipulation Predicates

The access mode for which files may be opened and the symbol to use in the open and p_open predicates are:

read	r	read or write	rw
write	w	read or append	ra
append	a		

create(H, Fname)	Opens a new file for writing. H becomes instantiated to the system assigned integer value of the file handle. If the file name contains characters other than letters and integers or begins with an upper-case letter, it must be enclosed in single quotes.
open(H, Fname, Access)	Opens file with the specified access mode.
p_open(H, Fname, Access)	Opens the file as does open, but, in addition to the current directory, searches (1) the directory of the .exe file of the current application, and then (2) the directories listed in the path command of the autoexec.bat file.
close(H)	Closes the file with the specified handle.

Figure 5.14 Predicates for file I/O

A File I/O Example

Listing 5.8 will read and display a text file. It first asks the user for the name of the file to use; the read_string predicate gets the file name. Next the file is opened for reading. The read_file/2 rule reads and displays the file. It reads each line of the file with the read_line/2 predicate. The nonvar/1 predicate is a check to see that a line has been read. If nonvar succeeds, the line is displayed by write/1, and there is a recursive call to read_file/2.

When nonvar/1 fails, the second read_file/2 succeeds and then execution resumes in the go/0 rule where the file is closed and the program ends.

5.7 PROGRAM CONTROL AND PROGRAM DESIGN

There are at least two ways to view a Prolog program. You can consider the program to be a database that describes some limited world. Alternatively, you can consider the program as a series of directions to Prolog. The first of these perspectives leaves to Prolog all concerns about how the program operates. However, at times you may be very concerned about exactly what Prolog does and when it does it. So far, with the exception of a few comments introducing the cut, we have said little about controlling execution in a Prolog program.

In this section we turn our attention to the workings of Prolog programs. The first portion of the section examines ways to control execution. The section's other main topic is program design.

5.7.1 CONTROL PROGRAM EXECUTION

There are a variety of steps you can take to control program execution. In this section we discuss the order of clauses in rules and the cut (!).

Clause Arrangement

You can increase the efficiency of your rules by putting the predicate with the fewest possible matches first. As an example, consider this rule, which determines if a menu is acceptable to Willi:

```
meal_for_willi(main_course, Beverage) :-
        willi_eats(Main_course),
        willi_drinks(Beverage).
```

The best arrangement for the clauses in the rule depends on the database. If there are relatively few main courses compared to beverages, the above arrangement is the one to use. On the other hand, if the database has many more main courses than beverages, the rule will run quicker if the beverages are tested first.

A similar bit of advice is to arrange entries in a fact set so that the ones to be used most often are listed at the top. When it is appropriate, you could have your program keep active data items at the top of the database list by retracting facts and then asserting them at the top of the fact list like this:

```
meal_for_willi(Main_course, Beverage) :-
        willi_eats(Main_course),
        willi_drinks(Beverage),
        !,
        retract(willi_eats(Main_course),
        asserta(willi_eats(Main_course).
```

Of course, you would want to do this only for very large fact lists and for queries like this one, which has a constant for each argument:

```
meal_for_willi(spaghetti, chocolate_milkshake).
```

Another, somewhat more practical example that illustrates the importance of clause arrangements is the grandparent/2 predicate:

```
grandparent(Grandparent, Grandchild) :-
        parent(Grandparent, Parent),
        parent(Parent, Grandchild).
```

This version of grandparent/2 is efficient at responding to queries like

```
grandparent(gertie, Grandchild).
```

In responding, Prolog will instantiate Grandparent to gertie, perform the necessary steps to instantiate the Parent argument in parent(gertie, Parent), and then find those arguments that cause the goal parent(Parent, Grandchild) to succeed.

Notice how much more work Prolog would have to do if the two conditions in the rule were reversed: Instead of just finding the children of Gertie's children, it would test every parent-child combination to see if the child were Gertie's grandchild!

This same inefficiency occurs when you use this rule to find the grandparent of an individual as in this query:

grandparent(Grandparent, rachel).

To respond to queries of this type, this form of the grandparent rule is much more efficient

grandparent2(Grandparent, Grandchild) :-
          parent(Parent, Grandchild),
          parent(Grandparent, Parent).

When you have rules like these that may be used for different types of queries, and clause order affects efficiency, consider having separate predicates for each query type. In this case, you could have two predicates, grandchild/2 for finding grandchildren, and grandparent/2 for finding grandparents. Be sure to arrange the clauses so that the clause with the fewest possible matches appears first.

One bit of advice we offered in section 5.4 was to put the recursive call at the end of a rule wherever possible. This form of recursion is called tail recursion. A tail-recursive rule is more efficient than other recursive rules in many Prolog implementations because they provide for tail-recursion (also called last-call) optimization.

The requirements for tail-recursion optimization are these:

1. The recursive call is in the last clause of the predicate.
2. The call is the last subgoal of the clause.
3. There are no untried alternatives for earlier subgoals in the clause.

This example of a rule that displays numbers beginning at N and ending at Limit satisfies the conditions:

count(N, Limit) :-   N =< Limit,
                      write(N), nl,
                      NewN is N + 1,
                      count(NewN, Limit).

Unfortunately, more often than not, the third condition for tail recursion optimization will be very difficult to meet. In the discussion of the cut that follows, we provide an example that uses the cut and some extra arguments to allow a recursive rule to meet that condition.

Using the cut (!) to control program execution

You have seen the cut, written as !, in some of the previous sections' rule examples. The cut is a goal that succeeds automatically, but only once. Whenever backtracking causes a return to the cut, the cut fails and so does its parent rule.

The cut thus gives you the ability to restrict Prolog to evaluating clauses in a rule only one time. As an example, consider the first restword/3 predicate from Listing 5.8:

restword(Ch, [NewCh | Char_list], Ch2) :-
          inword(Ch, NewCh),
          !,
          get0(c) ,

```
        name(Ch1, [C]),
        restword(Ch1, Char_list, Ch2).
```

Prolog will evaluate the clauses following the cut with the set of variables that were instantiated prior to the cut. The cut fences off any backtracking above (to the left of) it. However, be sure to notice that it has no effect on goals that follow it in a rule.

There are three reasons for using the cut. One is efficiency; you can use the cut to make your programs run faster by avoiding attempts to satisfy a goal that cannot contribute to a solution. The cut after the stopping conditions in recursive-rule sets usually serves this purpose. These rules to sum the first N numbers provide an illustration:

```
sum_to(1, 1) :- !.
sum_to(N, Sum) :- N1 is N - 1,
                  sum_to(NI, Sum1),
                  Sum is Sum1 + N.
```

The cut in the first rule tells Prolog not to bother trying the second rule when N is 1.

However, there is another way to prevent Prolog from executing all of the second rule when N is 1: add N > 1 as the first clause in the second rule. With that clause in place, the cut in the first rule is unnecessary. We prefer this alternative because it makes the second definition of sum_to complete.

A second reason to use the cut is to prevent duplicate answers. Suppose you want to know if two lists have at least one common member. As you saw in section 5.5, the member/3 predicate provides an easy way to determine that:

```
common_member(X, List1, List2) :-
        member(X, List1),
        member(X, List2).
```

However, if all you need to determine is the existence of one element in common, this predicate does more than is necessary. You can make it more efficient by stopping it when the common membership of an element is confirmed. Adding a cut after the second member/3 predicate does that:

```
common_member(X, List1, List2) :-
        member(X, List1),
        member(X, List2),
        !.
```

A third reason to use the cut is to stop Prolog's search after it has found the only possible answer. For this purpose, the cut is often used with another built-in predicate, fail. Fail is a goal that always fails; it prevents Prolog from examining another version of the rule that contains it.

To illustrate this situation, assume you are working on a database for St. Peter. In the database are predicates for sins and good works for each individual who has performed them. These are some examples:

```
shared_with_needy(alice).
shared_with_needy(lars).
shared_with_needy(billy_joe).
```

hot_fudge_twice_every_day(randolph).

hot_fudge_twice_every_day(juliette).

St. Peter wants a program that will let him enter the name of each soul that approaches the pearly gates and quickly determine if that person has performed some minimum level of good works and avoided some specific set of sins. After making that determination, he wants the program to simply tell him yes or no.

Prolog can avoid a lot of needless searching of the database if it immediately rules out individuals who have committed unacceptable acts. Suppose the predicate that evaluates the candidates is called enter; you can write a first rule that immediately excludes a person like this:

```
enter(Person) :-
        hot_fudge_twice_every_day(Person),
        !,
        fall.
```

Whenever the hot-fudge goal succeeds the enter/1 rule fails, and Prolog will not try any of its other versions. This is an example of a query and response:

```
?- enter(randolph).
no
```

Another example using the cut-fail combination is the definition for Prolog's built-in predicate not/1:

```
not(Whatever) :-    Whatever,
                    !,
                    fail.
not(Whatever).
```

[The first rule will fail if **Whatever** succeeds and then stops further searching. If **Whatever** failed, the second **not**-rule will be checked and it will succeed definitely, because the it has no conditions and is a fact. It will succeed if a match is found for the parameter **Whatever**, which is a variable and can match with anything.]

not/1 can often be used instead of the cut-fail combination. In the enter/1 rule, you can write:

```
enter(Person) :-
        not(hot_fudge_twice_every_day(Person)),
        ....
```

enter/1 will fail whenever Person is instantiated to a value that matches the argument in the hot_fudge_twice_every_day/1 fact list. We recommend this approach rather than the use of the cut because it makes the enter rule easier to understand.

A Tail-Recursive Factorial Predicate

The cut can help you to write a tail-recursive rule set for calculating factorials. The factorial rule in section 5.4 is this:

```
factorial(0, 1) :- !.
factorial(N, Nfac) :- M is N - 1,
                      factorial(M, Mfac),
                      Nfac is N * Mfac.
```

The second rule is not tail recursive because it fails condition (1). Making the recursive call as the last condition of the recursive rule requires some additional arguments so that Prolog doesn't try to do arithmetic with unbound variables. The tail-recursive rule looks like this:

```
factorial2(N, Nfac, I, Temp) :-
            I =< N,
            Temp2 is Temp * I,
            I2 is I + 1,
            !,
            factorial2(N, Nfac, I2, Temp2).
```

This rule serves as a stopping condition:

```
factorial2(N, Nfac, I, Nfac) :-
            I > N.
```

To provide an initial value of 1 for I and Temp and also to simplify queries to the rule, use another predicate as a driver:

```
factorial1(N, Nfac) :-
            factorial2(N, Nfac, 1, 1).
```

Which of its three roles does the cut play in this example?

Caution in Using the Cut

You need to be cautious in using the cut because it can change the way a rule works by limiting backtracking. As an example, consider this version of append/3:

```
append([], X, X) :- !.
append([H | T1], L2, [H | T3]) :- append(L1, L2, L3).
```

This will work fine if you are forming a new list from two other lists. However, with a goal of the form

```
append(X, Y, [a, b, c]).
```

Prolog's response will be only

```
X = []
Y = [a, b, c]
```

5.7.2 Programming Suggestions

This portion of the section offers some suggestions to help you design and write Prolog rules and programs. Some of these suggestions apply equally well to procedural language programming, but others are quite specific to Prolog.

Planning a Program

You can use traditional top-down design techniques to design a Prolog program. Implement the program modules with Prolog rules. The advantages of modularity exist here just as in procedural programming: program clarity, simplification of tasks, potential division of labor, and independent testing of program components.

With Prolog programs there is, however, one precaution as you create new modules: *Avoid duplicate names for rules*. This is an ever increasing hazard as programs get larger and as more people work on them.

Writing Code

The objectives in writing a Prolog program are the same as those in any other language: (1) Make it work, and (2) make it easy to read and understand. There are several things you can do to facilitate the second of these objectives.

1. Design your rules for readability. In particular, avoid the semicolon. Instead of or rules, write multiple rules.

2. Format your program so that it is easy to read: Begin each new relationship on a new line. Separate different relationships with blank lines. Indent each clause in a rule on a new line. Be consistent!

3. Organize your program: Group related rules. Describe major modules with comments. When appropriate, put facts with the rules that use them.

4. Make your program as self-documenting as possible. That requires using meaningful names for rules, variables, constants, and structures. There is no excuse for using cryptic names in Prolog programs.

5. Explain non-trivial relations in comments. For example,

```
Sum_to_N(N, Sum)
% N is an Integer
% Sum is the sum of all integers from 0 to N
```

6. Provide appropriate external documentation. This includes a description of the program's purpose, its structure, the files it uses, and instructions for using the program.

5.8 Additional Topics

By now you have gained a basic understanding of Prolog. You can extend your understanding on a few additional topics in this section, including pairs, recursion on lists, flow control structures, and the execution model of Prolog.

5.8.1 Representing Prolog Lists in Pairs and Writing Recursive Rules on Lists

Pair is a structured data type in Prolog. A pair is denoted by [X | Y], where X and Y can be any variables or literal values of any data type. When reading this section, please compare and contrast with Scheme pairs in section 4.4.6. Figure 5.15 lists examples of Scheme and Prolog pairs, and their full nations and simplified notations.

Scheme pairs: full and siplified nations		Prolog pairs: full and simplified nations	
(1 . 2)	(1 . 2)	[1 | 2]	[1 | 2]
(1 . (2 . 3))	(1 2 . 3)	[1 | [2 | 3]]	[1, 2 | 3]]
(1 . (2 . (3 . 0)))	(1 2 3)	[1 | [2 | [3 | []]]	[1, 2, 3]

Figure 5.15 Comparison between Scheme and Prolog pairs

Similar to a Scheme list, a Prolog list can be defined by pairs recursively, with an exception that the empty list is not a pair:

> <list> ::= [] (empty list)
>
> <list> ::= [<H> | <T>]

where

> <H> is a variable or a value of any type;
>
> <T> is a Prolog list.

Prolog does not really differentiate a list and a pair. The rules defined on lists can be applied on pairs, even if the pairs are not lists. For example, the member rule can be applied to pairs:

> member(1, [1, 2 | 3]). It returns "true"
>
> member(2, [1, 2 | 3]). It returns "true"
>
> member(3, [1, 2 | 3]). It returns "false" or "no".

Representing a non-empty list as a pair [H | T] is very useful when writing recursive rules, where T is in most cases the parameter to the size-(n-1) problem (see Scheme chapter on solving recursive problems). For example, when writing recursive rules to reverse a list, we can consider the following cases.

- Define the size-n problem: reverse(L, RL), where, L is the list to be reversed and RL will hold the result, i.e., the reversed list.

- Define stopping condition and its return value: If the list is empty (stopping condition), then the reversed list is an empty list (return value).

- Identify the size-(n-1) problem and assume the problem is solved: Since the list is not empty, it can be represented as a pair [H | T]. T is a list of size n-1 and thus, the size-(n-1) problem is reverse(T, RT). We assume that we have obtained RT, which is the reversed list of T.

- Construct the solution to the size-n problem based on the hypothetic solution in the last step: Since RT is reversed from T, and H is a first element of list L. If we insert H to the end of RT, we have the complete list reversed.

The complete recursive program (rules) for reversing a list is shown below:

```
reverse([ ],[ ]).              /* Stopping condition */
reverse([H | T],RL) :-         /* size-n problem */
    reverse(T, RT),            /* size-(n-1) problem */
    append(RT, [H], RL).       /* construct size-n problem's solution */
```

5.8.2 Flow Control Structures: Cut and Repeat

There are several built-in predicates that can be used to change the order of searching the Prolog database. We will discuss two important flow control predicates in this section: ! (cut) that removes the backtracking points and **repeat** that adds backtracking points.

A **backtracking** point is a point from which the Prolog runtime will re-start its search if the current search fails, or if the current search succeeds but a semi-colon is entered thereafter.

A cut (!) is a special control facility in Prolog that enables programmers to restrict the backtracking options. A cut will succeed when it is met (executed), however, it will remove all existing backtracking points, but new backtracking points may be added thereafter. Notice that a cut may cut off valid options and thus the search may not find all answers even if the semi-colon key is typed. Thus, use cut if you are sure there are no more answers or you don't want to have all possible answers.

Figure 5.16 shows the control structure (the solid lines) of a Prolog database, where a branch means there are two possible search branches at the point. The dotted lines show the actual search paths and the circled numbers are backtracking points. The search starts from the beginning of the database. When the first branch is encountered, it continues with, say, the left branch and makes a backtracking point ① to mark that the right branch has not yet been searched. When the second and third branches on the left are encountered, backtracking points ② and ③ are added, respectively. Then the search goes to the end at the leftmost branch and it returns to the latest backtracking point, which is ③. The search removes ③, goes to the end, and then returns to the latest backtracking point, which is now ②. The research process continues until a match is found, or the entire database has been searched.

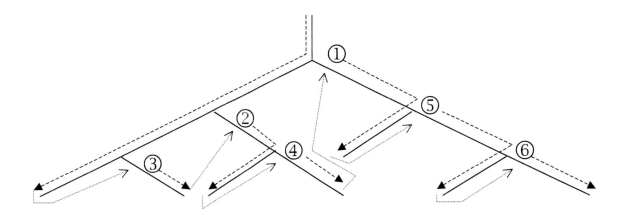

Figure 5.16 Adding backtrack points

Now let's exam what happens if a cut (!) is used in the rules of the database. As shown in Figure 5.17 (a), after backtracking points ① and ② are created and then a cut is executed, all existing backtracking points, in this example, ① and ②, will be removed, as shown in Figure 5.17 (b). A cut will succeed when it is executed and thus the search continues as normal. When the next branch is encountered, a new backtracking point ③ will be added. After the search goes to the left end, it returns to the latest backtracking point, which is ③ and continues from ③. Now when the search goes to the leaf, the search terminates and the remaining structure will not be searched, because there is no more backtracking points pointing to indicate what parts have not been searched.

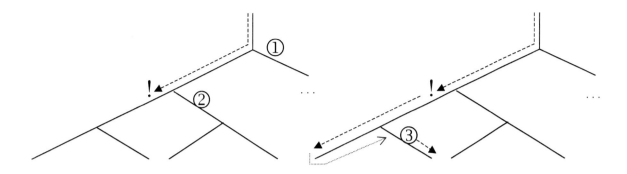

Figure 5.17 (a) A cut is executed after creating two backtracking points. (b) The existing backtracking points are removed and search continues.

The concept is simple. However, it is not trivial to understand what backtracking points are, and where backtracking points are added, and when they are removed. Consider the following simple database. To understand the effect of cut, we define four programming language rules: pl0 (no cut), pl1 (a cut as the first condition), pl2 (a cut as the second condition), and pl3 (a cut as the third condition).

```
language(english).
language(scheme).
language(prolog).
computer(scheme).
computer(prolog).
pl0(P) :- language(P), computer(P).      // no cut in the rule
pl1(P) :- !, language(P), computer(P).   // a cut as the first condition
pl2(P) :- language(P), !, computer(P).   // a cut as the second condition
pl3(P) :- language(P), computer(P), !.   // a cut as the third condition
```

Figure 5.18 illustrates the search process when the question ?- pl0(P) is asked. The first backtrack point is created when a match is found for the first condition "language(X)" and the search proceeds to matching the second condition. After the second condition fails, the research resumes from the backtracking point ①.

Thus, for the question ?- pl0(X), where no cut is applied in the rule pl0(X), it will find two answers, if a semicolon is typed after the first answer:

X = scheme
X = prolog

For the question ?- pl1(X), where a cut is put as the first condition of the rule pl1(X), the cut is executed before any backtracking points are created. Thus, no backtracking points will be removed and the answer to this question is same as that to the question ?- pl0(X).

For the question ?- pl2(X), the cut will be executed after backtracking point ① is created and before an answer is found. The execution of cut then removes the backtracking point ①. As the result, after the search failed (see the bottom right of figure 5.18), there is no backtracking point to return and thus, not a single answer can be found for the question.

```
?- pl0(X).
      ↓
language(englsih).    // no match
      ↓
language(scheme).     // no match
      ↓
language(prolog).     // no match
      ↓
computer(scheme).     // no match
      ↓
computer(prolog).     // no match
      ↓
   pl0(P).            // match P = X
      ↓
?- language(X).       // Check 1st condition: return to beginning of database
      ↓
language(english).    // match: X = english        ?- computer(english).  // restart
      ↓                                                        ↓
Backtrack point ①                                   language(english).   // no match
      ↓                                                        ↓
language(scheme). ──────────────→  . . .            language(scheme).    // match
      ↓                                                        ↓
Backtrack point ②                                   language(prolog).    // no match
      ↓                                                        ↓
language(prologe). ─────────────→  . . .            computer(scheme).    // no match
      ↓                                                        ↓
Backtrack point ③                                   computer(prolog).    // no match
      ↓                                                        ↓
    . . .                                                   failed
```

Figure 5.18 Adding backtrack points

For the question ?- pl3(X), the cut will be executed after backtrack point ① is created and after the first answer X = scheme is found. The execution will remove the backtrack point ①. As the result, the second answer will not be found, even if a semicolon is typed.

Not all the search-returning points in the Prolog database are backtracking points that can be removed by cut. There are other kinds of search-returning points: **composite condition returning points** and **recursive exit points**. These two kinds of returning points may not be removed by the cut.

For example, there are two conditions in the rule pl3(P) in the programming language example above. While searching for a match for the first condition, a search-returning point must be marked so that the search can continue from this point to find a match for the second condition after a match is found for the first condition. Obviously, this search-returning point may not be removed from semantics point of view. If such a search-returning point could be removed, a solution that only meets the first condition would be accepted as a "true" solution of the rule, which is incorrect.

For a recursive rule, there is a similar situation where a searching returning point must be marked. As shown in Figure 5.19, when a recursive call is made, the execution re-enter the rule, leaving the condition behind the recursive call not searched and thus, a search-returning point must be added every time a recursive call is made. Similar to the composite condition returning points, the recursive exit points may not be removed by the **cut**.

```
factorial(0,1) :-
               !.
factorial(N,F) :-
               N>0,
               N1 is N-1,
               factorial(N1,F1),
               /* Recursive exit point */
               F is N * F1.
```

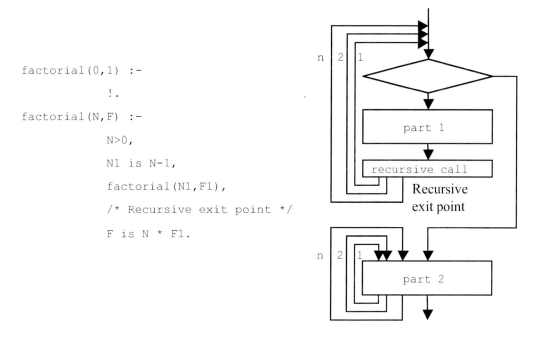

Figure 5.19 Recursive rule and recursive exit point

Now let's examine the next control structure **repeat** that always succeeds and always adds a backtracking point whenever it is executed. Figure 5.20 shows a simple application of **repeat** that creates an infinite loop: When the **repeat** is executed, a backtracking point is created and **repeat** succeeds. Then, the control enters the body of the loop to "do something". At the end, the build-in predicate "fail" is executed. The **fail** predicate does nothing but fail (return false). Since the rule fails, it automatically return to the latest backtracking point. The backtracking point is removed when the control returns to it. However, when the **repeat** is executed, a new backtracking point is created. The loop thus repeats forever.

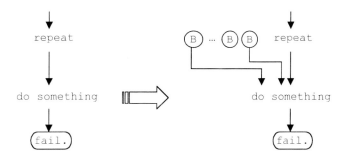

Figure 5.20 The "repeat" adds a backtracking point every time it is executed

The following program gives an example of this application. The program repeatedly gets a printable character from the keyboard and writes the character on the screen.

```
get_forever :-
        repeat,         /*      add a backtracking point */
        get(X),         /*      enter a printable char */
        write(X),
        nl,
        fail.           /*      to return to last backtracking point. */
```

Without the **fail** predicate at the end, the rule will succeed and not automatically return to **repeat**. It returns to the **repeat** only after a semicolon is entered.

Now let's examine another application of **repeat** that creates a loop and the loop exits when certain condition is met.

```
get_digit(X) :-
        repeat,                 /* add a backtracking point */
        write('enter a digit'),
        nl,
        get0(X1),               /* get any character */
        X1 > 47,                /* will fail if not digit */
        X1 < 58,
        X is X1 - 48,
        !.                      /* remove backtracking points */
```

When the rule **get_digit(X)** is executed, the first condition is a repeat, which succeeds and add a backtracking point. Predicates **write** and **nl** always succeed. Then a character is entered from the keyboard and instantiated to **X1**. If **X1** is a digit, its ASCII value must be between 48 and 57. If these two boundary conditions are met, the ASCII value is converted to the value it represents. Then the **cut** is executed, which removes the backtracking point created by **repeat**. Thus, the loop exits. On the other hand, if one of the boundary conditions is false, i.e., a non-digit character is entered, the composite condition fails and it returns to the backtracking point and another iteration of the loop starts.

5.8.3 The Prolog Execution Model

Prolog answers a question or executes a goal by searching the database. This section explains in detail how a goal is executed by the Prolog runtime (or called execution engine).

On the left hand side of Figure 5.21, a C-like pseudo-code program is given to outline the Prolog execution engine. On the right hand side, a general database, consisting of a set of facts and a set of rules, is given. Assume a goal "?- qst(a_1, ..., a_n)." is being executed.

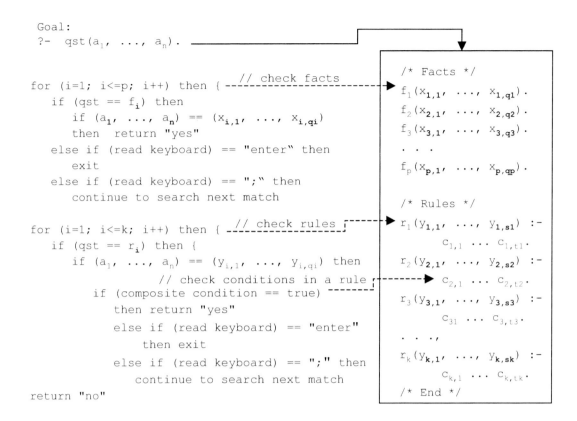

```
Goal:
?-  qst(a₁,  ...,  aₙ).

                                // check facts
for (i=1;  i<=p;  i++) then {  ------------------------▶
    if (qst == fᵢ) then
        if (a₁,  ...,  aₙ) == (xᵢ,₁  ...,  xᵢ,qᵢ)
        then  return "yes"
    else if (read keyboard) == "enter" then
        exit
    else if (read keyboard) == ";" then
        continue to search next match

                                // check rules
for (i=1;  i<=k;  i++) then {  ------------------▶
    if (qst == rᵢ) then {
        if (a₁,  ...,  aₙ) == (yᵢ,₁  ...,  yᵢ,qᵢ) then
                    // check conditions in a rule
            if (composite condition == true)  --------
            then return "yes"
            else if (read keyboard) == "enter"
                then exit
            else if (read keyboard) == ";" then
                continue to search next match
return "no"
```

Figure 5.21 Prolog execution model

First, the name of the goal is compared with the name of each fact. If a match is found, the parameter list in the goal is further compared with that of the fact that has the same name. If a match is found, an answer (a solution) is found for the goal. In this case, the user can decide to stop searching or continue to find more solutions by type the "enter" key or type the semicolon.

Having compared with all the facts sequentially, the search continues into the rules. The name and the parameter list of the goal are compared with the name and the parameter list of each rule. If a match is found, it does not mean that a solution is found because the rule is conditional. The conditions of the rule must be further compared one by one based on how the conditions are composed. If they are combined by logic AND operation, a solution is found only if all conditions are true. If they are combined by logic OR operation, a solution is found once a condition is found true.

Figure 5.22 presents a concrete example to demonstrate the entire execution process. Given the database consisting of four facts and one rule, a question "?- grandmother_of(jane, calvin)." is asked. The numbered arrows in the figure show the execution steps.

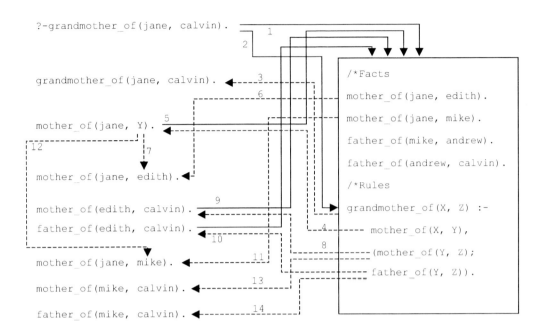

Figure 5.22 Demonstrating the execution model

1. The goal "?- grandmother_of(jane, calvin)." will be matched with each item in the database, starting from the beginning.
2. A match is found with the rule.
3. The match instantiates the variables X and Z to jane and calvin, respectively.
4. Since the match is a rule, in order for the rule to be true, the composite condition must be true. The sub goal is to check mother_of(jane, Y) is true. Y has not yet been instantiated.
5. The sub goal is matched with database from the beginning.
6. A match is found with the first condition. Notice here that the second fact has not been matched when it moves forward to check the second condition. Thus, a backtrack point needs to be set between the first and the second facts.
7. Variable Y is now instantiated to edith by the match.
8. Now we need to match the second condition mother_of(Y, Z), where Y and Z have been instantiated to jane and calvin, respectively.
9. The sub goal is taken back to the database. No match could be found throughout the entire database and thus the sub goal fails.
10. Since the second and the third condition are connected by an "or" operation, it can give a solution as long as one of the two conditions succeed. Thus, we need to check father_of(Y, Z), where Y and Z have been instantiated to jane and calvin, respectively. No match can be found for this sub goal and thus the third condition fails. Since both second and third conditions failed, the goal grandmother_of(jane, calvin) fails.
11. However, the entire database has not been completely searched. The control will return to the back-track point set at step 6. There is another match for the first condition: mother_of(jane, Y).
12. Variable Y is instantiated to mike and the sub goal becomes mother_of(jane, mike).

13. Now we need to match the second condition mother_of(Y, Z), where Y and Z have been instantiated to mike and calvin, respectively. No match could be found and thus it fails.

14. Now we need to match the third condition father_of(Y, Z), where Y and Z have been instantiated to mike and calvin, respectively. No match could be found and thus it fails.

After the 14 steps of exhaustive comparison, no match could be found for the goal grandmother_of(jane, calvin) and thus the goal failed.

5.9 SUMMARY

This chapter studied the fundamental concepts of logic programming and basic programming techniques. It covered:

- The structure of Prolog programs: At lexical level: composition of Prolog variables; at syntactic level: the syntax of constructing facts, rules, and goals; at contextual structure: the instantiation and scope of variables; at semantic level, there are two different programming models: the database-based unification model and arithmetic model.

- Recursive rules and application of recursion: The fantastic four abstract approach discussed in C and Scheme chapters can be applied to Prolog recursive programming.

- Lists and list operations: This section shares much of the common ground of list operations in Scheme chapter.

- Input and output: This section shows examples of interfacing Prolog programs with I/O devices.

- Advanced topics: Three topics are discussed. First, Prolog lists and Scheme lists are compared and the pair type defined in Scheme is used to explain the two different list representations used in Prolog. Then, the flow control structures of Prolog are explained in more detail, including the application of cut and repeat. Finally, underlying execution model of Prolog is described in a C-like pseudo language.

5.10 HOMEWORK, PROGRAMMING EXERCISES, AND PROJECTS

1.   Multiple Choice. Choose only one answer in each question. Choose the best answer if more than one answer is acceptable.

1.1   Which of the programming languages most closely follows the stored program concept?
❏ C   ❏ Lisp   ❏ Scheme   ❏ Prolog

1.2   There are three kinds of clauses in a Prolog program: facts, rules, and goals.
❏ A fact can be considered to be a special case of a rule.
❏ A fact can be considered to be a special case of a goal.
❏ A rule can be considered to be a special case of a fact.
❏ A rule can be considered to be a special case of a goal.

1.3   What mechanism cannot be used to pass values between clauses within a Prolog rule?
❏ call-by-value   ❏ call-by-reference   ❏ return value   ❏ All of them

1.4   If you want to pass multiple values out of a Prolog predicate, which of the following methods is valid?
❏ Use multiple return statements in the predicate.
❏ Use a single return statement to return a list that contains the multiple values required.
❏ Use multiple named variables to hold the values.
❏ Use multiple unnamed variables to hold the values.

1.5   A goal clause and a fact unify, if
❏ their predicates are the same.   ❏ their arities are the same.
❏ their corresponding arguments match.   ❏ all of the above are true.

1.6   The arity of a predicate is
❏ the head of the predicate.   ❏ the neck of the predicate.
❏ the body of the predicate.   ❏ the number of arguments of the predicate.

1.7   The scope of a Prolog variable is within
❏ a single rule.   ❏ a single clause in a rule.
❏ the fact/rule base.   ❏ the body of the next rule.

1.8   When the Prolog system is searching for possible matches between the goal and a rule in the fact/rule base and a cut "!" is encountered, the search
❏ stops immediately.   ❏ stops only after completing the current rule.
❏ stops at the end of the fact/rule base.   ❏ will continue, but existing backtracking points are removed.

1.9   A circular definition of a Prolog rule
❏ is an imperative feature that should be discouraged.
❏ will cause a dead-loop for every goal.
❏ will cause a dead-loop when no match can be found.
❏ will never cause a dead loop

1.10 An anonymous variable in Prolog is a
    ❏ constant.   ❏ placeholder.   ❏ predicate.   ❏ question.

1.11 What is the output when the following Prolog goal is executed?

    ?-member(cat, [dog, cat, mouse]).

    ❏ true?   ❏ X = cat   ❏ [cat, mouse]   ❏ None of them

1.12 Assume we have the following fact in a Prolog factbase:

    child_of(sadie, [alice, floyd, calvin]).

    What is the output when the following Prolog goal is executed?

    ?- child_of(sadie, [alice | T]).

    ❏ T = [alice, floyd, calvin]   ❏ T = [floyd, calvin]
    ❏ T = floyd, calvin   ❏ T = calvin

1.13 Assume that we have the following fact in a Prolog factbase:

    child_of(sadie, [alice, floyd, calvin]).

    What is the output when the following goal is executed?

    ?- child_of(sadie, [alice | [H | [calvin]]]).

    ❏ H = [alice]   ❏ H = [floyd]   ❏ H = floyd   ❏ H = [alice, calvin]

1.14 What is the output when the following Prolog goal is executed?

    ?- member(X,[81, 25, 9, 29]), Y is X*X, Y<400.

    ❏ X = [81, 25, 9, 29]   ❏ X = 9 Y =29   ❏ X = 9 Y = 81   ❏ X = 81 Y =400

1.15 Given the following Prolog recursive rules:

    foo(X, [X]).
    foo(X, [_ | T]) :- foo(X, T).

    The rules find
    ❏ the last element of a list.   ❏ the length of a list.
    ❏ whether an element is a member of a list.   ❏ the sum of all members in a list.

1.16 When Prolog is searching for possible matches and a cut "!" is encountered,

    ❏ all existing the backtrack points will be removed.
    ❏ all existing recursive exit points will be removed.
    ❏ all existing backtrack points and recursive exit points will be removed.
    ❏ none of the existing backtrack points and recursive exit points will be removed.

1.17 The built-in Prolog predicate **repeat** always

    ❏ fails immediately.
    ❏ succeeds and adds a backtracking point.
    ❏ fails at the end of the database.
    ❏ fails when it is visited (executed) for the second time.

1.18   What does the following code do?

```
go :- repeat,    get(X), write(X), nl, fail.
```

    ❏ It takes a single character from the keyboard and prints it.
    ❏ It repeatedly takes a character from the keyboard and prints it.
    ❏ It takes a character from the keyboard, prints it, and exits if the character is a digit.
    ❏ It takes a character from the keyboard, prints it, and exits if the character is printable.

2.   There are several data passing mechanisms between the calling function (caller) and the called function (callee): call-by-values, call-by-reference, return value, and global variable (global name). What data passing mechanisms are supported by imperative C, functional Scheme, and logic Prolog? Draw a table to summarize the supported mechanisms by these three languages.

3.   What are named and unnamed (anonymous) variables in Prolog? What are their differences?

4.   What is the scope rule of Prolog?

5.   What are the differences between the variables in imperative, functional, and logic programming languages?

6.   How is a Prolog program executed? What is the definition of a match?

7.   What is the difference between a circularly defined rule and a properly defined recursive rule? Can a recursive rule cause a dead loop? How can you avoid a dead loop in the definition of recursive rules?

8.   Does the order of the clauses in a rule matter? Does the order of the facts and rules in a fact/rule base matter?

9. How do you design a recursive rule? Is the following design process correct?
    (1) Formulate the size-N problem: choose the predicate name and appropriate arguments for holding the return value and the input values to the rule.
    (2) Design the stopping condition (normally, N = 0 or N = 1) and its solution.
    (3) Assume that you have already found the solution of the same problem with size N1, where, N1 < N.
    Use the solution of the size-N1 problem to define the solution of size-N problem.
    Verify the above design process using the "Hanoi Towers" problem discussed in chapter four as an example.

10. In a family database, will a problem a occur if we define the following recursive rules? Put these rules in a family database and test them.

    sister(X, Y) :- sister(Y, X).
    brother(X, Y) : brother(Y, X).
    parent_of(X, Y) :- child_of(Y, X).
    child_of(X, Y) :- parent_of (Y, X).

11. Using BNF notation, a Prolog list can be recursively defined as follows:

    <list> ::= [], where [] is an empty list
    <list> ::= [<X> | <Y>], where X is a variable or value, and Y is a list.

    In the definition, [<X> | <Y>] can be considered to be a pair defined in Scheme in chapter four.

11.1 Describe simplification rules that can be used to simplify the Prolog lists.

11.2 Apply the simplification rules to simplify [1 | [2 | [3 | []]]] into [1 2 3].

11.3 Is this structure [[1 | 2] | [3 | [4 | 5]]] a valid Prolog list? Explain your answer.

12. Define a rule to return the common members of two lists. Trace the execution manually and by the trace routine. Compare the two traces. The format of the rule is

common(X, List1, List2)

13. Define a rule to return the change (number of quarters, dimes, nickels and pennies) of a given amount *S*, where $0 <= S <= 100$. The format of the rule is

change(S, Q, D, N, P)

14. You are given the following Prolog factbase. The **familyquestions** rule is, in fact, a compound question. It will cause a number of goals (questions) to be called. You can consider the question as the "main" program that addresses the problem you want to solve. However, since the individual questions are connected by "and" relationship, the compound question will stop if a "no" answer is given to any individual question. You could use the "or" relationship to connect some questions. In this case, the compound question will stop if a "yes" answer is given to any individual question.

/* Factbase for family. It consists of facts and rules. */

/* Facts */
male(luke).
male(mike).
female(sarah).
mother_of(jane, edith).
mother_of(jane, mike).
father_of(mike, andrew).
father_of(andrew, calvin).
father_of(luke, mike).

/* Rules */
grandmother_of(X, Z) :-
            mother_of(X, Y),
            (mother_of(Y, Z); father_of(Y, Z)).

familyquestions :-
      grandmother_of(X, andrew),
      write('The grandmother of Andrew is '), write(X), nl,
      father_of(Y, mike),
      write(Y), write(' is the father of mike'), nl, nl.

14.1 Enter the program using a text editor under Unix operation system and save the file as family.pl. You can enter the program on your PC and upload the program into the Unix server.

You may enter the program on your PC and upload the program into your cse240prolog directory in *general* server.

14.2   Compile the program using the Prolog command:

> gplc famlly.pl

14.3   Enter GNU Prolog by executing the Unix command **gprolog**.

14.4   Execute the program family by typing GNU Prolog command

|?- [family].

14.5   Ask a few questions, for example,

|?- male(luke).
|?- male(X).
|?- grandmother_of(jane, mike).
|?- grandmother_of(jane, X).
|?- grandmother_of(X, mike).
|?- familyquestions. /* This will call all questions in the rule. */

14.6   Change the "and" operator "," after the first "**nl**" statement (newline) to the "or" operator ";" in the **familyquestions** and observe what differences are made in the output.

14.7 Manually trace the execution of the following goal. List all statements in their execution order involved in the trace.

|?- grandmother_of(jane, andrew).

14.8 Add the following set of rules that extend the relationships among the members: brother, sister, grandfather, grandparent, greatgrandfather.

14.9 Add 30 facts into the factbase showing the relationship between family members. These facts must ensure each rule defined on the facts can return a yes value for at least one set of parameters.

14.10 Compile the extended program and ask at least 10 different questions using GNU Prolog commands. Also use variables in these questions.

14.11 Add a rule called **morequestions** at the end of factbase to include the 10 questions that you have tested. Include sufficient write statements, so that the answers to individual questions are printed. Make sure that the compound question can terminate (will not cause a "dead loop").

14.12 Re-compile the program and call the following goal.

|?- morequestions.

15.   Define recursive rules to compute mathematical functions.

15.1 Compute $addexp(X, Y, N) = (X + Y)^N$, where X, Y, and N are non-negative integers, and X, Y, and N cannot be 0 at the same time, because 0^0 is undefined. You must add an argument to store the return value.

15.2 Test your program using different input sets (test cases) and verify (e.g., using your calculator) the correctness of the answer. Give five sets of inputs-outputs that you tested.

15.3 Compute fe(X, Y, N) = ((X + Y)^N)!. The function must call the function that you designed in question 15.1. You must include all functions that are used.

15.4 Test your program in question 15.3 using different input sets (test cases) and verify (e.g., using your calculator) the correctness of the answer. Give two sets of inputs-outputs that you tested.

16.   Fibonacci numbers are defined by

$$fib(n) = \begin{cases} 0 & n = 0 \\ 1 & n = 1 \\ fib(n-1) + fib(n-2) & n \geq 2 \end{cases}$$

Follow the fantastic four abstract approach to implement the function in Prolog rules.

16.1 Define the size-n problem

16.2 Define the stopping conditions and the return values.

16.3 Define the size-m problems

16.4 Construct the size-n solution from the size-m solutions

16.5 Give the complete rules that can be used to compute Fibonacci numbers for any given integer n ≥ 0.

17. You are asked to create a family tree according to the given tree in figure 5.23. In a tree we call a node **a** the **parent** of another node **b** if there is an **edge(a, b)** in the tree. Node **b** is also called a **child** of **a**. A node without the parent is the **root**. A tree must have a unique root. A node without any child is a **leaf**. For each rule you defined, you must write at least a line of comment, explaining what the rule does.

17.1 Define the factbase according to the given family tree, where a relationship **parent(a, b)** exists if there is an **edge(a, b)** in the tree. The names in the tree must be different.

17.2 Define a rule **sibling(X, Y)** which returns **yes** if **X** and **Y** have the same parent, where **X** and **Y** may not be the same, e.g., **sibling(mike, mike)** must return **no**.

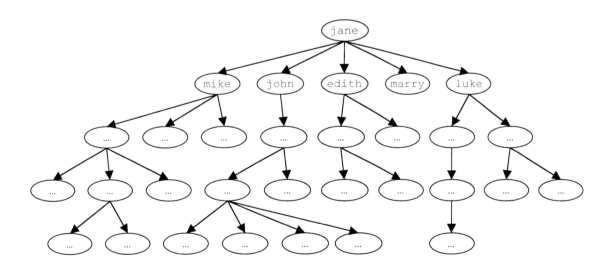

Figure 5.23 The structure of a family tree

17.3 Define a recursive rule **depth(D, X)** where D is the number of levels from the root to X. The depth of the root is 0.

17.4 Based on the depth relationship, define a rule **cousin(X, Y)** which returns yes if X and Y have the same depth. Note, this cousin relationship is slightly different from what the word cousin means. In this definition, siblings are cousins too.

17.5 Define the rule **cousin2(X, Y)** recursively without using the depth relationship. Hint: Use parent rule in the question.

17.6 Define a rule called **treequestions** that will call all rules that you have defined once. Make sure that all calls in the rule **treequestions** will be executed.

6

Fundamentals of Service-Oriented Computing Paradigm

This chapter introduces the fundamentals of the service-oriented computing paradigm, the basic concepts, principles, programming, and the software development process based on this paradigm. As a preparation, we first give a short introduction to C#. You need to read the C# section only if you want to program service components. C# is not necessary for application builder of service-oriented software.

6.1 Introduction to C#

C# is an object-oriented programming language, and it is one of the two major languages that are used to write Web services today. The other one is Java. In fact, the constituent services (components) of a service-oriented application are object-oriented. The object-oriented classes are wrapped with open standard interfaces to become services. A service-oriented application composes of services from different service providers. As the starting point, the following program prints the string "Hello, World!".

```
using System;
public class MyFirstClass {
    public static void Main() {
        Console.WriteLine("Hello, World!");
    }
}
```

C# inherits most of its syntax from the C/C++ family of languages and supports most features that Java supports. It is strongly typed with automatic garbage collection and a rich functionality set that empowers developers of both object-oriented and service-oriented software. This section introduces, from a C++ programmer's point of view, a small subset of this extensive language.

6.1.1 COMPARISON BETWEEN C++ AND C#

Table 6.1 compares and contrast the main features between C++ and C#. As can be seen, C# moves towards automatic management like Java, while trying to keep the C++ features where possible.

Feature	C++	C#
main()	global function	public static function in a class
Use of library functions	Header files (#include directives) and the **using** directive can be used	Header files may not be used. The **using** directive is used to reference types in other namespaces.
Preprocessor directives	Preprocessor directives and macros are allowed	Preprocessor directives are allowed, but cannot create macros. Directives can be used for conditional compilation.
Global functions or variables	Allowed	Not allowed. They must be contained within a type declaration (such as class or struct).
Inheritance	Mutiple inheritance is allowed	A class can inherit implementation from one base class only. However, a class or an interface can implement multiple interfaces.
Override	Declaring override functions does not require the **override** keyword	Declaring override methods requires the **override** keyword.
Garbage and destructor	No automatic garbage collector. Destructors are called automatically, but a programmer can call destructors.	There is an automatic garbage collector. Programmer cannot call the destructors.
long type	32 bits	64 bits
Array declaration	The brackets "[]" appear following the array variable, e.g., int myArray [] = {1, 2, 7};	The brackets "[]" appear following the array type, e.g., int[] myArray = {1, 2, 7};
string	An array of characters with a terminator	A string type is defined. One can use == and != to compare two string objects.
Pointer	Allowed	Pointers are allowed only in unsafe mode.
switch statement	support fall through from one case label to another. Use **break** to exit.	Does not support fall through from one case label to another.
foreach statement	Not allowed	Used to iterate through arrays and collections.

6.1.2 Namespaces and the Using Directive

The following code segment shows the most basic code template for a C# application:

```
using <namespace>
namespace <your optional namespace>
class <your class> {
    public static void Main() {
        ...
    }
}
```

Header files in C/C++ don't exist in C#; instead, namespaces are used to reference groups of libraries and classes. Programmers can define namespaces in order to prevent class naming conflicts, as well as reference namespaces, which define the .Net Framework SDK. For example:

```
namespace VirtualStore {
    namespace Customer {
        //define customer classes
        class ShoppingCartOrder( ) { ... }
    }
    namespace Admin {
        //define administration classes
        class ReportGenerator( ) { ... }
    }
}
```

The **using** directive tells the compiler where to search for definitions for namespace class's member methods that are used in the application. For example:

```
using VirtualStore;
```

Framework SDK UI functionality can be accessed by using a directive:

```
using System.Windows.Forms;
```

An alternative to using directives is to fully qualify each single reference like this:

```
private System.Windows.Forms.Button Button1;
```

6.1.3 The Queue Example in C#

To see concrete differences between C++ and C# and to get started with writing a C# program, we present the C# version of the Queue example given in section 3.1. From this example, you can see that it is easy to get started with C# after you have learned C++.

```csharp
using System;
namespace ConsoleApplication1
{    // class is defined within curly bracket
    class Queue {
        private int[] buffer;
        private int queue_size;
        protected int front;
        protected int rear;
        public Queue() {         // constructor
            front = 0;
            rear = 0;
            queue_size = 10;
            buffer = new int[queue_size];
        }
        public Queue(int n) {    // constructor
            front = 0;
            rear = 0;
            queue_size = n;
            buffer = new int[queue_size];
        }
        public void enqueue(int v) {
            if(rear < queue_size)
                buffer[rear++] = v;
            else
                if(compact())
                buffer[rear++] = v;
        }
        public int dequeue() {
            if(front < rear)
                return buffer[front++];
            else {
                Console.WriteLine("Error: Queue empty");
                return -1;
            }
        }
        private bool compact() {
            If(front == 0) {
                Console.WriteLine("Error: Queue overflow");
                return false;
            }
            else {
```

```
                    for(int i = 0;i < rear-front; i++)
                            buffer[i] = buffer[i+front];
                    rear = rear - front;
                    front = 0;
                    return true;
            }
        }
        static void Main( ) {
                Queue Q2 = new Queue(4);
                Q2.enqueue(12);
                Q2.enqueue(18);
                int x = Q2.dequeue();
                int y = Q2.dequeue();
                Console.WriteLine("X = {0} Y = {1} ", x, y);
                Console.ReadLine();
        }
    }
}
```

If you compare this program with the C++ program in section 3.1, you can see the two programs are very similar and C# is not difficult to learn.

6.1.4 CLASS AND OBJECT IN C#

Like Java, all C# applications require a unique program entry point, or **Main** method, implemented as a member method within a class. This differs from C++, where **Main** is a function that must be located outside any class. In C# programs, **Main**'s location is determined by the compiler, and it does not matter which class defines the **Main**. **Main** is required to be defined as **static**, and may optionally receive arguments or return a value. An optional **public** access modifier notifies the C# compiler that anyone can call this member method. The required **static** keyword means that **Main** is called without requiring an object instance.

A class is a user-defined type and a blueprint of functionality for variables of that type. An object is a named reference to that class with memory allocated. Instantiating a class with the **new** function creates an instance or an object with information about member methods and other members allocated on the heap. For both C++ and C#, a variable of a reference type takes values of the heap addresses required to locate those class members. Class members include anything defined inside a class, such as variables, constants, and functions.

In C#, accessing the members of a static object is accomplished like Java, with the "." dot operator.

```
<className>.<memberName>
Console.WriteLine("Hello World!");
```

where **memberName** is a method call or variable name, respectively.

Accessing the members of a reference object is also accomplished like Java, with the "." dot operator.

```
<referenceName>.<memberName>
time.printStandard( );
```

where **memberName** is a method call or variable name respectfully.

C++ offers a second way to define objects, not as reference types on the heap, but as local types on the stack. This is done by simply instantiating without the **new** function. In C#, the new keyword is the only way to create an object instance.

The class syntax can be described using the following syntax diagram, where the item in square brackets is optional.

```
[attributes][modifiers] class <className> [:
baseClassName]
{
    [class-body]
}[;]
```

Attributes can be thought of as inline notes and declarative statements that the programmer can attach to a class, members, parameters, or other code elements. Through a library called reflection, this extra information can be retrieved and used by other code at run time. Attributes provide a generic means of associating information with declarations, a powerful tool in numerous scenarios.

The access **modifiers public, protected,** and **private** have equivalent semantic in C# and C++. Both C# and C++ will default to **private** if no access modifier is explicitly defined.

Other possible method modifiers include **sealed, override,** and **virtual,** as well as the class modifier **abstract** that deals with class inheritance functionality and scope.

In C++, programmers have the choice of defining class members inside the class declaration, or outside the class declaration with use of the scope-resolution operator. In C#, programmers must define all class members inside the curly brackets of that class. The simple idea of grouping related objects inside the same class is designed to create more modular bundles of code.

6.1.5 Parameters: Passing by Reference With ref & out

In C#, parameter passing by reference, or giving the receiving method access to permanently changing the value, is done with the **ref** keyword, as seen in the example below:

```
using System;
class Point {
    public Point(int x) {
        this.x = x;
    }
    public void GetPoint(ref int x) {
        x = this.x;              // this.x refers to the class member
    }
    int x;
}
class Test {
    public static void Main() {
        Point myPoint = new Point(10);
```

```
            int x = 0;
            myPoint.GetPoint(ref x);              //x = 10
    }
}
```

C# offers a second way to pass parameters by reference, with the **out** keyword. The out keyword makes it possible to pass an uninitialized parameter by reference.

```
using System;
class Point {
    public Point(int x) {
            this.x = x;
    }
    public void GetPoint(out int x) {
            x = this.x;
    }
    int x;
}
class Test {
    public static void Main() {
            Point myPoint = new Point(10);
            int x;
            myPoint.GetPoint(out x);              //x = 10
    }
}
```

6.1.6 BASE CLASSES AND CONSTRUCTORS

C# takes after the C++ model for defining a parent class in the class header. Classes may inherit from one base class at most. The C# syntax for defining a base class and for calling the base class constructor might look like this:

```
class CalculatorStack: stack {
    public CalculatorStack(int n) :stack(n) {
    ...
    }
}
```

6.1.7 CONSTRUCTOR, DESTRUCTOR, AND GARBAGE COLLECTION

Like C++, if the programmer does not define a constructor, C# creates a default constructor for each class. This ensures that the member variables of the class are set to an appropriate default value, rather than pointing to random garbage. Multiple constructors can be overloaded for a class. Constructor header syntax includes the public modifier and the class name with zero or more parameters. Constructors are called automatically when the class object is instantiated and do not return a value.

In general, destructors release a reference an object holds to other objects. In C++, the programmer is responsible for implementing a class destructor to deallocate heap memory after the object is no longer referenced. Without manual clean up, memory leaks may ultimately crash the system. C# avoids this potential problem with automatic object clean up and tracking of all memory allocation by the .Net Garbage Collector (GC). The GC is non deterministic, it does not take up processor time by running constantly, it only runs when heap memory is low. There are some cases when the C# programmer wants to release resources manually; for example, when working with non-object resources like a data base connection or window handle. To ensure deterministic finalization, the Object.Finalize method can be overridden. C# does not have a delete function. Other than that small difference, overriding Object.Finalize method has the same syntax and effect as using a C++ destructor, as shown in the code below.

```
public class DestructorExample{

    public DestructorExample( ){
        Console.WriteLine('Woohoo, object instantiated!');
    }
    ~DestructorExample( ){
        Console.WriteLine('Yay, destructor called!');
    }
}
```

6.1.8 POINTERS IN C#

C# supports the following pointer operations, which will appear familiar to C++ programmers:

& The address-of operator returns the memory address of the variable.

* The primary pointer operator is used in two scenarios:

1) to declare a pointer variable;

2) to dereference, or access the value in the memory location the pointer points to.

The dereferencing and member access operator first gets the object the pointer points to, and then accesses a given member of that object. * can accomplish the same operation. These expressions equally access a member x of an object pointed to by pointer p.

```
(*p).x;
p->x;
```

Semantics for C/C++ pointers, as well as syntax for referencing and dereferencing their values, are upheld in C#. The main difference in C# is that any code using pointers needs to be marked as unsafe. The **unsafe** keyword is used as a modifier in the declarations of unsafe methods, and to mark blocks of code that call unsafe methods. Code written in the unsafe context is not explicitly unsafe—it simply allows the programmer to work with raw memory and sidesteps compiler type checking. Unsafe code should not be confused with unmanaged code; the objects in unsafe code are still managed by the runtime and GC.

Pointers in C# can point to either value types (basic data types) or reference types. However, you can only retrieve the address of a value type. Another thing to note, if you are working with the Visual Studio IDE, the code needs to be compiled with the /unsafe compiler option.

This example illustrates pointers in C#:

```
public class MyPointerTest {
    unsafe public static void Swap( int *xVal, int *yVal) {
            int temp = *xVal;
            *xVal = *yVal;
            *yVal = temp;
    }
    public static void Main(string[] args) {
        int x = 5;
        int y = 6;
        Console.WriteLine("Original Value: x = {0}, y = {1}"", x, y);
        unsafe {
            Swap(&x, &y);
        }
            Console.WriteLine("New Value: x = {0}, y = {1}", x, y);
    }
}
```

The console outputs are:

```
Original Value: x = 5, y = 6
New Value: x = 6, y = 5
```

6.1.9 C# Unified Type System

C# uses a **unified type system** that makes the value of every data type an object. Reference types (complex types) and value types share the same roots through the base class **System.Object**. Value types have a minimum set of abilities inherited through this hierarchy. The following are all valid C# code examples:

```
5.ToString( )                   //Retrieves the name of an object
b.Equals( ) == c.Equals( )  //Compares two object references at runtime
w.GetHashCode( )            //Gets the hash code for an object
4.GetType( )                    //Gets the name of an object
```

Because all types inherit from objects, it's possible to use the dot (.) operator on value types without first wrapping the value inside of a separate wrapper class. This solves some of the inefficient code that object-oriented programmers must write in C++ (and in Java) to wrap value types before using them like reference types.

In C++, if you want to create a method with a parameter that accepts any type, you have to write a wrapper class with overloaded constructors for each value type you want to support. For example:

```
class AllTypes {
public:
```

```
    AllTypes(int w);
    AllTypes(double x);
    AllTypes(char y);
    AllTypes(short z);
    //a constructor must be overloaded for each desired type
    //retrieving a value from this class would require overloaded functions
};
class CTypesExample
{
    public Example(AllTypes& myType) {
    }
};
```

In C#, whenever a value type is used where an object type is required, the compiler will automatically box the value type into a heap-allocated wrapper. **Boxing** is the compiler process that converts a value type to a reference type. **Unboxing** is explicitly casting the reference type back to a value type.

Boxing and unboxing example 1:

```
int v = 55;
Console.WriteLine ("Value is: {v}", v);        //Console.Writeline only accepts objects
//The compiler wraps value types for you
int v2 = (int) v;                              //Unboxing is like Java casting
```

Boxing and unboxing example 2:

```
int v = 55;
object x = v;                                  //box int value type v into reference type x
Console.WriteLine ("Value is: {0}", x);        // Console.Writeline
inv v2 = (int) x;                              // only accepts objects
```

A unified type system makes cross-language interoperability possible. Other benefits of the type system include guaranteed type safety, a security enhancement where each type in the system is tracked by the runtime. The overall effect is a safer, more robust code, with mainstream functionality creating a conceptually simpler programming model.

6.1.10 FURTHER TOPICS IN C#

The purpose of this section is to extend the object-oriented features discussed in C++. C# is a powerful programming language to which many books and Web sites have been dedicated. Key topics that are integral in C#, which are not covered extensively here include: generics, indexers, properties, event handling, delegates, attributes, and a long list of capabilities within the namespaces of the .Net Framework.

Section B.2.3 in Appendix B introduces how to use Visual Studio .Net to compile and run C++ and C# programs.

6.2 SERVICE-ORIENTED COMPUTING PARADIGM

The evolutional and technological shift from products to services means that the value of a technology is moving from the resulting product itself to how the technology is being received by its users. The value (in terms of increased productivity of using the product, total cost of ownership, improved efficiency and effectiveness, return on investment formula or benchmark, project completion time, and increased revenue) must be explicit and reflected from the technology's investment. For software products, the emerging Service-Oriented computing (SOC), including Service-Oriented Architecture (SOA) and Web Services (WS) technologies, reflects the shift from the product-oriented paradigm to the service-oriented paradigm. This paradigm shift is completely changing the way we develop and use computer software. In the near future, computer users may no longer need to buy hardware or software. All they need is to sign up a service contract with a service provider or broker. Hardware with necessary software can be provided for free. Users are charged for the services they use, similar to the models used by cable TV or cellular phone operators. The services can be provided online through the Web technology. Computer companies such as IBM, Microsoft, Micro Sun Systems, Oracle, and SAP have started to implement the new paradigm. For example, WebSphere (IBM) and Visual Studio .Net (Microsoft) platforms that support the development and applications of Web services. Software licensing model is also being changed from the previous model, which is a step towards this service-oriented direction: The users have to register the software or it stops functioning within certain period of time. Furthermore, the entire software is no longer stored on CDs. They are partially stored on the vendor's Web servers with appropriate access control.

In the traditional software development process, the developer takes the requirements, converts them into the specification, uses a programming language to code the specification, and then uses a compiler to translate the code into the executable. Service-Oriented Computing (SOC) paradigm evolves from the Object-Oriented Computing (OOC) and component-based computing paradigms by splitting the developers into three independent but collaborative parties: the application builders (also called service requesters), the service brokers (or service publishers), and the service providers. The responsibility of the service providers is to write program components, such as classes, and then, to wrap them into services with the open standard interfaces. The service brokers publish and market the available services. The application builders find the available services through service brokers and use the services to compose new applications. The application development is done via discovery and composition, rather than traditional design and coding.

6.2.1 BASIC CONCEPTS AND TERMINOLOGIES

Technically, a **service** is the interface between the producer and the consumer. From the producer's point of view, a service is a function module that is well-defined, self-contained, and does not depend on the context or state of other functions. In this sense, a service is often referred to as a service agent or simply an agent. These services can be newly developed modules or just wrapped around existing legacy programs to give them new interfaces. From the application builder or user's point of view, a service is a unit of work done by a service provider to achieve desired end results. A service normally does not have the human user's interface. Instead, it provides programming interface so that a service can be called (invoked) by other services. For human users to use the services, a user interface needs to be added. For example, the airline's services always have two sets of interfaces. The programming interfaces are used by programs for automated search, e.g., one can write a program to find the lowest fare across airlines from city A to city B with a given number of stops. The human user interfaces allow human users to manually browse through the airline's web pages to find the tickets they want.

Service-Oriented Architecture (SOA) considers a software system consisting of a collection of loosely coupled services (components) that communicate with each other through standard interfaces and via standard message-exchanging protocols. These services are autonomous and platform independent. They can reside on different computers and make use of each other's services to achieve their own desired goals and end results. A new service can be composed at runtime based on locally or remotely available services. Remote services can be searched and discovered through service brokers that publish services for public access.

Web Services (WS) implement a Web-based SOA and a set of enabling technologies, including XML (eXtensible Markup Language), the standard for data representation. SOAP (Simple Object Access Protocol) enables remote invocation of services across network and platforms. WSDL (Web Services Description Language) and OWL-S (Web Ontology Language for Services) are XML-based languages for service description. UDDI (Universal Description Discovery and Integration) allows WS to be published and listed in its WS registry for searching and discovering. Web services have three technical aspects:

- Services are functional building blocks. Multiple services can form a composite service and the composite service becomes a new building block. Service composition can be done at runtime when such a building block is needed.

- Services are software modules that can be identified by URL (Uniform Resource Locator) and whose interfaces and bindings are capable of being defined, described, and discovered as XML artefacts. Web services are often described by WSDL or OWL-S, accessed by the protocol SOAP, and published by UDDI. With an added human user interface, a single service or a composite service can form a Web application. Web services are normally accessed by computer programs while Web applications are accessed by human users.

- Services support direct interactions with other software agents using XML based messages exchanged via Internet based protocols; e.g., HTTP (Hypertext Transfer Protocol) and FTP (File Transfer Protocol) are independent of platforms and programming languages.

A **Service-Oriented Enterprise** (SOE) is an enterprise that implements and exposes its business processes through an SOA, and it provides frameworks for managing its business processes across an SOA landscape.

A **Service-Oriented Infrastructure** (SOI). To better support the operation of software developed in SOE, Intel proposed the SOI concept. The idea is to develop computing components, memory components, and networking components as virtual services, so that they seamlessly interoperate with software services. Another implication of SOI is that the hardware can be constructed as recomposable services which allow hardware components to be replaced or upgraded without stopping the operation of the system.

Service-Oriented Computing (SOC) refers to the paradigm that represents computation in service-orientation concepts and principles. SOC is also used an umbrella term for SOA, WS, SOE, SOI, etc.

Service-Oriented System Engineering (SOSE) is a combination of system engineering, software engineering, and service-oriented computing. It suggests developing service-oriented software and hardware under system engineering principles, including requirement, modeling, specification, verification, design, implementation, testing (validation), operation, and maintenance.

6.2.2 Web Services Development

Under SOC paradigm, individual services are developed independently based on standard interfaces. They are submitted to service brokers. The application builders or service requesters search, find, bind, test, verify, and execute services in their applications dynamically at runtime. Such service-oriented architecture gives the application builders the maximum flexibility to choose the best service brokers and the best services. Figure 6.1 shows a typical Web service architecture, its components, and the process of registering and requesting a service. The components and steps shown in the diagram are explained as follows:

1. The service providers develop software components (agents) to provide different services using ordinary programming languages such as C++, C#, or Java. SOC development platforms like Microsoft .Net and IBM WebSphere support the generation of standard interfaces in XML-based WSDL, which can be then registered to a service registry, such as UDDI.

2. The service providers register (publish) the services to a service broker and the services are published in the registry.

3. Current service brokers are UDDI or ebXML-based, which provide a set of standard service interfaces for publishing and discovering Web services. For UDDI, the information needed for publishing a service includes: (1) White page information: Service provider's name, identification, e.g., the company's DUNS number, and contact information. (2) Yellow page information (business category): industry type, product type, service type, and geographical location. (3) Green page information: technical detail how other Web services can access (invoke) the services, such as APIs (Application Programming Interfaces). UDDI's white and yellow pages are an analogy to the telephone white and yellow pages.

4. An application builder looks up, through the Internet, the broker's service registry, seeking desired services and instructions on how to use the services. The ontology and standard taxonomy will help automatic matching between the requested and registered services.

5. Once the service broker finds a service in its registry, it returns the service's details (service provider's binding address and parameters for calling the service) to the application builder.

6. The application builder uses the available services to compose the required application. This is higher level programming using service modules to construct larger applications. In this way, an application builder does not have to know low-level programming. With the help of an application development platform, the application code can be automatically generated based on the composition logic and the constituent services.

7. The code of certain services found through a broker could reside in a remote site, e.g., in the service provider's site. SOAP calls can be used to remotely access the services.

8. The service agents in the service provider directly communicate with the application and deliver service results.

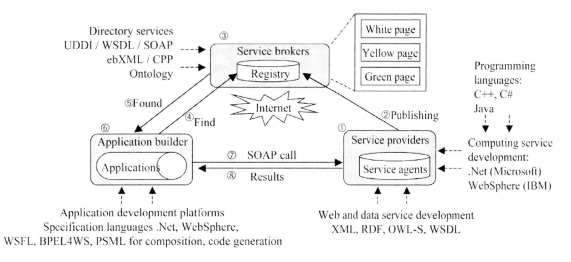

Figure 6.1 A typical Web service architecture

6.2.3 SERVICE-ORIENTED SYSTEM ENGINEERING

SOC uses services discovered over the Internet to compose applications. Trustworthiness of the discovered services, as well as the availability of remote servers and the connectivity to the Internet, are much bigger issues than those developed in the same house. Service-Oriented System Engineering (SOSE) techniques will play a bigger role in ensuring the trustworthiness of the discovered services.

Because SOC software is developed by three independent yet collaborative parties, SOSE will be different from the traditional software engineering. Table 6.1 lists typical SOSE techniques in the development phases of SOC software. Because the development process is collaborative, many of the SOSE techniques are collaborative too. For example, test cases may be contributed in a collaborative manner by all three parties. The service provider can provide sample unit test cases for the service broker and service requesters to reuse. The service broker can provide its own test cases via specification-based test case generation tool, and the broker may even make the tool available for all the parties. The application builder can use the sample test cases by the service broker, and contribute its own application test cases.

While the basic engineering principles remain the same, the way they are applied will be different in the SOC paradigm. Specifically, most engineering tasks will be done on the fly at runtime in a collaborative manner. Because systems will be composed at runtime using existing services, many engineering tasks need to be performed without complete information and with significant information available just in time before application. In this way, SOSE in some way may be drastically different from traditional engineering where engineers have complete information about the system requirements and thorough analyses can be performed even before system design is started.

Table 6.1 Different SOSE techniques

Development phase	SOSE techniques
Collaborative Specification & Modeling	Service specification languages, model-driving architecture, ontology engineering, and policy specification
Collaborative Verification	Dynamic completeness and consistency checking, dynamic model checking, and dynamic simulation
Collaborative Design	Ontology engineering, dynamic reconfiguration, dynamic composition and re-composition, dynamic dependability (reliability, security, vulnerability, safety) design
Collaborative Implementation	Automatic system composition and code generation
Collaborative Validation	Dynamic specification-based test generation, group testing, remote testing, monitoring, and dynamic policy enforcement
Collaborative Runtime Evaluation	Dynamic data collection and profiling, data mining, reasoning, dependability (reliability, security, vulnerability, etc) evaluation
Collaborative Operation and maintenance	Dynamic reconfiguration and re-composition, dynamic re-verification and re-validation

6.2.4 WEB SERVICES AND ENABLING TECHNOLOGIES

Web services and the enabling technologies form a perfect instance of the SOC paradigm, where available resources on the Web make full SOC possible and attractive. One part of Web services is the **Semantic Web**, which represents resources, and the other part is the service agents, which make use of available resources on Web to provide services requested by the application builders and service requesters.

Semantic Web is a vision for the future of the Web in which information is given explicit meaning, making it easier for Web services to automatically process and integrate information available on the Web. A specific domain of the semantic Web is called **ontology**, which defines a vocabulary of terms (words), their meanings (semantics), their interconnections (e.g., synonym and antonym), and rules of inference. The enabling technologies for Web services and semantic Web include the following:

XML (extensible markup language) is a universal meta language used to define other Web services standards, protocols, interfaces, document, data, etc. Like BNF (Backus Naur Form), XML is a context-free language that only defines the syntax of the language. The context and semantics of data and programs need to be defined in a detailed language or protocol based on XML syntax, such as SOAP, RDF, OWL, WSDL to be discussed in this chapter.

RDF (Resource Description Framework) can be considered a language that describes individual resources. An RDF document consists of a collection of statements. Each statement is a triple of (1) subject, (2) predicate, property, or relationship, and (3) object or value. The subject and the predicate are each a resource and the object can be a resource or a value. A statement makes an assertion that the subject is related to the object in the way specified by the predicate. An RDF document can be represented as a directed and labeled graph if we use a node to represent the subject or an object, and use an edge to represent the predicate. The subject is the source, the object is the target, and the predicate is the label of the edge.

RDF Schema (RDFS) extends RDF with frame-based primitives to specify class hierarchy and property hierarchy, with domain and range definitions of the properties, which can be used to define a simple ontology like a dictionary.

OWL (Web Ontology Language). In terms of the expressivity of describing the ontology or semantics, RDF and RDFS are very limited. OWL is built on RDF and RDFS to provide the description logic, including the classes and properties, as well as the constraints on the properties and their combinations using logic operators.

WSDL (Web Services Description Language) is an XML-based specification language for describing the Web services interfaces. It can be used to define data types, input and output data formats, the operations (methods) provided by Web services, network addresses, and protocol bindings.

SOAP (Simple Object Access Protocol) enables remote invocation of services across network and platforms. A SOAP packet is written in XML format and is normally embedded in an HTTP (Hypertext Transfer Protocol) packet to be sent to the destination using HTTP protocol. Once the receiver receives the SOAP packet, it calls the requested service and returns the result to the requester.

UDDI (Universal Description Discovery and Integration) [http://www.uddi.org] provides service directory service. The goal of UDDI initiative is to build a standard, open, global, and platform-independent framework to share a global business registry, let business entities find each other, and define how they access each other's services over the Internet. UDDI is implemented as a Web service that allows service providers to publish their Web services and for service requesters to search services by name, by business type, or by geographic region. When submitting a service to UDDI, the service provider must provide the provider's identity, contact information, geographic location, service type, and service APIs (Application Programming Interfaces) for the programs of the application builders to call the services. UDDI uses WSDL for service description and uses SOAP for service invocation.

ebXML (electronic business XML) [http://www.ebxml.org]. Similar to UDDI, ebXML also provides service directory but is more complex than UDDI. The goal of ebXML is more challenging, as it is to build a global e-business infrastructure, with the specific goal of letting small companies and companies in developing nations participate (with a very low entry cost). In ebXML, a central role is played by business processes. Every company publishes one or more Collaboration Protocol Profile (CPP), a description of the processes and the technical service interfaces to interact with them. The role of CPP is comparable to that of WSDL in UDDI, but CPP is more powerful, which allows users to define the semantics. ebXML also provides a messaging service to play the role of SOAP in UDDI.

Figure 6.2 shows the relationship among these techniques and their roles in creating service-oriented computing systems, where XML, XML Schema, DRF, RDF Schema, and OWL are used to describe resources, data, and semantics of resources and data, which form global and local ontologies. Programming languages such as Java, C++, and C# can be used to write the service agents. The IDE such as .Net and WebSphere can be used to wrap the program into standard service interface written in WSDL to form service agents, which make use of the resources, data, and ontologies to provide required services. UDDI and ebXML are used to publish services. SOAP is used for remote service invocation between services.

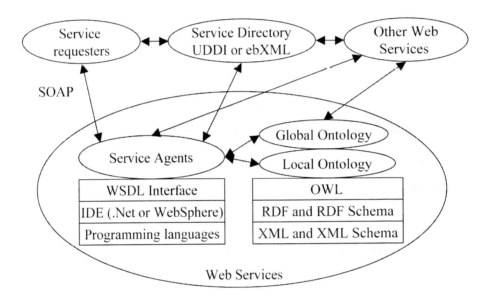

Figure 6.2 Overview of the techniques to be discussed in this chapter

In the remainder of the chapter, we will study creating Web services, registering Web services, and using Web services to build applications.

6.3 SERVICE PROVIDERS: PROGRAMMING WEB SERVICES IN C# AND .NET

Web services are platform independent. However, the agent that actually performs the computation tasks will still be written in a specific programming language. In other words, a Web service is an interface that coverts the service call (remote invocation) in an open standard language (e.g., XML/SOAP/WSDL) into the function-call of the programming language (e.g., C# or Java), in which the service agent is written, as shown in Figure 6.3.

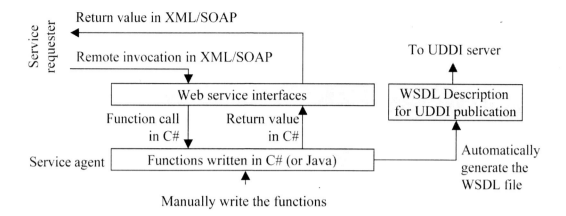

Figure 6.3 Service agent and Web service interfaces

In the previous section, we mentioned the standard interfaces in XML, SOAP, and WSDL. We did not study them in detail. In fact, we do not need to write the interfaces manually for the service agent. There are tools that can automatically generate the interface file. This is analog to writing a web page. You can either directly use the html language to write a Web page, or use a Web authoring tool to write a Web page.

There are different languages and development environments that can be used to develop Web services. In this section, we will use C# and .Net as example to show how to develop and access Web services. We will discuss:

■ How a service provider creates a Web service project, writes Web services consisting of a set of C# functions, and automatically generates the WSDL interface file;

■ How a service provider puts the Web services and its WSDL interface file online so that the service requesters (clients) can remotely invoke the services;

■ How a service requester (client) accesses the Web services by calling the functions remotely either in a Web application or in another Web service.

6.3.1 CREATING A WEB SERVICE PROJECT

ASP.NET is the built-in programming template in the Visual Studio .Net Framework's Common Language Runtime (CLR) that is used to create individual Web services on the service provider's server. It can also be used to create Web applications on the client site to consume the Web services. ASP.Net Web services tutorials for programmers and a downloadable version can be found in its official site at [http://www.asp.net/Tutorials/quickstart.aspx].

Similar to creating a C++ or C# programming project, you can create a C# and ASP.Net Web service template as follows:

■ In the "File" menu of Visual Studio .Net 2005, choose "New" and "Web Site ...";

■ A dialog window will be open. Choose the template "ASP.Net Web Service". Choose a location and a name for your Web service, for example, enter a name for the project, c:\inetpub\ wwwroot\WebStrar. Then a Web service project WebStrar with a stack of folders and files will be created;

■ In the project stack, the file with the name "Service.cs" is the file in which your C# code should be incorporated. Double click on the Service.cs file you will see the template of the service agent code. You can simply add your C# functions into the template. See the next subsection.

Once you added your code into the template, you can use the tools in .Net to compile your C# code, build the project, debug the code, and execute the code.

6.3.2 WRITING THE SERVICE AGENT

You still have to write the code of your service agent manually to perform the required tasks (services), for example, perform addition, sorting, etc. However, ASP.NET has provided a template with defined namespaces and classes to facilitate writing of Web services. Following code shows the template in the file **Service.cs**.

```
using System;
using System.Web;
using System.Web.Services;
using System.Web.Services.Protocols;

[WebService(Namespace = "http://tempuri.org/")]
[WebServiceBinding(ConformsTo = WsiProfiles.BasicProfile1_1)]
public class Service : System.Web.Services.WebService {
    public Service () {
            //Uncomment the following line if using designed components
            //InitializeComponent();
    }
    [WebMethod] // Make the following function accessible over Web
    public string HelloWorld() {
            return ("Hello World");
    }
    [WebMethod] // Make the following function accessible over Web
    public double PiValue() {
            double pi = System.Math.PI; // call lib function PI
            return (pi);
    }
    [WebMethod] // Make the following function accessible over Web
    public int abs(int x) {
            if (x >= 0) return (x);
            else return (-x);
    }
}
```

The program template starts with listing namespaces that could be used in the Web services. Not all namespaces listed are necessary for this small example. Since the project name is called **WebStrar**, the new namespace created for the project is called **WebStrar**. Then, a public class called **Service** is defined, which inherits the built-in class **WebService** in the namespace **System.Web.Services**. In the class definition, it starts with the constructor **Service()**, followed by a list of functions. A list of required system functions are omitted in the given program above. Three Web accessible functions are defined in the class:

The string HelloWorld() function simply returns a string "Hello World".

The double PiValue(int x) function returns a double value, e.g., 3.14159265358979.

The abs() function takes an integer value as input and returns an integer value, the absolute value of x: If x is nonnegative, it returns x, otherwise, it returns -x.

Before each function, an instruction [WebMethods] is used, which makes the following function Web accessible.

6.3.3 LAUNCH AND ACCESS YOUR WEB SERVICES

Once you have incorporated all your service functions into the C# program template Service.cs, you can build (compile) and execute the program.

When the program is executed using the option: "debug"—"start without debugging", it will immediately launch your Web services on your local host. If you are working on a Windows XP machine, the service will be launched as a local Web page located at: http://localhost:1262/WebStrar/Service.asmx. Figure 6.4 shows the Web page that contains the three services abs, PiValue, and HelloWorld, defined in Service.asmx.

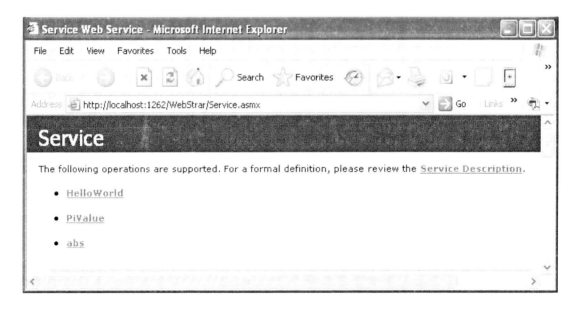

Figure 6.4 The Web service is launched on a service-hosting server

Click on a service, the function behind the service will be remotely invocated. For example, if abs is clicked, the Web page shown in Figure 6.5 will pop up. Since a parameter value is needed in the Web service, the Web page provides an input panel to take the parameter value. After a value, e.g., -1802, is entered and the button "invoke" is clicked, the Web service abs is remotely invoked. The return value will be shown in another web page containing the following information:

```
<?xml version="1.0" encoding="utf-8" ?>
<int xmlns="http://tempuri.org/">1802</int>
```

The return value **1802** is wrapped in the XML format.

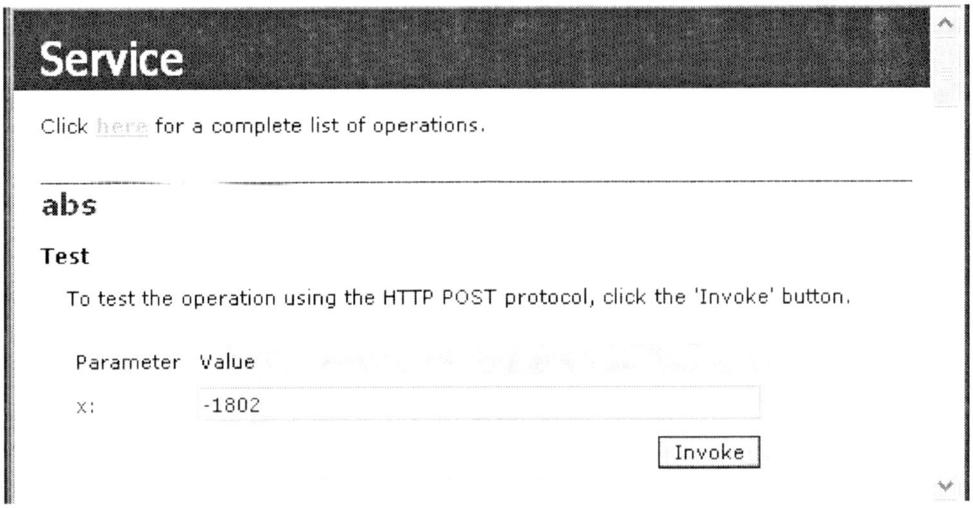

Figure 6.5 Enter the parameter value from a Web browser

The above process is in fact in the test mode. It is only possible when the services are launched on a local host. In this mode, the services cannot be remotely accessed by other application builders over the internet. They must be deployed on an Internet accessible server and be given a URL in order for them to be accessed by other Web services or applications on the Internet. If you want to make the services available on the internet, you have different ways to do it.

First, you can publish the services on your Windows XP computer by following these steps. In your .Net Web service project, you can choose menu item "Build" - "Publish Web Site". Then a dialog window will be open. You can choose a location in your computer to host the services, for example, you can choose the location: C:\Inetpub\wwwroot\WebStrarServices, where Inetpub\wwwroot is the Web directory managed by Internet Information Server (IIS), which is an optional component of Windows XP operating system. You need to install IIS, in order to run Web services from your Window XP machine. Once the Web Site is published, a Web page with the address http://localhost\WebStrarServices/Service.asmx will be open, which displays the same services shown in figure 6.4. Replacing the word "localhost" by the IP address of the local machine, you obtain the URL of the Web services, i.e., http://149.169.177.107/WebStrarServices/Service.asmx will be the URL of the services.

Second, if you have access to a Web server, e.g., a machine running Windows Server OS, you can move to the Web server once you completed testing your Web services. All you need to do is to "build" the program and "run" the program on the server, which will automatically deploy the Web services and assign a URL to them. In the example above, the URL given by the server is:

http://WebStrar.dhcp.asu.edu/WebStrarServices/Service.asmx

where WebStrar is the domain name we choose for the Web services.

Once the services are deployed on a server, the Web services can only be accessed through their programming interfaces. The following code shows an example of writing SOAP/HTTP request to call the Web service abs, and the response from the Web service to be sent back to the service requester.

In the code, the length needs to be replaced with the actual value.

```
POST /WebStrar/Service.asmx HTTP/1.1
Host: localhost
Content-Type: text/xml; charset=utf-8
Content-Length: length
SOAPAction: "http://tempuri.org/abs"
<?xml version="1.0" encoding="utf-8"?>
<soap:Envelope xmlns:xsi="http://www.w3.org/2001/XMLSchema-instance"
xmlns:xsd="http://www.w3.org/2001/XMLSchema"
xmlns:soap="http://schemas.xmlsoap.org/soap/envelope/">
    <soap:Body>
        <abs xmlns="http://tempuri.org/">
            <x>int</x>
        </abs>
    </soap:Body>
</soap:Envelope>
```

The SOAP response is

```
HTTP/1.1 200 OK
Content-Type: text/xml; charset=utf-8
Content-Length: length
<?xml version="1.0" encoding="utf-8"?>
<soap:Envelope xmlns:xsi="http://www.w3.org/2001/XMLSchema-instance"
xmlns:xsd="http://www.w3.org/2001/XMLSchema"
xmlns:soap="http://schemas.xmlsoap.org/soap/envelope/">
    <soap:Body>
        <absResponse xmlns="http://tempuri.org/">
            <absResult>int</absResult>
        </absResponse>
    </soap:Body>
</soap:Envelope>
```

Furthermore, in order to publicize the Web services, their URL and WSDL file must be registered to a service directory to make the services internet-searchable.

6.3.4 AUTOMATICALLY GENERATING WSDL FILE

When you execute the Service.asmx file on .Net, its WSDL file is automatically generated by ASP.Net environment and linked to the Web page in Figure 6.4. When you click on the link "**Service Description**", A Web page containing the service's WSDL file will be opened, as shown below:

```
<?xml version="1.0" encoding="utf-8" ?>
- <wsdl:definitions xmlns:soap="http://schemas.xmlsoap.org/wsdl/soap/"
xmlns:tm="http://microsoft.com/wsdl/mime/textMatching/"
xmlns:soapenc="http://schemas.xmlsoap.org/soap/encoding/"
xmlns:mime="http://schemas.xmlsoap.org/wsdl/mime/"
```

```
xmlns:tns="http://tempuri.org/"
xmlns:s="http://www.w3.org/2001/XMLSchema"
xmlns:soap12="http://schemas.xmlsoap.org/wsdl/soap12/"
xmlns:http="http://schemas.xmlsoap.org/wsdl/http/"
targetNamespace="http://tempuri.org/"
xmlns:wsdl="http://schemas.xmlsoap.org/wsdl/">
- <wsdl:types>
- <s:schema elementFormDefault="qualified"
  targetNamespace="http://tempuri.org/">
- <s:element name="HelloWorld">
  <s:complexType />
  </s:element>
- <s:element name="HelloWorldResponse">
- <s:complexType>
- <s:sequence>
  <s:element minOccurs="0" maxOccurs="1" name="HelloWorldResult" type="s:string" />
  </s:sequence>
  </s:complexType>
  </s:element>
- <s:element name="PiValue">
  <s:complexType />
  </s:element>
- <s:element name="PiValueResponse">
- <s:complexType>
- <s:sequence>
  <s:element minOccurs="1" maxOccurs="1" name="PiValueResult" type="s:double" />
  </s:sequence>
  </s:complexType>
  </s:element>
- <s:element name="abs">
- <s:complexType>
- <s:sequence>
  <s:element minOccurs="1" maxOccurs="1" name="x" type="s:int" />
  </s:sequence>
  </s:complexType>
  </s:element>
- <s:element name="absResponse">
- <s:complexType>
- <s:sequence>
  <s:element minOccurs="1" maxOccurs="1" name="absResult" type="s:int" />
  </s:sequence>
  </s:complexType>
  </s:element>
  </s:schema>
  </wsdl:types>
- <wsdl:message name="HelloWorldSoapIn">
  <wsdl:part name="parameters" element="tns:HelloWorld" />
  </wsdl:message>
- <wsdl:message name="HelloWorldSoapOut">
  <wsdl:part name="parameters" element="tns:HelloWorldResponse" />
  </wsdl:message>
- <wsdl:message name="PiValueSoapIn">
  <wsdl:part name="parameters" element="tns:PiValue" />
  </wsdl:message>
- <wsdl:message name="PiValueSoapOut">
```

```
      <wsdl:part name="parameters" element="tns:PiValueResponse" />
    </wsdl:message>
-   <wsdl:message name="absSoapIn">
      <wsdl:part name="parameters" element="tns:abs" />
    </wsdl:message>
-   <wsdl:message name="absSoapOut">
      <wsdl:part name="parameters" element="tns:absResponse" />
    </wsdl:message>
-   <wsdl:portType name="ServiceSoap">
-   <wsdl:operation name="HelloWorld">
      <wsdl:input message="tns:HelloWorldSoapIn" />
      <wsdl:output message="tns:HelloWorldSoapOut" />
    </wsdl:operation>
-   <wsdl:operation name="PiValue">
      <wsdl:input message="tns:PiValueSoapIn" />
      <wsdl:output message="tns:PiValueSoapOut" />
    </wsdl:operation>
-   <wsdl:operation name="abs">
      <wsdl:input message="tns:absSoapIn" />
      <wsdl:output message="tns:absSoapOut" />
    </wsdl:operation>
    </wsdl:portType>
-   <wsdl:binding name="ServiceSoap" type="tns:ServiceSoap">
      <soap:binding transport="http://schemas.xmlsoap.org/soap/http" />
-   <wsdl:operation name="HelloWorld">
      <soap:operation soapAction="http://tempuri.org/HelloWorld" style="document" />
-   <wsdl:input>
      <soap:body use="literal" />
    </wsdl:input>
-   <wsdl:output>
      <soap:body use="literal" />
    </wsdl:output>
    </wsdl:operation>
-   <wsdl:operation name="PiValue">
      <soap:operation soapAction="http://tempuri.org/PiValue" style="document" />
-   <wsdl:input>
      <soap:body use="literal" />
    </wsdl:input>
-   <wsdl:output>
      <soap:body use="literal" />
    </wsdl:output>
    </wsdl:operation>
-   <wsdl:operation name="abs">
      <soap:operation soapAction="http://tempuri.org/abs" style="document" />
-   <wsdl:input>
      <soap:body use="literal" />
    </wsdl:input>
-   <wsdl:output>
      <soap:body use="literal" />
    </wsdl:output>
    </wsdl:operation>
    </wsdl:binding>
-   <wsdl:binding name="ServiceSoap12" type="tns:ServiceSoap">
      <soap12:binding transport="http://schemas.xmlsoap.org/soap/http" />
-   <wsdl:operation name="HelloWorld">
```

```
<soap12:operation soapAction="http://tempuri.org/HelloWorld" style="document" />
- <wsdl:input>
<soap12:body use="literal" />
</wsdl:input>
- <wsdl:output>
<soap12:body use="literal" />
</wsdl:output>
</wsdl:operation>
<wsdl:operation name="PiValue">
<soap12:operation soapAction="http://tempuri.org/PiValue" style="document" />
- <wsdl:input>
<soap12:body use="literal" />
</wsdl:input>
- <wsdl:output>
<soap12:body use="literal" />
</wsdl:output>
</wsdl:operation>
- <wsdl:operation name="abs">
<soap12:operation soapAction="http://tempuri.org/abs" style="document" />
- <wsdl:input>
<soap12:body use="literal" />
</wsdl:input>
- <wsdl:output>
<soap12:body use="literal" />
</wsdl:output>
</wsdl:operation>
</wsdl:binding>
- <wsdl:service name="Service">
- <wsdl:port name="ServiceSoap" binding="tns:ServiceSoap">
<soap:address location="http://localhost:1262/WebStrar/Service.asmx" />
</wsdl:port>
- <wsdl:port name="ServiceSoap12" binding="tns:ServiceSoap12">
<soap12:address location="http://localhost:1262/WebStrar/Service.asmx" />
</wsdl:port>
</wsdl:service>
</wsdl:definitions>
```

This WSDL file contains the information for the UDDI server to match the service requests with the services provided by the Web services.

In the next section, we discuss the service directory and in section 6.5, we discuss how to use .Net framework to build application based on the Web services running on service providers' servers.

6.4 PUBLISHING AND SEARCHING WEB SERVICES USING UDDI

This section uses Microsoft UDDI Business Registry as an example to elaborate the service publication and searching processes.

Both IBM and Microsoft provide free UDDI services. Microsoft UDDI server is at: http://uddi.microsoft.com/. You can follow the following steps to register and use the services listed in the service directory.

1. Create a new account: This is a manual process using a GUI, as shown in Figure 6.6.

2. Publish a Service Provider: This is a manual process using a GUI, as shown in Figure 6.7.

3. Publish your Services: This can be a manual process using a GUI or automatic process using an API (Application Programming Interface), as shown in Figure 6.8.

4. Search for Services: This can be a manual process using a GUI or automatic process using an API, as shown in Figure 6.9.

Figure 6.6 Open an account at Microsoft UDDI registration page

Once an account is opened, the user can register as a service provider, as shown in Figure 6.7. A unique identity number will be returned to the service provider, which can be used by the service provider for publishing Web services.

Figure 6.7 Register as a service provider

Once a Web service is published by a service provider, a tModel key will be returned to the service provider, which can uniquely identify the Web service, as shown in Figure 6.8.

Figure 6.8 Publish a Web service

The Web services published in UDDI are organized in a category tree, as shown in Figure 6.9, which can be searched manually or through a programming interface.

Figure 6.9 Categorization of Web services in UDDI directory

6.5 BUILDING APPLICATION USING ASP.NET

In section 6.3, we discussed in detail how to use C# and ASP.Net to develop individual Web services. This section uses the same development tool to construct applications using the remote Web services available online.

6.5.1 CREATING A WINDOWS APPLICATION PROJECT IN ASP.NET

Similar to creating a C# and ASP.Net project as discussed in section 6.3, you can create a C# and ASP.Net Window application template as follows:

1. In the "File" menu of Visual Studio .Net, choose "New" and "Project . . .".
2. A dialog window will be open. In the project types panel, choose "Visual C#" language. In the templates panel, choose "Windows Application" as the template. Choose a directory, e.g., c:\inetpub\WebStrarAppWin, and enter a name, e.g., WebStrarApplication. Then a windows application project with a stack of folders and files will be created, as shown in Figure 6.10(a).

3. To use remote Web services in the application, mouse right-click on the "References" folder and choose "Add Web Reference". A dialog box will be open for entering the URL of the Web services, as shown in Figure 6.11.

4. The URL of Web services can be given directly by the service provider or discovered from searching a UDDI server. For example, if we want to use the services that we created and launched in section 6.3.3, we can enter the URL: http://149.169.177.107/ WebStrarServices/Service.asmx and name it "WebStrarServices", as shown in Figure 6.11. Once the reference link is added, the remote Web services is shown as "WebStrarServices" in the "Web References", as shown in Figure 6.10(b).

5. As a part of standard .Net function, the graphic interface is provided for Web application building. Mouse double clicks on the file "WebForm1.aspx". The Web form will be open and you can use your local functions or remote functions (Web services) to construct complex applications.

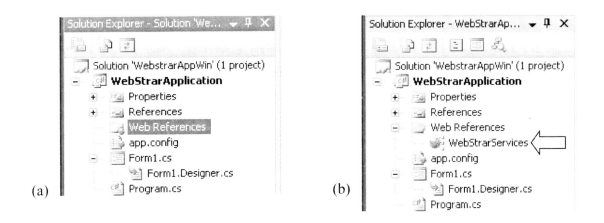

Figure 6.10 Project before and after the Web services are linked to the application

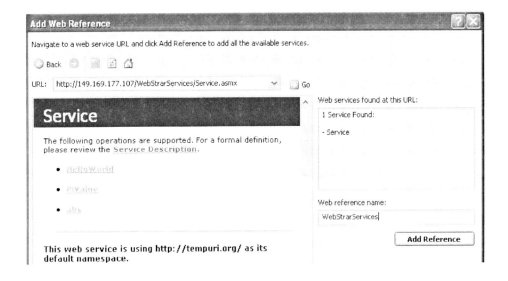

Figure 6.11 Add a Web reference in a windows application

Please notice that in step 2 above, you can also choose "New" and "Web Site", and choose ASP.Net Web Site as the template. In this case, the application created will run on a server and the users can use the application over the internet.

Both Web applications and Web services need to reside on a Web server. However, they are different. The former refers to an application with a human user interface. Users can use a Web browser to access the functions of the application. Examples of Web applications include online banking, online shopping, Web gaming, and online examination. The later refers to a piece of executable code that is accessed through a programming interface. Any Web service equipped with a human interface is considered a Web application. A Web application may use all local functions, all Web services, or both as its components.

6.5.2 CREATING AND COMPOSING A WEB APPLICATION BASED ON REMOTE WEB SERVICES

Creating a Web Application is very similar to creating Web services discussed in section 6.3, as shown below.

1. In the "File" menu of Visual Studio .Net, choose "New" and "Web Site . . .".

2. A dialog window will be open. Choose the template "ASP.Net Web Site". Choose a location and a name for your Web service, for example, c:\inetpub\wwwroot\WebApplication\ WebStrarApp. Then a Web application project with a stack of folders and files will be created.

3. In the menu "Website", choose "Add Web References".

4. In the menu "Website", choose "Add New Item", and then choose "Web Form", and we name the form WebForm1.

5. In the menu "View", choose "Toolbox", which offer various tools (graphic components) for building a graphic interface.

We will use the Web form as the design template of the graphic interface for our Web application and link the Web services to the graphic interface to perform various tasks. Figure 6.12 shows the graphic interface defined in the WebForm1.asxp of a Web application. You can drag and drop the Web Form components (label, button, textbox, etc) in the toolbox into the blank areas and add the names for them. In this example, we added four Buttons and named them:

■ Invoke String Service: This button will be linked to the Web service function HelloWorld() and the returned string will be displayed in the Label area named "Print String Value Here".

■ Get PiValue: This button will be linked to the Web service function PiValue() that returns the pi value, and the returned value will be displaced in the Label area named "Print Pi Value Here".

■ Get Absolute Value: This button will be linked to the Web service function abs() that returns the absolute value. The returned value will be displaced in the Label area named "Print Return Value Here".

■ Add Pi and abs Value: This button will be linked to the Web service functions that composed of PiValue() and abs(). The returned value will be displaced in the Label area named "Print Result Here".

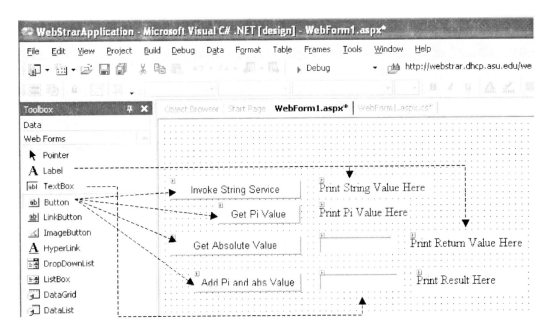

Figure 6.12 Web form layout that provides graphic interfaces to access C# functions

Once the graphic interfaces are designed, we need to link them to the respective Web services, so that the users can access the Web services through the interfaces (Web applications). Click on the tag **WebForm1.aspx.cs** in Figure 6.12 (or simply double click on the blank area, the C# code that implements the graphic interface will be opened, as shown below:

```
using System;
using System.Collections;
using System.ComponentModel;
using System.Data;
using System.Drawing;
using System.Web;
using System.Web.SessionState;
using System.Web.UI;
using System.Web.UI.WebControls;
using System.Web.UI.HtmlControls;
using WebStrarServices; // remote namespace Web reference
namespace WebStrarApplication {
    // Summary description for WebForm1.
    public class WebForm1 : System.Web.UI.Page {
            protected System.Web.UI.WebControls.Label Label1;
            protected System.Web.UI.WebControls.Button Button2;
            protected System.Web.UI.WebControls.Label Label2;
            protected System.Web.UI.WebControls.Button Button3;
```

```
        protected System.Web.UI.WebControls.TextBox TextBox1;
        protected System.Web.UI.WebControls.Label Label3;
        protected System.Web.UI.WebControls.Button Button4;
        protected System.Web.UI.WebControls.TextBox TextBox2;
        protected System.Web.UI.WebControls.Label Label4;
        protected System.Web.UI.WebControls.Button Button1;
        private void Page_Load(object sender, System.EventArgs e){
                // Put user code to initialize the page here
        }
        #region Web Form Designer generated code
        override protected void OnInit(EventArgs e) {
                // CODEGEN: This call is required by the ASP.NET Web Form Designer.
                InitializeComponent();
                base.OnInit(e);
        }
        // Required method for Designer support - do not modify
        // the contents of this method with the code editor.
        private void InitializeComponent(){
                this.Button1.Click += new System.EventHandler(this.Button1_Click);
                this.Button2.Click += new System.EventHandler(this.Button2_Click);
                this.Button3.Click += new System.EventHandler(this.Button3_Click);
//              this.TextBox1.TextChanged += new System.EventHandler(this.TextBox1_
                TextChanged);
                this.Button4.Click += new System.EventHandler(this.Button4_Click);
                this.Load += new System.EventHandler(this.Page_Load);
        }
        #endregion
        private void Button1_Click(object sender, System.EventArgs e){
                Service hw = new Service();
                this.Label1.Text = hw.HelloWorld();
        }
        private void Button2_Click(object sender, System.EventArgs e) {
                Service pivar = new Service();
                this.Label2.Text = pivar.PiValue().ToString();
        }
        private void Button3_Click(object sender, System.EventArgs e) {
                Service absvar = new Service();
                int number = Convert.ToInt32(this.TextBox1.Text);
                int result = absvar.abs(number);
                this.Label3.Text = result.ToString();
        }
```

```
private void Button4_Click(object sender, System.EventArgs e) {
    int number = Convert.ToInt32(this.TextBox2.Text);
    Service absvar = new Service();
    number = absvar.abs(number);
    double result = number + absvar.PiValue();
    this.Label4.Text = result.ToString();
}

}

}
```

The code that draws the graphic items such as buttons, labels, and textboxes are automatically generated by the library functions in .Net, which allow us to focus on the part of the code that performs the functions we wish to perform. In the code above, we have highlighted the part of the code we added into the template.

First, we added the namespace, which points to the remote Web service that we have developed:

```
using WebStrarServices;   //it contains a remote class service. See Figure 6.11.
```

Then, towards the end of the program, four functions are defined, each of which defines the action when one of the buttons is clicked by the user:

- Button1_Click(): The function first creates an object of the Web service Service(), and then it calls the method HelloWorld(). The returned string value is assigned to the Label1 area.
- Button2_Click(): The function first creates an object of Service(), and then it calls the method PiValue(). The returned double value is converted to string and then assigned to the Label2 area.
- Button3_Click(): Different from the first two functions, this function will take the input from textbox1, convert it into integer type, and then call the abs function in Service(). The returned value is displayed in Label3.
- Button4_Click(): The function will call two functions in Service(). It first calls the abs() function, gets the input from textbox2. Then it calls the PiValue(), adds the two numbers, and displays the result in Label4.

Compile and execute the program, a Web application will be generated, as shown in Figure 6.13(a). Click on the buttons, with proper input values, if required, the results will be displayed in the label areas, as shown in Figure 6.13(b).

Note, since this application is a Web application, it needs to be deployed to a Web server. On the other hand, the application does not have to be a Web application. It can be a Windows application. For example, if we develop a game based on Web services, the game can be either a Web application itself or a Windows application. In the latter case, the application can be downloaded to a Windows computer. However, the computer must have internet access when playing the game, because the game will contact the Web services at runtime.

*6.6 ADVANCED TOPICS IN SERVICE-ORIENTED SOFTWARE DEVELOPMENT

Service-Oriented Computing (SOC) is a new paradigm that is still under development. However, it has shown tremendous potential to revolutionize the software development process. This section discusses advanced topics in service-oriented software development, in which the authors of the book have been doing the research for many years.

Figure 6.13 Graphic interface of the Web application based on remote Web services

6.6.1 SIMPLE MODEL MULTIPLE ANALYSES VERSUS MULTIPLE MODELS MULTIPLE ANALYSES

Traditional object-oriented software development process is based on a process of Multiple Models Multiple Analyses (MMMA). The requirements of software are formalized into multiple models, describing different aspects of the software to be developed. Different analyses are performed on different models. The most well known MMMA development process is the UML (Unified Modeling Language) development [http://www.omg.org/technology/documents/formal/uml.htm], in which multiple models are used, as shown in figure 6.14.

The main problem with the MMMA approach is the maintainability of the models. If one model is modified, all the models will have to be modified, in most cases, manually. The models are usually

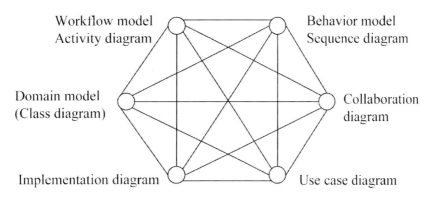

Figure 6.14 UML models

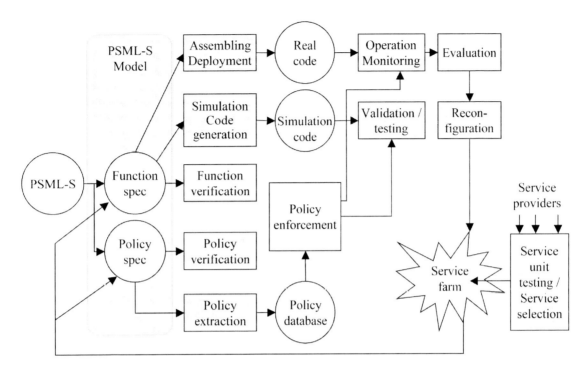

Figure 6.15 PSML-S-based SMMA development

managed and used by different personnel. If two or more models are modified simultaneously, it is extremely difficult to maintain the consistency among the models.

In the SOC software development process, it is possible to apply a Single Model Multiple Analyses (SMMA) process, that is, we use a single model as the basis of the entire development process. All analyses and evaluations are based on this model or its derived forms. A derived form is automatically generated by a tool from the original model or from a derived form. Figure 6.15 shows the PSML-S (Process Specification and Modeling Language for Services)-based development framework developed at Arizona State University. PSML-S is used to model the requirements to obtain a single model, the PSML-S model. Within the model, we separate the functional specification and the policy specification. All the analyses and evaluation will be based on this model. First, the functional specification and the policy specification will be verified by model checking, respectively. If they pass the verification, the functional specification will be used for simulation code generation. The simulation code will be used to validate the specification. If the code passes the validation, the functional specification will be used to generate the real code for deployment. In the meantime, the policies in the policy specification are extracted and stored into a policy database for runtime policy enforcement. During the operation, the execution is constantly monitored and evaluated. If a remote service is not reliable enough, the runtime reconfiguration service will select a better service from the service farm to replace an underperformed service. The service farm is maintained by the service management, that searches for newly available services and test these services. The qualified services will be stored in the service farm for later use by reconfiguration.

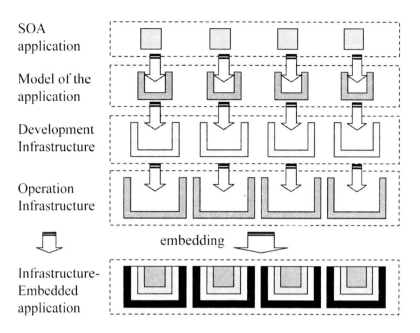

Figure 6.16 Infrastructure-embedded SOA application

6.6.2 INFRASTRUCTURE EMBEDDED DEVELOPMENT FRAMEWORK

PESOI (Process-Embedded Service-Oriented Infrastructure) is developed at Arizona State University. It integrates the development infrastructure into the operation infrastructure, so that the application can be re-developed during its operation. The PESOI is distinct from previous frameworks as it includes explicit Verification and Validation (V&V) activities and reconfiguration process. This section presents the overall design of PESOI, dynamic reconfiguration, and the dynamic architecture of the applications developed under PESOI. Figure 6.16 shows the layers related to an SOA application. First, the application is decomposed into the model consisting of patterns of sub models. Each of the sub models is developed using a tool in the development infrastructure, which in turn, maps the sub model into an executable code in the operation infrastructure. As a result, the user obtains an application that includes the development infrastructure, which make it possible for the users to revise or to redevelop the application during the operation.

Figure 6.17 outlines the lifecycle (development and operation phases) under PESOI development. These phases form a feedback loop, where the last phase reconfiguration is connected to the first phase modeling and specification.

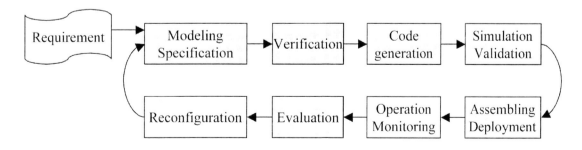

Figure 6.17 PESOI Reference Architecture

Each of the development phases in PESOI is elaborated as follows:

1. Modeling & Specification phase: This phase uses PSML-S process specification and modeling language to define the flow and conditions between the components.

2. Verification phase: It contains activities such as Completeness & Consistency (C&C) analysis, model checking, test case generation based on the functional and policy specifications.

3. Code generation phase: It automatically generates executable code from the process specification and binding of external services to obtain the executable code.

4. Simulation and validation phase: It runs the executable in a simulation environment and validates the code via testing.

5. Assembling and deployment phase: This phase assembles and deploys executable code into the operation environment. It involves binding the addresses of real devices into the code. Monitors and data collectors will be embedded into the code.

6. Execution and monitoring phase: The executable code is executed in the real environment. The monitors and data collectors will collect and record data for later analyses.

7. Evaluation phase: It analyzes the data, evaluates reliability and performance, and provides input for the reconfiguration phase.

8. Reconfiguration phase: It takes reliability and performance evaluation results as input and decide if a rebinding is necessary to replace a less reliable service or an underperformed service through rebinding to a better service. The service farm contains the backup spares needed for rebinding. The services in the farm are tested and ranked by an independent process such as group testing. If the application requirement is revised by the user, a re-composition or re-architecture needs to be performed. In this case, the composition or architecture of the application will be modified. The modified application need to go through the entire development process, and thus, the development infrastructure need to be embedded into the application to enable the reconfiguration.

6.7 HOMEWORK, PROGRAMMING EXERCISES, AND PROJECTS

1.   Multiple Choice. Choose only one answer in each question. Choose the best answer if more than one answer are acceptable.

1.1   What programming paradigm supports the highest level of abstraction?
❏ imperative   ❏ object-oriented   ❏ functional   ❏ service-oriented

1.2   What language supports automatic garbage collection?
❏ C   ❏ C++   ❏ C#   ❏ None of them

1.3   Who will need to have the detailed knowledge of programming languages in SOC paradigm?
❏ service providers   ❏ service brokers   ❏ application builders   ❏ None of them

1.4   What party in SOC paradigm needs to use an object-oriented programming language?
❏ service providers   ❏ service brokers   ❏ application builders   ❏ None of them

1.5   What feature C# does not support?
❏ preprocessor directives   ❏ macros
❏ overriding   ❏ switch statement

1.6   What feature C# does not support?
❏ multiple inheritance   ❏ array
❏ pointer   ❏ foreach statement

1.7   What do the C# **using** namespace directives replace?
❏ declaration in C++   ❏ printf statement
❏ pointer   ❏ header files

1.8   What is WSDL used to describe?
❏ control flow of Web services   ❏ interface of Web services
❏ syntax of Web services   ❏ semantics of Web services

1.9   What is UDDI used for?
❏ describing the interface of Web service   ❏ composing SOA applications
❏ publishing Web services   ❏ calling the remote Web services

1.10   What are the green pages in UDDI used for?
❏ describing contact information of service provide
❏ describing the service types of the Web services
❏ describing technical detail for remote invocation of Web services
❏ describing testing results on the reliability and trustworthiness of Web services

1.11   What is SOAP used for?
❏ describing the interface of Web service   ❏ composing SOA applications
❏ publishing Web services   ❏ calling the remote Web services

1.12 What is the difference between a Web service and a Web application?
  ❏ A Web service is intended for being accessed by a computer program
  ❏ A Web service is intended for being accessed by a human user
  ❏ A Web application is intended for being accessed by a computer program
  ❏ Web application is a synonym of Web service

2. Add a column in Table 6.1 to compare Java with C++ and C#.

3. Compare and contrast C++ and C#.

3.1 Can scope resolution operator be used in C#?

3.2 Does a C# program need a constructor? Does a C# program need a destructor?

3.3 Are there any global functions (functions that are outside any class) in C#?

3.4 Does C# support stack objects (objects that obtain its memory from the language stack)?

4. A part of the queue and priority queue example in C++ (the **Queue** class) in section 3.1 has been rewritten in C# in Section 6.1. Complete the priority queue class in C#.

5. Compare and contrast object-oriented programming paradigm and service-oriented programming paradigm.

6. What is the major differences between object-oriented software development and service-oriented software development?

7. Sorting an array or a list of numbers is a frequently used service.

7.1 Use an efficient algorithm, e.g., merge sort, and C# to write a sorting program for float numbers; wrap it as a Web service; and deploy it as a Web service;

7.2 Register the Web service to a free UDDI server;

7.3 Build a Window-based application that needs to use sorting service and use the Web service that you placed on the Web server to perform the required sorting tasks.

8. In this assignment, you will write a "Rescue Turtles" game in C#. As shown in figure 6.18, your program should display a random pattern with turtles, where an "M" represents a turtle on its feet and a "W" represents a turtle on its back. The goal of the game is to have all turtles on their feet use minimum time and minimum number of operations. The player can choose one of the following game actions:

- Select a column, e.g., c2: All turtles on the column will be inversed (M → W and W → M);
- Select a row number, e.g., r3: All turtles on the row will be inversed;
- Select a column AND a row number, e.g., c2r3: The turtle at the position will be inversed;
- Enter a q to exit the game.

The game should offer multiple levels of different size and complexity, e.g., different sizes (3×3), (5×5), (7×7), and (9×9) and different ways of placing turtles. The game starts with a player-selected level. After certain number of consecutive wins, the game proceeds to the next level, if there is a next level. At the highest level, the same level of the game will be continuously displayed until a "q" is entered.

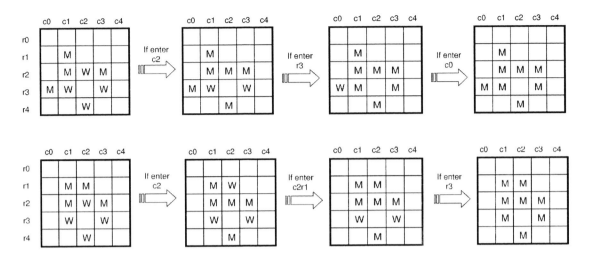

Figure 6.18 Two patterns and possible solutions

Score of at the end of each match (pattern) and total score will be computed by the following formulas:

Match score: MS = (1000 + L)/t - 5* Nm - 10* Ni. If MS < 0, then set MS = 0.

Total score: TS = TS + MS after each match, the initial value of TS = 0.

where,

L:　is the level of the GameLevel type and can take the values of easy, fair, tough, and extreme.

t:　is the time interval (in seconds) from the time point the pattern is displayed to the time point the player wins a match (all turtles are on their feet).

Nm: is the number of group invert actions when a column or a row number is entered.

Ni:　is the number of individual invert actions when both column and row numbers are entered.

8.1　Using C# to implement the Rescue Turtle game.

8.2　Convent the reusable functions into Web services and put them into a Web server. The game must use the Web services, instead of local functions.

8.3　Use the reusable functions to build another game and you may need to add some additional functions (Web services).

*8.4 Save the game in the Pocket PC or PDA format, so that the game can be played on a Pocket PC or PDA.

9. This is a group project. Figure 6.19 shows a Teaching Assistant Ontology (TAO) system that can be used for the instructors to keep their test questions, as well as for students to ask questions and obtain answers.

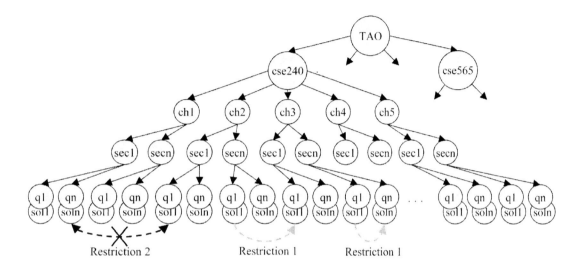

Figure 6.19 A Teaching Assistant Ontology

The system allows the instructor to add a new course, e.g., cse565, chapters, sections, questions, and solutions, into the system. It also allows the instructor to specify certain relations (restrictions) among the data in the ontology, for example, restriction 1: The two questions must be in the given order if they appear in the same test paper, and restriction 2: The two questions may not appear in the same test paper.

9.1 Implement the following functions as Web services and save the services on a Web server.
   1. addTreeNode(subRoot, name);

   2. removeTreeNode(nodeName);

   3. addTreeLeave(subRoot, name);

   4. removeTreeLeave(leaveName);

5. selectLeave(leaveName);

6. takeTest(testName);

7. gradeTest(testName, grade);

8. enterGrade(roster, testName, grade);

9. sort(roster);

10. display(roster, range);

11. login(userName, pwd);

12. logout();

9.2   Register these Web services to a free UDDI server.

9.3   Make use of the above Web services to build the following applications.

1. testPaper(subRoot, name);
   - login(userName, pwd);
   - selectLeave(name1) ... selectLeave(namen);
   - buildTest(testName);
   - logout();

2. testGiving(testName);
   - login(userName, pwd);
   - takeTest(testName);
   - gradeTest(testName, grade);
   - enterGrade(roster, testName, grade);
   - logout();

3. reportGrade(roster, key1, key2, key3);
   - login(userName, pwd);
   - sort(roster);
   - display(roster, range);
   - logout();

10. Figure 6.20 shows the component architecture model of an online bookstore.

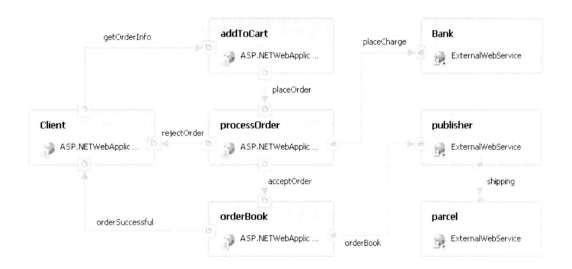

Figure 6.20 Components of an online bookstore

10.1 Use a process specification language, such as BPEL4WS, PSML-S, WSFL, or C# to define the flow of the bookstore.

10.2 Find existing services on Internet, where possible, or develop the services, and bind the services into your process model to perform required functions.

*10.3 Use a verification tool to check the properties of your process model, such as completeness, consistency, reachability, deadlock, etc.

*10.4 Use a test case generation tool to generate test cases and apply the test cases to test your program.

*10.5 Apply a reliability model to evaluate the reliability of your program based on the test data.

Appendix A

Basic Computer Architectures and Assembly Language Programming

In this appendix, we first introduce different computer architectures, and discuss how the architectures impact the way we write programs at the assembly language level. We then briefly examine how local variables are allocated on the language stack.

A.1 BASIC COMPUTER COMPONENTS AND COMPUTER ARCHITECTURES

At the highest level, a computer system can be abstracted as consisting of five components: control, datapath, memory, input, and output.

Control tells the other components, data path, memory, input, and output devices what to do according to the instructions of the program. In other words, the control component of a computer decodes instructions and sends the control signals to other components to perform the desired operations.

Datapath consists of one instruction register (IR), several data registers, and an arithmetic logic unit (ALU). The data registers buffer the data fetched from memory and the ALU performs basic arithmetic and logic operations on the data stored in registers and possibly in memory. Since all high level operations are decomposed into basic arithmetic and logic operations, datapath is the component that manipulates data in the required way. Datapath and control are also called the **processor** because they are closely related and are usually implemented on a single chip.

Memory stores the instructions (machine language code) and data translated from the programs.

Input and output components are the interface between the user and the computer. The input component writes user's input to memory and the output component reads data from memory and sends them to the user. Keyboard, mouse, and scanner are typical input devices, and screen, printer and speaker are typical output devices of a computer system.

Figure A.1 shows the five components and their interactions. A typical process is as follows. A computer program is entered through a keyboard and stored in memory. The program is compiled into machine code and stored into the memory. When this program is executed, a single instruction is fetched into the datapath at a time.

For example, assume that an addition instruction

add R1, R2, R3   // R1 = R2 + R3

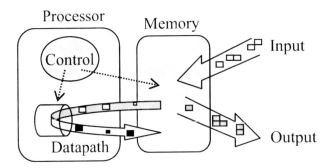

Figure A.1 Five-component model of a computer system

is fetched into instruction register in the datapath. The control reads the instruction from IR, decodes the instruction, and finds that the instruction is to add the content of register **R2** and **R3** and to store the result **R2+R3** back into register **R1**. The control then sends proper control signals to the datapath to complete the required operation.

In the following discussion, we will focus on the datapath, memory, and the organization of the two components, because they are directly related to imperative programming.

Figure A.2 shows four different architectures of computer systems. The **memory-memory architecture** in figure A.2(a) has no data registers in the datapath, and, thus, the ALU has to directly take operands from memory. Since memory access is very slow, this architecture is simple but extremely slow. The **accumulator architecture** in figure A.2(b) has one data register called accumulator. One of the operands is always in the accumulator and the data has to be fetched into the accumulator before any ALU operation. The result is written back into the accumulator too. In the **stack architecture** in figure A.2(c), the data registers are organized as a last-in first-out stack. The ALU can only take operands from the top of the stack. The result is pushed onto the top of the stack. The diagram in figure A.2(d) is called **load-store architecture**. It is a generalization of the stack architecture in which the ALU can take operands from any registers and write back the result into any register.

A.2 COMPUTER ARCHITECTURES AND ASSEMBLY PROGRAMMING

To see how the architectures impact the way we write programs, we show in table A.1 the assembly language programs on the four architectures that solve the same computation problem:

y = x1 * x2 + x3 * x4

where x1, x2, x3, x4 and y correspond to memory locations.

We now compare the instruction count (IC) and the memory access (MA) of the programs on the four architectures. Register or accumulator accesses are much faster than memory accesses and thus can be ignored in the analysis.

On the memory-memory architecture, the three instructions perform the following operations

y1 = x1*x2;
y2 = x3*x4;
y = y1+y2;

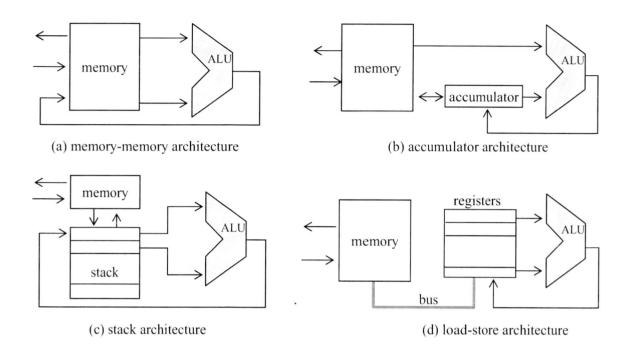

(a) memory-memory architecture (b) accumulator architecture

(c) stack architecture (d) load-store architecture

Figure A.2 Four major computer architectures

Since each instruction involves reading two operands from memory and writing the result back to the memory, the total number of memory accesses is 9.

Table A.1 Assembly language programs on the four architectures

Memory-memory		Accumulator		Stack		Load-Store	

mult y1, x1, x2
mult y2, x3, x4
add y, y1, y2
		Load x1
		mult x2
		Store y1
		Load x3
		mult x4
		Add y1
		Store y
				Push x1 (Load x1)
				Push x2 (Load x2)
				mult
				Push x3 (Load x3)
				Push x4 (Load x4)
				mult
				Add
				Pop y (Store y)
						Load R1 x1
						Load R2 x2
						Load R3 x3
						Load R4 x4
						mult R1 R1 R2
						mult R3 R3 R4
						Add R1 R1 R3
						Store R1 y	

IC 3	MA 9	IC 7	MA 7	IC 8	MA 5	IC 8	MA 5

On the accumulator architecture, one of the operands of all arithmetic operations is by default in the only register (accumulator) and the result is always written back into the accumulator. In this example, in order to perform x1*x2, x1 is first loaded into the accumulator, and the multiplication instruction multiplies the accumulator content with x2, and the result is written back into the accumulator. Then the content of the accumulator is stored in the memory location y1, making the accumulator free for the next multiplication. The program has seven instructions and each instruction has exactly one memory access, resulting in seven memory accesses.

On the stack architecture, operands of all operations are assumed to be on the top of the stack and the results are written back on the top. A **stack** consists of a set of registers or a block of memory in which a set of data can be stored and two operations can be performed on the data: **push x** and **pop x**. The former loads the data from memory location x and puts it on top of the stack and the latter takes (and removes) the data on the stack top and stores it into the memory location x. Figure A.3 shows the execution process of the stack-based program in table A.1. You can imagine that the stack is a storage compartment (or magazine) that only has one access (push and pop) point and a spring is used to hold the available item to the access point. When a new item is pushed onto the stack, all items already in the stack are pushed down one place. When the item on the stack top is removed, all the items in the stack move one place up.

For the example in Table A.1, the values of x1, x2, x3, and x4 are stored in memory. To compute:

$$y = x1 * x2 + x3 * x4$$

the value of x1 is pushed (copied) onto the stack by the operation **Push x1**. Then x2 is push onto the stack. The operation **mult** will pop the two values on the stack top (one after another) and perform the multiplication. The result of the x1*x2, assume to be (x12), is pushed back onto the stack. Similarly, x3 and x4 are pushed onto the stack, the result of the x3*x4, assume to be (x34), is pushed back onto the stack. The operation **add** will pop the two values on the stack top (one after another) and perform the addition. The result (x12+x34) is pushed back onto the stack. Final, the operation **pop y** will move the data on the stack top onto memory location y. The stack state returns to the state before it starts the operation.

In the real implementation, a stack has the same structure as a memory or an array. We use a pointer or an index variable "top" to hold the position of the stack top. Instead of moving all data in the stack up and down when pop and push operations are executed, we simply move the value of the variable top. Figure A.4 shows stack states by moving the position top variable.

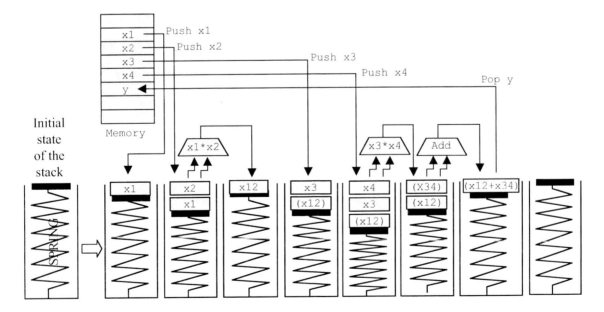

Figure A.3 Using a stack to compute y = x1 * x2 + x3 * x4

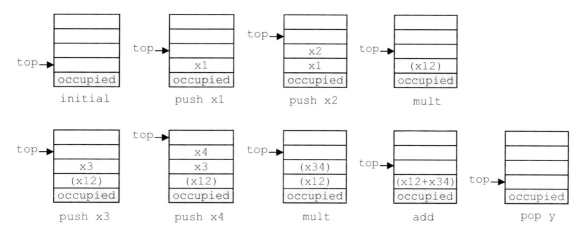

Figure A.4 Stack states during the execution

There are 8 instructions in this program; however, only push and pop instructions involve memory accesses. Thus, there are only 5 memory accesses.

The last architecture is a generalization of the stack architecture in which the registers can be accessed in an arbitrary way, that is, the ALU can take inputs from any two registers, instead of only from the two registers below the top pointer. This extra flexibility does not reduce the numbers of IC and MA in this example, but in general, it can reduce IC and MA. It also makes programming easier. Load-store architecture, also called RISC (Reduced Instruction Set Computer) architecture, is a mainstream architecture used in today's computer systems. In the following example, we will explain how we write programs on the load-store architecture and what are the roles of memory, registers and ALU.

Assume we want to organize a game involving a large number of teams and matches. In this example, we consider eight teams t0, t1, t2, ..., t7. We assume t0 plays t1 and t2 plays t3, and so on, in the first round, the winners in round 1 will play in round 2, and the winners in round 2 will play in round 3, as shown in figure A.4.

Now let's see how we organize the matches in an efficient way. We put the teams in a hotel where we have large number of rooms to accommodate large number of teams. However, the hotel is not close to the competition venue, and teams need to be transported, say by a bus, to the competition venue. To save time and eliminate unforeseeable traffic situations, teams will be transported (loaded) into waiting rooms close to the competition venue. The organization of the game facility is shown in figure A.5. The game facility is analogous to a load-store architecture. The hotel corresponds to the memory, the waiting rooms correspond to the registers, the competition venue corresponds to the arithmetic logic unit (ALU), and the bus route corresponds to the data bus connecting memory and the registers.

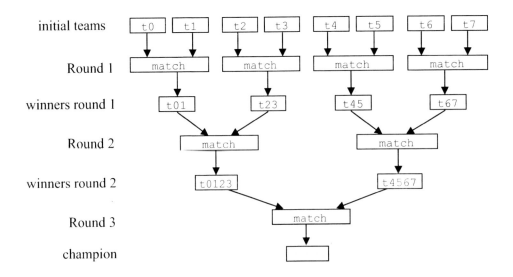

Figure A.5 The scheme of matches

The organization of matches in figure A.4 can be implemented by the following pseudo assembly language program. The comments after the double slash // explain what each instruction does. The instruction match(Z, X, Y) is, in fact, a procedure call and the definition of the procedure is given at the end of the program. The procedure simply chooses the larger value between X and Y and puts it in Z.

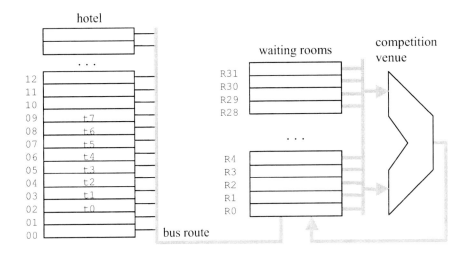

Figure A.6 The organization of the game facility

// This program implements the organization in figure A.4. The teams (data)

// are preloaded in the memory locations 21, 22, 23, 24, 25, 26, 27, 28.

//   round 1, four matches

```
load     R1, mem[21]    // load the content in memory location 21 into R1
load     R2, mem[22]    // load the content in memory location 22 into R2
match    R1, R1, R2     // call procedure match. The winner is put back into R1

load     R3, mem[23]    // load the content in memory location 23 into R3
load     R4, mem[24]    // load the content in memory location 24 into R4
match    R3, R3, R4     // call procedure match. The winner is put back into R3

load     R5, mem[25]    // load the content in memory location 25 into R5
load     R6, mem[26]    // load the content in memory location 26 into R6
match    R5, R5, R6     // call procedure match. The winner is put back into R5

load     R7, mem[27]    // load the content in memory location 27 into R7
load     R8, mem[28]    // load the content in memory location 28 into R8
match    R7, R7, R8     // call procedure match. The winner is put back into R7
```

// round 2, two matches

```
match    R1, R1, R3     // two winners in round 1 play and put winner in R1
match    R5, R5, R7     // other two winners in round 1 play and put winner in R5
```

// round 3, one match, and store the final result

```
match    R1, R1, R5     // two winners in round 2 play and put winner in R1
store    R1, mem[20]    // store the champion in memory location 20
```

// the "match" instruction is implemented as a procedure

```
match(Z, X, Y):        // match procedure needs 3 parameters
if X > Y branch G      // if X > Y, then jump to label G below
move Z Y               // Y is greater than X, put Y in Z
branch L               // unconditionally jump to L
G: move Z X            // X is greater than Y, put X in Z
L: return Z            // The larger value is put in Z
```

A.3 SUBROUTINES AND LOCAL VARIABLES ON STACK

Most operating systems today are capable of multitasking. A subroutine (procedure or function) may be interrupted before its completion and be called by a second caller (re-entrance). A subroutine may also call itself (recursion). In both cases (re-entrant) and (recursive), the subroutine needs to offer separate workspace (local variables) for each occasion of its execution. In other words, each time a subroutine is called, a new workspace must be created. In fact, it makes no difference at the assembly language level whether the call is a re-entrant or recursive call.

At the assembly language level, local variables are implemented by a **stack frame** and accessed through the **frame pointer**. A stack is usually a block of memory. As shown in figure A.6, the stack is accessed through a stack pointer **sp**. The stack pointer is usually stored in a register. When a subroutine is called, the return address, the address of the instruction next to the subroutine call, will be stored onto the stack and sp incremented. Then a stack frame (a block of memory) will be created and a register is used as the frame pointer fp to access the memory locations in the frame. The codes below illustrate the process of a subroutine call:

```
stack[sp] = PC;          // store return address onto stack. PC: program counter.
sp++;                    // increment stack pointer
fp = sp;                 // set frame pointer
sp = frame_size;         // create frame of frame_size
```

Then we have memory space between stack[fp] and stack[fp+frame_size] for local variables, as shown in figure A.6. When the subroutine complete and return to the caller program, following operation will be executed to return the stack to the state before the subroutine call:

```
sp = fp;                 // deallocate the stack frame
PC = stack[--sp]         // restore the PC and thus
                         // the control will return to the caller
```

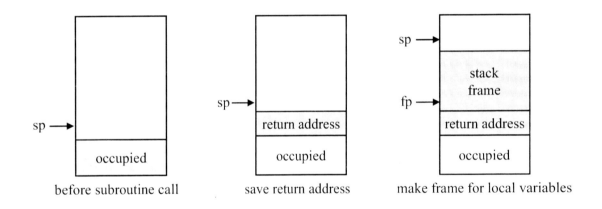

before subroutine call   save return address   make frame for local variables

Figure A.7 A stack frame is created for local variable in a subroutine

To support re-entrant and recursive subroutine calls, the frame creation and deletion described above can be executed repeated and, thus, created nested frames on the stack, as shown in figure A.7.

In fact, the value of the frame pointer associated to each re-entrance (recursion) will be stored in its stack frame, so that we only need one register for the frame pointers, no matter how many times the subroutine is called.

In summary, we discussed the following issues in this appendix:

- The major components of a computer system and the basic computer architectures.

- How to write assembly language programs on different architectures and how to write imperative programs: store data in memory, move data into registers, manipulate the data in ALU and put the result back into the register, and finally store data back into the memory.

- An examples of assembly language program on a load-store architecture.

- The process of subroutine calls and how stack frames are created for local variables in re-entrant and recursive occasions of the subroutine.

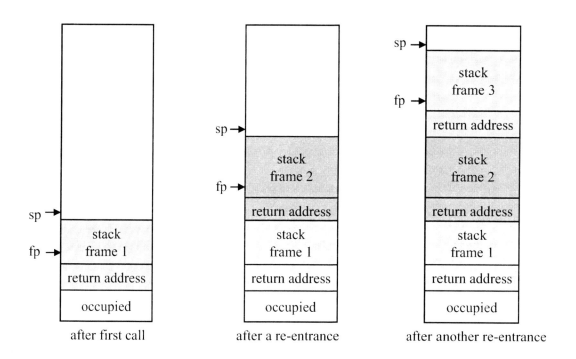

Figure A.8 Multiple re-entrances of a subroutine

Appendix *B*
Programming Environments Supporting C, C++, Scheme, Prolog, C#, and SOA

B.1 INTRODUCTION TO UNIX COMMANDS

Since we use GNU GCC and GNU Prolog under Unix operating system, we will briefly explain the basic Unix commands we may need to run our programs. We first explain a few commands that we will use immediately to get started. Then the most commands that you may need are listed in the table B.1 at the end of the section.

Current Directory

To find what directory you are currently in, you simply type

    pwd

pwd stands for "print working directory". The output shows the path from the root directory to your current working directory.

Creating a New Directory

To create a new directory within the current directory, type command

    mkdir newdirectoryname

Deleting a Directory

To remove (delete) a directory in the current directory, type command

    rmdir directoryname

Note that the directory to be removed must be empty.

List Directory and Files

To list all the sub directories and files in the current directory, type

    ls   ; only list directory or file names
    ls –l   ; will list details on directory and file, e.g., access permission

Change into a Directory

To change into a directory within the current directory, type

```
cd directoryname          ; enter the directory
cd ..                     ; return to the parent directory
```

Type **cd**, a space, and two full stops mean to move one level up in the directory structure or back into the parent directory.

Unix On-Line Manual

To read the description of a command, type

```
man commandName
```

For example, **man cd**. If you do not know the exact command, you may try apropos keyword and a list of possible commands relating to the keyword will be printed. A full help description of commands listed above can then be displayed using man.

Table B.1 below lists most commands that you may need. You can use the on-line manual to check the options available to each command and the full description of each command. The commands are alphabetically sorted.

Table B.1 Unix command table

Unix Command	Description
cat [options] file	concatenate and print on standard output
cd [directory]	change directory
chgrp [options] group file	change the group of the file
chmod [options] file	change file or directory access permission mode
chown [options] owner file	change the ownership of a file
cmp [options] file1 file2	compare two files and list where differences occur (text or binary files)
compress [options] file	compress the file and save it asfile.z
cp [options] file1 file2	copy file1 intofile2
date [options]	report the current date and time
diff [options] file1 file2	compare the two files and display the differences (text files only)
df [options] [resource]	report the summary of disk blocks free and in use
du [options] [directory or file]	report amount of disk space in use
echo [text string]	echo the text string to stdout
ed or ex [options] file	Unix line-oriented text editor
emacs [options] file	full-screen editor
file [options] file	report the file type
find directory [options] [actions]	find files matching a type or pattern

Unix Command	Description
finger [options] username@hostname	report information about users on local and remote machines
ftp [options] hostname	file transfer using file transfer protocol
gcc [options] file g++ [options] file	GNU C/C++ compilers
gplc [options] file	GNU Prolog compiler
grep [options] 'search string' argument	search a file for a pattern
gzip [options] file gunzip [options] file	compress or uncompress a file. Compressed files are stored with a .gz ending
head [-number] file	display the first 10 or the given number of lines of a file
hostname	display the name of the current machine
javac [options] file	Java compiler
kill [options] [pid#] [%job]	the process with the process id number (pid#)
ln [options] source_file target	link the source_file to the target
login logout, or exit	sign on exit
lpq [options]	show the status of print jobs
lpr [options] file	print to defined printer
lprm [options] cancel [options]	remove a print job from the print queue
ls [options] [directory or file]	list directory contents or file permissions
man [options] command	show the manual (man) page for a command
mkdir [options] directory	make a directory
mv [options] file1 file2	move file1 into file2
passwd [options]	change your login password
pico [options] file	text editor
ps [options]	show status of active processes
pwd	print working (current) directory
rcp [options] hostname	remotely copy files from this machine to another machine
rlogin [options] hostname	login remotely to another machine
rm [options] file	remove a file
rmdir [options] directory	remove an empty directory
sort [options] file	sort the lines of the file according to the options chosen
tail [options] file	display the last few lines (or parts) of a file
telnet [host [port]]	communicate with another host using telnet protocol

Unix Command	Description
tr [options] **string1 string2**	translate the characters in string1 from stdin into those in string2 in **stdout**
uncompress **file.Z**	uncompress **file.Z** and save it as a file
uniq [options] **file**	remove repeated lines in a file
uudecode [file]	decode a uuencoded file, recreating the original file
uuencode [file] new_name	encode binary file to 7-bit ASCII, useful when sending via email, to be decoded as new_name at destination
vi [options] **file**	visual, screen-oriented text editor
vc [options] [**file**(s)]	display word (or character or line) count for **file**(s)
who or w	report who is logged in and what processes are running

B.2 PROGRAMMING ENVIRONMENTS SUPPORTING C, C++, AND C# PROGRAMMING

In this subsection, we introduce three environments that support the development of C/C++, C#, and SOA programs.

B.2.1 GETTING STARTED WITH GNU GCC UNDER UNIX OPERATING SYSTEM

GNU GCC is a C/C++ development environment under Unix operating system. We assume that you have basic knowledge on Unix. A short introduction to Unix and basic Unix commands are given in section B.1. If you use the SSH Secure Shell, you can start a console window by choosing the menu item "Window" and then choosing "New Terminal".To enter and edit your program, you can use any Unix text editors, e.g., **pico** or **vi**. You enter, for example,

```
pico hello.c
```

A new text window will be opened and you can start to enter your program.

```
// My first program, file name hello.c
#include <stdio.h> // the library functions standard I/O will be used
main( ) {
    printf("hello, world\n");
}
```

After you have entered the program, type ctrl-X to exit the pico editor. Then you can use the GCC compiler to compile your program:

```
g++ hello.c -o hello
```

If no compilation errors are found, the command will create an object code (machine code) and store the code in the file **hello**. To run the program, you type

```
./hello
```

The program will be executed and the output printed on the screen.

The compiler g++ can compile both C and C++ programs. The name of a C program must have the extension .c while the name of a C++ program must have an extension .cpp.

B.2.2 GETTING STARTED WITH VISUAL STUDIO .NET UNDER MS WINDOWS OPERATING SYSTEM

Visual Studio .Net 2005 supports C, C++, C#, and SOA programming. C# and SOA programming in .Net 2005 is discussion in chapter six. To start a C or C++ project, you can follow the following steps to set up your system properly.

- Start .Net.
- Choose .Net menu "file" - "new" - "project...": A "New Project" dialog box will pop up.
- Choose "Visual C++ project" in the window on the left hand side, and then choose "Win32 Project" in window on the right hand side. Enter the project name. Assume your project name is MyProject1, in the text box below the two windows. Click OK.
- You can also choose "Visual C# project" in this step to start a C# project.
- A dialog box that "Win32 Application Wizard - MyProject1" will pop up. Before you click on "Finish", you must click on "Application Settings" on the left hand side of the window.
- Two setting options: "Application type" and "Additional options" will show up for you to choose.
- Under "Application type", select "Console application".
- Under "Additional options", select "Empty project".
- Click "Finish".

Now you have created an empty project that can be used to run your C/C++ programs. Assume that you have created a program called MyProgram1.c or MyProgram1.cpp and now you can add your program into the project following these steps:

- Start .Net.
- Choose .Net menu "file" - "open" - "project...". Browse to the location where your "MyProject1" is stored., and open the project.
- Choose the .Net menu "Project" - "Add Existing Item...". Browse to the location where your MyProgram1.c or MyProgram1.cpp are stored. Choose the program you want to add to the project, e.g., MyProgram1.c.
- Now you can compile, build and execute your program.
- Choose the .Net menu "Build" - "Compile..." to compile your program MyProgram1.c, or choose "Build MyProject1" to compile and build your project.
- Choose the .Net menu "Debug" - "Start" or "Start without Debugging" to execute your program. You can also choose the single step options to execute your program in single steps.

Using .Net, you can easily implement GUI (graphic user interface) in C++ and in C#: When you create a new C++ (or C#) project, instead of selecting an empty project, you can select "Windows Forms Application" as the project type. Then, the GUI tools and library will be included in your project stack. You can use the provided tools and library functions, such as buttons (for mouse click inputs), textboxes (for text inputs), and labels (for outputs), to implement different kinds of GUI. See chapter six for more detail.

B.2.3 Download C, C++, and C# Programming Development Tools

GNU home page:

http://www.gnu.org/

GNU GCC page:

http://www.gnu.org/software/gcc/gcc.html

.Net Framework page:

http://msdn.microsoft.com/netframework/

.Net Framework download page: Free .Net SDK command line tools to compile and run C#

http://msdn.microsoft.com/netframework/downloads/howtoget.asp

You can also go to Microsoft download pages:

http://msdn.microsoft.com/downloads/

http://lab.msdn.microsoft.com/express/

to find the latest C++ IDE and other downloads.

B.3   Programming Environments Supporting Scheme Programming

In this section, we first introduce how to write simple Scheme programs, and then explain how to use DrScheme programming environment to run Scheme programs.

B.3.1 Getting Started With DrScheme

A simple Scheme program is extremely simple. Most mathematical expressions in prefix notations are simple Scheme programs. For example,

(+ 1 2)

is a simple Scheme program that can be executed. To print "hello world", all we need to write is:

(print "hello world")

In the rest of the section, we will introduce DrScheme, a free Scheme programming environment for education purpose. DrScheme can be downloaded from http://www.drscheme.org/

After you downloaded and installed DrScheme, you can follow the following steps to use the programming environment to run your Scheme programs. We are referring to DrScheme version 208. Other versions may have slightly different interfaces.

1.   Start the program DrScheme. As shown in figure B.1, a window with two sections will be opened. In the upper section window, you can enter your program, and in the lower section, evaluation results and possible error message will be displayed.

2.   To have the full functionality, you need to choose the "full version" or the most advanced version through the menu (see figure B.1): language – choose language – full Scheme.

   By default, the system is set to the "beginning Student" version that works only for basic functions.

3. Enter your program in the upper window. For example,

```
(print "hello world")
(newline)                    ; start a newline for next print
(print (+ (* 3 8) 10))
```

4. Click on "Check Syntax" to check the possible syntax errors. Click on "Execute" to run your program. The single step execution option is only available when you choose the "Beginning Student" version. Click on "Break" to abort the execution.

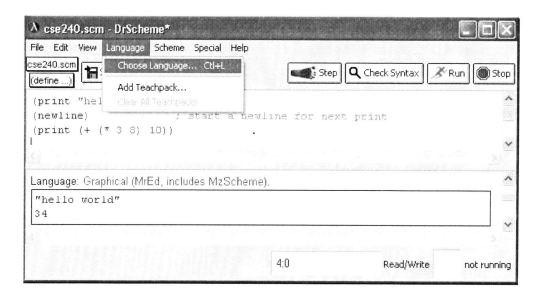

Figure B.1 DrScheme programming environment

B.3.2 DOWNLOAD DRSCHEME PROGRAMMING ENVIRONMENT

DrScheme home page:

http://www.drscheme.org/

DrScheme download home page:

http://download.plt-scheme.org/drscheme/

B.4 PROGRAMMING ENVIRONMENTS SUPPORTING PROLOG PROGRAMMING

In this section, we will explain how to use the GNU Prolog environment under Unix operating system to edit, to compile, and to execute Prolog programs. A short introduction to Unix and basic Unix commands are given in Appendix B.1.

B.4.1 GETTING STARTED WITH GNU PROLOG

After logged on a Unix server with GNU Prolog installed, you can create a new directory using command:

```
mkdir Prologfiles
```

Then you can put all your Prolog files and programs in this directory. You may create subdirectories in this directory.

Enter the directory by using Change Directory command:

```
cd Prologfiles
```

To write a GNU Prolog program, you can either use a Unix editor, e.g., **pico** or **vi** (**pico** is more convenient) or upload (e.g. using an FTP client software) a pre-edited file into the directory **Prologfiles**. The name of a Prolog program should have an extension .**pl**.

To compile a Prolog program, say myprologprog.pl, type the command

```
host> gplc myprologprog.pl
```

at the operating system prompt **host>**, where gplc is the GNU Prolog compiler.

The compiler will generate the machine code program, or called executable, stored under the name myprologprog.

Then you can start GNU Prolog by typing **gprolog** at the operating system prompt **host>**

```
host> gprolog
```

Having entered GNU Prolog system, you can execute the executable created by the **gplc** compiler. For example, you can type

```
|?- [myprologprog].
```

to execute your program, where, |?- is the GNU Prolog prompt. Then you can enter a goal (question) to search the database of **myprologprog**.

You can turn on and turn off the debugging tool (trace) by executing the goals, respectively:

```
|?- trace.        // turn on trace tool
|?- notrace.      // turn off trace tool
```

To exit from GNU Prolog system, type the end-of-file character at the Prolog prompt **^d**, i.e.,

```
|?- ^d
```

For more Prolog commands, please check the GNU on-line manual at:

```
http://gnu-prolog.inria.fr/manual/index.html
```

B.4.2 Download Prolog Programming Development Tools

To connect to a Unix server, you can use a telnet client software, or a secure telnet client software like SSH if your server requires secure connection. You can download a personal version of SSH program from **www.openssh.com**.

GNU Prolog page:

http://pauillac.inria.fr/~diaz/gnu-prolog/

GNU Prolog download page (Unix, Linux and MS Windows versions):

http://pauillac.inria.fr/~diaz/gnu-prolog/#download

I also tested the programs given in the exercises in chapter five using SWI-Prolog and Quintus Prolog. SWI-Prolog can be downloaded at

http://www.swi-prolog.org/

Quintus Prolog Web page:

http://www.sics.se/isl/quintuswww/site/

Appendix C
ASCII Character Table

ASCII stands for American Standard Code for Information Interchange. Table C.1 below lists the decimal, hexadecimal, binary and the corresponding character values.

Table C.1 ASSCII character table

Decimal	Hex	Binary	Char	Comment	Decimal	Hex	Binary	Char	Comment
000	00	000 0000	NUL	Null character	064	40	100 0000	@	
001	01	000 0001	SOH	Start of Header	065	41	100 0001	A	
002	02	000 0010	STX	Start of Text	066	42	100 0010	B	
003	03	000 0011	ETX	End of Text	067	43	100 0011	C	
004	04	000 0100	EOT	End of Trans.	068	44	100 0100	D	
005	05	000 0101	ENQ	Enquiry	069	45	100 0101	E	
006	06	000 0110	ACK	Acknowledge	070	46	100 0110	F	
007	07	000 0111	BEL	Bell	071	47	100 0111	G	
008	08	000 1000	BS	Backspace	072	48	100 1000	H	
009	09	000 1001	HT	Horizontal Tab	073	49	100 1001	I	
010	0A	000 1010	LF	Line Feed	074	4A	100 1010	J	
011	0B	000 1011	VT	Vertical Tab	075	4B	100 1011	K	
012	0C	000 1100	FF	Form Feed	076	4C	100 1100	L	
013	0D	000 1101	CR	Carriage Return	077	4D	100 1101	M	
014	0E	000 1110	SO	Shift Out	078	4E	100 1110	N	

Decimal	Hex	Binary	Char	Comment	Decimal	Hex	Binary	Char	Comment
015	0F	000 1111	SI	Shift In	079	4F	100 1111	O	
016	10	001 0000	DLE	Data Link Escape	080	50	101 0000	P	
017	11	001 0001	DC1	Device Control 1	081	51	101 0001	Q	
018	12	001 0010	DC2	Device Control 2	082	52	101 0010	R	
019	13	001 0011	DC3	Device Control 3	083	53	101 0011	S	
020	14	001 0100	DC4	Device Control 4	084	54	101 0100	T	
021	15	001 0101	NAK	Negative Ack.	085	55	101 0101	U	
022	16	001 0110	SYN	Synchronous Idle	086	56	101 0110	V	
023	17	001 0111	ETB	End Trans. Block	087	57	101 0111	W	
024	18	001 1000	CAN	Cancel	088	58	101 1000	X	
025	19	001 1001	EM	End of Medium	089	59	101 1001	Y	
026	1A	001 1010	SUB	Substitute	090	5A	101 1010	Z	
027	1B	001 1011	ESC	Escape	091	5B	101 1011	[	
028	1C	001 1100	FS	File Separator	092	5C	101 1100	\	
029	1D	001 1101	GS	Group Separator	093	5D	101 1101	]	
030	1E	001 1110	RS	Record Separator	094	5E	101 1110	^	
031	1F	001 1111	US	Unit Separator	095	5F	101 1111	_	
032	20	0010 0000	SP	Space	096	60	110 0000	`	
033	21	010 0001	!		097	61	110 0001	a	
034	22	010 0010	"		098	62	110 0010	b	
035	23	010 0011	#		099	63	110 0011	c	
036	24	010 0100	$		100	64	110 0100	d	
037	25	010 0101	%		101	65	110 0101	e	
038	26	010 0110	&		102	66	110 0110	f	
039	27	010 0111	'		103	67	110 0111	g	
040	28	010 1000	(		104	68	110 1000	h	
041	29	010 1001	)		105	69	110 1001	i	
042	2A	010 1010	*		106	6A	110 1010	j	

Decimal	Hex	Binary	Char	Comment	Decimal	Hex	Binary	Char	Comment
043	2B	010 1011	+		107	6B	110 1011	k	
044	2C	010 1100	,		108	6C	110 1100	l	
045	2D	010 1101	-		109	6D	110 1101	m	
046	2E	010 1110	.		110	6E	110 1110	n	
047	2F	010 1111	/		111	6F	110 1111	o	
048	30	011 0000	0		112	70	111 0000	p	
049	31	011 0001	1		113	71	111 0001	q	
050	32	011 0010	2		114	72	111 0010	r	
051	33	011 0011	3		115	73	111 0011	s	
052	34	011 0100	4		116	74	111 0100	t	
053	35	011 0101	5		117	75	111 0101	u	
054	36	011 0110	6		118	76	111 0110	v	
055	37	011 0111	7		119	77	111 0111	w	
056	38	011 1000	8		120	78	111 1000	x	
057	39	011 1001	9		121	79	111 1001	y	
058	3A	011 1010	:		122	7A	111 1010	z	
059	3B	011 1011	;		123	7B	111 1011	{	
060	3C	011 1100	<		124	7C	111 1100			
061	3D	011 1101	=		125	7D	111 1101	}	
062	3E	011 1110	>		126	7E	111 1110	~	
063	3F	011 1111	?		127	7F	111 1111	DEL	

References

Appleby, D., J. VandeKopple, *Programming languages: Paradigm and practice*, 2nd edition, McGraw-Hill Companies, Inc., 1997.

Bal, H., D. Grune, *Programming languages essentials*, Addison-Wesley, 1994.

Chen, Y., *Testing and evaluating fault-tolerant protocols by deterministic fault injection*, VDI-Verlag GmbH, Düsseldorf, 1993.

Clements, A., *68000 family assembly language*, Brooks/Cole Publishing, 1994.

Cormen, T., C. Leiserson, R. Rivest, *Introduction to algorithms*, 2nd edition, MIT Press, 2001.

Deitel, H., P. Deitel, *C++: How to program*, 3rd edition, Prentice-Hall, 2001.

Diaz, D., GNU Prolog, *A native prolog compiler with constraint solving over finite domains*, http://gnu-prolog.inria.fr/manual/index.html.

Gunnerson, E., *A programmer's introduction to C#*, Apress, 2001.

Hankins, Tom, Thom Luce, *Prolog minimanual*, McGraw-Hill, 1991.

Hennessy, J. L., D. A. Patterson, *Computer architecture — A quantitative approach*, Morgan Kaufmann, 2nd Edition, 1995.

Hull, R. G., *PC Scheme minimanual*, McGraw-Hill, 1991.

Kernighan, B., D. Ritchie, *The C programming language*, Prentice-Hall, 1978.

Kernighan, B., *Programming in C: A tutorial*, http://www.lysator.liu.se/c/bwk-tutor.html.

Lister, A.M., R.D. Eager, *Fundamentals of operating systems*, 5th edition, Houndmills, Basingstoke, Hampshire : Macmillan, 1993.

Manis, V., J. Little, *The schematics of computation*, Prentice Hall, 1995.

Mueldner, T., *C++ programming with design patterns revealed*, Addison Wesley, 2002.

Myers, G. J., *The art of software testing*, Wiley 1979.

Oualline, S., *Practical C programming*, 3rd edition, O'Reilly & Associates, Inc., 1997.

Patterson, D. and J. Hennessy, *Computer organization and design: The hardware/software interface*, 2nd edition, Morgan Kaufmann Publishers, Inc., 1998.

Powell, R., R. Weeks, *C# and the .Net Frameworks: The C++ Perspectives*, Sams Publishing, 2002.

Siewiorek, D., R. S. Swarz, *Reliable computer systems: Design and evaluation*, 3rd edition, Natick, Mass.: A K Peters, 1998.

Stroustrup, B., *The C++ programming language*, Addison Wesley, 1997.

Tanenbaum, A., *Modern operating systems*, 2nd edition, Prentice Hall, 2001.

Tsai, W. T., C. Fan, Y. Chen, and R. Paul, "DDSOS, Distributed Service-Oriented Simulation", to appear in Proc. of 39th Annual Simulation Symposium, (ANSS), Huntsville, AL, April 2006.

Tsai, W. T., R. A. Paul, B. Xiao, Z. Cao, Y. Chen, "PSML-S: A Process Specification and Modeling Language for Service Oriented Computing", 9th IASTED International Conference on Software Engineering and Applications (SEA), Phoenix, November 2005, pp. 160–167.

Tsai, W. T., "Service-Oriented System Engineering: A New Paradigm," IEEE International Workshop on Service-Oriented System Engineering (SOSE), pp. 3–8, Beijing, October 2005.

Tsai, W. T., X. Wei, Y. Chen, "A Robust Testing Framework for Verifying Web Services by Completeness and Consistency Analysis," IEEE International Workshop on Service-Oriented System Engineering (SOSE), Beijing, October 2005, pp.151–158.

Tsai, W. T., X. Wei, Y. Chen. B. Xiao, R. Paul and H. Huang, "Developing and Assuring Trustworthy Web Services," in Proceedings of 7th International Symposium on Autonomous Decentralized Systems, Chengdu, China, April 4–8, 2005, pp. 43–50.

Tsai, W. T., X. Liu, Y. Chen, R. Paul, "Dynamic Simulation Verification and Validation by Policy Enforcement", 38th Annual Simulation Symposium, April 2005, pp. 91–98.

Tsai, W. T., W. Song, R. Paul, Z. Cao, and H. Huang, "Services-Oriented Dynamic Reconfiguration Framework for Dependable Distributed Computing", Proc. of IEEE COMPSAC 2004, pp. 554–559.

Index

379

command line parameter, 118, 173
comment in Prolog, 239
comments, 7
common language runtime, 16
compilation, 15
composite condition returning points, 292
compositional orthogonality, 12
compound data types, 68
conclusion, 243
condition, 243
conditional expression, 43
conditional operator, 43
conditional statements, 7
const qualifier, 65
constants, 64
constructor, 133
containment mechanism, 143
contextual structure, 7
correctness, 23
correctness proof, 23
cout, 40
cut (!), 261

D

data type, 10, 49, 188
datapath, 353
debugging, 20
declaration, 49
declarative, 3
define, 185
    macro, 185, 205
dereferencing operator, 57
derived class, 144
design, 20
destructor, 133
directed graph, 183
directed tree, 183
dot-notation, 74
double precision floating-point, 51
DrScheme, 368
dynamic binding, 164
dynamic memory allocation, 74

E

eager evaluation, 187
early binding, 164
ebXML, 323
empty list, 193, 264
endl, 41
enum, 66
enumeration constant, 65
enumeration type, 66
EOF, 39
ESLPDPRO, 6
eta reduction, 201

exception, 164
execution engine
exhaustive testing, 20
expandability, 101
export, 203

F

factorial, 261
facts, 238
fantastic four abstract approach, 94
fclose, 84
feof, 84
ferror, 84
fgetc, 83
file close operation, 84
file open operation, 83
files, 80
filtering, 218
final method, 19
first-class object, 181
floating-point, 51
flowchart, 22
foo(), 142
fopen, 83
for statement, 47
for-loop, 48
foreach, 310
form of Scheme, 185
formatted input/output, 39
Fortran, 5
forward declaration, 51
FP, 6
fprintf, 84, 86
fputc, 83
frame pointer, 359
fread, 84
free, 200
Frolic, 6
fscanf, 84, 86
function, 185
functional, 2
functional programming, 179
functional testing, 21
fwrite, 84

G

garbage, 78
garbage collection, 139
getchar(), 39
glass-box testing, 21
global, 39
global variable, 74
GNU GCC, 366
GNU Prolog, 369
goal, 240

gplc, 370
GUI, 332

H

Hanoi Towers, 262
has-a relation, 145
head, 243
heap, 74, 139
higher order function, 217
higher order procedure, 195
Horn logic, 6

I

identifier, 6, 10
imperative, 2
implementation, 20
in-passing, 89
infix, 182
inheritance, 145
inheritance mechanism, 144
initializing, 59
inline, 17, 19
inorder traversing, 183
input case, 20
input component, 353
input/output, 39, 196, 272
instantiation, 241
instruction register (IR), 353
integer, 51
intermediate language, 16
interpretation, 15
interrupts, 164
is-a relation, 145

J

Java, 5
Java virtual machine, 15
jump-table, 46

K

keywords, 7
KRC, 6

L

l-value, 56
lambda, 186
lambda-calculus, 199
lambda-expression, 199
late binding, 164
lazy evaluation, 42, 187, 201
let-form, 203
lexical structure, 6
libraries, 38
Lisp, 5
list, 193, 263, 302

list simplification rule, 193, 302
literals, 7
load-store architecture, 354
logical operators, 43
long, 310
loop body, 47
loop invariant, 24
loop statements, 7

M

macro, 16, 205
malloc, 74
map procedure, 217
match, 240
member functions, 127
member predicate, 266
member variables, 127
memory component, 353
memory leak, 78, 142
memory-memory architecture, 354
methods, 127
Miranda, 6
ML, 6
modifiers, 314
multidimensional arrays, 55
multiple inheritance, 146

N

name, 56
name equivalence, 11
named procedure, 185, 202
neck, 243
non-terminal, 8
number orthogonality, 14
number type, 187

O

object, 132
object-oriented, 2
one's complement, 214
operators, 7
orthogonality, 12
out-lining, 17
out-passing, 89
output component, 353
overloading, 133
override, 310
OWL, 323

P

pair, 288
pair simplification rule, 192
pair type, 191
paradigm, 2
partial correctness, 23

symbol type, 191
syntactic structure, 7
syntax graph, 10

T

tail recursive, 92
tail-recursive procedure, 260
terminal, 8
termination, 23
test case, 20
total correctness, 24
Tower of Hanoi, 95
truncated initialization, 59
two's complement, 214
type casting, 12
type checking, 11

U

UDDI, 323
unboxing, 318
unified type system, 317
unify, 240
union, 70
Unix, 363

Unix Command, 364
Unix on-line manual, 364
unnamed procedure, 201

V

value, 56
value type, 51
valueless, 51
variable, , 56
variable in Prolog, 241
virtual base class, 146
Visual Studio, 367
Visual Studio .Net, 367

W

wchar_t, 51
weakly typed language, 12
while-loop, 47
white-box testing, 21
wide-character, 51
workspace, 359
WSDL, 323

X

XML, 323